French Fiction Revisited

French Fiction Revisited

Leon S. Roudiez

Dalkey Archive Press

for Jacqueline, always

Library of Congress Cataloging in Publication Data
Roudiez, Leon Samuel, 1917-
    French fiction revisited / Leon S. Roudiez.
    Rev. ed. of: French fiction today. 1972.
    Includes bibliographical references and index.
    1. French fiction—20th century—History and criticism.
I. Roudiez, Leon Samuel, 1917-   French fiction today. II. Title.
PQ671.R64   1991   843'.9101—dc20   90-14081
ISBN: 0-916583-73-2

First Edition

Partially funded by grants from The National Endowment for the
Arts and The Illinois Arts Council.

Dalkey Archive Press
1817 North 79th Avenue
Elmwood Park, IL 60635 USA

*Printed on permanent/durable acid-free paper and bound in the
United States of America.*

Contents

Introduction
to the 1972 Edition

"I must Create a System or be enslav'd by another Man's," William Blake wrote in his *Jerusalem*, expressing a necessity that will find its echo in an admonition by Philippe Sollers: "He who will not write shall be written" [which originally figured as the last sentence of my concluding chapter]. Blake is cited in Tony Tanner's introduction to his *City of Words* (New York: Harper & Row, 1971), a study in American fiction covering roughly the same period I am concerned with here—the one separating us from the Second World War. If my final quotation echoed my first it also distorted it, as any echo must in its reverberating process, which takes place in this instance through the pages of my book. Echo and distortion: the two images aptly convey the impression one receives after setting contemporary French and American fiction side by side.

Basic assumptions and concerns are shared by the postwar generation of French and American writers. All realize that their work is primarily in language, and each of their works of fiction is a structure of words. Many of them also have a sense of being constricted, possibly determined, by the cultural, social, and linguistic patterns of the country in which they happen to have been born; escaping from such patterns is often at the core of their literary travails.

On the whole, however, French writers have shown a greater preoccupation with giving their work a social dimension, that is, with being socially or politically effective. There are of course exceptions on either side of the Atlantic. Still, I do not detect in French fiction writers that strong individualistic concern apparently characteristic of their American counterparts (verging on egomania in the case of Norman Mailer, even when he adopts a clearly political stance); nor does French fiction reflect with the same intensity the search for an illusive identity. As Richard Poirier has noted, "We all see images of ourselves performing, on candid camera as well as on soap opera, until it is hard to know what is left in

speech or gesture that can be truly claimed as one's own."[1] Philippe
Sollers might have made that statement his own but for the final clause.
To be free from the patterns imposed by society is certainly to be striven
for; as to claiming any gesture or speech as truly one's own, he would
probably ask, *Qu'est-ce que cela veut dire?*

Walter Kaufmann has written that France has, "more often than not,
produced men who stand at the borderline of philosophy and literature."[2] It has become almost a cliché to accuse French writers of
being overly interested in abstract theory. Today, however, except
insofar as political theory is concerned, I am not sure that this would
constitute an essential difference between them and American writers.
Possibly they have at their disposal a larger body of continuously
evolving source material produced by the speculations of French intellectuals, which are more widely disseminated than the books of American
speculative thinkers. Perhaps French publishers have been (in the past
at least) more receptive to the idea of bringing unorthodox, iconoclastic
views into the open. Also, while French periodicals have more than their
share of tradition-bound, myopic reviewers, there are enough intelligent
critics writing for noncommercial publications who are willing to
examine seriously new theories and new experiments in fiction.

If, then, there is a similar awareness of linguistic and cultural structures
among fiction writers of both countries, eventual reaction to them varies
considerably. The reasons for the difference appear to be in part
political. . . . As I see it, it lies in an unwillingness, on the part of a new
generation of French writers, to separate literary (or linguistic) activities
from any other human activity. Such an attitude goes hand in glove with
the abandonment of old middle-class illusions about the "humanizing"
effect of literature or the compelling values of "authentic" style. Richard
Poirier once marveled at the way Spiro T. Agnew (or his speech writer)
illustrated an ability "to appropriate the language of one's enemies in the
act of defeating them." That exemplified the recourse to patterns in
order to stimulate a reaction, a device constantly used in nearly all
societies but to which our eyes had been closed for too long. Poirier
continues, "Herein is a lesson for those who like to imagine the power of
the word or of literature: power as a property, power of the kind at
Agnew's command, can do what it wants with language, and language
can do practically little to it."[3] Philippe Sollers's answer to that sort of
abuse of power is clear: subvert the patterns by dismantling them from
within, so to speak, making them ineffective, by means of a conscious
operation of language, changing the act of reading into a productive act.
If I read him correctly, Poirier seemed to be moving in the same direction, but without the imposing theoretical structure upon which Sollers
and others of the review *Tel Quel* based their textual practice, when he
urged that we acquire "a feeling for the power, still generating in those

works [of literature], of the retraceable act of writing, composition, performance."[4] We shall indeed be encountering some of those very words in several chapters of this book.

In the spirit of what the writers themselves have been doing, those chapters will deal with works of fiction rather than with authors. No intentions, no biographies, no gossip. In discussing the fiction, I shall generally make no reference to anything outside the fiction except in my final chapters; the reasons for doing so will be obvious enough. I should like to emphasize that I have no desire to sever the ties that bind a writer to his work; his active presence is what gives it a unity of sorts, and in all my essays but one (the concluding survey) a single writer is involved. That unity, however, is more important than what made it possible, and it is less so than the meanings that radiate from such a unified cluster. What goes into a work of literature or art matters less to me than what comes out of it.

Having just used the term *literature*, I should now like to dissociate myself from it to a certain degree. My quarrel is not so much with what has gone under that label; it is rather the use to which it has been put. Too often, in what must surely be a degradation of its function, literature has been, in practice if not in theory, viewed as a delightful pastime for the idle rich. Some literature unfortunately lends itself to that only too well. Of course there should be pleasure in reading as well as in writing, but there are degrees in the quality of pleasure—of which Faust experienced the gamut. There is also a necessity, an urgency that drives a person to write (intransitively, as Roland Barthes said) and attracts others to his books. The shock of recognition, of which Melville spoke, where ordinary readers are involved becomes the shock of discovery: the discovery of words used in a fashion not attempted before, of the new approach to reality that they afford, perhaps even the liberation of thought from an earlier linguistic confinement. It is a pleasure of the highest kind.

The writers whose works I examine here bear several common traits, which will become obvious along the way. They also exhibit differences, and the aggregate of their books does not reflect the doctrines of any school, nor does it illustrate the evolution of any genre. If anything, it shows that the concept of genre is not as useful as it was in the past. Actually, if the trend . . . persists, the death of all literary categories may be at hand. For those reasons, I have avoided the use of the word *novel;* I can see no point in joining in the arguments of those who keep worrying whether this or that is "really" a novel. Likewise, I have eschewed the phrase *new novel* or *nouveau roman* as it is much too slippery and serves little purpose aside from fanning controversies. Some writers, such as Philippe Sollers, actually use the term *roman* with a subversive intent; others, like Jean Ricardou, favor the phrase *nouveau roman* precisely because of its provocative, exclusive possibilities.

While my concern is for those who have written the major portion of their fiction since the Second World War, I nevertheless include an earlier writer. Raymond Roussel belongs here, in my opinion, since he was not really "discovered" until the fifties and many contemporary writers and critics refer to his works. Others might also have been included (and were, in an earlier draft) when their works, like those of Valery Larbaud or Jean Giraudoux, begin to reveal some of the concerns germane to contemporary fiction. I finally decided to omit them, for what is most interesting in French writing today is its revolutionary character, its desire to effect a break with the past. Although I shall [on occasion refer to] some of their antecedents, I do not wish to present today's writers as the latest link in a long chain in French literary tradition, into which they will eventually be assimilated. Theirs is not another instance of the romanticists' fight against classicism, of the Parnassians' against romanticism, of the symbolists against Parnassus, and so on. This generation of writers is attempting to break away from *literature*.

Surrealism tried to do that very thing [seventy] years ago and failed. That there must be some connection between the two enterprises is obvious. That there is also a difference, giving today's writers some hope of success, is also clear. As a matter of fact, the importance that surrealists have had for writers who came after them is no longer a topic for debate. Identifying the influence and tracing it, however, is another matter; it is a vast enough undertaking for at least a full-length study. I shall do no more than allude to it in several instances. . . .

Clearly, too, I have not presented a comprehensive picture of present-day French fiction. A place might have been found for texts by writers like Alain Badiou, Maurice Roche, Jean Thibaudeau, or Pierre Guyotat, for instance; or even better known ones such as Julien Gracq, Raymond Queneau, or J. M. G. Le Clézio. Yet, unwilling to compile an encyclopedia, I had to stop somewhere, at an arbitrary point established by means of a personal equation. Hence also some deliberate omissions–the writings of Pierre Klossowski, among others, in spite of the esteem in which they are held by intelligent French readers.

I began writing this study during the summer of 1967, in Santa Monica, while teaching a summer course in French fiction at UCLA; I finished the first draft in the summer of 1968, while helping to "restructure" the French Department at Columbia after the revolt. Revisions then began; but the text had reached something close to its present shape when books by John Sturrock, *The French New Novel* (New York: Oxford University Press, 1969), and Vivian Mercier, *The New Novel from Queneau to Pinget* (New York: Farrar, Straus, and Giroux, 1971), appeared. Sturrock discussed only Claude Simon, Michel Butor, and Alain Robbe-Grillet, and his presentation is primarily intended for a

British audience. Mercier, in addition to Raymond Queneau [whom I omitted] took up six of the writers I present here. In either case, as it was too late for me to benefit from their pioneering work, I was relieved to note that the critical viewpoint and the prejudices are not the same as mine. These have changed since 1967, as so much around us has. I have not written what I intended to then, nor have I done it in the way I thought I might. For one thing, as my work progressed I became more and more attached to its object, gradually sharing more and more of the assumptions of the writers I was studying. I believe now that what some of them are doing is of greater moment than anything that has been written in the past.

Anything. If I have not succeeded in having others share that feeling, that is of course due to my own shortcomings. As soon as you can, go to a bookstore or a library and read these writers' texts—... and look for your role within them.

1990 Postscript

There is little, if anything, of what I wrote in the 1972 introduction that I would now disown. The great majority of the writers I discussed seem as important to me today as they did some twenty years ago. During the two intervening decades, however, they have written many more books and my various chapters have been brought up to date: my text now accounts for all the significant works of fiction published by them up through December 1990.

Younger writers have also come into their own and my original plan in revising this volume was to present the works of at least half a dozen noteworthy new writers. As I surveyed the field I decided that there were indeed many writers of talent, dedication, and promise active today but none, so far, comparable in stature and innovative practice to the leaders of the previous generation. In order to be fair to writers of undeniable quality, including a number of remarkable women writers, I would have had to contribute twelve to eighteen additional chapters. Clearly, the book would have been unmanageable from a practical, financial standpoint. I have therefore limited myself to providing, in a conclusion, a brief survey of the writers of the eighties.

Even without the addition of individual essays on younger writers, the established ones have been so productive that the book was still in danger of getting out of hand. Cuts had to be made and I reluctantly decided to omit chapters on Samuel Beckett, Claude Mauriac, and Marc Saporta. By the time Beckett died, in December 1989, he had become so well known, his works had spawned a body of criticism that had assumed such enormous proportions, that a few more pages on his French fiction would make little difference. Claude Mauriac does not seem as significant now as he did in the sixties and Marc Saporta has retreated from writing fiction altogether. On the other hand, I believe I should have brought Maurice Roche into the concluding chapter of *French Fiction Today;* to atone for that lapse I am now giving him a short chapter in *French Fiction Revisited.* Georges Perec did not have enough to his credit to warrant including him earlier (or else I was not perceptive enough to detect what his early work portended); the critical interest he has aroused and an untimely death that has allowed one to view his work as a whole made it imperative that he be given a chapter. Finally, the previous concluding chapter, "Jean Ricardou and French Writing Today," has been recast in order to give greater emphasis to Ricardou's own work.

A number of the writers I examine have also written for the theater, the cinema, radio, and television. Some have expressed disappointment because I did not discuss such activities. Having suggested in my original introduction that I held no brief for the notion of genre, I should like to emphasize that what I had in mind was the traditional division into genres. There is thus no more than an apparent contradiction between that statement and my concentrating on works of fiction. The latter category is made up of texts that one reads in a solitary situation and, in many cases, one can complete the reading in a single continuous sitting or, exceptionally, in a definitely limited number of sittings (Proust, Joyce, and a few others). A work that is performed on a stage by live actors in the presence of hundreds of spectators functions in a very different way, and so does a movie, a radio performance, or a television show. The text read by someone who is alone in a quiet room, no matter what the appearance of the letters on the page, constitutes, in my opinion, a legitimate genre, and that is what I call *fiction* (it also includes some of what most people call *nonfiction,* since *reality,* as opposed to the *real,* is a form of fiction).

Within such a category, the one I call fiction, a new practice may well be developing. It is one that combines what used to be called the novel with autobiography, the personal essay, commentaries on various forms of art (music, painting, sculpture), and so forth. Michel Butor, Maurice Roche, and Philippe Sollers, for instance, have been working in that direction, each in his own different way.[5] What is now even more patent than it was in the sixties is that there was not then, and certainly there is not now, any "school" unifying the work of those writers in spite of Jean Ricardou's efforts to ground one more firmly than journalists had done.[6] The phrase *nouveau roman* was useful, up to a point, in calling attention to a number of important young writers and sparking discussions about what they were contributing to the art of writing. Without the tag and controversies, readers might not have been attracted to them, nor would they have become aware of a new way of approaching the written text. It was detrimental to the extent that it allowed some readers who disliked the practice of one writer to project their criticism indiscriminately on all others. All that, however, is past literary history (another genre that could be dispensed with): these writers' accomplishments are now an established and accepted fact.

○

All translations from the French are mine unless otherwise noted. Titles of French books are translated in parentheses on their first appearance —and in italics if published in English—unless the titles are self-explanatory. (Initials are used in page references if the source isn't obvious.) Notes follow at the end of each chapter, and full publishing details for the books discussed in the bibliography at the end.

Several small sections of this book have previously appeared, in slightly different form, in the following publications: the *Review of Contemporary Fiction* (Claude Ollier), *World Literature Today* (Claude Simon), *Modern Philology* (Conclusion), and *Three Decades of the French Novel* (Urbana & Chicago: University of Illinois Press, 1986; Conclusion).

NOTES

1 Richard Poirier, *The Performing Self* (New York: Oxford University Press, 1971), 6-7.
2 Walter Kaufmann, *Existentialism from Dostoievsky to Sartre* (New York: Meridian, 1957), 41.
3 Poirier, 82-83.
4 Ibid., 84.
5 I have developed this point in "Un Texte perturbé: *Matière de rêves* de Michel Butor," *Romanic Review* 75, no. 2 (1984): 242-55.
6 See Jean Ricardou, *Le Nouveau roman*, rev. ed. (Paris: Seuil, 1990).

1

Raymond Roussel

Alain Robbe-Grillet, while working on *Le Voyeur*, had occasion to take a trip to the Brittany coast; on the way, he decided that the journey would provide a fine opportunity to refresh his memory, to take a good look at the sea, the fishing ports, and the gulls—all of which might enter into the setting of his forthcoming book. "But no sooner had I glimpsed the first sea bird than I realized my mistake: on the one hand the gulls that I now saw had only the vaguest connection with those I was describing in my book, and on the other, I could not have cared less."[1] He cared only for the gulls that soared out of the pages of his fiction. Several decades earlier, Jean Giraudoux had led one of his characters to the seashore, this time to the coast of Normandy. Simon, as Giraudoux called him, was about to leave Paris for extensive travel in continental Europe, but he had never experienced the ocean: "I should have been ashamed not to know the sea before plunging into Europe.... That was exactly it, at least as I imagined it, with its foam of gulls. All who think of the sea know it.... I was delighted to have guessed right. Quite probably, I also knew before-hand what the glaciers were like, and the desert, and the void. From now on, there would be no point in checking such things too closely."[2] It is not difficult to detect a vague affinity with Oscar Wilde's remark about nature imitating art; in more apposite fashion, it implies that nature, or reality, assumes shape according to a model that language proposes. Relationship between language and reality lies ever at the core of the writer's care.

Roussel pointed out that he had traveled all over the world; he had seen the Near East and North Africa, India, China, Japan, Australia and New Zealand, the South Sea Islands, and most of Europe. For his creative activity, however, he claimed that such experience did not count: "Now I have not, from all my travels, ever used anything for my books ... with me, imagination is everything."[3] A silly statement, if one were to take it at face value. Had Roussel not traveled all over Europe and the Orient, he would have been a different person and his works would also have been different. What he probably meant was to establish a separation between the world as it appears and the fictions he elaborated. Along with Robbe-Grillet and other contemporary writers, he is interested in subjectivity and a person's will (or propensity) to distort, transform, or deny the outside universe. As a matter of fact, he was as much a victim of that propensity as an observer of it. What is so fascinating about Roussel is that nearly everything he wrote either rejects or ignores what most of us, by tacit consent, construe as reality—even when he appears to concentrate on a minute description of it. His was an inner world, conditioned by language just like ours, but where verbal creation feeds upon itself in the manner of a snowball. Replacing the "inner world" metaphor with a different one, the "world of language" for instance, would bring us very close to the concern of writers such as Philippe Sollers and others, whom I shall examine in later chapters.

If Roussel was not lured into the realm of surrealism (to which Giraudoux and Robbe-Grillet are also close), he occasionally skirted it and came near enough to be recognized and praised. André Breton himself was intrigued, proclaiming, "Roussel is, along with Lautréamont, the greatest magnetizer of modern times."[4] That Roussel had few readers until the 1960s is irrelevant in this context, for the magnetism Breton referred to has to do with the creative process—what he has called the alchemy of words. Roussel, on the other hand, showed little interest in the surrealists (he thought their works rather abstruse).[5] His own works are also lacking in two major surrealist preoccupations: the linking of surreality with reality and the desire to change life. Nor is it clear if any portion of his work could truly be interpreted in terms of a quest for the lost paradise of childhood. He remembered his own with great fondness: "I have delightful memories of my childhood. I may say that I then experienced several years of perfect happiness."[6] It was possibly less urgent for him to seek such a paradise again, for, in some ways, he carried it with him. Pierre Schneider has distinguished his attitude from that of the surrealists by saying, "His entire work is a kind of child's play . . . he plays while they pretend to play."[7] Michel Butor was led by what he calls Roussel's "salvaging of childhood" to mention Proust rather than the surrealists.[8]

It is true that the surrealists were attracted by his commonplace description of the preposterous. As J. H. Matthews puts it, "Roussel's inventiveness catches the imagination and disturbs most when, entirely without comment or interpretation, his storyteller merely relates without sign of emotion what he says he has witnessed."[9] But this does not so much imply an acceptance of the surrealists' *merveilleux quotidien* as it does an exclusion of accepted reality, a placing it within parentheses. What remains is a self-sustaining verbal universe, which Breton recognized as one of the very few created in his day. It is a complete one, "a world recreated from scratch by a man fully set on following only the bent of his own mind, insofar as such bent might be unique."[10] This led Roussel along a one-way street, beyond mere exclusion of other people's reality, toward total denial. As he showed no interest in transforming reality, it is tempting to call him an escapist. Still, there are virtues in this escape into language, virtues of which he was in all likelihood unaware. Most of his contemporaries were equally blind and their judgment of him was unduly harsh. If the variety of his more recent admirers seems surprising, it could perhaps be explained by one feature of his works: one could almost describe his production as the establishment of a void. His logical, consequent, and seemingly matter-of-fact universe appears enchanted because of its availability. There is something in it for almost every reader.

As is often the case with writers, Roussel's first published work, *La Doublure* (1897; The Understudy), displays some of the basic threads that run through everything he wrote. The narrative deals with an episode in the life of Gaspard Lenoir, a mediocre actor. As an understudy (one of the meanings of *doublure*) he is unable to win the audience; after a humiliating failure on the stage, he and his mistress, Roberte, decide to put their savings together, leave Paris, and spend a few carefree weeks on the shores of the Mediterranean. All goes well at first; they have a grand time at the carnival in Nice, but just before funds run dry Roberte walks out on Gaspard. He returns to Paris alone and in worse straits than before, for the only employment he can find is at a street fair in Neuilly. Such a plot outline reveals nothing startling or even original (although one might note its circularity, a recurring feature in Roussel's fiction and other twentieth-century texts as well). Some of the details are significant, but it is in the structuring and shaping of the material that Roussel displays unusual characteristics. Two of these strike the reader at once: the fiction is in verse, and two-thirds of it consist of a meticulous description of the street scene—floats, costumes, and various incidents—during a few hours of the carnival. Were I to judge this verse according to traditional standards, I would surely be inclined to label it as doggerel of the worst sort. Actually, the word *verse* is somewhat misleading. A glance at the text gives one the impression that *La Doublure* is written in rhymed alexandrine couplets, whereas it is really prose with pairs of rhymes every twelfth and twenty-fourth syllable. There is no rhythm; there are few of the pauses that characterize the French classical alexandrine; and enjambment is the rule rather than the exception. If the text were printed as prose, there is a good chance that most readers would be unaware of the rhymes. Here, for an example, are the first three sentences of the book:

Le décor renaissance est une grande salle au château du vieux comte. Une
portière sale sert d'entrée. Un vieillard, en beaux habits de deuil et l'air grave, est
assis sur le bord d'un fauteuil à dossier haut.
[The Renaissance setting shows a large room in the castle of the old count. A
soiled portiere serves as an entrance. An old man, wearing fine mourning clothes
and a sober mien, is seated on the edge of a high-backed armchair.]

When the text is set in such a fashion, its "verse" features are almost
completely obliterated. Only a very astute reader would detect the
rhymes *salle/sale* and *deuil/fauteuil*, even though they constitute a
rhetorical generator in the composition. What matters is that the twenty-
fourth syllable of the narrative, as well as the word incorporating it, is
determined by the twelfth syllable; the forty-eighth is then determined
by the thirty-sixth, and so on, and objects, features, or incidents in the
text are similarly determined. Such a process is not absolutely new:
André Gide has remarked, for instance, that "The demands of versifica-
tion have inspired Racine with some of his most subtle notations; these,
as well as the most original and daring ones, were almost dictated to
him."[11] With Roussel, however, the emphasis is obviously much greater.

In ordinary writing, words generally are intended to express or convey
some aspect or understanding of reality; here, in part at least, they are
used to create that reality. One is again on the frontiers of surrealism,
remembering Breton's "words that produce energy" and are able to
command thought.[12] In later works, Roussel increased the creative role
of words, but in *La Doublure* they already serve to orient the progression
of the narrative. It seems likely, for instance, that in the few lines I have
quoted the count's mourning (*deuil*) required him to be seated in an armchair (*fauteuil*), and that later on a character's great sensitivity to the
breeze (*souffle*) called forth a carnival float in the shape of a slipper
(*pantoufle*)—or vice versa. More recently, writers such as Jean Ricardou
have used purely verbal generators to produce a large number of events
in their fiction.

The carnival description occupies the entire third chapter out of the
six that make up the text, a disproportionately large one comprising 116
pages of the Pauvert edition as against 13, 5, 7, 20, and 24 for the others.
The length of that chapter is puzzling at first, and the purpose of the
description is obscure. The book's slim plot is not advanced one bit: the
episode seems a gratuitous parenthesis in the lives of Gaspard and
Roberte. Then one realizes that the interruption is more important than
the life, just as Roussel's inner reality is more important than everyday
exterior reality. Gaspard, a ham who thought he could act, is so mediocre
that he himself begins to realize the impossibility of his ever breaking
through; he has nowhere to go but down. Even his mistress is not all his:
Roberte de Blou (her name is an anagram of *double*), who maintains
herself a few rungs above the prostitute level, has been attracted to him

through what the text calls "perverse love" after seeing him play the part of a shady underworld character. While she has been drawn to a mask that is worse than its wearer, he, ironically, thinks she is too good for him. Each one sees in the other a figment of his or her own imagination—a double. Their love itself is a denial of things as they are. And when they leave Paris, it is to forget more than one bad performance on the stage. Gaspard wants to forget everything that he is, and the possibility of having Roberte all to himself during their spree represents another negation of reality. Thus he plunges into the carnival.

From the moment we begin to follow him and Roberte through the streets of Nice, we enter a world of make-believe where everyone is different from what he or she is in everyday life. All wear costumes and masks, and while we see everything through the eyes of Gaspard and Roberte, there is nothing in this chapter to contradict the impression that they are two lovers having the time of their lives. Even when Roberte runs into a friend of hers who is watching the excitement from a balcony, an actress whom Gaspard might logically be expected to know, he says the name means nothing to him; and Roberte, sensing that her friend is curious about her presence in Nice with Gaspard, says she will tell her all about it some other time. The refusal to let reality intrude upon the carnival could hardly be more explicit. A number of men accost Roberte as she and Gaspard walk along the streets, and they, too, are completely in the spirit of the carnival. They make up preposterous stories about themselves and their supposed love for Roberte, changing their lines shamelessly as occasion seems to warrant. On the whole, Gaspard takes it all with good grace—except when fantasy threatens to become reality. The most obvious illustration of this occurs when one of the amateur Don Juans pinches Roberte's waist. Gaspard intervenes and tells the offender "in a curt and abrupt tone of voice" that he has had enough. He reacts in like manner to those whose disguises allude to the harshness of the world instead of contributing to the general atmosphere of harmless fantasy— grotesque or ugly as its players might be. A man made up as a beggar and displaying references to a financial scandal, or a lame boy who pretends to be lamer than he really is, likewise provoke his ire.

Some readers have found this section overlong and tedious, but in truth it could never be long enough, since the carnival suspends Gaspard's downfall. Contrasting it with Victor Hugo's descriptions in *Notre Dame de Paris*, the anonymous reviewer for the *Times Literary Supplement* pointed out that, "What happens at the festival [in Hugo's work] carries the story a long way forward. In *La Doublure* the story is merely postponed."[13] Of course, but not "merely": this is essentially the way the meaning of the text is established. Ideally, the carnival and Roussel's description of it should go on for a thousand days and a day, for we know that when it ceases the final catastrophe will be close, as it would be for Scheherazade if she stopped telling her tales. (I shall return to this image in the chapter on Michel Butor.) In the end, at the Neuilly fair, as a barker drums up customers for the show that is about to begin, Gaspard cannot bring himself to be a part of the concomitant hustle and bustle. The last line of the book has him gazing at the stars in the sky and thinking, in all likelihood, of a more definitive way of escape.

Shorter works such as *La Vue* (1903), *Le Concert* (1903), and *La Source* (1904), also written in verse, effect the same kind of rejection, without even the pretext of a meager plot. Each one has a framework, in the guise of what one might call a brief introduction and conclusion, and that framework is precisely the reality that is being blanked out. Two dozen lines or so at the beginning of *La Vue* describe the narrator's pen, the tip of which contains a miniature photo mounted in a magnifying glass. He applies his right eye to the glass, closes his left to prevent his being distracted by anything taking place outside the window by which he is seated—and a sixty-two page description (*invention* would of course be a more appropriate word) of the scene in the photo gets under way. In a brief conclusion he explains that he must stop because passing clouds have darkened the room and the photograph, and he muses on a period of the past that the picture has vividly resurrected but that is now "already dead, already far removed from me, swiftly carried away." Just as in *La Doublure* a realistic "description" of the carnival, that is, of unreality, masked reality, in *La Vue* a meticulously realistic presentation of the impossible helps the narrator flee the present. The photo supposedly represents an ocean-resort town seen from the sea. Among other patent impossibilities, the narrator depicts a thick vein on a hand resting on the handle of a cane, the hand belonging to an old man who is seated in a carriage being driven uphill on a road that is hidden from view by a row of houses in the background of the picture.

Such discrepancies, which belong in the realm of literary plausibility, should not obscure an equally significant denial: in this text the aspect of reality that is most emphatically rejected is the passage of time. Naturally enough, it is happiness that is associated with the past, and the gathering clouds in the "actual" landscape at the end of *La Vue* are an obvious enough correlative for present reality. The beginning of *Le Concert* is quite explicit about the same process: "Forgetting present time, I plunge again into old memories of happy bygone days." The narrator, at midnight (!), is rereading old letters; one was written from a hotel, and the letterhead has a picture of it and its immediate surroundings, including a bandstand where an orchestra is performing. Roussel needs a mere thirty-two pages to account for its details, completely obliterating the contents of the letter (even though he says it is especially dear to him) and shifting the emphasis of the letterhead from the hotel to the concert in the bandstand. The pretext for *La Source* is even more trivial, but it again produces the same motion away from reality. The narrator is in a restaurant, his order is taking too long, and he is getting impatient. On his table, however, there is a bottle of mineral water. On the bottle there is a label with a picture depicting the spa where the water came from. About thirty pages take care of that.

The two works that have done most for Roussel's reputation are *Impressions d'Afrique* (1910) and *Locus solus* (1914). More ambitious than his earlier fiction, written in prose, they exhibit, with varying degrees of emphasis, the same concerns or obsessions. Like *La Doublure*, *Impressions d'Afrique* centers on the elaborate narration of a spectacle, this time quite an extraordinary one. It is presented to the reader as a series of what seem like outlandish and gratuitous happenings, the pretext for which is the coronation of Talou VII, emperor of a most fictitious African realm. As the show goes on, the narrator witnesses and relates a number of elaborate, impossible performances and a display of contraptions that would have put Rube Goldberg to shame. Because of a flaw in one particularly difficult recital, the emperor rules that it must be repeated the following day. *Felix culpa:* the interval allows the narrator a long flashback (thus prolonging the literary feast) during which everything is explained in detail, everyone's background is thoroughly accounted for, and good and evil meet their just rewards. Everything, from beginning to end, is made plausible but in a totally unrealistic fashion.

It appears that a shipwreck off the coast of Africa is what made the narrative possible—just as a stage flop got things under way in *La Doublure*. A liner bound for South America, the *Lynceus*, named after one of the Argonauts who was famous for his keen sight, is driven aground;[14] one remembers the sharpness of the narrator's eyes in the preceding fictions and notes the irony (or pessimism) involved in thus naming a ship unable to find its way to its original destination. At any rate, all passengers come ashore safely (I assume there were officers and crew aboard, but they are a realistic irrelevancy and therefore not mentioned),[15] only to be held captive by Talou. While waiting for ransom money to come from Europe, the stranded travelers prepare for a celebration that will mark both their liberation and the coronation of the African emperor, who has just added another kingdom to his possessions. To him, that latest victory represents freedom from a succession of hereditary wars, and for a number of individual participants the occasion also signifies various kinds of releases—from bondage, exile, or illness. In the end, the flawed performance is repeated, this time to the emperor's satisfaction, and the Europeans return home, thus completing a circle (as in previous narratives). *Impressions d'Afrique* is a fairy tale for adults written by an admirer of Jules Verne, hence a tale where supernatural magic has been displaced by science (or what is presented as such). In this instance, however, science, rather than serving life, liberates it, just as it frees the emperor's son from the earth and allows him to soar into the air for a few brief moments. It also serves art, as in the case of rockets that reproduce paintings in the sky, for art itself, as Roussel appears to conceive it, effects the same kind of liberation. But freedom is a fleeting thing: the young man must soon come back to the ground, the pictures disappear into the night, the literary fantasy draws to a close.

The title lends itself to a pun. In English as in French, *impressions* can convey the notion of imprints as well as of sense perceptions. Upon reading the title, most people would probably opt for the latter meaning and expect an account of the writer's travels to several African countries. Clearly, however, the words of the fiction do not refer to any African reality or even to likely events. More apposite is the meaning of imprints where words are imprinted upon one's consciousness without being tied to any definite referent. This comes close to the more recent concept of the floating signifier—which might also be called the fuzzy sign, the sign that simultaneously points in several directions. As a result, while the narrative as a whole conveys a meaning (rejection of commonplace reality, for instance), its segments usually have no meaning beyond their necessary existence within the verbal framework of the text. While each performance that is described, as I have indicated, constitutes a microcosm of the pattern of the whole, the details and nature of any performance rarely signify anything beyond themselves. If one character has an affair with a woman named Flore in the Algerian city of Bougie, it is because (or in order that) another character has invented (or might invent) a vegetal candle (Flore = flora, and *bougie* is also a word for candle).[16] Each episode is verbally dependent on every other one and signifies nothing beyond that dependence. Such a complex system of interdependence constitutes the unity of the text, a feature that, for reasons very different from Roussel's, will be of considerable interest to writers like Sollers or Ricardou.

In *Locus solus* we are also treated to a sequence of extraordinary performances. The difference here lies in the fictional frame that surrounds them. They are not created, so to speak, by a fictitious event that gives them an excuse for being; nor, if they exist independently of that event, as in *La Doublure*, is the narrative set in motion by it. The performances have been going on for some time, and a number of them are to be repeated in the future, perhaps, as Michel Butor has suggested, in the hope of attaining a Kierkegaardian perfect, decisive repetition, "Liberating at the same time from death and from these vain, perpetual recurrences, but perpetually imperfect."[17] The story accounts for their existence but attempts no serious justification for the narrator's becoming a spectator and then relating his experience: it simply happens that way.

Martial Canterel, a wealthy scientist, has transformed his country estate into a gigantic performing laboratory in which his discoveries are given spectacular, although not very practical, applications. A negation of time, similar to that implied in the earlier *La Vue*, may be detected in the sequence dealing with the refrigerated human bodies, frozen in the midst of a significant decor, that mechanically reenact a crucial period of their lives when set in motion by the scientist. The reader is told about these and other performances because the narrator, a friend of Canterel's, has been invited to visit the estate along with other intimates. I do not believe the lack of any sort of motivation for the withdrawal from reality is particularly significant, for there is nothing in the text to indicate a changed attitude towards life. At the end of the visit, the guests get together for a "cheerful dinner" in Canterel's country house, but this is part of the ceremonial of the visit.

What has taken place amounts to a rhetorical shift through which the framework for the narrator has nearly been reduced to zero. Concomitantly, the author's indirect presence has switched from the framework to the main event. He was felt to be with Gaspard Lenoir in *La Doublure*, with the narrator of the subsequent fictions, but he seems now much closer to Martial Canterel, the organizer of the spectacle. The complicated machines Canterel has devised are analogous to the intricate fictions elaborated by Roussel. With each successive work (all were published at his own expense), he hoped to obliterate the failure of the preceding ones. As each one failed either to sell or to be noticed (let alone praised) by critics, with very few exceptions, his hopes for the next one must have grown more and more desperate and, in a form of defiance, caused him to emphasize its gratuitous, antirealistic aspects. Little excuse is thus provided for what is narrated in *Locus solus* and none whatsoever for the last fictional work that Roussel published, *Nouvelles impressions d'Afrique* (1932).

The compositional method used by Roussel in *Impressions d'Afrique* and *Locus solus* has much in common with the one he adopted for his other fiction. The process, which is also applied to his plays, was explained in detail in the posthumous *Comment j'ai écrit certains de mes livres* (1935; *How I Wrote Certain of My Books*). Had Roussel remained silent about them, the chances are that these particular devices would have remained a secret for a very long time, if not forever. Revealing such a secret was perhaps hard to resist, especially for him, considering the compulsive way every detail in his fiction is accounted for: what the narrator does for the fictional performances of *Impressions d'Afrique* Roussel emulates in order to account for his own textual performance. As a result, however, a number of critics have tended to wallow in the revelations (something similar has taken place in the case of Georges Perec) and forget that the elaborate explanations given in, say, the fiction of

Impressions d'Afrique stop short of the final revelation, which must remain a mystery. Likewise, *Comment j'ai écrit certains de mes livres* gives only the preliminary steps of his compositional devices. Critics have also tended to take too literally his affirmation that the method he described had nothing to do with the composition of *La Doublure, La Vue, La Source,* or *Nouvelles impressions d'Afrique.* Technically, he is right. But he himself has also pointed out that the method was related to verse composition: "It is essentially a poetic technique."[18] In both cases Roussel placed upon words, regardless of meaning, a large share of the creative burden. As the choice of words was sometimes arbitrary, this also has meant giving a greater role to chance. "In either case, there is unexpected creation due to phonic combinations."[19]

Roussel would take a sentence at random (but under what personal or contextual constraints?), say from a nursery rhyme or even from one of his own works, and consider it exclusively from a phonetic point of view. As in a sort of extended pun, he would then try to think of other words that might approximate his phonetic scheme. "J'ai du bon tabac dans ma tabatière" thus becomes "Jade tube onde aubade en mat à basse tierce": the new words then serve to generate elements of a story, in this case a tale told in *Impressions d'Afrique* that involves a Persian who serenaded his beloved every morning sitting by a basin where water spouted from a jade tube. Michel Butor has termed this "a sort of hallucinatory reading that consists in asking oneself, when faced with any kind of text, if it would not be possible to read it differently."[20] Marguerite Duras has done something similar, but only once, in passing as it were, when playing with the sounds of *la menthe anglaise.* Jean Ricardou, on the other hand, seems to do it as a matter of course. According to Michel Leiris, "Roussel has, much more than anyone else before him, drawn on the creative power of words. What is involved is a magical nominalism giving words the power to create things and enabling one to recreate the universe through the dislocation of a series of ordinary sentences."[21] One should remember, however, that this re-created universe negates the existing one.

Another aspect of the process involves taking two nouns, each of which could have two different meanings, and linking them with a preposition. For instance, "palmier à restauration," which could mean either a cookie for a meal or a palm tree for a restoration. The problem then was to work up a story around the ideas suggested by the two (identical) phrases as well as utilizing the words themselves. Such a problem is analogous to the one faced by the writer of a sonnet who must fit his or her statement into a given rhyme scheme, meter, and a set number of lines. It is identical when the verse form actually suggests the statement. One might recall Paul Valéry's comment on his *Cimetière marin:* "It was born, like most of my poems, out of the unexpected presence in my mind of a given rhythm."[22] Nor is the problem unrelated to that of Martial Canterel, in *Locus solus*, when, for instance, he is led to bring together two unrelated discoveries: an absolutely painless method for extracting teeth (without the use of anesthetic) on the one hand and a totally accurate formula for predicting the weather down to minute shifts in the wind and exact location and size of clouds on the other. The plight of the oversuccessful dentist faced with ever-growing mounds of extracted teeth he cannot dispose of could easily have developed into a hilarious situation. It is not hard to imagine what Marcel Aymé or Raymond Queneau might have done with such an idea, but Roussel had little sense of humor. Finally, the incongruous consequence of juxtaposing the two inventions results, perhaps, as in the case of a surrealist metaphor, in a work of art: a giant mosaic made of the thousands of variegated, discarded teeth, put together by a complicated machine activated by wind and sun. While this was already perceptible in *Impressions d'Afrique*, in *Locus solus*, just as the spectacle overshadows the framework, production of the fiction and production of the spectacle are brought closer together. The latter is the metaphor of the former.

In *Nouvelles impressions d'Afrique* the evolution is brought to a close; the fiction is the spectacle. Framework, narrator, fictional performances have completely vanished; the text requires no justification, the pretense of plausibility has been discarded. As Julia Kristeva put it, "In that universe of translinguistic productivity there is no room for plausibility—the notion remains outside, being the provincial monopoly of a consumer, data-oriented society."[23]

What confronts the reader is a 1276-line "poem" in four cantos that demanded seven years of Roussel's life. Like the mosaic in *Locus solus*, it strikes one at first as being a somewhat gratuitous tour de force. Africa, limited to Egypt, is present in the thematic headings of each canto: the house in Dumyat where Louis IX is kept prisoner, the scene of Napoleon's victory over the Turks near the pyramids, the mosque of Abul Ma'ateh, and the gardens of Rashid (Rosetta). The statement of the theme, however, occupies no more than a few lines at the beginning and a few more at the end of each canto (merely one at the end of the third and the fourth). In two instances the statement is expressed in one sentence; but in all cases the sentence that ends the canto has begun on its first page— it simply has been interrupted by another parenthetical, associative statement. That statement, in turn, is interrupted by one enclosed in double parentheses. The latter is then broken up by one or more passages within triple parentheses. As one reads on, one encounters quadruple and quintuple parentheses and also footnotes that continue the rhyme- and verse-scheme of the main text. A footnote to a line enclosed within quadruple parentheses also contains single, double, and triple parentheses and within the latter a sentence separated from the rest by a dash.

It would take a mathematician working with a computer to figure out the precise relationship of that statement to the main theme of the fourth canto, in which it occurs.

There are in *Nouvelles impressions d'Afrique* several instances of enumerations (more recent writers like Raymond Queneau or Michel Butor have also evidenced a fondness for catalogs). One in particular illustrates the device Roussel used elsewhere, but not in the composition of this last fiction, as it lists a number of words with two distinct meanings (the theme of the double is ever present). The final example of that series is the word *faute*, and its two meanings are not only distinct but opposite —negative, when it means "lack," and positive, when it means "blemish." Roussel's obsession with verbal ambiguities might well be symbolic of a more general quest, analogous to André Breton's hope (expressed at the beginning of the second surrealist manifesto) of reaching a point from which opposites would no longer be perceived as such. Michel Foucault, without suggesting this analogy, has called *Nouvelles impressions d'Afrique* a "treatise on lost identity" and a "cosmology of the Same."[24]

The line commenting on the word *faute*, with the meaning of "absence," is located not far in the poem from the one that, given the system of parentheses around which the work is built, might be considered its center: "—De se taire, parfois, riche est l'occasion" [There are sometimes great opportunities for silence]. That sentence contains the same kind of verbal antithesis that accompanied the mention of *faute:* the contrast between the profusion of *riche* and the emptiness of *taire.* At the same time, its immediate context displays a proliferation of words either suggesting or referring to fire (*feu, flambeau, grille, cendre, brûler,* and so on). It is a tantalizing statement, when one considers the role the concept of silence has assumed in contemporary criticism such as that of Maurice Blanchot, or the void that some commentators have discovered at the heart of much postwar fiction, burning away the fabric of conventional literature. It is also an ominous one when one realizes that it was followed by Roussel's own silence. Less than a year after the publication of *Nouvelles impressions d'Afrique*, all his books having been written (and instructions for the posthumous *Comment j'ai écrit certains de mes livres* carefully given), his wealth dissipated and his health gone, drink or drugs no longer effective, literally burned out, he was found dead in Palermo under circumstances as mysterious as his life and as puzzling as his works.

NOTES

1   Alain Robbe-Grillet, *Pour un nouveau roman* (Paris: Minuit, 1963), 139.
2   Jean Giraudoux, *Simon le pathétique* (Paris: Grasset, 1918), 31-32.

3 Raymond Roussel, *Comment j'ai écrit certains de mes livres* (Paris: Pauvert, 1963), 27.

4 André Breton, *Anthologie de l'humour noir* (Paris: Pauvert, 1966), 384.

5 François Caradec, *Vie de Raymond Roussel* (Paris: Pauvert, 1972), 191.

6 Roussel, *Comment j'ai écrit*, 28.

7 Pierre Schneider, "La Fenêtre ou piège à Roussel," *Cahiers du Sud*, no. 306 (1951): 470.

8 Michel Butor, "Sur les procédés de Raymond Roussel," in *Répertoire* (Paris: Minuit, 1960), 184.

9 J. H. Matthews, *Surrealism and the Novel* (Ann Arbor: University of Michigan Press, 1966), 43.

10 André Breton, "Fronton Virage," preface to Jean Ferry, *Une Etude sur Raymond Roussel* (Paris: Arcanes, 1953), 11.

11 André Gide, *Divers* (Paris: Gallimard, 1931), 45.

12 André Breton, "Les Mots sans rides," in *Les Pas perdus* (Paris: Nouvelle Revue Francaise, 1924), 169.

13 "Revival of a Writer," *Times Literary Supplement*, 9 January 1964, p. 18.

14 See Carolyn A. Durham, *L'Art romanesque de Raymond Roussel* (York, SC: French Literature Publications Company, 1982), 95.

15 This is so from the point of view of the text; if I were to consider the author's point of view, I should have to say that, as a wealthy member of bourgeois society, he would not consider the crew worth mentioning.

16 See Christiane Veschambre, "Sur les impressions d'Afrique," *Poétique* 2 (1970): 64-78.

17 Butor, "Sur les procédés de Raymond Roussel," 182.

18 Roussel, *Comment j'ai écrit*, 23.

19 Ibid.

20 Butor, "Sur les procédés de Raymond Roussel," 175.

21 Michel Leiris, "Comment j'ai écrit certains de mes livres," in *Brisées* (Paris: Mercure de France, 1966), 58-59.

22 Quoted by Jean Hytier in his notes to *OEuvres de Paul Valéry*, Bibliothèque de la Pléiade (Paris: Gallimard, 1957), 1:1674.

23 Julia Kristeva, "La Productivité dite texte," in *Séméiotiké/Recherches pour une sémanalyse* (Paris: Seuil, 1969), 244.

24 Michel Foucault, *Raymond Roussel* (Paris: Gallimard, 1963), 189, 186.

2

Nathalie Sarraute

By her own account, Nathalie Sarraute started writing in 1933—several years before Philippe Sollers was born. Within a span of five decades, from 1939 to 1989, she has published nine works of fiction, two volumes of essays, several short plays, and one text of fictionalized childhood memories. Quantitatively, that may not be too impressive, and her audience has been a rather small one. The imprint she has left, however, is undeniable. Through her effective evocation of a new level of consciousness, she has, directly or indirectly, encouraged other writers to explore new directions in fiction, to bring forth statements of their own views or transformations of reality.

Out of the tightly knit pages of her early narratives an inner world of gelatinous beings emerges under a pallid light. All anxiously groping for identical satisfactions, her creatures alternately experience pleasure and pain as tumorlike feelers either mingle with similar excrescences or become bruised by hostile reactions and are forced back into their own transparency and nakedness. Nathalie Sarraute is not primarily concerned with individual characters, for these she sees as but fictions of the mind. She is not interested in molding a conventional plot into a perfect edifice; she would agree with Sartre that "adventures" lie outside ordinary life. She cares little for polite, rational discourse, for she believes it cannot account for what goes on beneath its surface.

After quoting Katherine Mansfield's reference to "this terrible desire to establish contact," Nathalie Sarraute wrote in one of the essays of *L'Ere du soupçon* (1956; *The Age of Suspicion*), apropos of Dostoyevski's characters, that "their being continuously and madly in need of establishing contact . . . is what seizes them like a dizzy spell."[1] Dizziness might be experienced as one sways on the edge of a precipice—and, indeed, when in the same passage she alluded to Dostoyevski's statement concerning

28

the "identical permanent stock" (36) from which he had extracted the substance of all his works, she seemed to be playing on the two meanings of the French word *fonds*, which (spelled without the *s*) also means depth. The implication is that only in the depths of one's being is it possible to reach the level where any actual contact, either pleasing or painful, is possible. That is the level of truth, revealed when the protective coating of society's lacquer is removed, where the slightest impulse is registered, and the faintest perception is a scar. This level is well known by psychologists and also by traditional novelists; but Nathalie Sarraute has shunned psychological descriptions or analyses in favor of the sensations themselves, however minute or occasional they might be.

Her first book of fiction, *Tropismes* (1939), consists of nineteen disconnected descriptions (twenty-four in the 1957 edition) of that kind of event. According to biologists, a tropism is the involuntary movement of an organism in response to outside stimuli such as light, heat, or chemical agents. An American scholar has suggested that her title, in spite of its scientific tenor, might actually have a literary origin: the word appears, in a satirical context, in the early pages of André Gide's *Les Caves du Vatican.*[2] Be that as it may, Sarraute's tropisms, as she explained in the *Listener* some years ago, are those instinctive movements within one that are caused by other people or by the outside world: they "glide quickly round the border of our consciousness, they compose the small, rapid, and sometimes very complex dramas concealed beneath our actions, our gestures, the words we speak, our avowed and clear feelings."[3] At first sight, the various sketches of *Tropismes* are less "tropistic" than some of her subsequent texts. One can understand why Max Jacob, in 1939, wrote to her, "You are a profound poet, and I am placing your heavy volume (I say 'heavy volume' in the sense that one says a 'heavy heart') in a section with those poets that I reread."[4] They are prose poems, often tinged with melancholia or irony. The opening twenty-six-line sketch describes people walking in the streets, stopping in front of store windows, gazing, hardly capable of going any further, while their bored small children wait patiently for them to move on. Absorption of the individual into an aimless crowd, druglike effects of vulgar window displays, resignation of children in the face of an incomprehensible adult world—such might be the unexpressed reactions the reader could detect after giving the matter some thought. These, however, being passively observed, are apt to be overshadowed by active feelings of compassion.

Consider also the eighteenth sketch, framed in an English suburban setting. A dignified lady sits reading a magazine, knowing that "in a few moments they are going to ring the bell for tea," while in the kitchen the cook is peeling vegetables, knowing that "soon it will be time to warm the buns and ring the bell for tea." There is no outward activity of mind, for again it may be assumed that nonconscious anticipation is the reaction provoked by the approach of a given time of day, by awareness of another person's presence. But it is hard not to read irony into the scene, to ignore the more delicate tropisms in favor of social criticism. In the ninth sketch, on the other hand, there is no distracting interference. When "he" comes to visit "her" and begins at once to talk compulsively for fear that "she" might talk about herself, show her hidden self, there is no problem in identifying the inner impulses of the psyche.

Constantly, Sarraute has displayed signs of being wary of her readers: her next three works of fiction may be viewed in part as stages in an attempt to educate her audience as well as to master her own craft. As she has written in *L'Ere du soupçon,* "The reader, indeed even the most sophisticated one, as soon as he is left to his own devices, tends to create types; he simply cannot help it" (70). Not only does the reader create types, corresponding to people or characters he thinks he knows, he will also create situations, plots, or themes. He will latch on to anything in order to bend the text he is reading into the stereotyped forms provided by his culture and education. As a tentative response to that sort of reader aggressiveness, characterization, plot, and setting are reduced to a bare minimum in *Portrait d'un inconnu* (1948; *Portrait of a Man Unknown*). One might call it naked fiction, or perhaps abstract fiction (as Monique Wittig suggested, by analogy with abstract painting), for decor, social masks, and Sartrian "adventure" are stripped away, leaving us, presumably, with what actually takes place. The title, which refers to a painting by an anonymous artist the narrator has seen in a museum, is a metaphor of the fiction—as well as its generator. The anonymous "I" attempts a portrait of an unknown "he"—and both painting and text stare at the reader, sounding a call that is "pathetic, demanding" (86) and at the same time desperately silent.

In that silence lies a major theme of Sarraute's entire output: the urgent need for communication, which can be detected deep within every human being, is constantly being thwarted or crushed by falsehood, artifice, and social codes. The fronts people put up and the conventions they adhere to provide a semblance of security and communication, but they merely disguise the reality of human solitude. Silence and lies correspond to the two poles between which her texts oscillate: that for which there are no words, and that which is rendered in clichés. Success lies somewhere in the middle, in the adequation of language with elementary sensation; failure lies at either pole.

The opening pages of the book describe precisely such a failure experienced by the narrator with two different groups. With the one he encounters outright rejection, with the other a more complex misunderstanding. As a fictional device, the extremely sensitive, anonymous "I," whom we see from the inside, is pitted against characters, also nameless, who are seen only from without. Unable to break through their protective casing, the narrator has been forced back upon himself to a pathological degree. Throughout what I shall call the first part of *Portrait d'un inconnu*, up to and including the fifth chapter (actually, chapters in this and other fictions by Sarraute are unnumbered), the narrative stress is on him: everyone else, even the other two main characters, "elle" and "lui," are merely opportunities for him to display his sensitivity, and digressions give him occasion to present his views. (The latter naturally tend to give the work a slightly didactic tone.) Except for the portrait of the title (also described in the text) and two references to Utrillo, cultural correlatives in this part belong to the most introspective of all arts, literature.

The fifth chapter, which takes the narrator to a Dutch city, amid evocations of Baudelaire's "Invitation au voyage," ends with his visit to the museum. There, the *Portrait of a Man Unknown*, striking mainly because of its eyes ("his glance took hold of me"), perfects the false cure begun earlier by a psychiatrist: "I was free. My mooring lines were cut. I sailed, driven towards the open sea" (87). Liberating him from an obsession with self, the painting opens his mind to others. Specifically, it causes him to identify with the unknown artist and attempt to understand the man unknown—"lui," who is the father of "elle." The second part lays stress on this other character. The cultural correlatives, with the sole exception of Lewis Carroll, are painters. The woman of the story, who, at first reading, might appear to hold a central position, the object of the narrator's advances, stands revealed as a catalytic agent enabling both her father and the narrator to bare their own selves—through the writer's exposure of tropisms. All three are sensitive people; that is what, at this point, makes the revelation possible. A concluding chapter introduces a man named Louis Dumontet, who is engaged to "elle." He is all solid surface and shielded, as it were, by his name; no tropisms emanate from him.

Martereau, the character who has given his name to Sarraute's third work of fiction (1953), appears more solid and secure (like Louis Dumontet), especially when confronted with the delicate, nameless narrator and his equally nameless relatives. When his name is first mentioned, it suggests a "distant homeland," a "peaceful haven" (85, 86) from which the narrator has been banned. Gradually, that name is shown to be no more than a mask: the manner in which it is associated with Holland in the text actually suggests a trompe l'oeil quality. As it crumbles away, Martereau's uncertain gropings and ambiguous feelings are brought to light—or, it may be better to say, into the twilight.

In addition to Martereau, about whom a plot of sorts evolves, more than half a dozen episodic or referential characters are also given names. Cultural correlatives, no longer exclusively taken from the realm of art and literature as in *Portrait d'un inconnu*, also come from history or legend. Both changes help to anchor the book in the reader's familiar reality, even though that may not have been intentional, and, at times, the anchor seems to drag a bit. It is clear that Sarraute intended to reveal Martereau as being as much the locus of tropisms as anyone else: "He is as people are, not in traditional novels, but in real life."[6] Somehow, she does not quite bring it off, and it is hard to blame those who see Martereau as more "authentic"[7] than the narrator—precisely because he fits conventional reality and appears unaffected by the wild fancies the latter's imagination indulges in.

The inadequacies of first-person narrative, here really a modified interior monologue, are more obvious in *Martereau* than in *Portrait d'un inconnu.* There we were dealing with a set of relatively homogeneous beings. The problem as to the reality of some of the descriptions is only a minor one: other people's reactions, as supposed or imagined by the narrator, are always plausible within the atmosphere of the book. But in *Martereau* two different worlds are involved, that of "solid reality" (the masked people) and that of the semiconscious tropisms (the unmasked, hypersensitive people). To penetrate Martereau's protective shell the reader needs an intelligence other than the narrator's. Since Sarraute does not provide it, Martereau's inner reality and the narrator's imagination become confused. What, from an ordinary reader's point of view, "saves" the book, ironically, is the element of suspense and ambiguity contained in the plot. Will Martereau, who has agreed to go along with a tax-evasion scheme and bought a house in his own name but with money from the narrator's uncle, consent to relinquish the house? Such a question, however, is obviously irrelevant to Sarraute's concern.

In *Le Planétarium* (1959)—a false sky in which stars merely appear to be located—she has wisely adopted a stance halfway between omniscient writer and recorder of different points of view, thus entering the consciousness of a large number of characters without creating confusion. Some of these are readily identifiable by name, and their activities seem to converge into a gossamer plot, which, metaphorically, is represented by the dome of the planetarium. The successful efforts of the main character, Alain Guimiez, to deprive his spinster Aunt Berthe of a spacious apartment so that he and his wife might move into more comfortable quarters make up the merely superficial sound and fury of middle-class life. Hidden to the naked eye like quasars in space, tropisms manifest their parallel existence as everyone responds or seeks a response, strives for approval or identification. On the plane of such movements it matters little which character is involved, for, as one of them says, "Everyone is alike, everyone resembles everyone else" (34)—and this is supposedly true regardless of sex or social standing.

Actually, in *Le Planétarium,* there seldom is any lasting doubt as to which character is involved at any given moment; when there is, as in the case of the woman who bursts out laughing at the party given by the Guimiez's in-laws, the uncertainty does not apply to any of those one has decided to call "principal." An excuse is thus provided for a gradual attempt at characterization, and the attention paid to such matters is easily diverted to the anecdotal dealings of characters with one another and thus to the elaboration of a significant plot. One critic has described the process as follows: "Gradually the pronouns begin to germinate, the bones take flesh, the flayed psyches acquire expression, and, for one reader at least, the metamorphosis is complete. Immediately the whole novel slips into a new perspective: good, sound construction appears, faintly reminiscent of Angus Wilson, with a coherent plot . . . and characters!"[8]

Again it appears that Sarraute was aware of having allowed such interpretations of her fourth work of fiction, of the difficulties involved in getting her point across. In *Les Fruits d'or* (1963; *The Golden Fruits*) she gives evidence of having acquired an even greater degree of control over her technique and material. This work has very little extraneous decor, and it is remarkably successful from the point of view of her aesthetic aims. The slender plot involves the rise and fall of a novel's reputation, thus bringing plot and topic closer together. Tropisms within an indeterminate number of characters and presented, as in *Le Planétarium*, from as many different points of view, grow in intensity as the imaginary work, "Les Fruits d'or," becomes quite the rage among members of the Paris literary set. As the opinion makers impose their views those tropisms reach their highest level of intensity and then recede as the novelty wears off and a new fad takes its place, eventually pushing the book into oblivion. If such a plot can be called slender, however, it is also a serious one. It does not seem, as in the previous fictions, a mere pretext allowing the writer to deal with what she is really interested in. The doorknob and plate of *Le Planétarium* could have been a mirror or a chandelier; the apartment could have been any other valuable possession; and the book would have remained essentially the same.

The making and unmaking of a novel's image as contrasted with its intrinsic nature and merit raise questions as to what constitutes a literary masterpiece (assuming that the term still has meaning, as it does within the framework of that book) or, in more general fashion, as to what criteria may be used to assign value to any given text. Such matters must be of considerable concern to a writer as dedicated as Sarraute, even more so after the publication of several controversial works, when comments from admirers may well have been as embarrassing as attacks by detractors were exasperating. These matters should also be of great interest to readers who expect more from a book than a temporary diversion.

In *Les Fruits d'or* the anecdote can no longer be called trifling, for it has reached a plane of significance that is comparable to the new aspect of human reality revealed through tropisms. These again take place within characters that are not always named and are seldom identified; readers are thus frustrated in their desire to create a set of characters and link them along in the chain of a linear story. Three unnamed persons, two men and a woman, are clearly involved in the first ten pages of the book. Others (but are they really "others"?) named Marcel, Lucien, and Jacques appear in subsequent pages. A man named Bréhier is obviously the author of "Les Fruits d'or." Brulé, Orthis, and Mettetal are critics. Their interrelationship and who speaks or reacts to whom at any given moment could possibly be determined by painstaking analysis—but that would no longer constitute creative reading, it would amount to sheer pedantry.

   Entre la vie et la mort (1968; *Between Life and Death*) gives one the other side of the picture: no longer concerned, as in *Les Fruits d'or*, with the fate of a novel after it has been published, Sarraute turns the spotlight on what is called the "creative process." In the words of Mary McCarthy, "Nothing of the sort—a rending of the veil—has been attempted before, and one would have said in advance that it was impossible, short of demonstration, to show how an author composes, that is, to create with words a sort of program music imitating the action of other words as they assemble on a page."⁹ Somehow Sarraute succeeds, perhaps because, to her, verbal composition is the most interesting side of the literary phenomenon, just as hidden tropisms fascinate her more than outward gestures—and there is a definite link between tropisms and productivity. As Yvon Belaval wrote with reference to her earlier volume, *Tropismes*, "Nathalie Sarraute has chosen as her topic creation as it comes to life."¹⁰ Indeed, finding appropriate words to match sensations, emotions, or events is what most writers have usually been concerned with.

   The setting of *Entre la vie et la mort* is absolutely barren except for metaphors expressing inner psychological states or actions that transport one to a king's court or a military encampment. The technique is as effective as, if not more so than, in *Les Fruits d'or*. Surnames are few and even less conspicuous than in the preceding work. There is Régier, a famous writer, Frémiot, the publisher, and Burel, his editor; the rest are utilities. All play inconsequential parts compared to the anonymous writer, whose composition the book is about, his family, friends of prepublication days, and the new ones he has made after the work he has been struggling with has appeared. Each provides a stage for the manifestation of tropisms. Broad outlines of a narrative can be detected: the writer, whose book has given him notoriety, explains to his admirers how he works; then a series of flashbacks reveal his developing sensitivity as a boy, encouragements from his mother, his efforts at writing, literary discussions with friends, acceptance of manuscript by the publisher, his mother's and father's reactions, and the book's success; again explanations of himself and the way he composes. Of course, my suggested outline becomes rather blurred when one actually reads the book, and chronology is not faithfully adhered to.

The title refers to the precarious state of the writer in the presence of the deep, essential fountainhead within himself, out of which his activity flows: he must withdraw from society into the self (where there is silence, darkness, and the danger of death) but cannot go too far or too long lest contact with others (life) be severed. Sensitivity leads the writer to that spring, and the problem is to stay close to it while still remaining in touch with the world, for if it is lost or runs dry the creative artist in him dies. (Sarraute sees herself as a writer who happens to be a woman, and she favors the masculine pronoun when referring to writers.) Such preoccupation with the background of the work and stress on sensitivity to the material would set Sarraute apart from many of the leading writers of the postwar generation. *Entre la vie et la mort* affirms her independence from the most recent trends. Even more so than in *Les Fruits d'or*, she relies on irony to define her position. Toward the end of that work, after the noise made by fashionable fakers has subsided, one reader manages to establish a rapport with "Les Fruits d'or," and his attitude is conveyed in straightforward fashion. But here, such positive statements as exist are dispersed throughout the text and presented in tentative manner: "everything here should assist in the unfolding, the asserting of—what should I call it? This activity of a fragment of living substance?" (EVM 104). The writer, as the romanticists had already decided, suffers more than other people. *Entre la vie et la mort* might well have been subtitled, "Portrait of the Artist as a Young Martyr."

The quality of writing evidenced in *Vous les entendez?* (1972; *Do You Hear Them?*), "*Disent les imbéciles*" (1976; "*fools say*"), and *Tu ne t'aimes pas* (1989; *You Don't Love Yourself*) is the highest she has achieved. A small pre-Columbian sculpture is central to the setting of *Vous les entendez?* as a painting was to that of *Portrait d'un inconnu* and a book to *Les Fruits d'or*; as it is owned by one of its fictional beings, it again suffuses the text with the upper middle-class aura of earlier works. The sculpture functions as a sort of textual generator (to use Jean Ricardou's terminology) as it occasions the tropisms of this particular text. As it is pre-Columbian (or perhaps Cretan—an indeterminacy that is frequent with Sarraute) it originated in another culture, in a distant time period, where it was not considered as "art" but was probably a ritual object linked to religious or magical practices; it has now been desacralized and wrapped in the cloak of "art." This involves a different kind of sacralization, characteristic of our own time. Selected artifacts and written works are viewed with awe and reverence; they become the models with which new ones are compared and often found wanting. As a consequence, the traditional and the stereotype are encouraged, the innovative and the unconventional are disparaged—and these attitudes are what Sarraute has been struggling against in her own work. Here, she examines cultural stereotypes through a clash of generations; this is hardly original, but by using her tropisms to pit the young's iconoclastic feelings against the complacent, tradition-bound attitudes of older people, she brings out a broad range of individual psychic actions and reactions. Broadly speaking, spontaneous, nearly uncontrolled, "crystallike" laughter ("Just listen to them!") is the repeated response to the standardized cultural training the young are subjected to. Their parents, however, give a peculiar twist to their own aims: "Haven't they acquired this immediate self-control, this perfectly natural attitude that at first glance enables one to recognize manners that have become similar to reflexes, which an accomplished education provides?" (VLE 200). Ironically, the owner of the statue (no one bears a name in this book) almost becomes appealing as he ages and dies, and the statue is given to the Louvre; the young, on the other hand, his own children, as they age in turn, start wearing the same masks they thought so silly.

"Disent les imbéciles" reads like a purified version of *Le Planétarium* or a more integrated writing of *Tropismes*. There are no names, there is no plot, no artifact (painting, apartment, book, or sculpture) to draw one's attention away from the essential. The fragmentary aspect of *Tropismes*, which is once more in evidence, is worth stressing, as critics and writers alike have recently become interested in the notion of the fragment in literature. Here again, Sarraute assumes the position of a forerunner. A sequence of a dozen narrative pieces of unequal length, each presents a consciousness confronted with what others seem to say about it, which is also the way they give it shape (and this, incidentally, is supported by Lacanian psychoanalysis). Lacan also spoke of "the possibility I have . . . to use [language] in order to signify *something quite other* than what it says."[11] In related fashion tropisms suggest that we understand the speech of others as signifying something different from what it says—something that nurtures our unconscious fears.

Tu ne t'aimes pas carries the refining work even further. It is fragmentary, there is no plot and no setting; very few names are mentioned, almost inadvertently it would seem—Cézanne and the fictitious Robert and Galion (123, 45, 108). Everyone else is anonymous and, what is even more striking, the narrator (the term is somewhat inadequate) is plural, fragmented as well. What others see as a person, the narrator(s) consider(s) to be "one of our possible embodiments, one of our virtualities," sometimes a "delegate" or "envoy" (9, 59, 111). This function is related to the masks worn by some of the characters in the earlier novels. The narrator(s) is (are) aware of the complexity of their own being, qualities and faults included. One day, after the "delegate" had displayed an unattractive trait, one of the "others" said, "The trouble with you is, you don't think highly of yourself" (12). In French, of course, since the "other" is not an intimate friend, the formal "vous" was used, which is also a plural. This allows for constant ambiguity as meaning fluctuates between singular and plural—unified and complex personality. "Others" are seen as being fond of themselves, they have fabricated a mask out of what they deem their best features, they have hidden or repressed everything else, they give the impression of being made of a piece, and this, ironically, is the impression the narrator(s) give(s) others, through the "delegate." Like the earlier Dumontet and Martereau, they are solid and secure, they bask in Love, Success, and Happiness (47-52). The narrator(s), on the other hand, seem like a representation of the writer— hypersensitive, aware of everything, and suffering. In several ways, this writer is related to Baudelaire's *Heautontimoroumenos,* although there is enough irony in *Tu ne t'aimes pas* to keep one from identifying him with Nathalie Sarraute herself.

Tropisms take place, according to her own definition, beneath the level of actions, gestures, and words. Words, on the other hand, whatever the writer in *Entre la vie et la mort* may say, are the basic components of fiction. The problem of expressing those wordless events is perhaps no greater than that involved in rendering violent emotions that transcend normal powers of expression. One might even say, with Yvon Belaval, that "a word is no more profound if it has been uttered silently rather than articulated aloud; when a novelist or poet uses it to depict feelings, its nature does not change whether it refers to the shadow cast by a post on a terrace or the shadow of a doubt, whether it conveys a truism or a subtle remark."[12] Nevertheless, though the nature of words is not affected, difficulties are increased when a writer endeavors, as Sarraute does, to have readers participate in the activity rather than to give them a description of it. In all cases, of course, the choice of words must be appropriate and effective. Where tropisms are concerned, the choice of imagery can also pose a number of problems.

I have already alluded, in the case of Martereau, to the fictional link Sarraute establishes between a character's name and the social masks he dons. Direct, conventional use of the word *mask* thus occurs, as when it is defined as "that individual, artificial, fixed expression people often assume when they look at themselves in a mirror" (PI 63). It is also a "heavy, hard cast" (M 32) that they fashion in order to portray others, like the "grotesque and outmoded mask of a musical-comedy mother-in-law" (P 52) that Alain has placed on Gisèle's mother. The use of a name as metaphor for such masks, fairly obvious in *Portrait d'un inconnu* and *Martereau,* is somewhat more complex in *Le Planétarium.* There, most characters bear only one name, with the exception of Alain Guimiez, Germaine Lemaire, and a minor personage, Professor Adrien Lebat.

Germaine Lemaire's protégé, René Montalais, Alain's wife, Gisèle
Guimiez, and his father, Pierre Guimiez, also have full names, but their
first and last names are never associated. We know Alain's mother only
by her maiden name, Delarue; his aunt is Tante Berthe, his late uncle,
Henri; Gisèle's father and mother are merely Robert and Madeleine;
Germaine Lemaire's other disciples appear as Jean-Luc, Lucette, and
Jacques. Secondary characters appear only as names, that is, as masks or
silhouettes that enter fleetingly the main characters' range of perception. Major characters (whose names are, on the whole, infrequently
mentioned) carry their names as they might an artificial excrescence that
is either emphasized or not, according to the needs of the fiction. It
would appear that, for instance, "Germaine Lemaire" and "Maine," her
nickname, are two very different masks; or that "Alain Guimiez," "Alain,"
"he," "son," "nephew," and "son-in-law" correspond to different levels of
reality. What previous novelists had usually restricted to dialogue (and it
requires an entire novel for Jane Eyre to go from "Mr. Rochester" to "my
Edward") Sarraute diffuses throughout the whole text. A similar,
although simpler device is used in *Les Fruits d'or* where characters
evolve on three separate levels: they are anonymous (baring their sensations), bearers of given names (indeterminate), or bearers of last names
(hiding or repressing sensations). Even though *Les Fruits d'or* appears
more effective in this respect, the device is not carried to *Entre la vie et la
mort*, in which the reader is not allowed behind the masks of named
characters; anonymity returns with *Vous les entendez?*

Ordinary words, too, are but the proper names for objects, actions, or
thoughts—in common usage, at least; like them, they can be bearers of
masks. Frequently, one finds Sarraute skillfully shifting back and forth
between stereotypes and what might be called a person's idiosyncratic
language. As with characters, the device is more obvious in the first two
works of fiction following *Tropismes*. Stereotyped words or phrases are
occasionally found within quotation marks or even capitalized in *Portrait
d'un inconnu* and *Martereau:* "We have entered the Sacred Domain of
'Life,' as they call it, of 'Practical Matters,' of 'Hard Facts,' as they say with
a sigh" (PI 58); "Money that I have earned 'by the sweat of my brow,' just
imagine" (M 23). In *Le Planétarium*, however, a comment like "such fine
workmen who know their job thoroughly, who love it, too, one should
always patronize the better stores" (P 10) bears no sign of emphasis—no
more than its opposite number, "idiots, big brutes, without an ounce of
initiative, no interest in what they are doing, not the slightest intimation
of good taste" (13), made, of course, by the same person about the same
workmen who have come to install a new door. Stereotyped words and
phrases are both protective, in that they help to establish a character in
his or her accustomed role, and harmless because they have no more
significance than what happens in the course of a parlor game: "Happy

smiles . . . sympathetic glances . . . exquisite scene" (149). What takes place on the level of sensations, on the other hand, is linked at times to the "bloody games of the Roman circus" (M 75); or to a bullfight when "a bull, dripping with blood, lowers its head and confronts the matador" (P 143); or to the experiences of early Christians in the catacombs— "they are surrounded by pagans, hunted down, they will be martyred, humiliated" (FO 110); or to scenes of torture, with "a sadist relentlessly torturing his victim" (EVM 55). In all such instances, words are no longer harmless; they harbor pernicious germs (M 133). As the narrator in *Martereau* expresses it, "There are no harmless words between us, there are no longer any harmless words" (283).

The metaphor of protective shell is but a short conceptual step from that of mask. There are, in Sarraute's first three full-length works of fiction, at least forty specific references to a shell (either *coquille* or *carapace*, depending on the connotation desired). We witness characters who "struggle, forehead against forehead, clumsily ensconced in their shells, their heavy suits of armor: 'I am the Father, the Daughter, my Rights' " (PI 48). The analogy between the two groups of metaphors is made obvious through juxtaposition. In addition, there are even more numerous uses of such related adjectives as *hard, smooth, solid,* and the like, applied to characters when their guard is up and they have taken refuge behind society's props. Louis Dumontet is thus represented as "Extremely sure of himself. Impassive. Imposing. A reef. A rock that has withstood all of the ocean's onslaughts. Unassailable. A compact block. All smooth and hard" (PI 222). Even the syntax is adapted to the metaphor of rocky solidity. There is also a kind of shell that protects not only the wearer but others as well, the uniform. Related to stereotyped phrases, it enables everyone to play his or her part and identify others in unthinking security. "He is undressed, they give him his underwear to put on, it is part of the prescribed dress. They have him don his uniform" (EVM 25). The issuing of a uniform constitutes a sort of exorcism. Opposed to hardness and relative safety, there is softness and vulnerability. Correspondingly, one finds many adjectives describing such a state, as in the following example: "At his feet, she was there before him, thoroughly soft, at his mercy, always within reach" (PI 196).

Earlier, when quoting a passage from *L'Ere du soupçon,* I suggested the image of a precipice to express the feeling of those about to establish contact on a deeper level. As a character totters on the edge of the abyss (there are about fifty references to *bottom, hole, void,* and so forth), he is overcome by dizziness and then usually sinks into the chasm. The process is a slow one, and characters are agonizingly conscious of it: "That time, as it almost always happens when things have gone a bit too far, I had the impression of 'hitting bottom' " (PI 25). They do not fall precipitously; rather they slide (the verb *glisser* alone appears about sixty times), as the old man and his daughter do in *Portrait d'un inconnu:* "Their shells, their armor are splitting up all over, they are naked, without protection, they slide downward, they go down as if to the bottom of a well" (185). On their way down, some occasionally manage to catch hold of something solid and chin themselves up to the surface again. More than fifty instances of verbs conveying the idea of clinging to, holding on to, testify to their reluctance to leave their accustomed level. What they most want is security. There are thus many references to the verb *to cuddle up (se blottir)* in a warm, safe place, often in a *nest*—a word having similarly cute, stereotyped overtones in French as in English.

Unwillingness to let go of a solid, artificial world is also conveyed by the usually unfavorable connotations of the words used to describe what is found beneath. Fearful characters find that level markedly suspicious (as evidenced by the frequent appearance of the word *louche*—"shifty, suspicious"). They picture it as an amorphous world of undefinable, slightly repulsive motions (*remous* and *grouillements*—"swirls" and "swarmings"), where all things are soft and gluey (*gluant*), where living entities are reduced to the condition of larvae. Ironically, one of the literati praising the fictitious novel in *Les Fruits d'or* emphasizes that it contains "no swarming of larvae, no floundering in some miry depths or other emitting asphyxiating miasma, in some undefinable slimy ooze where one sinks in" (60).

Such uneasy sensations as characters experience when viewing the depths of their being lend a mysterious, almost magical aura to the nether regions. Those are the primitive areas of mankind, also the archaic space of the psyche (but Sarraute is leery of psychoanalytic connotations), where our artificial civilization has not penetrated, and strange, terrifying powers appear to reign. Their demoniacal nature is implied by Nathalie Sarraute's occasional use of the verb *to exorcise.* One instance occurs when she is speaking of Dumontet's use of clichés: "Those words he seems to reel off mechanically must eventually have the soothing, exorcising effect that simple, monotonous words of prayer have upon non-believers" (PI 236); and another, when a disappointed Alain returns from the apartment of Germaine Lemaire and invokes his masks: "Gisèle ... my love, my wife ... Gisèle ... That name exorcises" (P 111). Waiting to be exorcised, so that they might enter the Sacred Domain of a previous quotation, are several ghouls, vampires, dragons, and a sorceress. Complementing this exorcistic process, a certain amount of religious imagery might be expected; there are hints of it, as when Martereau's cordial handshake and backslap have a soothing effect on the narrator, like "the imposition of hands, exorcism, the sign of the cross that causes the Evil One to flee" (M 91); but it becomes significant mainly in *Les Fruits d'or.* I shall return to that point presently.

Once they have reached the realm of sensations, characters can truly communicate. They do so either through a devious utilization of words that become like "tiny safety valves releasing heavy gases, unhealthy emanations" (M 283), when something about the tone, the sound of a person's voice, even the pauses between utterances suggests suspicion or hatred. They can also confide more directly, through a mysterious, instantaneous process. Here we reach the crux of Sarraute's problem, for, as I indicated earlier, and as the narrator in *Martereau* makes clear, "All this and even more is expressed not through words, of course, as I must express it now, lacking other means" (34). She, too, as supernarrator, must use words. Her answer, in the composition of her fiction up to and including *Le Planétarium*, and again in *Entre la vie et la mort*, seems to have resided in extensive recourse to animal imagery. Basic, semi-conscious actions and reactions taking place below the polished level of civilized life are thus pictured as analogous to the instinctive comportment of animals.

Animal metaphors occur in instances that number in the hundreds. Some thirty-odd references are to animals in general (*bête* or *animal* with an appropriate qualifying phrase). There are in addition at least one boar, two toads, two horses, four tigers and hyenas, four mice, four bulls, five pigs or piglets, six foxes, six monkeys, seven cats, seven wolves, a dozen snakes, a flock of sheep, and forty-odd dogs or packs of dogs! One also detects half a dozen larvae, a dozen or so more developed underwater creatures, forty birds, and close to fifty insects of various kinds. All that in addition to the reference to animals in common sayings or proverbs such as *il n'y a pas de quoi fouetter un chat* ("not worth making a fuss about"), which occurs several times.

Closely related to such metaphors, numerous implicit or explicit appeals to the sense of smell catch the reader's attention. They do, in a way, belong to the group of animal actions, beasts commonly being credited with acutely developed olfactory abilities; but human beings, too, register scents with varying degrees of intensity, small children more so than adults (and the early life of the psyche is again suggested). It is also more difficult here to draw the line between an obviously intentional use of an animal characteristic and the perhaps unconscious use of a figure of speech. When, for instance, does *flair* really mean "scent," and when does it mean something like "instinctive feeling"? What matters, in the final analysis, is the effect on the reader. Because of the sheer number of references involved, it is quite likely that many of the clichés in Sarraute's fiction have been contaminated, so to speak, and reactivated by proximity to live metaphors. At any rate, smells are linked to the more primitive, uncivilized activities of man, and it is significant to find about one hundred fairly specific references to odors or to the act of smelling, in addition to or associated with some fifty references to "emanations" that may or may not be perceived with the nose, ranging all the way from an "exquisite, cool scent" (M 51) to "the miasmas that emanate from us" (EVM 24) and a "vague carrionlike stench" (M 175).

The olfactory appeal is dominant although far from exclusive; but when made in combination with appeals to other senses, it would seem to make the most lasting impression. For instance, in *Martereau*, the uncle on his way home thinks of his wife and pictures her as "silky and pink, wearing perfume" (*soyeuse et rose, parfumée*, 55). The words convey tactile, visual, and olfactory impressions, and all three adjectives are general in nature. *Soyeuse* has connotations that tend to make it overlap into areas of sight (silk is shiny, and the metaphorical connotation of "radiance" may well be aided in French by the near homonym *soyeuse/ joyeuse*) and hearing (silk swishes). *Rose* is not a particularly original or distinguishing attribute, especially considering that the human eye has the ability to register phenomena with great precision. *Parfumée* is pleasantly vague, but olfactory perceptions in man are rather imprecise. The scent, however, is amplified by a nearly automatic throwback to *rose*, now perceived not as a color but as a fragrant flower—the net result being that the third qualifier seems the most effective, the most likely to be remembered. Stylistically less subtle but perhaps more typical of the undertow that occasionally catches the reader off balance is the account of Pierre, in *Le Planétarium*, as he approaches his sister: "He gives off a kind of radiation, like a fluid, it flows out toward people, out of his narrow eyes, out of his Buddha-like smile, out of his silence" (136).

Visual elements are present throughout the fiction, although less strikingly, and visual imagery as such is relatively rare. There is an obvious connection here with the world of outward appearances as opposed to the realm of sensations. More visual references appear in *Le Planétarium* where the surface of life is given greater emphasis than in both the previous and the most recent fiction, and also in *Les Fruits d'or*. Very little can actually be *seen* in *Portrait d'un inconnu* or *Martereau*. Characteristically, visual sense impressions are most precise and frequent in those pages of *Portrait d'un inconnu* that deal with the narrator's travels, after he says he has been exorcised (81); and a number of them are directly inspired by Baudelaire's "Invitation au voyage" (the references to Holland and to painting are significant in this respect). In *Martereau*, they are more noticeable wherever Martereau and his wife are involved. In *Les Fruits d'or*, the metaphorical connection between sight and mask is illustrated in the "recognition" scene: "We are, after all, among people of our class. . . . Same flower in the buttonhole, same spats and satin vest, same eyeglass" (12). A visual picture emerges, one sees a kind of masquerade. That is in contrast to the unusual instance of a technically visual image that leaves practically no visual impression, such as "the semidarkness of what is poetically called the inner landscape" (Pl 25).

Finally, tactile references also appear in noticeable numbers in Sarraute's fiction. This is consistent with what we have seen so far, since, like olfactory ones, they correspond to a more primitive means of perception and communication. If there are fewer tactile than olfactory references, it is probably because actual contact may be considered a metaphorical representation of Sarraute's supposed goal for her characters. A tactile metaphor conveys the satisfaction felt during one of those rarely achieved moments: "The two of us are there, as we used to be, huddled together, isolated from all others. I experience the delightful, comfortable feeling one has upon plunging into a lukewarm bath" (PI 46).

Many of the metaphors either suggest violence or are explicitly linked with it. Roman circuses and bullfights have already been mentioned. The contemporary circus provides an image of mental torture as characters are made to play the clown, and they make themselves ridiculous under the floodlights, before a crowd of spectators (M 259; EVM 234). Military imagery and an accompanying array of wounds, humiliations, and conquests, within contexts ranging from the Turkish overthrow of Byzantium to attacks by American Indians and armored vehicles prowling through a conquered city, serve to render the feeling of psychological torture that people experience in confrontation with others. Animals, in many instances, are preying upon other animals, fleeing before them, or fighting. The vocabulary of the hunt provides a ritualistic element, enabling related metaphors to mirror the complexity of human relationships, those hardly perceptible but sudden shifts from the instinctual to the polite. All that violence is, in the main, essentially negative: it is almost invariably depicted from the point of view of the victim or of someone in sympathy with him or her. The aggressor is basically the Other. Nearly every one of Sarraute's main characters could exclaim with Alain Guimiez, "There is only one victim here, myself" (P 86)—and in *Entre la vie et la mort* that becomes the writer's own cry.

None of Sarraute's imagery is unusual per se. The emphasis on certain image categories is perhaps more so, but even in that respect there are precedents. A striking analogy exists between the imagery of her fiction and François Mauriac's. Martin Turnell has noted the older Mauriac's preoccupation with the sense of smell, his "use of the language of violence," his frequent references to mud, squalor, and decay, his predilection for animal and insect metaphors.[13] It is not too important that the two writers were probably drawn to those categories for analogous reasons: a portrayal of the base nature of man when unaided by God on the one hand, a description of instinctive, preconscious phenomena on the other. In each case, a very different value judgment is implied. What may be more significant is the effect upon readers of types of images that they are made to absorb in greater proportion than usual.

Timorous Catholics have denounced Mauriac for being obsessed with sin, perhaps even enjoying it, and attracting perverse readers to his books. One critic has accused Sarraute of defining human relationships through her insect comparisons.[14] Another has referred to her "sadism" and characterized her view of human relations as being "at the same time a gluey aggression and a somewhat vile collusion."[15] This is but one more illustration of the power of stereotyped cultural ideology, such as the simple one that determines the connotations of "high" and "low";[16] it is likely that Sarraute herself sensed the danger in her use of such imagery.

While her stress was already more attenuated in *Le Planétarium*, in *Les Fruits d'or* she tilted the scales away from her menagerie, while in *Entre la vie et la mort* and even more so in *Vous les entendez?* she has achieved a balance that is far more effective, considering the cultural context. In *Les Fruits d'or*, the Sacred Domain conjures up visions of religious rites, ecstasies, and persecutions. Literature, or rather its false front embodied in Parisian literary cliques, has become "a sacred abode" (48). Sarraute presents one with visions of an orthodox, dogmatic, church hierarchy, supplemented with well-meaning innocents to whom the kingdom of heaven belongs (108), who are shaken by heretics who roam the streets in their bare feet, beating their breasts, calling for repentance, and preaching the gospel of Christ (124). Establishment critics and their salon henchmen are the high priests of a hollow religion in which the faithful are concerned only with being in step with the authorities; the work of art is far less important than one's attitude toward it. The critic is the one who allows the crowd of worshipers to "file silently through the sacred halls filled with the relics that [he] has presented for their veneration, that [he] has offered, imposed upon them as objects of their piety" (52). The metaphorical religion is not necessarily Christian, and one of the opinion makers exhibits the "smile of a Hindu deity" (92). Other categories have not completely disappeared; they came to the fore again in *Entre la vie et la mort*, only to be toned down in *Vous les entendez?* and *"Disent les imbéciles,"* where, for instance, animal "shells" give way to man-made "partitions" (60, 61).

The relative emphasis on religious imagery in *Les Fruits d'or* led Dominique Aury to observe that "Literature has assumed the sacred character of Religion or Party, it harbors Inquisitors and Stalinists."[17] This was perhaps placing too much stress on particular moments in the text and disregarding Sarraute's irony. It again illustrates the danger inherent in an unbalanced use of imagery. In this instance, the emotional impact of a series of related images obliterated the appeal directed by irony at the intellect. The spread of imagery in *Entre la vie et la mort*, in my opinion, does better justice to the topic. Religious imagery is present, but more subdued than in the previous book, as when the writer exclaims: "Flaubert . . . Baudelaire . . . just like them . . . you understand nothing . . .

I take upon myself all the sins of the world" (83). Sarraute's control is close to its peak. Indeed, Dominique Aury had previously reproached her with being too much a master of her topic, too much a master of her craft.[18] I believe readers are apt to notice craftsmanship to the extent that they are unable to enter into the writer's fictional structure. In the case of Sarraute, a sizable part of her potential literary audience was apparently left outside. The perceptive readers she has had are found, in the main, among a select number of critics and fellow novelists as different in their practice as Claude Mauriac or Philippe Sollers, for instance. Mauriac, in one of his texts, has his fictional novelist state, "his friend Nathalie Sarraute alone had been able to express those silent exchanges that are so little known even though everyone has experienced them."[19]

In her essays Sarraute has accurately diagnosed the reader's tendency to manufacture characters, even when given the slightest of clues, as an obstacle to the understanding of a text based on tropisms. Making up characters, however, is but one particular aspect of the reader's imaginative potential, which writers recently have encouraged rather than hindered. It is, after all, even in its more limited, traditional scope, such an ability that makes reading an active, fruitful pursuit. But somehow she has felt the compulsion to structure her fiction so that readers are not encouraged to "create." It might perhaps have been better to take advantage of the readers' potential, guiding it in order to lead them to the discovery of her "truth." Readers tend to be more willing to accept what they themselves have partly made up. Even had they distorted it to some extent, the consequences would not have been catastrophic. At this point one might well recall Proust's remark concerning distortion in literature: "Fine books are written in a kind of foreign tongue. Each one of us, over the words of a text, places a meaning, or at least an image, which is often a misinterpretation. But in fine books, all such misinterpretations are beautiful."[20]

As things stand, with the reader as enemy, Nathalie Sarraute is at the mercy of her own errors and weaknesses, which can lose her a battle or even the war. Success depends on her maintaining him or her constantly within her grasp, fighting on her own terms. As has been pointed out, a book of hers "attacks us where we are most vulnerable: not in the rational regions of the mind, but somewhere beyond, or on the very fringes of consciousness, destroying our assumptions and beliefs before they are so much as formulated; and we have no defense."[21] The reader must then be kept in a state of hallucination, literally fascinated—but this is only an extreme variation on the traditional suspension of disbelief. No writer, of course, can maintain such hallucinatory powers for any great length of time. Sarraute's evident, although limited success is ample testimony to her ability. She has been rewarded by the strength of her convictions and her determination to translate them into fiction. To a lesser degree, just

as she may be seen as the forerunner of some of the most interesting
contemporary novelists, she has also benefited from the publication of
their works and from the acceptance of a number of psychoanalytic
notions by a more knowledgeable audience.

Like a number of other writers discussed in this volume, Sarraute has
deemphasized the part played by characterization and plot in conveying
the sense of a novel.[22] But in spite of the importance she attributes to
language, to its creative or evocative powers, she finds herself at quite
a distance from Jean Ricardou's theory and practice: for her, not only
perceptions and sensations come first (and this is hardly controversial)
but even representations and reflection. Her attitude toward literary
genres is ambiguous: on the one hand, she rejects the distinction made
between poetry and the novel, and on the other she seems to maintain
that between fiction and nonfiction. Her seemingly autobiographical
volume, *Enfance* (1983; *Childhood*), does indeed, at first, read like a
book of childhood memories even though, as suggested in the text itself,
the role of the imagination is difficult to dismiss (21)—but it differs very
much from the way (auto)biography has been fused into the writings of
Alain Robbe-Grillet, Michel Butor, or Philippe Sollers. In the final
analysis, *Enfance* does have much in common with her fictional works,
and the people mentioned in it are never fleshed out the way Sartre's
mother and grandparents are in his autobiography, *Les Mots*, which is
also somewhat fictional. She herself claimed that in *Enfance* there was
only the stirring provoked within the child by confrontations with adults
—stirrings that she remembers or imagines. Such stirrings or sensations
somehow help to define the child she was and make the book seem,
thematically at least, like the counterpart of her first novel. It might well
have been subtitled "Portrait of a Child Unknown."

All this might imply a certain precariousness in her leadership
position. Lucien Goldmann, for instance, while praising her work,
presents her as "a novelist belonging to the period we have characterized
as presiding over the disintegration of the character,"[23] and that would
place her toward the end of a tradition; Stephen Heath, however,
suggests that "such an assessment . . . is deeply problematic; perhaps
literally a *misreading* of the novels, a misreading which is a refusal to
understand a fundamental change in the novel form."[24]

As to a possible misreading, I would refer to the above quotation from
an essay by Proust and to what Sarraute herself has said: "Any reading of a
text is legitimate [except the one] that draws the text toward what it
refuses to be, toward what it seeks to fight against."[25] Nevertheless, I am
inclined to side with Stephen Heath, perhaps because I have as little
respect for "periods" as Sartre had for the notion of "adventure." Seen
within the context of the works of younger writers, Sarraute's books
appear to have performed the necessary, albeit negative, function of

helping to clear fiction of some of its superficial, culture-bound paraphernalia. Perhaps all they need, in order fully to come into their own, is a new generation of readers with a different creative bent. Innocent of today's prejudices, they will not need to be indoctrinated by her essays, nor guided or misguided by critics. In the not-too-distant future, her theories on fiction-writing might matter as little to those readers as Zola's notion of the experimental novel matter to people today.

NOTES

1 Nathalie Sarraute, *L'Ere du soupçon* (Paris: Gallimard, 1956), 33. Within this chapter, all references to Nathalie Sarraute's works will appear in the text with these abbreviations: *Portrait d'un inconnu*, PI; *Martereau*, M; *Le Planétarium*, P; *Les Fruits d'or*, FO; *Entre la vie et la mort*, EVM; *Vous les entendez?*, VLE.

2 Justin O'Brien, "Sarraute: 'Tropisms,' " in *The French Literary Horizon* (New Brunswick: Rutgers University Press, 1967), 333.

3 Sarraute, "New Movements in French Literature," *Listener*, 9 March 1969, pp. 428-29.

4 Quoted in Mimica Cranaki and Yvon Belaval, *Nathalie Sarraute* (Paris: Gallimard, 1965), 96-97.

5 The revised version of this chapter has benefited from the colloquium "Autour de Nathalie Sarraute" held at Cerisy-la Salle between 3 July and 13 July 1989. The conference was chaired by Valérie Minogue; Nathalie Sarraute and Monique Wittig were present for one day.

6 Sarraute, "New Movements," 429.

7 I have avoided the word *authentic*, which was used by Sartre in his preface to the 1956 edition of *Portrait d'un inconnu* and, in the context of Sarraute's work, could be misleading. It is the result of a questionable translation of Heidegger's *eigentumlich*, a word that corresponds to the French *propre*— "one's own particular nature," "one's peculiarity."

8 Richard N. Coe, "The Anti-Reader Novel," *Time & Tide*, 29 March 1962, p. 28.

9 Mary McCarthy, "Hanging by a Thread," in *The Writing on the Wall* (New York: Harcourt, Brace, and World, 1970), 183.

10 Yvon Belaval, "Nathalie Sarraute: *Tropismes*," *Nouvelle Revue française*, no. 62 (February 1958): 337.

11 Jacques Lacan, *Ecrits*, trans. Alan Sheridan (New York: Norton, 1977), 155.

12 Belaval, 336.

13 Martin Turnell, *The Art of French Fiction* (New York: New Directions, 1959), 348ff.

14 Georges Anex, "Nathalie Sarraute: *Portrait d'un inconnu*," *Nouvelle Revue française*, no. 54 (June 1957): 1115.

15 Ludovic Janvier, "Nathalie Sarraute ou l'intimité cruelle," in *Une Parole exigeante* (Paris: Minuit, 1964), 78.

16 See Georges Bataille, "La 'vieille taupe' et le préfixe 'sur' dans les mots

'surhomme' et 'surréaliste.' " *Tel Quel*, no. 54 (Summer 1968): 5-17.

17   Dominique Aury, "La Communication," *Nouvelle Revue Française*, no. 127 (July 1963): 96-97.

18   Aury, 97.

19   Claude Mauriac, *La Marquise sortit à cinq heures* (Paris: Albin Michel, 1961), 70.

20   Marcel Proust, *Contre Sainte-Beuve* (Paris: Gallimard, 1954), 303.

21   Coe, 27.

22   See Nathalie Sarraute, "Ce que je cherche à faire," in *Nouveau Roman: hier, aujourd'hui*, ed. Jean Ricardou and Françoise van Rossum-Guyon (Paris: 10/18, 1972), 25-40.

23   Lucien Goldmann, *Pour une sociologie du roman* (Paris: Gallimard, 1964), 195.

24   Stephen Heath, *The Nouveau Roman: A Study in the Practice of Writing* (Philadelphia: Temple University Press, 1972), 65.

25   Sarraute, "Ce que je cherche à faire," 39.

3

Maurice Blanchot

Between the fiction of Maurice Blanchot and that of his contemporaries, Beckett and Sarraute, there are noticeable bonds. Like Molloy, Malone, and their various synonyms, the characters of Blanchot's early narratives wander about in an incomprehensible world, find themselves victims of unjustifiable circumstances, and deteriorate physically without apparent reason, attempting all the while to communicate with others. Like the semianonymous beings of Sarraute, they seek to exteriorize what lies beneath the surface in the twilight zone that either precedes language or lies beyond it, using words in a desperate attempt to verbalize that for which there are no words—a fairly "normal" situation that is hidden by our constant use of stereotypes. Differences are no less perceptible. Blanchot's writings do not emphasize the grotesque, and his attitude toward language is far more complex than either Beckett's or Sarraute's. He does not punctuate the failures of his characters with humor ranging from slapstick to scatology, nor is he concerned with the somewhat instinctive nature of tropisms.

A struggle with language, not as an inadequate tool but as an element both distinct from and distinctive of human reality, capable of endowing the literary work with generative qualities, actually brings Blanchot closer to the surrealists and writers such as Raymond Roussel and, especially, Mallarmé. The latter's efforts to remove words from too close an adhesion to the material objects they commonly designate—that is, to free signs from their banal referents—interested Blanchot very much. Of the many statements Mallarmé had made concerning language, he thought that "the most remarkable pertained to the impersonal aspect, the kind of independent and absolute existence" the poet attributed to it.[1] According to Blanchot, the surrealists went one step further: they "understood, in addition, that [language] is not an inert object: it has a life of its own and a latent power that we do not control."[2] These and many other remarks scattered through his critical essays clearly indicate that Blanchot has pondered at length over the nature of language, as have twentieth-century linguisticians with whose works he is presumably acquainted. He is well versed in philosophy, as his references to Hegel and Heidegger attest. He is also a critic and a theorist of literature. But we need not at this point investigate that background material in depth, important as it may be to an understanding of his thought.[3] His practice is what counts: Blanchot's fiction must stand as fiction and be examined for what it might yield to the steady gaze of a receptive reader, with only occasional references to his critical texts.

Of the numerous volumes of fiction he has published, two offer promising paths of investigation to the critic, for they are openly presented as different structures of the same material. The first one, *Thomas l'obscur*, published in 1941, was again offered to the public in 1950 under the same title, to which the words "new version" were added. It was accompanied by a prefatory note explaining that "the present version adds nothing, but as it omits a great deal it can be called other and even quite new." One may (and many do) keep writing the same book over and over again, using different materials to state the same theme or express the same "truth" (a word viewed with increasing disfavor by contemporary writers), which he believes his previous work has not adequately portrayed—or he may unconsciously be getting rid of an obsession. Here the process is a conscious one; the material of the new book was all contained in the old, and the architecture is roughly the same. The reader's attention is no longer directed toward examining the different ways in which a "truth" might be "expressed." He is led to focus on the different meaning suggested by a new arrangement of words. (Something similar is suggested by Marc Saporta's loose-leaf *Composition No. 1*, in which different meanings come out of different arrangements of the pages.) Even though one might argue that the theme is identical in the two versions, the effect upon the reader must by necessity be different.

The original *Thomas l'obscur* was followed by two other works of fiction, *Aminadab* (1942) and *Le Très-haut* (1948; The Almighty), that quite obviously belong to the same rhetorical system. Also in 1948, *L'Arrêt de mort* (*Death Sentence*) appeared, which marks a change in direction, confirmed by the new version of *Thomas l'obscur* as well as by more recent texts. It appears as if Blanchot had sensed he had been on the wrong scriptural track and by publishing a reworked version of his early fiction wanted to stress that the switch was less radical than one might think, while at the same time enabling one to see precisely what differences there were between the two approaches. I believe this is confirmed by the 1951 publication of two short pieces from the midthirties,

"L'Idylle" and "Le Dernier mot." Their brevity links them to the narratives of the fifties and sixties, but they are much closer in spirit to *Aminadab* and *Le Très-haut* on account of their fantastic, nightmarish features. There might possibly be a connection between Blanchot's political evolution and his rhetorical one, but going into that would be beyond the scope of this essay.

In its original state, *Thomas l'obscur* was over 100,000 words in length while the new version has less than 30,000. Cutting out more than two-thirds of a narrative's basic ingredients cannot fail to have a pronounced effect. Gauging that effect is more difficult if one reads the two versions in their chronological order, for referents of the words that have been left out will almost inevitably remain as a halo in the mind, affecting the structure of what one is reading. I shall therefore use the second version as a point of departure.

From the standpoint of the narrative, which is told in the third person, there are two characters, Thomas and Anne; we witness their developing relationship, the death of Anne, and the effect of that death upon Thomas. Other characters are mere utilities; the setting is vague and nameless—a beach, woods, a hotel dining room, the countryside, various rooms; the time is unspecified. At the beginning we find Thomas alone, sitting on the beach. He decides to go in for a swim that lasts the length of the first chapter. As Thomas swims out to sea, in a direction he had not taken before, fog hides the coast from him; he feels alone with the sea, then alone in "an absence of sea,"[4] and such a phrase is characteristic of Blanchot. As sudden gusts of wind stir up the ocean, Thomas struggles and has the sensation of actually becoming the sea. Eventually, he strives to reach a special region, "something like a sacred spot, so well suited to himself that it was enough to be there in order to be; it was like an imaginary hollow into which he sank, because before being there his shape had already been imprinted into it" (TO/2 13). After that he returns to the beach, and stares at the sea and at a distant swimmer. He contemplates the expanse of ocean with a kind of sorrow, as if he had felt "a freedom that was too great, a freedom obtained by breaking all bonds" (TO/2 15). The experience has been an unusual one, to say the least, bearing the earmarks of an initiation.

From the outset, emphasis has been laid on the exceptional; but what distinguishes this narrative from other related accounts (for instance, the murder committed by Tchen in the first chapter of Malraux's *La Condition humaine*, which is also an initiation) is that the aesthetic experience is as unusual for the reader as the physical one is for the fictional character. The well-known process of "identifying" with the protagonist of a fictional text can give birth to considerable emotional response, perhaps even involvement. Rarely does it constitute, strictly speaking, an experience, that is, rarely does the reader feel as though he himself had gone through an ordeal in the character's stead, so to speak. To facilitate such a transference, assuming this was Blanchot's intention, he has omitted all references that would tie the event to any specific time or place; one is thus prevented from projecting it into a familiar aspect of reality, hence away from oneself. In addition to abstracting it from reality, Blanchot also removes the action from the commonplace. Finally, he gives key words a denotation that is different from the one we would normally give them. As with Mallarmé, this means loosening the bonds that link signs to their referents.

There is, strictly speaking, nothing revolutionary about that, to be sure. He himself has pointed out, within the context of an essay on Kafka, that "a narrative written in the most simple prose already assumes an important change in the nature of language";[5] and the innumerable consequences and controversies resulting from Aristotle's having written that the personages of Homer and of tragedy were better (that is, other) than we are need no further stress. What is new here is the intensity with which language is removed from its utilitarian use and the direction taken by the removal from the commonplace. Swimming in a river or in the ocean is a fairly ordinary activity. As described by Jean Giono, however, at the beginning of the second chapter of *Le Chant du monde*, it departs from the commonplace. Because of the character's outstanding physical features, his sensitivity to the river, the account takes on an epic quality. There is, however, nothing fantastic about it, nor are any supernatural forces involved. Not only is Blanchot's account out of the ordinary, but one is tempted to say that it enters the domain of the fantastic.

I call this a temptation, as it is a reaction of the analytical mind, looking back at the text from outside and considering the point of view of the story and its degree of plausibility, after the reading has been completed. The temptation needs to be resisted, for it is the textual experience that matters rather than any rational examination coming after the fact—an irrelevant procedure on account of the way the narrated event has been abstracted from everyday reality. When calm seas, fog, high wind, and turbulent waters are presented in very close succession, one might marvel at the kind of "reality" that has thus been described, but one actually senses that no real description is involved: the words in this text are not the usual signs pointing to referents of everyday experience. "The water revolved as in a whirlpool. Was it really water?" (TO/2 11). Statements appear self-contradictory and, as Jean Starobinsky has pointed out, abstract and concrete terms, objective and subjective approaches, central and peripheral points of view, active and passive verbs are all used almost interchangeably.[6] Language is as much unsettled as "reality" is. In a way, it becomes the reality of fiction. For those readers who tend to be more affected by the language of a narrative than by its topic, reading *Thomas l'obscur* can be a profound experience.

The second chapter takes Thomas into a wooded area and down into a cave. His underground sojourn seems even more outlandish than his stay in the water. Trapped for hours in darkness and solid rock, he nevertheless is able to proceed forward and perceive things with his eyes; but what he sees appear to be materializations of his own thoughts, and as he moves ahead a whole world of matter penetrates him physically. His thought becomes exterior to himself, and he finds he is inhabited by his own corpse, which he attempts to vomit. At the end, Thomas's thoughts reintegrate a body that has been bereft of its senses. The word *sacred,* which appeared in an earlier quotation from the first chapter, does not figure in the text of the second. While the first experience might be termed a purification, the second is literally a descent into hell. An integral part of initiation procedures, it also prefigures the events to follow.

The reader, too, has been initiated. He has been transported into a world utterly different from his own. A few comparisons between corresponding portions of the two versions of *Thomas l'obscur* should illustrate this.

On the whole, the physical setting of the first chapter in the second version is barely noticeable—it has been abstracted into nonexistence. In the earlier 1941 version, it is apparent (in addition to a more elaborate style, a point to which I shall return) that the setting had some importance. There is another swimmer, to whom Thomas calls out but who does not respond. There is also an empty boat that drifts by. Both incidents occur before Thomas's stranger experiences, and their eerie flavor adumbrates what is to follow. The setting thus plays an introductory role. It contains, to use Julien Gracq's phrase, "warning signals" similar to the Gothic novel trappings of *Au chateau d'Argol.* Remembering André Breton's praise of "Monk" Lewis in the first surrealist manifesto, I believe such details may properly be interpreted as a first, albeit superficial, indication of surrealist presence in Blanchot's work. The original version of the underground journey contains analogous signals, with odd-looking trees and strange-sounding birds contributing to the atmosphere; and, as the main portion of the narrative unfolds, differences between the two renditions become more obvious.

In the 1950 edition, Thomas and Anne are not only the main characters, but statements by or about them dominate the book. Where other characters appear, they are usually nameless and their role is minimal. The anecdote becomes thinner and thinner, and even such simple actions as swimming (except, of course, Thomas's initiatory experience in the sea), walking in the woods, or sitting down with others at a hotel dining-room table are eliminated. The major event of the work, Anne's illness and death, also occurs in the abstract. She is found asleep on the garden bench (which garden and by whom are irrelevant questions); she lies ill in her room, is visited by friends and by her mother (only one friend bears a name, Louise, and she is only mentioned once); and eventually she dies without doctor or priest having been summoned, without any material cause of her death having been suggested. In the 1941 version of *Thomas l'obscur* we see anecdotes and characters playing a much larger role.

The first half of the book is set in a resort town, the second in a large city—and it is clear that the trip between one and the other is made by train. In the city, such mundane places as restaurants and museums are easily identified. Another major character is involved in the action, a woman called Irene, and something close to a love triangle appears to take shape. As in more conventional writing, all this is metaphorical, incidents and minor characters being vehicles of a single tenor—the meaning toward which the fiction is structured. With Blanchot, however, their metaphorical nature is emphasized by his keeping them at greater distance from everyday reality. Many "warning signals" are instrumental to that effect: when Irene first meets Thomas, for instance, she is described as having "faithfully kept, for the first time, the date set by destiny and, moreover, by Anne that very morning" (TO/1 121). Words and phrases such as "destiny" or "for the first time" are the kind that normally lead the reader to expect some extraordinary transformation in the narrative. In more extended fashion, when Irene walks the city streets, she is presented as being so obsessed with Thomas that she sees his likeness, or part of it, in every person she encounters; but Blanchot, as would Robbe-Grillet more than a decade later, offers such fancies as if they were "real," refusing to intrude upon the text with an extraneous message to the effect that a switch from the plausible to the implausible (or imaginary) has taken place; as a result, when Irene sees Thomas in a restaurant, one is no longer sure at what level the encounter takes place (TO/1 148ff.). The subsequent meeting between Irene and Thomas is hardly questionable, upon reflection, but it follows the other one so closely that its fanciful treatment tends to appear realistic by contrast. Something close to a fusion of the real and the marvelous (Breton's *merveilleux quotidien*) has been accomplished, when one considers the level of the story.

On the verbal level, I am reminded not so much of surrealism as of Jean Giraudoux, nor am I the first to associate the latter's name with Blanchot's. Claude-Edmonde Magny, in her book on Giraudoux, had detected similarities between *Thomas l'obscur* and *Aventures de Jérôme Bardini* (1930).[7] Although she does not refer to them, those pages dealing with the museum visit offer most striking analogies. Metaphors and conceits are perhaps not handled with as much agility, but every now and then a sentence crops up that, with a change in pronoun, might not have been out of place in *Suzanne et le Pacifique* (1921). The suggestion that art-loving museum attendants wax floors with greater ardor in front of anonymous paintings in order to slow down the visitors' pace—that is almost worthy of Giraudoux. The same might be said of a statement concerning the unique nature of a work of art (in this instance a painting by Titian): "Anything that might be used to seduce plants, to flatter stars, such as magic words or metaphors, left the picture unmoved; what is more, it became radiant, and it obstinately refused, at least in a figurative sense, to be a picture" (TO/1 156). The phrase "magic words" belongs to Suzanne.[8] She, however, refusing, as she puts it, the outlook of a German or a Russian, will not lend a tragic note to her situation, stranded as she might be on her deserted Pacific island. Blanchot's characters show no such compunction. Kind fate, in the shape of a group of wandering Englishmen, restores Suzanne, virtually intact, to her native land, while Anne's destiny is to experience solitude, illness, and death—and death is a common topic or metaphor in Blanchot's writings.

Both the museum passage and the three excerpts quoted by Magny have disappeared from the revised version of *Thomas l'obscur*—and with them those obviously "precious" aspects of style that suggest Giraudoux. In the examples just quoted, the verbs *to seduce* and *to flatter* as well as the parenthetical phrase "at least in a figurative sense" would almost certainly, had the episode not been deleted, been replaced or suppressed. On the other hand, the unqualified statement about the picture that "refused to be a picture" remains characteristic of Blanchot, as an illustration of his removal of language from its utilitarian function. As with elements of the narration, actual stylistic changes made in the revised version point toward a greater economy of means and a more considerable break between fictional reality and the reader's reality.

In the following sequence, taken from the episode of Anne's illness, those words maintained in the second version appear in italics (and within brackets if added or changed), all others having been deleted:

Elle seule vit s'approcher, à la vitesse d'un bolide [*d'une étoile*], *ce moment* idéal, le dernier peut-être, *où* elle allait reprendre [*reprenant*] *contact avec la terre*, [*elle ressaisirait*] avec *l'existence banale*, ou elle *ne verrait rien*, [*ne sentirait rien*], seule existence véritable. *A travers des nuées rapidement chassées au-dessus d'elle*, elle prit tragiquement conscience de l'instant unique où elle embrasserait son frère qui ensuite cesserait d'être son frère, *où elle pourrait vivre, vivre enfin*,—rien n'était perdu—se marier, finir son écharpe à l'aiguille, *et peut-être même mourir*, mourir d'une mort imprévue, *épisode merveilleux*. (TO/1 195-96; TO/2 106)

[*She alone saw this* ideal *moment approaching with the speed* of a fireball [*of a star*], it might well be the last, *during which* she would resume [*resuming*] *contact with the earth*, [*she would again hold on to*], with *commonplace existence*, where she *would see nothing*, [*would feel nothing*] the only genuine existence. *Through fast-driven clouds above her*, she became tragically conscious of the unique instant when she would kiss her brother, who would then cease being her brother, *when she might live, live at last*—nothing had been lost—get married, finish knitting her scarf, *and perhaps even die*, die of an unexpected death, *a marvelous occurrence.*]

Furthermore, in the revised text, the phrase that begins the second sentence has been transferred to the beginning of the first, which now reads: *"Elle seule, à travers des nuées rapidement chassées au-dessus d'elle, à la vitesse d'une étoile, vit s'approcher . . ."* Originally, the two sentences each contained one image that complemented the other. Merging the two sentences into one caused a fusion of the images, while replacing "fireball" (*bolide*) with "star" (*étoile*) added an element of unreality to the vague mystery suggested by "clouds" (*nuées* traditionally signals poetic connotations, as opposed to the prosaic *nuages*). *Bolide* is no longer a live metaphor; it is a cliché applied to almost any fast-moving object, a racing car for instance. *Etoile*, on the other hand, gives the image an unusual quality of the sort one so often finds in Blanchot. Intellectually, we know that stars move at incredible rates of speed, but our experience suggests that they are stationary. As a result, *vitesse d'une étoile* produces tension. Deleting a few explanatory words or phrases, particularly the qualifier *idéal*, again emphasizes the unique nature of the approaching moment and also divorces it from the more traditional realm of the ideal. References to an existence in which basic attributes of life, such as seeing and feeling, are absent contributes to the same effect, and this renders the phrase *instant unique* superfluous. Finally, by removing concrete illustrations, the words *vivre* and *mourir* are not only restored to an abstract level, they are brought close to juxtaposition within that moment the sentence produces. Such a time, when speed and immobility, life and death, appear to coincide, is at the end of the sequence characterized by the word *merveilleux*. Again one is reminded of surrealism, but this time at a deeper level, and of the emphasis André Breton placed upon that word in the surrealist manifesto.

A sentence from the previous paragraph of the text of *Thomas l'obscur*, identical in both versions, reinforces the analogy: "Dark night where there were no more contradictory terms, where those who suffered were happy, where white and black shared a common substance" (TO/1 194; TO/2 104-5). That sentence, in turn, may be matched with a statement from Breton's second manifesto: "Everything leads me to believe that there is a given viewpoint in the mind, from which life and death, the real and the imaginary, past and future, what is communicable and what is not, high and low, cease to be perceived as contradictory terms."[9] Anne's "moment," the approach of which she senses, is very much like Breton's hypothetical "viewpoint in the mind." The annihilation of being that he professes to seek has its metaphorical counterpart in Blanchot's fiction: Anne's death, through which Thomas is able to attain a higher level of existence. The situation resembles that described by Breton in his *Nadja* (1928). Nadja disappears into a psychiatric ward while Anne vanishes in a more radical fashion, but each woman acts as intercessor for her narrator and protagonist. In each instance there is an effort to transcend the limitations of conventional reality and traditional behavior (in the broadest sense of the term). Anne's death results in illumination for Thomas (Breton had associated annihilation with brilliance),[10] in his becoming aware of the presence, within himself, of another Thomas "whose genuine existence would consist in not being" (TO/1 216). In other words, he too will partake of an aspect of death. Just as dream and reality may be said to fuse into the "surreal," Thomas will attempt to integrate light and darkness, to assimilate that obscure part of himself; "the more the shadow of my thought receded, the more I conceived of myself, in this flawless light, as a possible host, full of desire, of that obscure Thomas" (TO/1 217; TO/2 144). He then adds that, in the fullness of reality, he believes he can come into contact with the unreal—and that is what surrealism was essentially about. As Breton sought to explore the deeper recesses of the mind, *Thomas l'obscur* represents a quest for the obscure regions of the self.

As those observations indicate, and I feel confident a more detailed comparison between the two texts of *Thomas l'obscur* would confirm this, rhetorical changes evident in Blanchot's work do not manifest a rejection of surrealism after an early infatuation. Quite the contrary, his later fiction reveals an affirmation of its more basic tenets. André Breton condemned commonplace reality and favored the "surreal"; other contemporary writers, especially those of the next generation, are more inclined to condemn stereotyped reality in the name of the "real." The two gestures might seem to lead in opposite directions, and the processes are often quite different; in the final analysis, however, they may well be doing the same thing.

What one finds in the two works that followed the original *Thomas l'obscur, Aminadab* and *Le Très-haut*, is a stress on the more obvious aspects of surrealism, on the signposts calling attention to its domain, rather than on the domain itself. This, however, has not resulted in a kind of Gothic novel similar to Julien Gracq's first. The writer that readers of *Aminadab* were reminded of was Franz Kafka. Sartre, one of the first to make the connection, was also quick to point out that Blanchot had not read Kafka at the time. Instead of having been affected by him, he was probably led to the Czech writer through the devices of *Aminadab*.

A man named Thomas is again the main character. The name had first appeared in the prewar story "Le Dernier mot" as that of a somewhat mythical person who somehow had not been included in the general census of the population. "So he stayed, as a supernumerary, and one took to considering him as if, with respect to mankind, which was itself demented, he had been deprived of reason" (RE 123). A discussion as to whether this is the same Thomas as before seems hardly relevant. Neither one is given background, family, friend, or even a home. Beckett's Molloy at least had a mother, to whose room he at last returned. Thomas first appeared on a beach, as we have seen, out of nowhere, was transformed by an extraordinary experience, and is last seen on the shores of the ocean. In *Aminadab*, he or another Thomas arrives alone in a small town where he is obviously a stranger (this basically repeats the beginning of "L'Idylle," in which the main character, simply called "the stranger," is upon his arrival immediately taken to an institution). No reason is given for his being there, no indication as to where he has come from, and, even more than in *Thomas l'obscur*, the events that follow appear to be determined almost exclusively by chance. Thomas allows himself to be chosen, somewhat as Breton, the narrator of *Nadja*, did in the streets and movie theaters of Paris, letting people and programs come as they might.[11] Nevertheless, he does not answer a call unless there is some element of mystery involved. When a man issues a straight-forward invitation, Thomas is not interested. When a woman in an upstairs window across the street makes an ambiguous sign, he is intrigued. Not knowing if he should interpret it as a summons, a friendly wave, or a dismissal, he hesitates. When he makes up his mind and crosses the street, he has unknowingly embarked upon a quest that will fill the 240-odd pages of the book. Perhaps he finds the woman eventually, but whom he found and what meaning it might have for him the reader is not explicitly told, for the narrative ends as Thomas asks her who she is.

The inception of the narrative in *Aminadab* suggests an analogy with the writer as he or she is about to begin writing, as Blanchot conceives of that position. He is a stranger because he does not use language as others do, in a utilitarian way, and when he begins to write he does so without motivation or purpose.[12] When Thomas enters the house in answer to something he does not know how to interpret, he finds himself caught in an endless series of frustrating, Kafka-like experiences. He gets lost in hallways, cannot communicate in any satisfactory fashion with the people he meets, becomes a tenant in the building, is manacled to another man whom he drags along in his wanderings (he is not sure whether he is prisoner or captor), befriends another woman (perhaps a servant), is told contradictory things about the occupants of the house and their relationship to one another, cannot decide whether his fate is to be determined on the basis of an unknown crime or he is to judge others in equal ignorance of what they may have done—and eventually he becomes ill. As in the 1941 version of *Thomas l'obscur*, two women are involved, one subservient to the other, who guide the main character toward a kind of salvation. Again, illness plays a crucial role; it is because of that illness that he is able to reach a region hitherto unattainable. After he recovers, he penetrates into the room of the woman named Lucie, who, he thinks, is the one who beckoned from the window. She, bearing a name suggestive of light, prepares him for the annihilation of his being, for a darkness in which everything will become clear—metaphors similar to those I quoted in connection with *Thomas l'obscur*. Here the protagonist hesitates, and his last question, "Who are you?," may represent an ultimate effort, perhaps futile, perhaps not, to reject such an arcane form of understanding. The answer to his question is of course not provided, nor would it seem to matter much, for the text concludes, "It was as though that question might allow him to clear up everything." We shall never know whether it was the right question or not.

Aminadab, in its general outline, even more than *Thomas l'obscur*, lends itself to allegorical interpretations. Sartre considered that to be true of a number of episodes and proceeded to give his own interpretation of them.[13] While they are quite plausible, they are not those that first occurred to me, nor are they identical with those proposed by Georges Poulet.[14] One probably tends to see allegories to the extent that one remains outside the fiction and fails to participate fully in the textual experience. I am inclined to blame Blanchot himself for the reader's failure, for in multiplying incidents that, although decidedly strange, are specific, sequential, and certain—therefore constituting a narration that may readily be retold or summarized—he gives the reader no opportunity to share in the productive process. The reader merely listens to the narrator and interprets what he hears.

With *Le Très-haut* the narration moves into slightly more recognizable surroundings, and the narrative shifts from third to first person. One detects a number of thematic echoes from the earlier texts in *Le Ressassement éternel* (1951; *Vicious Circles*). The events described are probably no more implausible than those of Albert Camus's *La Peste* (1947); they exude nightmarish qualities because accepted laws of causality, progress, and transformation do not apply. The atmosphere is much less Kafka-like than in *Aminadab*, and this may well be the result of a conscious effort on Blanchot's part to achieve a distinctive manner. The first-person narrative also helps to bring the action closer to home. *Aminadab* described another world, which could be interpreted either as the distorted image of the reader's or as being Other in an absolute sense; but *Le Très-haut* shows one's own world gone awry.

The easiest way to account for this third work is to call it the story of a plague in a large city. The theme of illness is thus once again restated, but it is treated more extensively than before. Already in *Aminadab* there was illness among the tenants and rumors of an epidemic in the mysterious upper stories of the house. A distance was nevertheless maintained between those incidents and Thomas's own experience, while in *Le Très-haut* the epidemic is more like a maelstrom that engulfs everything, including the narrator. Individual illness, here that of the narrator, is no longer the central element of the narrative: when the story begins, it is already a thing of the past. The action moves from the individual to the collective, ending with the annihilation of the narrator. It begins with a brief affirmation and a rhetorical question: "I was not alone, I was an ordinary man. How could I forget such a phrase?"

Reminiscent of attempts by traditional novelists to suggest that the unusual or shocking experience of their characters might well have been those of the reader, as with Duhamel's Salavin or Camus's Meursault, that statement, by being placed at the outset of the narrative, acquires ironic overtones, for what obviously stands out at first is the narrator's strangeness, even though mitigated by the first-person point of view. He is called Henri Sorge; the family name does not have a French ring to it. One thinks, rather, of the German word meaning "anxiety" or "concern." That connection has led Pierre Klossowski, in an interesting but abstruse essay, to a possible interpretation of the book's title (to appreciate it one should remember that "le très-haut" is the French equivalent of "the almighty"): "God, deprived of his name, or existence deprived of being because it is deprived of God's name, would become 'anxiety.' "[15] The narrator has become the metaphor of God, whose creation has become his illness or perhaps his sin, and whose disappearance is suggested at the end. Something similar had already occurred in "Le Dernier mot" when children ask the anonymous narrator, "Are you the teacher or are you God?" (RE 119-20). He looks at them sadly and tells them that he, too, is but a child in the cradle "who needs to speak by means of screams and tears." Later as he reaches the last tower to remain standing in a nightmarish landscape, its owner tells him, "If you can hold out until the cock crows . . . you will see that I am the All-Powerful" (RE 142). He laughs, but in the end he cannot hold out: the tower crumbles. In that text, the narrator questioned God's existence and perished.

A resident of the city, Sorge seems as new to it and its inhabitants as Thomas was in the fantastic house of *Aminadab*. That is partly due to his illness. He himself speaks of the "revelation" it has afforded him: "Until recently, men were only fragments, and they projected their dreams toward heaven. . . . But now, man exists. That is what I have discovered" (TH 29). It is perhaps such existence that spells the death of God. A series of encounters or conversations serves to establish Sorge's distance from those who have not risen to his own level of awareness. They also point to a converging pattern of ills of various sorts. Like the beggar who, according to Sorge, exists only in order to "give the impression that things are not really going like clockwork" (17), they might be indicative of a concern (*Sorge*) that literature is meant to communicate and simultaneously of the distance between the language of literature and that of the marketplace. Eventually, the plague emerges as a possible metaphor for the condition of this world.

In addition to the epidemic, disastrous fires break out in several sections of the city, and there is also evidence of considerable political and social unrest if not of actual uprisings. Social or political matters, however, are not, in my opinion, the focus of the book. Like the plague and the fires, they, too, are metaphors for something else. Vague and unsatisfactory as the phrase might sound, the book seems essentially a statement about the human condition—or, to refine this a bit more, it represents a writer's attempt to utter the human condition rather than speak about it. The narrator's affirmation concerning the existence of man is one of several pieces of evidence pointing in that direction. Not that politics is unimportant; rather it is a symptom or consequence of more fundamental matters.

Connected with the theme of social unrest is that of the underground (the book was published soon enough after the German occupation of France for this concept to have been highly suggestive at the time) and of darkness. Again we meet with a recurrent motif: previously there had been the descent into the cave, in *Thomas l'obscur*, and the concluding episode in *Aminadab* when Thomas was told that the path toward salvation lay in a direction that would have led him gently but deeply into the caves of the earth. His mistake had been to seek the upper regions of the house, projecting, as Sorge confesses to have done, his dreams toward heaven. The myth of Orpheus, a favorite of Blanchot's, is not very far in the background, along with his perpetual return with, and loss of, Eurydice; and also close is André Breton's "depth of the mind," where there are "strange forces capable either of joining with those that exist on the surface or struggling victoriously against them."[16] Jacques Lacan, starting from Freud's remark that dreams are organized like picture-puzzles, has asserted that the structure of the unconscious was the structure of language.[17] If true, this would make the probing of language, which is the concern of so many contemporary writers, analogous to an exploration of the unconscious—but only in very approximate fashion. Maurice Blanchot sees Orpheus as the writer whose skill enables him to undertake his voyage to Hades, that is, into the unconscious regions of his being. His supreme accomplishment would consist in bringing back Eurydice to the light of day. For him, she represents a possibility akin to Breton's "viewpoint of the mind," which the writer necessarily strives to reach and contemplate—at which point Eurydice vanishes. "The sacred night encloses Eurydice within its shadows, it encloses within the song [of Orpheus] all that transcends his song."[18] His is a necessary failure, for, had he succeeded, his "masterpiece" would have resembled a Eurydice stripped of her meaning, of her nocturnal essence.

L'Arrêt de mort (1948) appeared almost simultaneously with *Le Très-haut.* A two-part narrative, each one corresponding to a different reading

of the title—"the stopping of death" or "the death sentence"—it marks
the rhetorical change that prompted a revision of *Thomas l'obscur*. Like
Le Très-haut, it is told in the first person, as are the three books of fiction
following the second version of *Thomas l'obscur*. The narrator is nameless; one usually thinks of this as a means of removing part of the literary
screen between writer and reader. Other characters are occasionally
referred to by the initial letter of their names—a traditional device, it
would seem, to give fiction a semblance of reality. The book is a short one,
the two stories extremely simple, and the more spectacular aspects of the
previous works have been discarded. What remains is again in the spirit
of Breton's *Nadja*, with one important difference: the reader is very
specifically made aware of the book's being a product of language. Whatever his first impressions might have been, he soon realizes that the
narrator's anonymity is but a correlative of his nonexistence; if the characters' names are reduced to their initial letters, it is because they do not
have enough substance to carry more than that.

Throughout *L'Arrêt de mort*, death as the end of physical life is viewed
intellectually rather than emotionally, even on the superficial level of the
anecdote. Death, in other words, is basically a metaphor, as it is in so
many of Blanchot's seemingly paradoxical essays.[19] One might also view
death as correlative to the writer's involvement with language (in traditional terms, Orpheus did venture into the kingdom of the dead), during
which language ceases to be a practical function, and the writer himself
refuses a world in which objects and people alike have become commodities and ventures into a realm that is absolutely Other.

L'Arrêt de mort and the second version of *Thomas l'obscur* constitute
the pivots of Blanchot's evolving rhetoric. With *Au moment voulu* (1951;
When the Time Comes), we enter his privileged domain without the
benefit—or the hindrance—of warning devices, signposts or semblances
of conventional plot. What action there is takes place in a small apartment, presumably in Paris, shared by two young women. A man, the
narrator, a friend of one of them, appears at the door of the apartment as
the narrative unfolds; the text then goes on to account for what may be
their changing relationships. The setting for *Celui qui ne m'accompagnait
pas* (1953; *The One Who Was Standing Apart From Me*) is a house in the
country, surrounded by a garden of sorts. The narrator is alone with
someone else, perhaps. In *Le Dernier homme* (1957; *The Last Man*) we
are transported to what appears to be a large resort hotel, close to or on
the seashore. There are hallways, doors, individual rooms, lounges, and a
gambling room. The existence of two other characters seems reasonably
well established: a woman friend of the narrator and another man,
probably older. It may well be that *L'Attente l'oubli* (1962; *Waiting
Forgetting*), no longer a first-person narrative, has the same setting, but
only hallways and a room remain identifiable. While the earlier fiction

bore a label, either *roman* or *récit*, this story carries none. It might well be called a poem. Comprised of two parts followed by what could pass as epilogue, it is subdivided into stanzas or sequences varying in length from a single sentence to several pages. The larger portion of the text constitutes a dialogue between a man and a woman—the only characters involved, if such a term may be applied. In this dialogue, they use either the *tu* or *vous* forms; in the first part, the man is mostly designated by *il*, sometimes by *je* or *tu*, but in the second part he is always *il*. This interchangeability of pronouns seems to reflect the disappearance of the narrator. There remain anonymity, waiting, and forgetting, words that are both necessary and futile. In a way, the evolution that took Blanchot from, say, *Le Très-haut* to *L'Attente l'oubli* is analogous to the evolution in painting that goes from André Masson's surrealistic *Le Labyrinthe* (1938) to the abstract impressionism of Jackson Pollock's *Autumn Rhythm* (1957).

The reader cannot help feeling disoriented, and, as Blanchot himself argues in another context, he may be forced to become actively involved in the text. "Without a fulcrum, deprived of the pleasure of reading, he can no longer view matters from afar, maintaining a distance that goes with the act of observing, for remote elements, in their presence without presence, are available neither at a distance nor at hand, and they cannot be objects of observation. Henceforth, we can no longer talk of sight. The narrative ceases to be what may be seen by means of a chosen actor-spectator and from a given point of view."[20] Writers of the next generation might say that the solitary "pleasure of reading" should make way for the collective activity of writing.

The movement that carries Blanchot's fiction forward is similar to that evidenced by the work of Samuel Beckett, especially the French trilogy —from the towns, countryside, seashore, and forest of *Molloy* to the eerie nothingness of *L'Innommable*. Beyond what I have indicated above— and I may well have superimposed my own fables on his texts—to identify a plot or simply a coherent, sustained narrative in those books by Blanchot is just not possible. Paraphrasing them would be harder and even more pointless than paraphrasing a poem by Mallarmé. Characters gradually lose what little fabric they had. Names are discarded first; the last narrator to be named was Thomas, in the second version of *Thomas l'obscur*. Other characters retain them in *L'Arrêt de mort* and *Au moment voulu*, although in the latter, Judith is a name that is given a woman by each of the other two characters in turn—it is not actually hers, it exists only to establish transitory relationships as suggested by the biblical connotations of that name. After that, one finds merely pronouns.

One of the women in *Au moment voulu* tells the narrator after a long discussion, "I hardly believe in you" (18). The other character in *Celui qui ne m'accompagnait pas* affirms, "You know, there is no one" (65). In that instance, the reference appears to be to a third person the narrator thinks he has seen in the house, but in the more general context of this text the statement reverberates ad infinitum. It comes as no surprise, later on, to read the narrator's questions regarding his hypothetical companion: "Would he still hear me? Where is he now? Perhaps very close by? Perhaps he is at hand? Perhaps it is he that my hand slowly pushes back, thrusts aside once more?" (173); or to be confronted with the book's final statement, "Everything had already disappeared, disappeared with the day" (174). The reader's right to generalize the questionable aspect of characters is implicitly given in *L'Attente l'oubli:* " 'Don't you have faith in me?' She meant her truthfulness, her words, her behavior. But I was thinking in terms of a greater disbelief" (37). In another conversation, the man will profess that he has no doubts as to the woman's "presence"—and she then reproaches him for preferring that presence to herself. It would seem that his attitude at this point is analogous to that of readers who believe in characters: they clutch at every possible straw that appearances present to them in order to force a strange reality into more comfortable, familiar structures. At some point, however, characters, readers, and the writer himself are bound to echo the woman's lament at the end of the early text "Le Dernier mot": "Alas, she said, don't you feel the ground giving way beneath us?" (RE 146).

Two-thirds of the way into *L'Attente l'oubli,* one detects an attempt to organize "events" into some kind of linear, coherent story. Toward the end, it is clear that the endeavor has not been very productive: "What point have we reached in the story?—There probably isn't much of the story left, right now" (153). Such groping for a "story" is a correlative to the quest characters engage in. Male protagonists or narrators throughout Blanchot's fiction are the seekers, the unsure, the stumblers, reaching for a light (or a darkness), to which female intercessors might lead them. The surrealist cult of woman as standard-bearer of the irrational seems in evidence here, in addition to Blanchot's own modified myth of Eurydice. Whether it is Thomas or one of the subsequent nameless ones, from the ambiguous signal in *Aminadab* to the "words that were also perhaps intended for him" of *L'Attente l'oubli* (7), the protagonist encounters an interruption, a call away from complacency or routine. (It is true that in *L'Attente l'oubli* the man signals first; but his is a commonplace action, and it is she who irritatedly rushes into his room, asking for "the meaning of a gesture about which there is obviously nothing to say" [117].) Thomas cannot be persuaded that the hard road upward is not the right way. The narrator of *Au moment voulu* has to be warned that "No one here wishes to tie himself to a story" (108), and although that affirmation makes a strong impression on him, his successor, the man of *L'Attente l'oubli,* while he repeats it verbatim (22), has to be persuaded all over again. The earlier narrator had come to realize that "Whoever wants to live needs to relax within the illusion of a story, but such relaxation is not allowed to me" (AMV 156); the protagonist of *L'Attente l'oubli* has to experience the same truth on his own until it can finally be said of him, "He is no longer protected by the hidden aspect of things" (AO 136). The life referred to is the same *vie réelle* of which Breton spoke so sarcastically in his first manifesto, and *histoire* ("story") may be equated with "adventure" (in the Sartrian sense of the word), myth, quest, or anything that attempts to impose a satisfying, linear, logical, and therefore artificial explanation on a complex reality. The comfort it provides is a false security that isolates one from true existence.

I suppose it is a sense of that existence that Blanchot tries both to experience and to have his readers experience. His repeated efforts have their corollary in those of his characters as they attempt to communicate with one another. The means of communication that is at their disposal, language, is on a par with story and characters: it is a part of the fiction and a conventional counterpart of reality, but it is not reality. Hence the peculiar nature of Blanchot's texts, since he must at the same time use language and distrust it—and this, as I have shown, is also Sarraute's problem. If story and language sometimes appear as vehicles in a metaphor of which reality is the tenor, that situation is complicated by the former's being dependent upon the latter for their existence: "If things were divided between things that are seen and things that are said, language might endeavor to erase that division, to make it deeper, to leave it intact while giving it speech, to disappear within it. But that division upon which language is operative is still only a division in language" (AO 143).

Language appears to betray reality, and it also betrays the speaker. At the outset of *L'Attente l'oubli*, the man reads back to the woman those notes he has taken while she was speaking. She listens, but fails to recognize herself: " 'Who speaks?' she would say. 'Who speaks anyway?' " (7). It is the same question that has been asked so often, in criticism and works of fiction, particularly at the end of Michel Butor's *Degrés*, with similar implications as to literary production. Instead of emphasizing and striving for authentic communication between individuals, as did Sarraute, Maurice Blanchot appears to be carried beyond that to a question about, and a questioning of, man's being. In so doing, because of the intimate relationship between man and his language, he faces a similar problem in finding words for what cannot be put into words. If he conceives of himself as being in the same situation as the narrator of *Au moment voulu*—"And what was I really, if not the reflection of an appearance that did not speak and to whom no one spoke, only capable of (relying on the endless quiet of what was outside) questioning the world, silently, beyond a window pane?" (AMV 94)—he must nevertheless translate his silence into writing.

This brings us back to an observation by Blanchot, quoted earlier in this chapter, concerning the essential difference between the language of fiction and everyday language. Taking one further step, if one remembers that ordinary language exists for the purpose of simple communication (as opposed to the sovereign communication effected by literature, as defined by Blanchot's friend, Georges Bataille),[21] one might say that, the opposite of communication being silence, the language of fiction is a form of silence. "At the outset, I do not speak in order to say something, but there is something that needs to speak."[22] Such a need is analogous to a compulsion. "I cannot describe the misfortune that befalls the man who once has begun to speak" says the narrator of *L'Arrêt de mort*, adding nevertheless, "I must speak" (65). But a number of years and books later, the text of *La Folie du jour* (1973; *The Madness of the Day*) ends with the statement: "A narrative? No, no narrative. Never again."

Like Beckett's *L'Innommable*, whose last words are, "You must go on, I can't go on, I'll go on," Henri Sorge, the narrator of *Le Très-haut*, a gun pointed at him, his back against the wall, forever poised between life and death, closes that book by shouting, "Now, it is now that I speak." If we can, however, imagine Beckett's character in the act of continuing, Sorge's speech is beyond the range of normal perception. He has come close to that hypothetical point in space and time of which I have already spoken, and, like Thomas in the preceding books, he has done so through a series of fantastic and horrible experiences. In the *récits* that follow, the mood shifts to a calm from which joy is not excluded. We even read, in *La Folie du jour*, "When I die (perhaps before long) I shall experience a tremendous pleasure" (9). The "point" is ever present: witness the emphasis on a unique moment implied in the very title of *Au moment voulu*. In *L'Attente l'oubli* characters grope for a condition in which they would experience expectancy of past time and oblivion of the future. As with surrealists, there are intimations of a lost paradise, and if it is more abstract than that of childhood it is that more difficult to conceive. Blanchot demands a great deal from the reader.

NOTES

1   Maurice Blanchot, "Le Mythe de Mallarmé," in *La Part du feu* (Paris: Gallimard, 1949), 48.

2   Blanchot, "Réflexions sur le surréalisme," in *La Part du feu*, 95.

3   For a different approach, see Geoffrey Hartman, "Maurice Blanchot," in *The Novelist as Philosopher*, ed. John Cruickshank (London: Oxford University Press, 1962), 147-65. His political thought has been scrutinized more recently; see Jeffrey Mehlman, "Blanchot at Combat," in *Legacies of Anti-semitism in France* (Minneapolis: University of Minnesota Press, 1983), 6-22.

4 Blanchot, *Thomas l'obscur*, deuxième version (Paris: Gallimard, 1950), 12. In this chapter, references to Blanchot's works of fiction will henceforth appear in the text with these abbreviations: *Thomas l'obscur*, TO/1 (first edition) and TO/2 (revised edition); *Le Très-haut*, TH; *Le Ressassement éternel*, RE; *Au moment voulu*, AMV; *L'Attente l'oubli*, AO.

5 Blanchot, "Le Langage de la fiction," in *La Part du feu*, 80.

6 Jean Starobinsky, "Thomas l'obscur, chapitre premier," *Critique*, no. 229 (June 1966): 498-513.

7 Claude-Edmonde Magny, *Précieux Giraudoux* (Paris: Seuil, 1945), 13.

8 Jean Giraudoux, *Suzanne et le Pacifique* (Paris: E. Paul, 1921), 120.

9 André Breton, "Second Manifeste du Surréalisme" (1930); rpt. in *Manifestes du Surréalisme* (Paris: J.-J. Pauvert, 1962), 154.

10 Ibid., 154.

11 Breton, *Nadja* (Paris: Gallimard, 1928), 38ff.

12 See Blanchot, "La Littérature et le droit à la mort," in *La Part du feu*, 308.

13 Jean-Paul Sartre, "*Aminadab* ou du fantastique considéré comme un langage," in *Situations I* (Paris: Gallimard, 1947), 122-42.

14 Georges Poulet, "Maurice Blanchot, critique et romancier," *Critique*, no. 229 (June 1966): 485-97.

15 Pierre Klossowski, "Sur Maurice Blanchot," *Les Temps modernes*, no. 40 (February 1949): 306-7.

16 Breton, *Manifestes*, 23.

17 Jacques Lacan, *Ecrits* (Paris: Seuil, 1966), 267, 495.

18 Blanchot, "Le Regard d'Orphée," in *L'Espace littéraire* (Paris: Gallimard, 1955), 183.

19 See Blanchot, "La Littérature et le droit à la mort," in *La Part du feu* and various essays in *L'Espace littéraire*.

20 Blanchot, "La Voix narrative," in *L'Entretien infini* (Paris: Gallimard, 1969), 563.

21 See Georges Bataille, *La Littérature et le mal* (Paris: Gallimard, 1957), 203ff. and passim.

22 Blanchot, "La Littérature et le droit à la mort," 327.

4

Marguerite Duras

The work of Marguerite Duras came to the attention of critics, especially outside of France, at the time of the publication of her sixth book, *Le Square* (the translation of which was closely followed by the release of her first movie, *Hiroshima mon amour*). An unusual text, it seemed related in some mysterious way to the works of Sarraute and Robbe-Grillet. It also appeared to break with the continuity of style and technique of her previous ones. As more of her fiction was published, the link with those writers who were receiving considerable attention throughout the fifties grew more and more tenuous. As a result, she soon found herself somewhat isolated from literary trends or circles. She herself was somewhat reluctant to discuss literature or even her own works. She did develop a following for her dramatic and film productions, but critics were slow to give her the recognition she deserves. In 1984, however, with *L'Amant*, she won a major literary prize and a much wider audience.

A definite evolution can be detected in her fiction, with three "deflection" points (rather than turning points) identifiable: *Le Marin de Gibraltar* (as much as *Le Square*), *Le Ravissement de Lol V. Stein*, and *L'Amant*—thus defining four periods. Such classifications, because in part arbitrarily imposed on the work by a critic (who is no more than a distant witness to the productive process), should not be taken too seriously. They are like navigation aids, subject to revision.

Be that as it may, Duras's early works tended to be dictatorial in their rhetoric. They were also diffuse and contained many descriptions in the conventional mode, such as that of the picturesque "père Bart," the tavern keeper, in *Un Barrage contre le Pacifique*, together with much analysis and explanation. The opening paragraph of the same book, stating what meaning the purchase of a horse had had for the three main characters ("And they felt less isolated, now that they were linked by that horse to the outside world"), and the prediction made on the second page that "they were about to meet someone, and that meeting would change the lives of all three," are typical of what she would later eschew. In her attempt to keep the reader's imagination in check, she revealed a probably unconscious acceptance of traditional aesthetics. Nevertheless, some of the themes and preoccupations that run through her better-known works were already present from the beginning.

The three works of her early period, *Les Impudents* (1943; The Shameless), *La Vie tranquille* (1944; The Quiet Life), and *Un Barrage contre le Pacifique* (1950; *The Sea Wall*), are essentially analytical. The latter two might even be viewed as allegory and parable, respectively. Like those that follow, they present the reader with an identical predominant condition that generates incidents of the narrative: a stifling, nearly unbearable situation from which characters cannot escape on their own. Here, especially in the first two, Marguerite Duras is concerned with the plight of the young who are imprisoned within the family group, which attracts them and repels them at the same time. Maud, the twenty-year-old daughter in *Les Impudents*, is rescued from her family by a stranger, but even after she has become pregnant she feels compelled to return to the family cell. Only when she seizes the initiative and breaks her bondage by denouncing an older brother to the police does her mother reject her, liberating her so to speak. This work, in which freedom is obtained partly through an impulse coming from within, is unique. It contrasts sharply with *L'Amante anglaise*, written almost a quarter of a century later, where a similar impulse inspires a murder, dooming the character instead of liberating her.

Maud was the central intelligence of *Les Impudents*, a third-person narrative. *La Vie tranquille*, with its view of hard, unrewarding life on an isolated farm, presents a picture of the human condition as seen through the consciousness of a first-person narrator, Francine. While she is not responsible for the plight they find themselves in, it is an uncle who, through some misdeed that also involved her father, caused a scandal, forcing the family to flee the town where they were well-to-do and respected. In contrast to Maud in *Les Impudents*, she does not expect a savior—but he does show up, somewhat enigmatically, in the person of a man named Tiène, who seeks work at the farm. He will help her to find herself and perhaps save herself. When the two first meet and become acquainted, their talk expresses much more than the words they use would indicate. Duras, however, does not attempt to "show" the dialogue—she describes it: "That conversation was not actually a conversation. . . . He seemed absentminded and I, too, would answer him absentmindedly."[1] Later, he questions her intensely in order to discover the underlying motives for her first act (which indirectly caused her uncle's death), to reach her own truth, which he knows to be "pure and coherent" (85)—but it is he who says so; the reader is not made to sense it. After her brother commits suicide, she goes to the seashore at Tiène's suggestion, to a resort called T . . . (which anticipates T. Beach in *Le Ravissement de Lol V. Stein*). She engages in much self-analysis and has a pointless encounter with a mediocre man that prefigures the meeting of *Le Square*, although here her indifference results in the man's drowning. The entire episode enables her to discover who she is, and she then discourses at length on what has happened, there and at the farm. Her account, given in a form that is close to that of Duras's middle period, reveals a feminine sensuality to be displayed only in the later works. Shortly after her return to the farm, her engagement to Tiène is announced. They will be married soon, because he must leave before winter comes. Having played his role, the savior disappears as unaccountably as he had come. The allegory might be reconciled both with Christian myth and with existentialism, but while Duras is undoubtedly acquainted with the writings of Sartre, she surely is no Christian believer.

With *Un Barrage contre le Pacifique* metaphysical overtones are laid to rest and replaced with social ones; the atmosphere in this book has reminded at least one critic of the works of Erskine Caldwell.[2] While an oppressive family situation is still the cause for individual misery, the economic ruin that befalls the mother and her two children is directly traceable to the corrupt colonial administration of prewar French Indochina. The mother continues madly to wage a losing battle both against the all-powerful administration and the Pacific Ocean, but the children know that it is useless to fight. They wait for someone to rescue them and take them away. The daughter turns down a rich suitor, but her brother meets a wealthy married woman who will be the "savior" of both.

With this work Duras actually was in the running for a Goncourt prize, which, instead, went to a now-forgotten writer. Ironically, she did receive that award, nearly a quarter of a century later, for a book that draws its material from the same period of her life in what is now Vietnam —*L'Amant* (1984; *The Lover*). The two texts could hardly be more dissimilar, for after all what they have in common is unimportant. What does matter is the way the same material has been shaped into works that obey different aesthetic laws and are produced by different psychic conditions. *Un Barrage contre le Pacifique* is told as a straightforward narrative whose subject knows and imposes meaning—even though it might be a false one (and this does not detract from the quality of the book). *L'Amant,* even though it displays the more open, indeterminate writing that is found in the works of Duras's middle period, retains enough of a linear, "autobiographical" narrative to appeal to a greater number of readers. Here, however, it is not the young woman who rejects the son of a wealthy Chinese real-estate speculator (in the earlier work one could

assume he was French); it is he who refuses to allow his son to marry a
white woman, that is, a woman of an inferior race, instead of the Chinese
bride who had been chosen for him. At a time when racist feelings were
being exploited by right-wing politicians against North African immi-
grants, telling her readers about a "reverse" kind of racism might well
have appealed to Duras. What is more significant is that *Un Barrage
contre le Pacifique*, written in the realistic tradition, practically invited
political and sociological readings but censored a manifestation of
racism; even more importantly, it wiped out the rejection the young
woman suffered. It points to a deep wound (as deep or perhaps deeper
than that caused by events of the Second World War and the occupation
of France) that may well have been the wellspring of Duras's writing,
which, on the surface, repressed the pain while displaying the other
wrongs that she endured.

A man and a woman meet in a public square. They talk at length, and
we learn of their helplessness, of their longing for a love and a freedom
they have never known. At last they part company, perhaps to meet
again, perhaps not (*Le Square*, 1955). A lonesome mother accompanies
her child to his piano lessons. During one lesson a crime is committed in a
café nearby, and for the rest of the narrative the mother tries to understand why a man murdered his mistress, wishing that she, too, could be
loved by a man passionate enough to kill her (*Moderato cantabile*, 1958).
Three French tourists in Spain, a married couple (with a small child) and
their woman friend, are forced by a storm to spend the night in a small
town where a man has just shot his wife and her lover. The murderer is
still at large but the French wife, who is as lonesome as the protagonist of
the previous story, finds him by chance and tries to save him. She fails,
losing her husband to the other woman as well (*Dix Heures et demie du
soir en été*, 1960; *10:30 on a Summer Night*). An old man waits for a contractor outside the house he has bought for his daughter. The contractor's
child comes to warn him that her father will be late. The old man continues to wait, and the contractor's wife comes to say that he will be later
still. They both wait and despairingly talk about his daughter and her
husband, whose love they sense they are losing (*L'Après-midi de Monsieur
Andesmas*, 1962; *Afternoon of Monsieur Andesmas*). As Germaine Brée
put it in her introduction to the American edition of those four works,
"Each novel concentrates on one central relationship that gives it its
dramatic cogency, but it is not an isolated relationship, for implacably it
draws all other relationships into its orbit, modulating them as it were."[3]

The man in *Le Square* is a peddler, traveling from town to town,
hawking small articles in public markets; he is perhaps thirty years old,
and he has accepted mediocrity as his lot. She is twenty; she is maid and
governess for a bourgeois household that lives not far from the square.
Unlike him, she finds her lot intolerable and lives only for the day when

she can cast it away. The dialogue between the two nameless characters develops then as a dialogue between two attitudes toward life, between two situations, both oppressive. Ironically, it is the man, to whom our culture has assigned an active role, who has adopted a pessimistic, passive outlook. His partner, predisposed by temperament toward positive action against the social injustice of which she is a victim, is forced into passivity by a situation as a woman. Like Maud, Francine, and others, she too is pushed into the seemingly unrealistic position of waiting for a savior from abroad.

As fiction, *Le Square* offers the unusual feature of being written almost exclusively in dialogue form—something no major writer in France had attempted since Roger Martin du Gard's *Jean Barois* (1913). In later works Duras periodically came back to an emphasis on dialogue, although not as exclusively. Brief descriptive sections provide a framework for each of the three parts into which the work is divided. Within the descriptive pages a child appears—also a recurrent motif in much of Duras's fiction. This child, a boy, is the one the young woman is supervising in the public square. He is the pretext for bringing her and the man together. Concerned only with his own desires, he plays, expresses hunger, thirst, and exhaustion, thus punctuating the dialogue and marking the passage of time between 4:30 in the afternoon and dusk. As the man and the woman become acquainted and tell each other about their jobs, one soon notices the unrealistic features of their language. No ordinary French people of their social status, meeting on a bench in a *jardin public*, ever talked in such a manner. The words themselves are commonplace (although there is no slang), but they are seldom specific. Describing the objects he sells, the peddler says they are varied and small, the kind one always needs but usually forgets to buy (12). Later he speaks of a trip he has taken to a city in a foreign country, but without ever mentioning names (34 ff.). On the other hand, a specific reference is occasionally made when either none or many more would have been expected. Asked if any qualifications are necessary for his job, the man suggests literacy, although he says that is not indispensable—but one should be able to read the name of the town when arriving at a railroad station! The young woman notes that because of her employment she always has enough to eat. At the place where she works they often eat very good things, sometimes leg of lamb.

This device, which on occasion borders on the humorous (more so, of course, when quoted out of context, that is, out of style), gives enough implicit particularization to preserve some semblance of individuality for the book's two characters, thus balancing the effect of the first device. It can also give symbolic value to a specific detail. The peddler remarks that although he travels a lot he keeps returning to the same towns, but sometimes he notices that a change has taken place: in spring, for instance, there are cherries in the marketplace (27). Those splotches of red keep cropping up throughout *Le Square,* acting as correlatives to the feeling of hope one traditionally associates with spring, but also to the memories of a lost paradise of childhood. Both man and woman have vivid memories of the days when they used to steal cherries from orchards. In the foreign city described by the man, even though he himself emphasizes the honey-colored light that impregnated the atmosphere, his references to the setting sun and words such as *feu* ("fire") and *incendie* ("conflagration") are likely to bring back the color red in the reader's mind. Because of the emotional charge contained in that description, there is no strain involved in linking such redness to that of the cherries—they, too, have acquired symbolic value. The recurrence of red underlines the intense passion felt by the young woman, a passion that loses none of its fire for being repressed. It corresponds to the inner wounds she has suffered, but the life-giving principle it symbolizes might well be what sustains her. The objects that give off the color, through the ambiguous directions they suggest, convey a feeling that might be termed oppressive when one thinks of the characters' lives (the fiction generated in the reader's mind) or circular if one considers the book's architecture (the text itself), even though the narrative may be structured toward a breaking away from the circle. Indeed, setting sun and childhood cherries fail to cancel out the cherries of spring and the radiance of the foreign city, nor can a reader be blamed for thinking of that color's political connotations.

The peddler's visit to the foreign city has had for him the effect of a quasi-mystical experience. He has been deeply marked, and he shares that complexion with many other protagonists of Duras's writings. Their experience might be active or passive; in either event it constitutes a trauma that affects them permanently. Early works suggest the trauma caused by what Duras has called the absolute injustice of childhood.[4] The murder scene at the outset of *Moderato cantabile* and the jilting of Lol V. Stein in the book that bears her name are perhaps the most striking cases of a later trauma. In his strange city, the man of *Le Square* has undergone a sense of being at one with the world, of being as worthy as other men. He felt a sort of happiness that he cannot describe and also the welling up in himself of a strength that could not find its object. The young woman identifies it with hope; he adds that it is the hope of hope. In other words, as the context of the book bears out, it is undistinguishable from despair. As she says, immediately after he recounts the foreign city experience, "If there were only people like you, we would never succeed" (57).

What the man and woman actually say strikes one at first as being as insignificant as their stations in life. But the tone that is given to their utterances, the serious consequences they deduce from matter-of-fact statements, the emotions they arouse—all conspire to channel the reader's imagination into his or her own psychological storehouse, enabling each reader to create two human beings that far transcend the particularities of those given by the writer. The characters talk and talk, seemingly saying nothing, while laying bare the secret recesses of their being. Referring to the young woman's part in the dialogue, Maurice Blanchot remarked: "In everything she says with such extreme reserve and restraint, one detects the impossibility that lies at the core of human lives and that her own position impresses upon her every moment of the day: that job of being a domestic, which is not even a job, which is like a disease, a lower form of slavery, preventing her from having a bond with anyone, not even the slave's bondage to the master, not even one with herself."[5] After the young woman describes how unpleasant it is to take care of a senile, eighty-two-year-old woman, weighing about two hundred pounds, the reader is moved rather than surprised by her saying, "And please note that I haven't murdered her, even two years ago when I came back from a visit to the union local . . . and that I still don't murder her, still not, although it would be easier and easier to do" (105). That does not surprise the reader because such an expression of feeling comes two-thirds of the way through the book, and it has been adequately prepared by considerable implied feeling that was left to be developed by his or her imagination.

The characters themselves are shown to be aware of the revelatory nature of their statements. As I see it, this is made quite clear by the extraordinary politeness to one another. They know that their questions or their comments can inflict serious psychic wounds, and they handle their words with extreme caution. (This suggests an obvious analogy with what takes place in Nathalie Sarraute's narratives on the level of the fiction or the anecdote, but not on that of the text.) Such unrealistic precautions also constitute a signal: the reader, whose sensitivity has been alerted, is in a better position to pick up the overtones. Another indication is a character's (almost always the woman's) occasionally urging the other to speak, to talk some more—rather than asking a specific question (*dites voir*, 27; *Et encore? . . . Et encore?*, 86; *dites-moi encore*, 134; *encore une fois, vous, vous?*, 138). She seems to imply that he will reveal important matters, regardless of what he talks about. The analogy with psychoanalysis does come to mind, but I do not believe it should be pushed much further, at least not in a conventional fashion. It, too, is primarily a signal. One might conceivably argue that it calls for the application of psychoanalysis to textual interpretation as practiced by Julia Kristeva or by Hélène Cixous, following a reading of Freud that is advocated by Jacques Lacan.[6]

The idea that banal words and even silence could be a means of mean-ingful communication was not new to Duras at the time of *Le Square*. More than twelve years earlier, when describing a scene between the two lovers of *Les Impudents*, she had affirmed that possibility: "From now on, they understood each other completely. As soon as they outlined a gesture, which need not be completed, through the most ordinary words, which they no longer felt obliged to speak. Silence, charmingly pregnant, began to be possible. They had ceased being two" (132). In *Le Square*, however, such a process is no longer explained by a narrator and rendered somewhat trite by that explanation—the reader experiences it.

Much of that invites comparison with a later book, *Détruire, dit-elle* (1969; *Destroy, She Said*). Both pieces of fiction demonstrate the same narrative concision, the same emphasis on elliptic, disturbing dialogue. In the latter, the social milieu is that of most of her other fiction, the middle class, and the locale is a resort hotel patronized mainly by the ill or the convalescing. It is the milieu of those who, in *Le Square*, were the unseen oppressors, mirrored in the mind of the maid. *Détruire, dit-elle* could be said to depict the other side of the picture, with a revolutionary ferment being introduced into the midst of a sick and frightened bourgeoisie by Alissa, an eighteen-year-old woman, who speaks the words of the title (34). Other characters are much older. One is her husband, Max, a professor of history—of future history, a time when there will be nothing left. He is therefore silent and his students sleep (122). There are also Stein, an acquaintance who, like Max, is trying to become a writer, and Elizabeth, a convalescing guest at the hotel, who fascinates Max in the fullest sense of the word. The narrative line could, I suppose, be interpreted exclusively on the level of purely personal, emotional, and sexual relationship, a tale of eroticism and madness, and this would be congruent with a reading of other recent texts such as *L'Amour, La Maladie de la mort*, or *Les Yeux bleus cheveux noirs*. But a sense of impending revolution can also be read into it. The latter is far from obvious, but nothing is ever obvious in Duras's writings. There is no allegory to be deciphered, rather, a mood is to be felt. Thus, the tennis games that are being played in the background, although not by hotel guests, do not "stand" for any struggle or riot threatening the establishment. Nevertheless, the words that are used to describe the sound of the balls (especially in French, where the same word *balle* is used both for "ball" and for "bullet") lend an ominous tone to what the reader imagines, and in his or her mind the tennis court itself could benefit from an unconscious association with the *Jeu de Paume* hall, where the so-called Tennis Court Oath of 1789 was sworn. The surrounding forest, which is dangerous "because" the guests are afraid of walking into it (34), a cracking sound heard in the air (133), and the final surge of music that shatters trees and strikes down walls permit the initiated reader to elaborate his or her own political or social creation out of the strands, both subtle and corrosive, tendered by the writer.

If one examines an earlier work such as *Le Marin de Gibraltar* (1952; *The Sailor from Gibraltar*), it is not hard to see in it a prefiguration of the books of the middle period and indeed a modification in Duras's concept of fiction. One is confronted with two main characters who show some resemblance to those in *Le Square.* The man, who in this instance is the narrator, is a petty government clerk; basically passive, he nevertheless triggers the events of the story. The woman, eldest of five children, whose father owned a small-town café, is an activist who, like Suzanne in *Un Barrage contre le Pacifique* and the narrator of *L'Amant,* believes that she must be chosen by a male savior. She therefore institutes what might be termed a negative search wherein the apparent seeker offers herself as a quarry. Anna has run away from home at nineteen; at twenty, she has taken a job as bartender on an American millionaire's yacht. Eventually she marries him and still later inherits the yacht. When she enters the story, she is imbued with a legendary aura. She is a beautiful, wealthy American who sails the seven seas looking for a man she used to know. It is as though a spell had been cast on her, for she is unable to abandon her search for the elusive being she calls the sailor from Gibraltar. How could such a romantic impersonation fail to attract a savior? He turns up in the guise of the narrator, a most unlikely candidate for the part, as Anna's yacht is anchored off the beach of a small Italian resort. He has been vacationing with his mistress (also an employee at the ministry where he works). He neither likes his job nor loves his mistress, but he lacks the willpower to walk out on either one. When he encounters Anna, however, something happens within him, and he does exactly that—not that he acquires any special power; rather his mistress and his job drop off like ripe fruit from a tree. He then sails off with Anna, in pursuit of the sailor.

This is Duras's longest work of fiction and probably the richest, but in art, wealth is not necessarily an asset. *Le Marin de Gibraltar* is structured on dialogues, an important change in technique from that used in *Un Barrage contre le Pacifique* and a device that is featured in many of her later works. The trouble stems from having to rely on too many different contributing dialogues in order to establish the book's meaning. Often, too, the dialogues are overburdened with material that tends to generate minor digressions, hence distracting the reader. As the story develops, one overhears successively a series of dialogues between the narrator and a truck driver, an Italian girl, an innkeeper, and the narrator's mistress as well as several involving the narrator with Anna and a number of minor characters, sometimes individually, sometimes in a more general conversation. In one of the latter instances, a man relates a story that requires several thousand words. Anna herself, in a more controlled dialogue, is twice allowed to speak some eight hundred words without being interrupted (141-42, 144-46). At the same time, the reader is aware that all that is not "just talk," no more than it is in *Le Square.* Conversation is a process by which people disclose what they are, not only to others but to themselves as well. Within the framework of the narrative, characters become what they are through subjection to such a process (which, it should be clear, goes beyond the traditional one of characterization by means of dialogue, often a mere revelation of essence rather than a becoming). Significantly, there are already some instances of one person's urging another to "say something," no matter what (e.g., 158). At the outset of *Le Marin de Gibraltar*, the narrator is a nonentity. He talks very little. Of his fellow employees at the ministry we learn that he feels more like killing them than speaking with them (24). It is the narrator's conversation with the truck driver that makes him realize that he must leave both his job and his mistress. Each succeeding conversation gives him a bit more substance, and in the end he has become the sailor that Anna has been seeking.

The first dialogue between Anna and the narrator takes place at a popular outdoor dance. The ballroom or dance motif is one that runs through Duras's work from *Les Impudents* to *Le Vice-consul*. Its significance might well reside in its being a ritual that requires active participation by an indeterminate number of people, involves a minimum of set rules, is accompanied by music and wine, and brings together man and woman in a culturally accepted communion of erotic gesture. All of that transforms public dancing into a celebration that temporarily eradicates drabness or suffering. At the dance, the narrator does what the young woman of *Le Square*, who keeps talking about the forthcoming Saturday dance, hopes the peddler will do—he chooses her. Ironically, he becomes her "savior" by displaying a signal of distress (MG 121) in a narrative metaphor of what the mythical sailor "actually" did when, adrift in a small boat off Gibraltar, he was taken aboard the yacht. He does that quite simply, by describing his own life. But as he casts his lot with Anna's he soon understands that he must join her in the mysterious chase even though they have become lovers and their love is genuine. Late in the narrative, when she asks him, "And what if I had made up the whole thing?" (275), he answers that it would not change things much. The search has been revealed as a ritualistic quest, and, without such a ritual, love between Anna and the narrator could not endure. For it is what characters in this book refer to as *un grand amour*, but it does not possess the characteristics lovers normally associate with it—it is not a secure, long-lasting state. As one character comments, a state like that "is something sad to behold" (320). The protagonists of *Le Marin de Gibraltar* are in a dynamic situation, their love is not guaranteed, it must be tested continuously. The men who preceded the narrator on Anna's yacht failed the test, partly because they did not take it seriously. Some embarked as if going on an ordinary cruise, bringing books, cameras, and so on; one tried to convert Anna, another was foolish enough to suggest that she forget the sailor from Gibraltar. The narrator has left everything behind, pursuing the legendary sailor, first near Marseilles, then in Central Africa, in all seriousness. When the narrative is about to close, they are off to the West

Indies. As Anna remarks, it is a joyful life. It will remain so as long as the two lovers are seriously playing their dangerous and fanciful game.

While the motif of the savior appears with great constancy throughout Duras's fiction, ritual connected with intense erotic experience, an embryo of which was noticed in *La Vie tranquille*, is dealt with at length in *Moderato cantabile* and *Le Ravissement de Lol V. Stein* and several subsequent works. In the first, Anne Desbaresdes, who is "happily" (if conventionally) married to a successful manufacturer, has the revelation of a love so great or so unusual that it could only be fulfilled in death. This is analogous to Anna's experience in *Le Marin de Gibraltar* (the similarity of the two names could be more than coincidental, and one might note that the main characters in *Dix heures et demie du soir en été* and *Le Vice-consul* are respectively Maria and Anne-Marie, the latter being once referred to as Anna Maria), except that in *Moderato cantabile* the event is objectively presented by the writer. Of Anna's discovery of love we know only what she herself is willing to tell—and she is inclined to mythify.

The contact, even though accidental, with a love that leads to death opens up an entire new world for Anne Desbaresdes. She symbolically deserts the fashionable section of town where she lives in favor of the proletarian café where the murder was committed. She engages in conversation with a former employee of her husband's manufacturing concern. With his assistance, through a series of revelatory dialogues, she attempts a ritual identification with the slain woman. He tells her about the woman, she tells about herself (it is he who uses the characteristic *Parlez-moi* or *Inventez* [MC 55, 79]). She drinks a lot of wine, as do characters in *Le Marin de Gibraltar* and those of several other texts, in part because drinking is good, but also, here especially, because of the underlying analogy with a Dionysiac ritual. As suggested by a reference to her *ventre de sorcière* (137), Anne is a sorceress who partakes of the blood of the god. With it she will acquire some of that natural power that he wields, from which civilization, culture, and social status have estranged her. It enables her to penetrate into a region where reason is of no avail: "There is no point in trying to understand. One cannot understand to that extent" (150). Eventually the lives of the two women— Anne and the victim—merge in a "ritual of death" (153). When the man says to her, "I wish you were dead," Anne answers, "It has been done" (155), and walks away into the setting sun.

Le Ravissement de Lol V. Stein (1964; *The Ravishing of Lol Stein*), the second of the two ritualistic love stories, is far more complex. Lol has been so severely affected by the public rejection she suffered at the hands of her fiancé, Michael Richardson, that she sinks into severe depression for about ten years. Even though she marries and has children, she barely exists. Then, through a casual encounter with the narrator, she is given a chance of coming back to life. It may be possible to see the recovery from her trauma as being effected by her stealing Jacques Hold, the narrator, away from his mistress, Tatiana: she would be cured by the realization that she could do to others what had been done to her, that she is not insignificant compared to other women.

But the process might well be more complicated than that. Lol had been discarded, so to speak, in the most casual fashion. Her love story had not been brought to its ritual conclusion. While she had been rejected at a public dance, it is the woman her fiancé walks away with who is presumably involved in the ceremony of love. Lol dreams of a conclusion in which her fiancé would begin to undress her. As her clothes were removed, her body would gradually be replaced with that of the other woman; a "velvetlike annihilation of herself" would occur (56). When, after ten years, Lol looks up her childhood friend, Tatiana, and meets Hold, she somehow senses that with their help she can bring her story to a satisfactory end. Lying in a field of rye she watches the lighted hotel room where Tatiana and her lover meet, and she identifies with her friend—for that, in her world of fantasy, is the indispensable first step. Only from such an annihilated position in another woman's body can she cry out to her fiancé and beg him to take her back. The narrator, like the one in *Le Marin de Gibraltar*, is aware of the game being played, and he accepts his role within it. He and Lol go back to the scene of her shattering experience. They become lovers, and that night the identification is perfected: "And there no longer was any difference between her and Tatiana Karl, except for her remorse-free eyes and the way she referred to herself . . . the two names she used: Tatiana Karl and Lol V. Stein" (219). All is over between Hold and Tatiana, but they will meet one last time at the hotel to bring their own story to a conclusion. When they arrive, Lol is outside, sleeping in the rye.

The end of Duras's narrative is left open. Lol may well have destroyed herself or, more likely, have succeeded in destroying the ghost that had been haunting her. The role of Jacques Hold (he is a doctor) has perhaps been played out, and a reborn Lol will be given back to her husband. Perhaps not. Because of the psychological implications of this work, one of Jacques Lacan's comments is worth noting: "We should remember with Freud that in his subject the artist always precedes us and that we are not called upon to play the psychologist where the artist has cleared the way. That is precisely what I acknowledge in the ravishing of Lol V. Stein, where Marguerite Duras reveals, without being acquainted with my work, a knowledge of what I teach."[7] What may also give this work the power I believe it has is the resonance produced by Duras's own trauma, as recounted in *L'Amant* twenty years later. In 1964 the reader could not, and did not need to, know the later work—but something undefinable could be sensed working through the text.

In another respect, *Le Ravissement de Lol V. Stein* marks a change in that problems inherent to the very nature of fiction are now being emphasized. Generally speaking, in the works published before *Le Marin de Gibraltar*, the fiction was both closed and certain—closed in the sense that the reader's contribution did not significantly affect its meaning, certain in the sense that the reader's willing suspension of disbelief was expected. *Le Marin de Gibraltar* and the five works that followed could be characterized as open but certain. *Le Ravissement de Lol V. Stein* is both open and questionable. Needless to say, once again, such divisions cannot be considered rigorous, for there are questionable as well as open aspects to *Le Marin de Gibraltar*. Contrariwise, the oppressive circularity of *Les Petits Chevaux de Tarquinia* is relieved by the characters' existential assumption of their situation, which is explicitly conveyed to the reader: "As to love, one has to love it completely with its boredom and everything, there is no possible escape from that" (258). The way the characters reach that conclusion and the manner in which their lives are affected by it are not analyzed. Otherwise, the reader's freedom is restricted by the writer. The questionable portion of *Le Marin de Gibraltar* pertains to what is narrated by Anna rather than to the fiction presented by Duras: although one might not believe what Anna says, one accepts the existence of that character in the story and believes that she speaks the words that are reported as hers. Obviously, what is open results from the ambiguity of Anna herself. In *Le Ravissement de Lol V. Stein*, on the other hand, such questionable aspects are an integral part of the structure.

As in *Le Marin de Gibraltar* the story is presented from the point of view of a first-person narrator. When the narrative begins and for a long time afterwards, the connection between narrator and narration is uncertain. It is not until more than a third of the story has been told, when Lol comes to visit Tatiana after ten years of silence and is introduced to Jacques Hold, that the latter identifies himself as the narrator. He had begun by giving a few facts concerning Lol's youth, stating, on the second page of the book, that those were the things he knew—and implying that he knew little more. On the fourth page he confesses, "I no longer believe anything of what Tatiana says, I am not convinced of anything." He then prefaces the next narrative sequence with this warning: "Here are, in full, intermingled, simultaneously, the fabrication told by Tatiana Karl and what I invent" (12). As one continues to read, one finds an expression of uncertainty constantly maintained. At the start of the fourth (unnumbered) chapter, the still-unidentified narrator explains the kind of approach he has selected in order to deal with his topic, "since I must invent the missing links in the story of Lol V. Stein" (41).

But why must he? As a character, he is under no compulsion. As the writer's surrogate, he must indeed reveal the story of Lol. Can the writer make a distinction in her invented material between fictional reality and fictional falsehood? Considering that reality is a form of fiction, what does this question mean? Later on, the narrator, who apparently thinks he is able to differentiate between the one and the other, prefaces some of his remarks with the statement, "I see this," others with, "I invent" (62, 64), or with the combination, "I see, I invent" (62, 64). After Jacques Hold has identified himself, he relates only those events he has witnessed. One readily accepts his observation, when transcribing Lol's words in a conversation, "This woman lies," or when giving the presumed thoughts of Tatiana, "I invent" (124, 178). On the other hand, it is disturbing to have him admit, "I am lying" or "I want to avoid going to the Hotel des Bois, I am going there" (140, 147). At one point, Tatiana herself shouts at Jacques Hold, "Liar, liar" (185). When the narrator and Lol are together, toward the end of the story, he places the whole narrative in questionable perspective: "I deny the ending that will probably come to separate us, its ease, is desolating simplicity, for since I deny that one I accept the other, the one that needs to be invented, the one I don't know, that no one has yet invented: the ending without an end, the beginning without end of Lol V. Stein" (214).

With that statement the writer's surrogate withdraws, expressing a willingness to play the role of a mere character. He relinquishes all his powers to the reader, who must now invent what "no one has yet invented." Lol now belongs to that reader—she has been his or hers, of course, from the beginning, but the ritual of reading, of her being turned over to the reader, has been completed. At the same time, the title acquires its full meaning. The secondary sense of *ravissement* fits Lol's ecstatic states and her contemplative attitudes outside the hotel, but she has never been forcefully abducted, not even by Jacques Hold, whom she chose as her "savior," as other female characters in Duras's fiction had done. The narrative stands in part as metaphor of the act of literary production: Lol V. Stein has been abducted from the writer's domain by the reader.

In *Le Vice-consul* we are confronted with an even more complicated affair, for two narrations are involved instead of one. A character, Peter Morgan, tells one story, but not as the writer's surrogate: she has a very different story to tell. The scene is set in Calcutta. Peter Morgan is one of several English friends the wife of the French ambassador has gathered about her. He has been obsessed by the sight of an insane female beggar, presumably from Cambodia, who shares the life of Indian lepers, eating scraps from the embassy garbage cans. Spurred by an anecdote the ambassador's wife has told him, Morgan invents a background for the woman, depicting a miserable chain of injustice and suffering extended along a ten-year journey, on foot, from Battambang to Calcutta. To him, as to the other Europeans in Calcutta, she is an object of scandal. It is, however, relatively easy to keep her at a safe distance: fences and armed guards protect the *vie tranquille* of the well-to-do. Even though this is Morgan's story, I cannot help feeling Duras's sympathy for the beggar, as memories of her own youth in Indochina haunt her, turning the insane woman into a transmuted mother figure in whom she has unconsciously poured her love and hatred.

There is, however, another cause for scandal, and this is the topic of Duras's own overt tale, so to speak. The French vice-consul at Lahore has been recalled to Calcutta, pending further investigation, because of his shocking behavior. Matters are not very clear: at night, he would shoot at lepers and dogs from the windows of his residence; he would cry out in the dark and also fire his gun inside the house. As in the case of the mad beggar, a search for antecedents gets under way. Begun on the two opposite sides of the earth, one following the course of abject poverty and the other a privileged existence, two lives follow different paths to Calcutta where they explode in madness and scandal. Both biographies represent tales from the outside. The sanctuary they disturb, which constitutes the reality of the book, is the European colony of that Indian city or, at any rate, of the portion that gravitates about the French embassy. At its center, there is a woman—the ambassador's wife.

Someone asks Peter Morgan if the beggar from Battanbang is to be the only character in his book. He answers no, there will also be Anne-Marie Stretter (183). That was the name of the woman for whose sake Lol V. Stein's fiancé walked out on her. That is now the name of the wife of the French ambassador, and at a formal embassy party she wears the same dress that the other woman wore when she appeared at the fateful dance, accompanied by her daughter—in other words, she shows up as a mother who brings misery to others.[8] The halls of the embassy are like "those of a casino in a seaside resort town, in France" (93), which describes the place where Lol was abandoned by Michael Richardson. In *Le Vice-consul*, Michael Richard has been one of Anne-Marie's lovers. While this in my opinion represents a belated effort on Duras's part to build a fictional world of recurrent characters and places in the manner of Robert Pinget or William Faulkner (the change from Richardson to Richard is probably the tip-off), it is symptomatic of the way in which later works will keep echoing features of earlier ones. Half a dozen years later, for instance, *L'Amour* (1971) accounts for the experience of three individual beings divorced from story, recognizable location, or characters. The reader is presented with an unnamed woman and two men (one identified as "the traveler," the other as having blue eyes), on and near a beach, somewhere. Clues to a connection with *Le Ravissement de Lol V. Stein* are the peculiar name of the seaside town, S. Thala, and a visit to the dance hall where Lol had been jilted. Stripped of the usual novelistic paraphernalia (like some of Blanchot's shorter texts), *L'Amour* is a sequence of haunting, poetic dialogues on love and death. *L'Homme*

atlantique and *La Maladie de la mort* (*The Malady of Death*), both
published in 1982, belong in the same category.

In *Le Ravissement de Lol V. Stein* Anne-Marie replaces Lol in Michael's
affection. In *Le Vice-consul* she replaces Lol from a functional point of
view—she is not the same woman, but she plays the same role. Like Lol,
she may also be said to belong to the reader, and she is truly at the center
of the text. In the light of a changing aesthetics, one might call her a
transfigured Jamesian central intelligence. As Peter Morgan has related
her to the beggar, someone else relates her to the vice-consul: "By the
way, the vice-consul at Lahore, whom does he resemble? . . . He hears the
answer: me, says Anne-Marie Stretter" (204). Without her, the book
would fall apart, leaving only two disconnected narratives; but she is a
void, a "blank,"[9] at the center of things. "At the club, other women talk
about her. What goes on in that life of hers? Where can one discover her?
One does not know" (109). She needs no protection from the two Calcutta
scandals, for she is, morally speaking, an outsider. Characteristically
enough, her final position is left ambiguous. When one of her close
friends suggests that they must all forget about the vice-consul lest they
lose their image of Anne-Marie, another friend says, "Here, someone is
lying" (193), but he does not specify who.

The story of the beggar is an outright fabrication but it bears its own
truth, as did the story of Anna in *Le Marin de Gibraltar* and both are told
by one of the characters. The story of the vice-consul is a puzzle, with
many pieces missing. The story of Anne-Marie will be as true as the
reader is able to make it. Duras contributes her truth, the reader his or
hers. If the two join in harmony, the book succeeds. The writer, however,
cannot directly attain a truth that is not within herself. An awareness of
such a limitation goes hand in hand with the development of an aesthetics
that shifts a sizable part of the productive burden over to the reader.
Unless there is some intuitive resonance, as in the many dialogues scattered throughout Duras's fiction, from those in *Le Marin de Gibraltar* to
the one between the vice-consul and Anne-Marie Stretter and those in
later texts, people can understand one another only up to a point. All this
is explicitly brought forward in *L'Amante anglaise* (1967).

A modified version of an earlier play entitled *Les Viaducs de la Seine-
et-Oise*, and later readapted for the stage as *L'Amante anglaise*, the narrative bearing this title, like the original play, takes its point of departure
from a rather ghastly crime actually committed in France in 1954. The
culprits were found, they confessed; they were brought to trial and
sentenced; but no one, including the criminals themselves, could give an
adequate motive for the crime—and thus, in Duras's view, it remained
"unsolved." (In the previous text, the vice-consul was also unable to
provide an understandable reason for his mad behavior in Lahore.) In
the narrative of *L'Amante anglaise* the criminals are reduced to one, for

better focus; she is a woman named Claire. The text consists of a series of three interrogations, conducted by a narrator who says he intends to write a book about Claire. (Contrary to what happens in a few other works, the book the character is writing or plans to write is not the book we are reading.) He has a tape recording of the scene in a café that led to Claire's admission of guilt and her arrest. He plays it back in the presence of the café owner and questions him about the people involved, especially about Claire. He then talks to Claire's husband, and finally he sees Claire herself.

At the very outset, the café owner raises the question of truthfulness: "The difference between what I know and what I shall tell you, what are you going to do about it?" The narrator does not answer within the context of the narration but within that of the reader's act: *"That constitutes the share of the book the reader must contribute. It is always present"* (9-10). As one progresses through the three narratives, one notices not only discrepancies between the characters' memories or interpretations concerning the same fact, but also the different views they have of one another and themselves. When Claire is reached, she turns out to be very different from what one expected, almost likable in spite of her crime. But the narrator eventually reaches a stage beyond which he cannot go: his truth and hers are no longer compatible. She proposes to tell him some of the things she had concealed; she might even succeed in explaining why she committed the murder but he is no longer interested (193). She keeps talking, practically to herself. Her last lines, also the last lines of the text, constitute an appeal to the reader disguised as an admonition to the narrator: "If I were you, I would listen. Listen to me" (195). The main character is thus abandoned to the reader, as had been those of the two previous works. The title comes from a plant grown in the garden where Claire was fond of staying. It is *la menthe anglaise* (peppermint), but her spelling was poor, and she had various ways of transcribing that phrase. Sometimes it would come out as *l'amante anglaise* (the English mistress), which produced the title. One transcription she did not think of would have come out in English as "the clay mistress" (*l'amante en glaise*): to be abducted and fashioned by the reader.

For reasons about which one can only speculate, Marguerite Duras did not pursue her experiments in that same direction. After *L'Amante anglaise* came *Détruire, dit-elle,* upon which I have already commented, and *Abahn, Sabana, David* (1970). Because of its concision, its emphasis on dialogue, the unrealistic nature of characters and setting, the latter rightly belongs to what I have been calling loosely the writings of Duras's middle period. On the other hand, the very stress that is placed on symbolism, a nearly extreme refusal to allow the text to be contaminated by "literary" style, and the more explicit references to politics relate the book to some of her later texts. Actually, calling the references explicit is somewhat of an overstatement. At first, the book seems to deal with the condition of Jews. Abahn, who lives in an isolated house outside the city and is known as Abahn the Jew or Abahn the dog, has been sentenced to die. Sabana and David come to stand guard over him until Gringo, his executioner, arrives. The howling of dogs outside is heard intermittently. Soon another man, also named Abahn, joins the group. From there on, there is nothing but talk.

At this point I hardly need to stress the importance of talk in a text by Duras. The device operates as before, only the dosage is much heavier. But what about the Jews? One does not have to read far into the book before noticing the symbolism. At first, it seems that while some of the references fit the Jewish situation, others do not. Suddenly everything becomes clear, and the text reads like an amplification of the retort made by students in Paris in 1968 to the accusation leveled at Daniel Cohn-Bendit. When authorities, delighted at the opportunity to blame an "outside agitator," said that Cohn-Bendit was a foreigner on two counts, the students chanted, "We are all German Jews!" As I read it, *Abahn, Sabana, David* turns out in effect to be a prose poem in praise of the *gauchistes* ("New Left," perhaps), of all those who proclaimed solidarity with a German Jew (at first Sabana, then David, through a series of dialogues that are often highly ritualistic, go over to the side of the two Abahns), of all who refuse the "establishment," whether communist or capitalist. "On his body, says Sabana, on his arm, there is something written. . . . It is the word NO, says Abahn" (123). The references that allude to the persecution of Jews are those to the Nazi gas chambers and to the Russian salt mines (22-23). It is, nevertheless, the transparent allusion to a Nazi concentration camp, that of Auschwitz, that transforms the Jew into a broader symbol. When Sabana has gone over to Abahn's side, David accuses her, "People say that she is Jewish, that she comes from far away." Abahn then adds, "From German Judea . . . from the city of Auschstaadt" (101). It is then explained that Auschstaadt is everywhere. "We all come from the city of Auschstaadt, says Abahn." That is very similar to the Paris students' chant. It might also be a way of saying that a new kind of political consciousness arose when the atrocities of the concentration camps were disclosed, one that demanded solidarity with the victims.

The three names that Duras uses in her title move the text in the same direction. All three, to a non-Jew, leave a vague impression of being Jewish, but upon investigation neither Abahn nor Sabana reveals a Semitic etymology. There is of course no question concerning David but, ironically, he is the last to identify with Abahn the Jew. The name David is doubly ironic as it means "the beloved" and he has come as an agent for a killer. The executioner is Gringo, a name that, on this continent, is applied by Mexicans and others to foreigners, who are usually seen as oppressors or exploiters, from the United States. In the book's context, however, Gringo is a communist party official. He gives speeches at the Maison du Peuple—even speaking all night at the twenty-second congress (79). His name is Gringo because in the point of view from which this text was written, the communist establishment is no longer distinguishable from the capitalist one. The party, the businessmen (*les marchands* [14-15]), the Société Immobilière (82—probably meaning the giant multinational corporations), are all united in their fear of those who will not fit into the system. The latter are the "others," and they are called Jews (20). Abahn is (or are) conscious of it, even to the point of assuming that position: "Do you come to shatter unity? David asks . . . / Yes. / To divide? To inject confusion into unity? / Yes. / To sow doubt into people's minds? / Yes" (104). He is (or they are) also willing to take the consequences: "it is normal for them to kill you, to seek you out like a plague. / Yes, says the Jew" (ibid.). Men such as Abahn, who cannot live with the establishment, used to be communists: "You used to belong to Gringo's party before this? / Yes" (45). But now they are thoroughly disillusioned. Their attitude is epitomized by that of the Jew; he once spoke of freedom, then of despair, and now he has lost all certainty. "He is a different man, says Abahn. He is a communist who believes communism is impossible; he adds, Gringo thinks it is [possible]?" The question is addressed to David, who came to the isolated house as Gringo's man; he answers, "Well, yes" (94). They have no positive values to propose, nor do they know where their actions might lead them. They do know that the existing system must go: "Look carefully about you: destroy!" (136). That is an obvious echo from the preceding *Détruire, dit-elle*. Love, nevertheless, is what unites them. The final exhortation given to the group, at last joined by David, is paradoxically one implying unity: "REMAIN TOGETHER . . . DO NOT LEAVE ONE ANOTHER ANY-MORE" (149). Lucien Goldmann once told me that there were two major romantic writers in contemporary France, one on the right, the other on the left. To the right stood Henry de Montherlant; to the left Marguerite Duras, and it is hard to believe that either one would have been pleased to be associated with the other in this or any other way. I do not know whether or not Goldmann was able to read *Abahn, Sabana, David*, which appeared shortly before he died. If he did, he must have been amply fortified in his assessment.

I have mentioned *L'Amant* as the third "deflection" point in Duras's evolution and discussed it briefly. The writing is similar to that of *Moderato cantabile* or *Le Vice-consul* except that dialogue has been almost completely eliminated and the biological subject of the text speaks more directly. What is in evidence here might perhaps be described as the return of the repressed, in that the wound suffered by the writer as a teenager can now be revealed. It may be significant that fourteen years separate the publication of *L'Amant* from that of *Abahn, Sabana, David;* during those years Duras produced films, plays, a series of conversations with Xavière Gauthier (*Les Parleuses,* 1974; Woman to Woman) and a few brief texts that feel like aftershocks from previous fictions. On the one hand we have the sound of plays, films, and conversation, on the other the silence of texts. Julia Kristeva might well be right when, considering the reader's or the viewer's point of view, she asserts that, "If Duras uses the screen in order to burn out its spectacular strength down to the glare of the invisible by engulfing it in elliptical words, she also uses it for its excess of fascination, which compensates for verbal constriction. As the characters' seductive power is thus increased, their invisible malady becomes less infectious on the screen because it can be performed."[10] She goes on to recommend that Duras's books not be put in the hands of oversensitive readers. With minor changes, those statements would equally apply to the writer who might find it less painful to translate emotions into pictorial images rather than inscribe them in a text. That may be why the film *Hiroshima mon amour* could come out in 1960, but the texts of *L'Amant* and *La Douleur* had to wait until 1984 and 1985. The latter book includes several narratives that deal with incidents of the Second World War and it is clear that "La Douleur," the one that gives it its title, describing the narrator's detailed feelings and actions while waiting for her husband's release from concentration camp and after his return, was written long before 1985 and then put aside. When it resurfaces, Duras, in prefatory note, states, "I have absolutely no recollection of my having written it." From the viewpoint of the subject of writing the text is thus completely "other."

La Douleur is an important, disturbing piece of writing, but it did not prevent Duras from going on with "literature"—or at least with the new form of it that she herself has shaped. Her recent book, *Emily L.* (1987), is both testimony to a kind of return (or perhaps it had best be called renascence) and a fitting exemplar of her writing power. It is a first-person narrative in which the woman narrator is a writer and is thus close to Duras herself. Soon after the beginning of the text she says, "It seems to me that when it is put into a book, that is when it will no longer cause suffering . . . it won't be anything anymore. It will be erased" (23). I cannot help reading this as an indirect commentary on *L'Amant* and *La Douleur* and on the additional suffering brought upon herself by repressing the events. Justification for this can be found in a later statement where she speaks of "those other things, about which I then thought that I should have remained silent, and about which I now believe on the contrary that I should have stayed with my entire life" (48). And those are not isolated statements on matters of writing: the narrative ends with an impassionate sort of *art poétique* covering a little over a page. It is not a rational, analytical, or didactic presentation, but it meshes with her own practice quite well.

There are two couples involved, as in *Moderato cantabile;* there are ocean voyages on a yacht, as in *Le Marin de Gibraltar;* and there are other echoes as well. The narrator/writer and her friend are the observers, although they are experiencing an affective crisis of their own; the narrator knows she will write about it. They discuss her writing, her fears, her memories of Indochina. She is becoming not quite serene but detached although sympathetic toward the other couple, and that is the tone of the book—except where writing is involved. The couple under observation is British. She is from the Isle of Wight where her parents owned a yacht. He had been hired to take care of it; they fell in love, married against her parents' wishes. Ten years later the parents died; she inherited the yacht, he became its captain, and they traveled the seven seas. It is a great, beautiful love—but it is flawed just the same. The flaw resides in his inability to understand her. She used to write poetry, stopped when they were married, started again a few years later —but those poems reveal an otherness he cannot penetrate. After she gave birth and the child died she wrote another poem; upon reading it the captain felt as though he had been erased, and he secretly burned it. "It must have been after the loss of that poem that she discovered ocean voyages, that she decided to waste her life away on the ocean, to do nothing else with her poems and with love except to waste them on the ocean" (89). Her life from then on is a form of death; a young man who has been hired to look after the estate understands her quite well after a brief meeting, and in his view the captain murdered Emily L. when he burned her poems. He comes too late to save her, however, although he seeks her and her yacht as far as Singapore, without success. As the story is told to or by the narrator (it is often hard to say who speaks), the reader is made to realize that the observing couple is breaking up. She thinks he never really loved her, although she did but no longer does. And at the source of their misunderstandings lies her writing activity.

Thematically, and with varying degrees of intensity, all of Duras's works are reflected in *Emily L.* Most emphatically, however, it needs to be read in conjunction with everything from *La Maladie de la mort* onward. Blankness, as the center of one's being, is linked with that malady of death; Eros no longer vies with Thanatos but sinks into emptiness. The very brief (20 pages), self-deprecating *La Pute de la côte normande* (1986; The Normandy Coast Hooker) is told by the same first-person narrator to the same narratee (anonymous in *Emily L.*), named Yann, to whom *La Maladie de la mort* had been dedicated, and it lays stress on writing, on its near-impossibility. The title is what Yann calls the writer in one of his raging outbursts—and she assumes the epithet, perhaps as a form of catharsis, perhaps also with the painful memories of *L'Amant* and Indochina still present. Thinking of the setting of *Emily L.* she wondered why she liked to go to that river port: "I thought it was because of the Siamese sky, here yellow from the crude oil aura, but everything Siamese was dead" (PCN 17).

All this brings back to mind Duras's own remarks presented at the outset of *La Douleur:* "How was it possible for me to write this thing, for which I still cannot find a name, and which terrifies me when I read it over again." Stressing that "La Douleur" is one of the most important things in her life, she concludes: "I was in the presence of an extraordinary confusion of mind and feeling, which I did not dare tamper with, and in the sight of which literature made me feel ashamed." That is emblematic of the position reached by a number of writers today, recognizing the split nature of the human subject and rejecting the notion of literature as mere entertainment for those with time on their hands. It also echoes some of the pages of Nathalie Sarraute's *L'Ere du soupçon* concerning the worthiness of stories completely made up from whole cloth (as if such an accomplishment were possible).

In her most recent book, *La Pluie d'été* (1990; Summer Rain), Duras returns to a topic that permeated her earliest texts—what I have called the plight of the young who are imprisoned within the family group. It is based on her own film *Les Enfants*, which she shot in 1984 in Vitry-sur-Seine, a Paris suburb. In her postscript to the narrative she stressed the things she did not make up: "Again I forget: the children's names I did not invent. Nor the love story that extends through the length of the book" (155-56). The two children who matter most are named Ernesto and Jeanne but they are also called Vladimir and Giovanna—which ones did she not invent? Other things she says she did not invent are tied to the physical reality of Vitry, which is not really essential to the story compared with the interactions between the family and the world and even more so within the family. In a profound way *La Pluie d'été* is one of the most autobiographical of Duras's texts: what she did not "invent" in the story of the Italian immigrant who met and married a Polish refugee in a Paris suburb must have struck a deep resonating chord. The relationship between Jeanne and her brother Ernesto, between Ernesto and his mother and to a lesser degree between Jeanne and her mother, and the aloofness of the father did, in all likelihood, and in a complex manner, reactivate Duras's own childhood memories. In the fiction the family is separated and Ernesto, whose progress without the help of schools is nothing short of miraculous, goes abroad to become a renowned mathematician and scientist. In actual life Duras's family disintegrated and her brother was a failure. *La Pluie d'été* is the refreshing summer rain of a fictional narrative that relieves the sultry, storm-laden atmosphere of life. It is a sublimation, almost a fairy tale that tells the impossible story of what life might have been—a compensation for the tone of much of her work, with, perhaps, the signal exception of *Le Marin de Gibraltar*, which puts forward a similar concept of love and places an analogous emphasis on make-believe.

NOTES

1   Marguerite Duras, *La Vie tranquille* (Paris: Gallimard, 1944), 74. Henceforth, all references to the works of Marguerite Duras will appear in the body of the text with the following abbreviations: *Les Impudents*, I; *Le Marin de Gibraltar*, MG; *Moderato cantabile*, MC; *Le Pute de la côte normande*, PCN.

2   Armand Hoog, "The Itinerary of Marguerite Duras," *Yale French Studies*, no. 24 (Summer 1959): 68-73.

3   Germaine Brée, introduction to Marguerite Duras, *Four Novels* (New York: Grove Press, 1965), viii.

4   Cf. Pierre Hahn, "Marguerite Duras: 'Les Hommes de 1963 ne sont pas assez féminins,'" *Paris-Théâtre*, no. 198 (1963): 34.

5   Maurice Blanchot, "La Douleur du dialogue," in *Le Livre à venir* (Paris: Gallimard, 1959), 192.

6   Cf. Jacques Lacan, *Ecrits: A Selection*, trans. Alan Sheridan (New York: Norton, 1977); Julia Kristeva, *Desire in Language*, trans. Jardine, Gora, & Roudiez (New York: Columbia University Press, 1980) and several subsequent works; Alan Roland, ed., *Psychoanalysis, Creativitity, and Literature: A French-American Inquiry* (New York: Columbia University Press, 1978); and the *Yale French Studies* double issue no. 55-56 (1977) on "Literature and Psychoanalysis."

7   Jacques Lacan, "Hommage fait à Marguerite Duras du ravissement de Lol V. Stein," *Cahiers Renaud Barrault*, no. 52 (1965): 9.

8   Cf. Julia Kristeva, "The Malady of Grief: Duras," in *Black Sun: Depression and Melancholia*, trans. Leon S. Roudiez (New York: Columbia University Press, 1989).

9   Trista Selous, in her recent work, *The Other Woman: Feminism and Femininity in the Work of Marguerite Duras* (New Haven: Yale University Press, 1986), has devoted a full chapter to the notion of "blanks," which she picked up from the book by Marguerite Duras and Xavière Gauthier, *Les Parleuses* (Paris: Minuit, 1974). See especially 113-22.

10   Kristeva, *Black Sun*, 227.

5

Claude Simon

Surveying the seventeen works of fiction Claude Simon has published, one becomes aware of several stages in his aesthetic development, as was the case with Marguerite Duras. In his earliest writing, which is relatively conventional, from *Le Tricheur* (1945; The Cheat) to *Le Sacre du printemps* (1954; The Rites of Spring), he appeared to be searching for the right focus and style to give to his work. With *Le Vent* (1957; *The Wind*) he seemed to have found it, at least temporarily, and the next three books, through *Le Palace* (1962), reveal a highly disciplined concentration on a single character, theme, or setting, coupled with a distinctive style. Meanwhile, *La Route des Flandres* (1960; *The Flanders Road*) had begun to evidence a preoccupation with textual matters. *Histoire* (1967), which came out after a five-year silence, showed a confident and relaxed Simon—a writer who could allow his fiction to become more complex, letting textual and thematic developments intermingle, without having to fear its getting out of focus. *La Bataille de Pharsale* (1969; *The Battle of Pharsalus*), with its emphasis on textual operations, was the sign of yet another renewal, as it aligned itself with the most up-to-date trends in French writing. There was convergence with the theories of Jean Ricardou, and such a congruence lasted through *Les Corps conducteurs* (1971; *Conducting Bodies*) and *Triptyque* (1973). Simon reasserted his independence with *Leçons de choses* (1975; *The World about Us*) and even more so with *Les Géorgiques* (1981) and *L'Acacia* (1989; *The Acacia Tree*).

Critical recognition came to Simon only after *Le Vent*, official consecration after *Les Géorgiques* as he was awarded the Nobel Prize in literature for 1985.[1] While feeling no compulsion to attempt a rehabilitation of his previous works, some of which read like dry runs for later ones, I believe they are well worth examining, both in the context of the writer's developing craft and in the context of their times. Of the writers who have found eminence after the end of the Second World War, he is one of the few to have allowed history as such to intrude into his fiction. Jean Pierre Faye is another, but he belongs to a more recent literary generation. Claude Ollier allows the reader's consciousness to be affected by a specific aspect of contemporary events such as the French colonial problem. Michel Butor maintains a general sense of history as an oppressive presence. But in a number of Claude Simon's books historical events, like the Spanish Civil War, function as they did in those of Malraux, a generation earlier—and not at all as they did in Sartre's fiction and drama. In spite of chronology, Malraux actually might be said to stand at midpoint between Sartre and Simon in this respect. Sartre was interested in a person's "project," the existential choice when confronted with a historical situation; Malraux was more concerned with using the situation in order to give meaning to a person's life; Simon, who has no sympathy for either of his two predecessors, emphasizes the situation mainly as it fills one's consciousness.

During Simon's first two stages his fiction could be characterized as being structured by time. But in the time–space equation, it is the spatial element that receives more attention. Rather than progressing in linear fashion, gathering experience as they go, his characters seem more like giant, interlocking receptacles: time fills them relentlessly, and there comes a moment when they can take no more. A balance is destroyed and they come crashing down, carrying others with them or, at the very least, damaging the equilibrium of the structure of which they are part. The past is felt as a material presence that can be inventoried. There is no need to go in search of lost time, for it weighs on characters only too heavily.

Seen in retrospect, it is no gratuitous impulse that triggers the very first act of the main character in *Le Tricheur:* he throws his watch away.[2] A denial of conventional chronology, characteristic of all of Simon's work, is already in evidence in the jumbled narrative sequences of that text. The protagonist is a man who refuses to be governed by chance. He takes matters involving life and death into his own hands, and that can be described as a form of cheating—hence the title. There is much that is traditional here, especially in the handling of both narrative and descriptive sequences, much also that is typical of the later Simon, although sometimes only in embryonic form. Thematically, of course, it cannot be separated from what follows. But while the performance is a creditable one, such that a lesser writer might justifiably be proud of, the master's imprint is not sufficiently strong to make a detailed examination as rewarding as it will be in the case of *Gulliver.* Simon himself said that he had been disconcerted by the critical reception of *Le Tricheur* and, unsure of himself, wanted to prove that he could write a conventional novel: "The result was edifying, I could not do so!"[3] The statement is ambiguous, for in spite of many conventional features *Gulliver* is not an ordinary, conventional novel.

The setting of *Gulliver* (1952) is postliberation France. Its mood is one of disillusionment and cynicism, in consonance with the mood that prevailed in the country after the initial euphoria had subsided. It is a mood that had already been conveyed by Marcel Aymé in *Uranus* (1948)—except that Aymé, because of a different political orientation, sensed the mood earlier and sympathized with it. Not sympathy but bitterness pervades Simon's book, and its title refers to the tone of Swiftian satire, not, as I see it, to any particular detail of the fiction. While he has given two of his main characters strikingly large bodies, their physical traits seem only a reminder of satirical intent. The giants are twin brothers. One collaborated with the Germans, the other joined the Free French Forces in London as a pilot—but neither one is respected back home. Both are involved with a group of peculiar individuals, and one of the major events of the narrative consists in their going to a party that ends up with what might be described as gangland murder, followed by the suicide of the principal character, known as "le beau Max." (The theme of suicide was also present in *Le Tricheur*.) A number of other characters are thrust into the limelight, each in his or her turn, and all are morally demolished when the narrative ends. What, in part, turns this book into such a scathing satire is the manner in which the various subplots and individual biographies are linked to, and made dependent on, the story of Max. He is somewhat despicable, and this negative value infects everything else.

The events that constitute the more immediate action take place during two consecutive days and nights; others cover a number of years; the longest sequence deals with Max's life since childhood. There is, however, no narrative distinction between the various episodes. Nearly always, the same verb tenses are used—imperfect and past definite, as required by conventional syntax. This in itself is an indication of Simon's individual concern with time. His placing the several sequences on the same syntactical level implies a denial of chronology similar to the one found at the outset of *Le Tricheur* but expressed by different means. The two exceptions to an otherwise consistent verb usage, although barely noticeable, actually reinforce that denial. Three paragraphs (totaling less than a page), dealing with Max as a small child, the most remote time period in the book, are dominated by verbs in the present tense, with a sprinkling of past indefinites and one future (236-37). Later, some eight pages, involving a significant moment in his life, are also told in the present (248-56). Strictly speaking, the only events taking place in what might be called the reader's present are those of the first and last chapters.

Chapter 1 begins late in the afternoon of the second day and continues into the night, for less than thirty pages, ending with the first violent death—chronologically the third and last. The time perspective is given on the second page: "during the previous night . . . a man had died, perhaps murdered, another had killed himself. They did not know that yet another was going to die." After the end of that chapter, almost every-thing is a flashback: main flashback for what I have termed the immediate action, secondary flashbacks for biographies of the principal characters, or at least for those fragments of their past that converge on the present locale, and, in the case of Max, tertiary flashbacks presented from his own point of view. The final chapter, balancing the initial one, provides the reader with a sense of relief—at first: "It was a quiet, silent, and halcyon day" (374). Such a mood, however, is merely a vehicle for irony. Gradually dissipated, it is replaced with feelings of antagonism among the char-acters, and the novel ends with an expression of hatred.

Between the initial and final chapters, the flashbacks are quite orderly. The main one proceeds in strict chronological fashion, interrupted only by the secondary narratives that are necessary to account for the accumulation of events within a character's spatial consciousness, when they have welled up to the point of making violent action inescapable. Just before the shooting begins, Max realizes that there is no point in asking himself questions, for he clearly sees himself "proceeding now towards the logical, inescapable consequences of a series of actions that had not begun merely a few hours earlier in the locker room at the soccer field, nor even the previous day, nor the month, nor the year; as a result it was useless to wonder what had driven him to follow Bobby tonight, what was driving him now as, in complete and scornful ignorance of what he was going to do, he once again turned his steps toward the silent house squatting in the dell's hollow" (170). The present time implied by "tonight" (*ce soir*) is possibly a slip, but it is a significant one. Coupled with the present participle "proceeding," which governs most of this sentence, it affirms the permanence of past within present. Critics have expatiated upon the proliferation of the present participle in Simon's more recent fiction; the tense appears infrequently in *Gulliver*, but when it does it is so closely associated with a major theme as to make its sub-sequent development appear absolutely organic. This same passage, while showing the vitality of the past and the character's being conscious of its force within himself, also makes it clear that the same character is blind as far as future consequences are concerned.

Looking forward to Simon's utilization of the myth of blind Orion, one is tempted to see here a prefiguration, in all likelihood an unconscious one, of his present view of the writer who, when he begins to write, has no inkling where his writing might lead him, but knows that something within him urges him to write on. His character's blindness justifies another characteristic Simon device, the withholding of information from the reader. Aside from providing an element of suspense, this lessens what has come to be considered the artificiality in third-person narrative technique, in that the writer's omniscience is not so obvious. There is also the possibility that, in this instance, the writer is not omniscient. As early as this, he may have allowed words some initiative in shaping the narration. Or else the concealment was dictated by problems related to theme and characterization. Not only does he have to step back in order to inform the reader that Max is ignorant of the future that his past has built up for him, but his characters' lack of awareness makes it difficult for them to conduct their own flashbacks. If they were able to do so, this would amount to giving them the power of introspection and self-analysis in a moment of crisis, something of which they are not capable. The result is that Simon removes himself from his characters even more than François Mauriac did in his own flashbacks (in *Thérèse Desqueyroux*, for instance). Thus the long flashback of Max's life is inserted between the shooting scene and his suicide a few hours later, at a moment when "he could feel pressing on him the steady weight of that thing, its odor of darkness." He can no more analyze the "thing" than he can fight it, and the examination of his past must be done from without. Even the point of view is not consistently his, shifting from Max to several episodic characters. Nevertheless, the impression of being very close to Max is given the reader at the end of this episode, when feeling and gestures immediately before suicide are described in detail and then cut off without any intimation of intent or consequences. Skillfully as such incidents are handled, the fact remains that the devices used are traditional tricks of the trade.

The opening line of *Gulliver*, "At aperitif time, on Monday evening, in a small café near the station, three regular customers were seated," is as old-fashioned as anything that could be found in a novel by Paul Bourget. When the first few sentences of *Le Vent* (1957)—a work that owes a great deal to *Gulliver*—are compared with it they provide a most striking contrast: "A fool. That's all. And nothing else. And everything people have been able to tell or invent, or try to deduce or explain, all that can only confirm what anybody could see at first glance. Just a plain fool." We are not only plunged in medias res, a commonplace in fiction today, but we are given no immediate indication as to the identity of the speaker. We know neither about whom nor to whom he is talking. The words pour out, almost compulsively, breathlessly, and continue to do so with minor variations in intensity, carrying with them images of people and events, until the end of the book some 230 pages later. They are like the wind that gives the book its title, blowing fiercely through the southern French town where the action takes place, "an unleashed force, aimless, condemned to exhaust itself incessantly, with no hope of ending" (241).

The style of *Le Vent*, developed in the fiction of the middle period and emphasizing continuity and accumulation, is one of the techniques Simon was searching for. Like the symbol of the unrelenting wind, it is part of a structure that aims at creating within the reader a sense of the past's dynamic pressure. But this style did not originate in *Le Vent*. There are many pages in *Gulliver*, especially those describing the more significant episodes, that show Simon's ability to write in such a manner, almost, one might say, naturally. His problem was one of unity. In *Le Vent* it was solved by having the story told in the first person by a narrator who has put together information gathered from the main character and a number of others with whom he happened to be acquainted. Simon pays his respects to conventional verisimilitude, for the writer's surrogate teaches in a lycée and is doing research on Romanesque churches in the region. He is well qualified to assemble the various pieces of the puzzle created by the sudden appearance and strange behavior of the protagonist in the town.

Le Vent bears a curious subtitle: "Attempted Restoration of a Baroque Altarpiece." It is of course linked to the narrator's profession. The first two words offer no difficulty; the reference to a "Baroque Altarpiece" becomes clear only in the context of Simon's spatial concept of the past. An altarpiece usually depicts, through painting or sculpture, an assemblage of characters and scenes that represent the culmination of a tradition, that is, of a past, without which they could have no meaning for the viewer—legends dealing with the lives of Christ and of the saints, for instance. That tradition, with all its details, has irrevocably solidified them as well as divorced them from chronology, by juxtaposing the Crucifixion, the Last Supper, and knights in medieval armor, thus joining the realism of details to the fantasy of the aggregate. The attitude toward reality implied here is specifically set forth on the opening page of *Le Vent*. What we know of reality is "merely that fragmentary, incomplete knowledge, made up of a sum of brief images, themselves incompletely apprehended by the eyes, of sayings, themselves poorly grasped, of sense perceptions, themselves poorly defined, and all of it vague, full of holes, of blanks, which imagination and something like logic attempted to correct with a series of risky deductions." That is the problem of the narrator, one that did not exist for the omniscient writer of *Gulliver*, and he is thereby, along with the reader, brought into closer intimacy with the characters, who retain the relative blindness they had in *Gulliver*. Instead of blindness one might well say innocence. The religious undercurrent of the subtitle becomes even clearer when one realizes that Antoine Montès, the protagonist of *Le Vent*, comes rather close to being a Christ figure—although drawn with irony.

The relationship between this work and the earlier one becomes apparent. *Le Vent* represents a refining, perhaps even a sublimation of a pattern encountered in *Gulliver*. At first a variation on the theme of the prodigal son, it now appears as a veiled allusion to the life of Christ. Set in the context of Simon's other works, however, the value of such cultural references diminishes to a large extent. At least a change of emphasis should take place. The absence of the prodigal son, Christ's stay in Egypt and Galilee, both serve to establish a distance. Translated into Simon's fiction, it becomes the distance between generations, between youth and old age, promise and fulfillment, innocence and corruption. The cry of Christ on the cross, "Why hast thou forsaken me?" could be uttered by any number of Simon's characters, especially by older ones addressing their former selves.

The reappearance of the son in *Gulliver* and *Le Vent* reflects the same theme as the confrontation between son and stepfather in *Le Sacre du printemps* or between the protagonist and his younger self in *Le Palace*. It is expressed again in capsule form in the description of an old photograph in *L'Herbe*, contrasting "the well-behaved child with gnarled knees . . . and the old man, overrun, crushed, smothered" (226). In *Gulliver*, Max cut himself loose early from his wealthy, presumably corrupt family. He volunteered (and was wounded) in the First World War, after assuming both the name and the place of someone who did not want to fight. He showed up again in his hometown only after his father's death. Dissatisfied, alienated, he transformed his life from an affirmation of innocence into a corrupted quest for value and satisfaction, and he finally acts as a magnet for catastrophes. Antoine Montès disappeared even earlier in life than Max did (he was still *en ventre sa mère!*) and comes back likewise after his father's death; but although giving him similar catalytic powers to trigger disasters, Simon shows him while he still possesses an innocence rather like that of Parsifal. To the reader, if not to the townspeople, he is more understandable than Max because less complex. As Max had returned about six years before the main action in the book takes place, he had had a chance to become a part of the town's life again and to appear as one of several intriguing characters—this, of course, from the standpoint of plausibility, which is still a valid one as far as these works are concerned. Montès, on the other hand, is as strange to the townspeople as he is to the reader. His appearance on the scene coincides with the beginning of the narration (even though the narrative is a flashback). As far as knowledge of the town and its inhabitants is concerned, he is as innocent of it as the reader is. The latter can readily sympathize with his troubles.

In *Le Vent*, the reader's present time is posterior to the narrated events, as the narrator reminisces. First, one is in a lawyer's office, and it is the lawyer who makes the first statement, but he soon fades away, and one concentrates on Montès as seen through the narrator's consciousness. In a number of instances, the narrator dissolves into omniscient writer as he relates what only Montès himself could have seen or experienced. The device of inserting brief statements like "as Montès told me later" only calls attention to the implausibilities. That is particularly noticeable in those moments of emerging awareness, after some shock or trauma, when the outside world impresses itself gradually upon the character's consciousness: "It was only after a while that Montès felt the priest's hand upon his arm, saw quite close by a mass of flabby, greyish flesh that seemed to flow around the nose and mouth, forming a series of meandering, flaccid folds, studded with grey hair." At this point Simon throws in a protective statement, "He told me it took him a moment to realize it was a face" (192). That does not actually spoil the paragraph that follows, but it does not help either. Simon, when writing *Le Vent*, was apparently not fully convinced that superficial matters of verisimilitude could and indeed must be subordinated to the organic, aesthetic necessities of the work of art. That he was at least partly aware of the precedence that should be given the latter is evident from his treatment of dialogue.

Not at all affected by Nathalie Sarraute's condemnation of "the monotonous, clumsy, 'said Jeanne,' 'answered Paul,' with which dialogue is usually strewn,"[4] he keeps the device and modifies it for greater effectiveness. He uses it not only in run-in dialogues, as Faulkner did, where it is perhaps less noticeable, but also in indented forms, where he appears to flaunt it at the reader. Using no verb, only a conjunction and a pronoun, he presents them as though they were substitutes for the traditional French dash that precedes indented fragments of conversation. But since he also uses the dash on occasion, it would seem that the sequence "And he: . . . / And she: . . ." serves an emphatic purpose, characterizing those exchanges in which there is opposition or a momentary emotional clash between two characters. The device is both unrealistic and effective. Another feature of Simon's dialogues is that they are often interrupted, not merely in the middle of a sentence, but also in the middle of a word. While one could agree that this realistically reflects what happens in rapid-fire conversation, at least for the first kind of interruption, such a chopping-off process relates to the refusal to accept a linear concept of time. It is in harmony with the "breathless" impression created by Simon's style in this group of works and mirrors the constant accumulation of experience within a consciousness, ever increasing and ever present.

Neither of these aspects of dialogue originated with *Le Vent*. Fragmentation was already present in *Gulliver* and, in one instance, in *Le Tricheur*; emphatic dialogue-identification appeared in *Le Sacre du printemps*, which embodies a different approach to the problem Simon was attempting to solve. This work is also the forerunner of *Le Palace* (1962), for in both instances he is dealing with a Spanish Civil War experience confronted with a much later situation. Simon must have sensed that a temporary aesthetic salvation lay in the direction of the first-person narrative, but perhaps he did not realize that the traditional, plausible first-person narrative was merely one of several possibilities. He was still, in part, a victim of the realistic fallacy.

Le Sacre du printemps (1954) focuses on a time quite close to that of the writing and on a young man named Bernard. In the background loom his stepfather and the latter's experience of the Spanish war. Essentially, the book describes a confrontation between the two men, a clash between two receptacles of experiences. Simon handles the matter by dividing his narrative into two parts of two chapters each. Chapter 1, part 1, is told by Bernard himself; in chapter 2, a shift to the third-person narrative presents a more detached view of Bernard. Chapter 1, part 2, begins in the third person, but only to introduce the stepfather as a secondary narrator, who relates his civil war tribulation to his new wife, in the first person of course. The final chapter, again in the third person, brings Bernard and his stepfather together. Unity is achieved by means of a family relationship, involvement of both Bernard and his stepfather with the same young woman, and, even more artificially, with a coincidence of dates. "Contemporary" events take place on December 10, 11, and 12, 1952; Spanish war events occur on December 10, 11, and 12, 1936. Obviously, this is not organic unity, nor is it good collage, for no great spark leaps forth from the juxtaposition of the various elements. What interest there is in this book emerges from the situation created by Bernard, that is, by the sum of his experiences, even more so by his lack of them (for, in some way, he, too, prefigures Montès), when confronted by a no-longer so innocent outside world. The Spanish experience appeared, until quite recently, to have obsessed Simon even more than what he underwent during the Second World War. To him, it may have been a necessary ingredient of consciousness, and here, because of the Madrid government's failure, it was a source of disappointment and pessimism. The stepfather is a disillusioned idealist rather than the cynic Bernard perceives him to be. The conflict between the two is inevitable but ill-founded. In *Le Palace*, the conflict is resolved by fusing the two consciousnesses into one, and the same person confronts his own civil war experience in Spain with the total experience of what he has become some years later.

The narrative elements in *Le Palace* are more closely woven together. A Frenchman goes to a Spanish city (which one identifies as Barcelona for reasons that lie outside the text), has a glass of beer in a café across the street from a modernistic bank building. Where the bank now stands there used to be a luxury hotel, the "palace" of the title, which burned down during the final stages of the Spanish war. As he looks at the bank and thinks back to the few days he had spent in the hotel, apparently as a volunteer for the loyalists, when it was requisitioned by the Republican forces, he reexperiences both the events and the material objects of that particular past. Central to his recollections is the hotel room where he had been with four other men during most of a sweltering summer afternoon in 1936. With him were a talkative American, a gun-toting Italian, a man who looked like a schoolteacher, and one who was wearing what resembled a policeman's uniform. Outwardly, it would seem that five men of different backgrounds were accidentally brought together, then scattered in various directions, each to his own life or death, but the reader is viewing things from within the mind of the Frenchman, then a university student. Even though none of the four others has left a name in the Frenchman's memory, thus ceasing to exist as a "real" person, each has become a quasi-material component of his consciousness.

It is therefore his own past he takes stock of as he contemplates the building that has replaced the hotel. The narrative proceeds from an initial chapter called "Inventaire" to a final one entitled "Le Bureau des objets perdus," where the possibilities that might have changed his life have been lost, overwhelmed by the accumulation of events that followed his Spanish experience, thus leaving him only with a minor modification of his being. It is within himself that the encounter between the all too innocent and the all too wise takes place, and in the process his inner perspective is changed. At first, he considers his former self as "this remnant of himself, or rather this trace, this blotch (this excrement as it were) that had been left behind: a derisive character seen to stir about, ridiculous and presumptuous" (20). The last lines of the book, however, suggest a similar concept by means of a very different image, as the boxes of the shoeshine attendants are likened to "ancient and mysterious little chests, tiny and ridiculous child coffins" (230). That ending conveys a taste of ashes, and it is tempting to see in the ruins of his former self both a thematic adumbration of the narrator's eventual disintegration (as a concept in fiction) and an inner correspondence to the now-destroyed palace, itself an objective correlative to the Spanish Republic. That might tend, thematically, to place the Civil War in the forefront—instead of where it belongs, in the background of the protagonist's consciousness. The narrative is so structured as to make of the war not an outside reality, an absolute that might be used as a standard by which past actions might be evaluated, but a fragmented series of events, of which several become the components of an inner reality.

In similar fashion, *La Route des Flandres* (1960) is not about the French army retreat in 1940; rather, it describes the attempt by one participant to make some sense out of the life and death of another (a death that occurred during the military rout of 1940, a time of intense psychological stress). As in *Le Palace*, the historical event is viewed from a later point in time, on the occasion of a purely personal experience that releases a previously repressed trauma. What in the later work triggers an inventory of the past is an emotional shock, but also a somewhat arbitrary one: the Frenchman did not have to return to Barcelona. The catalytic event of *La Route des Flandres* is deliberately sought by George, who is the central consciousness of this story. He thinks sleeping with Corinne, the dead man's widow, will provide him with certain clues he is looking for—although he does not realize how much his own memory will yield on that occasion. From that point of view, it is almost a necessary event and one to which the narrator comes back regularly. That is one of several reasons that leads me to place this book a few rungs above *Le Palace*, which follows chronologically. Other reasons include the emphasis placed in *Le Palace* on the funeral of the slain Republican leader and the long narration of how the Italian eliminated a political enemy in a Paris restaurant (which takes up an entire chapter, over one-fifth of the book)—both of which, in spite of their being closely related to the main character's experience in Barcelona, captivate the reader's attention and prevent the book from being as narrowly focused as it might have been. What may have happened is that Simon was becoming more and more interested in textual motifs but had not yet found an effective way of weaving them into the fictional architecture, as he later succeeded in doing in *Les Corps conducteurs*.

Indeed, the success of *La Route des Flandres* is in large part the result of Simon's having built a very rigorous architecture for his narrative. He was thus able to achieve a more complex interweaving of thematic elements than the fundamental plot of *Le Palace* allowed. An episode of the 1940 retreat provides the framework: remnants of a battered cavalry unit roam the countryside amid corpses, burning trucks, and carcasses of horses; the unit commander, Captain de Reixach, gets killed, and George is eventually taken prisoner. In the meantime, the men are lost and keep returning to the same place in spite of themselves; each time they recognize the same dead horse. Such wandering is correlative to the processes of George's imagination, some years later, as he spends the night with Reixach's widow, Corinne, and tells his tale. Within the narration, horses, dead on the battlefield, alive in Reixach's peacetime stables, or metaphorical in relation to George's and his captain's common ancestor, are the verbal (textual) means that give his imagination unity. What obsesses George is the manner in which Reixach died (so peculiar as to suggest a form of suicide) and the sort of life that made that death necessary. The captain is thus as much the central character of the fiction as George is. The latter is the consciousness through which the events in the captain's life acquire significance. The real disaster in *La Route des Flandres* (Simon had considered subtitling it "Description fragmentaire d'un désastre") is that of Reixach's life. Looming historically larger is the French army's disaster in Flanders—aesthetically a mere objective correlative—and the catalytic agent that helps in bringing everything into focus is George's erotic disaster with Corinne. Just as the cavalrymen keep encountering the dead horse, George's narrative keeps wandering back to Corinne.

George enjoys a peculiar position in this story, part narrator (but much more integrated into the narration than his predecessor in *Le Vent*), part protagonist (but somehow subordinated to Reixach). It is he who speaks at the outset of the narrative, but less than twenty pages later he is replaced by an anonymous narrator who refers to George in the third person. From then on, the narrative shifts back and forth between first and third persons, sometimes in traditional fashion with the opening or closing of quotation marks, at other times with no typographical indication that a change has taken place. In the second section the ambiguity is compounded when part of the narrative is taken over by Blum, another member of Reixach's unit, who has also been taken prisoner. (In at least one instance the anonymous narrator intervenes to explain that there is no way of telling whether George or Blum is speaking.) There is also some uncertainty as to the person George is talking to. One supposes at first that he is either reminiscing silently or talking to Reixach's widow, but near the end of the first part everything is put into question. "Then he stopped. It was not to his father that he wanted to speak. It was not even to the woman who lay unseen next to him, perhaps it was not even to Blum that he was explaining, whispering in the dark, that if the sun had not been hidden they might have known on which side their shadows traveled. Now they no longer rode through the green countryside, or rather the green country path had suddenly vanished and they [Iglésia and he] stood there, stunned, stopped" (100-101). George, of course, whatever he is, is talking to the reader, or better, the text addresses itself to the reader as text rather than as communication. This heralds the beginning of the evolution that leads to Simon's third manner.

In the passage just quoted, four separate scenes are fused, all centered upon George: the basic scene with Corinne, always implied when not specifically mentioned; one with Blum in a freight car on his way to prison camp, a third one with his father; and a fourth with Iglésia, another cavalryman (and former jockey), as they are about to come upon the dead horse. *La Route des Flandres* thus exhibits a tripartite confusion affecting narrator, narration, and listener, destroying the three indispensable elements of traditional storytelling. What remains is no longer a story, properly speaking, but something that one might conveniently call a text—an assemblage of words that functions according to linguistic laws. As Bernard Pingaud wrote about one of its features, "transition from fictitious scene to real scene (and vice versa) is in most instances effected by surprise, the narrative turning not on a fact, not even on an analogy (thereby giving up all logical links), but on a word, as in music a simple chord is enough to indicate modulation."[5] Going one step further, Jean

Ricardou gave such pivotal words the designation of "structural meta-phors," since what enables the transition to take place is often the shift from one meaning of that word to another. The most striking example he gives concerns the reference to *traditions ancestralement conservées comme qui dirait dans la Saumur* ("traditions ancestorially preserved as if they had been soaked in brine") where the meaning "brine" immedia-ately gives way before "French officers' cavalry school," located in the town of Saumur (which lacks the final *e* of *saumure*, meaning "brine").

Claude Simon had previously written and published *L'Herbe* (1958; *The Grass*), not as accomplished as *La Route des Flandres* but a text in which his concept of time is given clear emphasis. Aspects of style, dialogue, and narrative technique previously noted are present here to the extent and quality one might expect, considering the chronological position of this work in relation to others. The central consciousness is Louise, who, along with her husband, lives with her in-laws. The main character is Marie, her aunt by marriage, who is in a coma and near death. Necessarily, then, the greater part of the narrative consists of a series of flashbacks. One also encounters familiar patterns: variations on the theme of confrontation between young and old (Louise's husband and his father, Louise and Marie, her husband as he is now and his former self), and attempted restoration of the past. The instrument of this attempt is a small tin box, given by the dying Marie to Louise during a scene that has definite mystical overtones. This box contains "the very web of her existence" (123); it is all that is left of her, it is Marie—and it is also Louise. The box, an old cookie tin, is decorated with the picture of "a young woman clad in a long white dress, partially reclining in the grass" (11). At the beginning of the book, Louise is standing in the grass, talking to her lover, ready to elope with him. At the end, she is lying in the grass, again talking with her lover, but now a defeated woman, unable to leave. She has become the image on the box, she is tied to it, as Marie was to its contents.

The tin box is Marie's "pyramid," her "monument," and what it contains has spatial quality. Inside, there are items of inexpensive jewelry and a number of notebooks. These notebooks, however, do not constitute a diary, a linear record of spent time; they are much closer to an inventory, a record of objects and money acquired or surrendered. The acquisition of canned goods balances the loss of a sister, and the sale of walnuts is compensated by the purchase of an umbrella. Undoubtedly this is, in part, a commentary on middle-class life analogous to the satire found in such works as François Mauriac's *Génitrix*—with a bit more compassion on Simon's part. More generally, though, it expresses time as a "frightful accumulation" (140) of matter that stifles not only innocence but life itself. In a pointed paraphrase of what old Gisors says in Malraux's *La Condition humaine* about the fifty years it takes to make a man, Louise reflects "on all that is needed not to make a man or a woman, but a corpse —one of those things one wraps up in airtight boxes" (140). The actual coffins that are buried in the ground are but objective correlatives to the more significant ones. Marie's real coffin, her "mausoleum" (141), is her tin box. Louise's father-in-law's is his own body, bloated with food and self-indulgence. Perhaps Simon would say that we all have the coffins we deserve. We build our mausoleums very gradually, no one can see them grow—not even ourselves—any more than one can watch the growth of a blade of grass.

The epigraph of *L'Herbe*, a statement by Boris Pasternak ("No one makes history, one cannot see it any more than one can see the grass grow"), extends the analogy beyond the life (or death) of a person, making of each one an imperceptible part of history. This specifically broadens the significance of the dying Marie: "If to endure History ... is to make it, then the drab existence of an old lady is History itself, the very stuff of History" (36). It also points toward Claude Simon's *Histoire* (1967), which stands as an engrossing synthesis of several previous themes and achievements and is equaled only by *Les Géorgiques* (1981) and *L'Acacia* (1989). The tin box of *L'Herbe* is with us again—metamorphosed into a chest of drawers full of old postcards. Its role in the work remains similar from a thematic standpoint. Within the framework of the story, it is more effective since, belonging to the narrator's grandmother, its falling into his hands can be taken for granted, and it reinforces a natural link instead of creating a seemingly artificial one.

The entire emphasis of *Histoire* is on integrating the architecture of the narrative into a natural framework, something *La Route des Flandres* had already attempted and partially accomplished. The basic unit here is a day in the narrator's later years, from early morning until after midnight. Both his parents and the relatives of their generation are dead. He has been married and the marriage has just broken up. The account of his day is divided into twelve chapters, although there is not, as in Butor's *Passage de Milan*, any precise correspondence between chapters and time of day or night. They are unnumbered, possibly to avoid such a suggestion, and untitled, for there is no theme, image, or event each one might be tied to exclusively. (The device, used in *Le Palace*, of having a sentence begin at the end of one chapter and continue at the outset of the next is again in evidence.) If we consider the day of the narrative to constitute the present time of the fiction, the first and last chapters then belong outside of time and serve a purpose similar to the corresponding chapters in *Gulliver*. The second chapter starts with the narrator's awakening; the eleventh chapter closes as he watches the stars from his bedroom window. In the meantime he has gone out into the street, encountered a former beau of his mother's, visited his bank, had lunch in a restaurant, returned home for an appointment with an antique dealer, driven out to the shore to get a cousin's signature on a legal document, driven back to the city, had a sandwich in a café, and taken a stroll before going home to bed. A completely uninteresting day, a mere canvas on which to weave the drama of a single person against the backdrop of history. Colonialism, two world wars, the Russian revolution, and the Spanish Civil War are inescapably present throughout the pages of *Histoire.*

What sets things in motion is the narrator's decision to sell a chest of drawers and the ensuing necessity to empty it of its contents—the mass of postcards. They were sent by various members of the family, but those that spur his memory most were mailed to his mother from all over the world by his father before their marriage. Much of his life is resurrected in the process, modified by present obsessions. That, at least, is how things might appear to the reader at first; but if one looks at this work with the insight gained from reading subsequent ones, the reader sees a need to modify the order of those events. If one will refrain from allegorizing, from attempting to fit matters into a plausible story, and remain on the textual level, it should become clear that the postcards are at the very source of the fiction. Their aggregate has generated the chest of drawers and the reason for its being where it is. Each individual card has generated an incident or series of incidents that eventually create the narrator's life and all the aspects of the fiction—down to its recurring words and metaphors.

To go back to the narration and the fable it allows readers to elaborate, one does not get the impression of a series of flashbacks as in the preceding books; the narrative seems closer to an interior monologue. It even includes something like a parody of Joyce's *Ulysses* as the narrator, remembering indecent transliterations of Latin responses a schoolboy friend used to make at Mass, says when approaching his washbasin in the morning, "Introibo in lavabo" (43). Buck Mulligan is not far behind. (Not too close, either, and this could be no more than a tongue-in-cheek device to establish a distance from Faulkner, with whom Simon must have become tired of being compared.) As the day of the narrative unfolds, the narrator's life is spread out before us, some of it in chronological order. There are actually three planes of development: the present time, the narrator's life, and incidental forays into the past. The first two constitute the fixed, arbitrary elements of the architecture, which nevertheless correspond to biological realities. The third is, aesthetically speaking, a chance element; it is the one more obviously determined by the reality of the thought process, that is, by the nature of language. That sort of freedom under a close-fitting harness is an essential virtue of this book.

As in previous works, the theme of *Histoire* is the accumulation of time, its accelerating encroachment upon innocence and life, the increasing weight it places upon a person until it eventually destroys him or her.

A concomitant theme is that of decay. The selling of the chest of drawers, together with the indication that other items in the narrator's house will be sold in the future, is related to his obtaining a mortgage on another piece of property. All are objective correlatives for something that is constantly implied but never specifically mentioned: his whole life is breaking up. The narrative is motivated by a sense of catastrophe and the need, compulsive and partially subconscious, to determine its causes. That was also the reason for the flashback account of Max's life in *Gulliver* and for other subsequent narratives as well. But with the exception of *Le Palace*, all were conducted from the outside or, in the case of the stepfather in *Le Sacre du printemps*, presented as a formal, conscious recollection. The recourse to interior monologue or to what gives the illusion of being one (for the narrator as subject leads a precarious existence here) permits greater involvement on the reader's part, as he has the impression of "living" the story instead of merely listening to it, and gives more plausibility to Simon's withholding of information. It is no longer simply an effective technique that creates suspense. It is, as in Robbe-Grillet's *Le Voyeur* or in Ollier's *La Mise en scène*, an integral part of a person's tendency to suppress undesirable events from conscious thought. The blank that lies at the center of *Histoire* and keeps sucking everything else in its direction is the fate of the narrator's wife, her probable suicide. That such a suicide is indeed the hidden *histoire* the title alludes to in one of its connotations is suggested not only by the narrator's fascination with a newspaper headline about a woman who jumped to her death, but by frequent references to Reixach's death on the battlefield of *La Route des Flandres* and the implication that the latter allowed himself to be killed because of his wife's infidelities. Furthermore, he suppresses until the last chapter the memory of a very suggestive sleeping-pill scene. Thus the list of suicides in Simon's work grows longer.

Reixach's reappearance is symptomatic of his creator's assurance, the new-found ease with which he roams over the texts of his fictional works. George, in *La Route des Flandres*, was a distant cousin of Reixach's. The narrator of *Histoire* refers to an old "tante de Reixach" (12), but Corinne, Reixach's wife, is also the narrator's first cousin, and they were brought up together. He also seems identical with the narrator of *Le Palace*, for an incident that took place in Spain during the civil war comes to the surface again. His sacrilegious friend, Lambert, who goes through a communist phase, recalls Abel (all the letters of whose name are in "Lambert"), the communist student in *Le Sacre du printemps;* the locale is Pau, a southern city, as in *Le Vent.* The situation does recall that of the traditional fictional universe, of which Balzac's is typical. In it, characters (seen as people), their preoccupations, and the setting in which they carry out their activities constitute the ingredients of a familiar world, spread out over a number of fictional works. On the other hand, one is also reminded of what has more recently and misleadingly been called "intertextual" activity, where "quotations" from other works, considered as texts rather than stories, increase the creative potential (the productivity) of those into which they are inserted.[7] The narrator of *Histoire* is also placed in a curiously ambiguous position. As the writer's surrogate, he has created the world that is presented to us, but he has also inventoried it and thus discovered himself as the product of the past he has described. More accurately, he is the product of his language, the result of everything he has written. The last word of the book, "me?", toward which everything has been building up, expresses his astonishment, or perhaps his horror, at such a discovery.

When *Histoire* was published the book seemed such a felicitous culmination of Simon's writings, restating and relating so many of the earlier themes, that it was hard to visualize the work that might follow. This was *La Bataille de Pharsale* (1969), a text that heralded the third stage in his fictional development. One of many factors that apparently prompted the change was Simon's first visit to the United States, especially to New York, which he made in the fall of 1968. There he was struck by the kaleidoscopic variety of the metropolitan area—lower Manhattan, Brooklyn Heights, industrial sections of New Jersey, fall colors in Bear Mountain Park and in Westchester, various lookout points and bridges over the Hudson and other waterways, which he saw in quick succession and also telescoped together from the top of the Empire State Building. Another factor was a growing interest in the process that Claude Lévi-Strauss has called *bricolage* (the act of pottering, of making objects with whatever materials are at hand), a term that, I have been told, had also been previously applied to language at the Linguistic Circle of Prague. The term might actually be superfluous, for Lévi-Strauss himself has remarked that "the intermittent interest in 'collages,' which arose at a time when craftsmanship was dying out, might well be no more than a transposition of 'bricolage' to the plane of speculative ends."[8] As the interest in collage has been more than a passing one, that term might well suffice for our needs. Be that as it may, it is still useful to remember the comparison Lévi-Strauss has made between bricolage and mythic thought, which operates by means of analogy and proximity, and constitutes "an intellectual aspect of 'bricolage.' "[9]

The new manner revealed in *La Bataille de Pharsale* does not signify a complete break with the previous fiction, for one of its important features was already noted in connection with *La Route des Flandres*. The work is a text: not a linear narrative but an assemblage of words ruled by linguistic laws (as discovered by people like Freud and Lacan as much as by linguists) rather than by those of plausibility and everyday logic. An indication of the evolution that had taken place since *Le Palace* may be conveyed by the contrast between "Inventaire," a chapter heading in that book, and "Lexique," the title of the second chapter of *La Bataille de Pharsale*. The shift is from representation of an objective exterior reality as absorbed by a subjective consciousness to a display of the reality of language as constituting the subjective world of an individual. That aspect of the book has been dwelt upon by Jean Ricardou, who presents it almost as if it embodied characteristics of his own texts. Noting that "Pharsale" is an anagram of "La Phrase," he entitled his essay on Simon's book "La Bataille de la Phrase."[10] One is naturally reminded of Ricardou's own *La Prise de Constantinople*, in which the back cover is an exact duplicate of the front one, except for the substitution of one letter in the title, "La Prose de Constantinople." What Ricardou says is generally accurate, but, in my opinion, his own interests have led him to overemphasize the purely linguistic features of Simon's book.

As the logic of the fiction is removed from the domain of reality (involving, say, considerations of psychological plausibility) to the linguistic one, generative elements become more noticeable. Ricardou has shown, for instance, how words in Paul Valéry's stanza (taken from "Le Cimetière marin"), which Simon used as an epigraph for the first part of *La Bataille de Pharsale*, are picked up in the first few paragraphs of the narrative and then allowed to reverberate throughout the text; how the first word of the book, *jaune* (yellow), is disseminated, not only as a color (that is, as meaning, also summoning words such as *safran, bananes, urine, soleil,* and the like) but by means of anagrammatic or homonymic processes (generating, for instance, words such as *nuage* [cloud] and *Jeanne*); or how the shooting of an arrow into an adversary's mouth (*pénétrant dans sa bouche ouverte*) calls forth, because of one connotation of *bouche*, a description of people emerging from a subway entrance (*la bouche du métro*).

Nevertheless, while agreeing with Ricardou that one should not restrict Simon's work to purely lyrical and sensorial aspects and pointing out that a similar analysis could be carried out on the basis of the first words and pages of *Histoire*, I am reluctant to see the latter ignored. Indeed, a section of the second chapter entitled "Le Guerrier" (The Warrior) shows the presence of such aspects. Here, the narrator describes a cavalryman gone berserk in a military barracks; when the soldier takes his sword out of the racks, one hears "a metallic, icy rustling sound" (138). The narrator recalls a similar auditory sense impression received when, as a child at the circus, he watched a magician unsheath the swords with which he would pierce the box in which a beautiful woman was locked. This second scene has been activated by a sensory stimulus coupled with an emotional response. The sound has caused the narrator to feel a "shudder" analogous to the one he felt as a child. A sword is involved in both scenes, but the word *sword* alone, either materially or semantically, would not have been sufficient to bring the second scene to light. The link between "rustling" and "shudder" is phonetically closer in French, *froissement/frisson*, but neither is that linguistic analogy enough to conjure up the earlier scene. It is actually the (involuntary) memory of the first shudder experienced at the circus and associated with an identical sound that produces the scene. Articulation might also be thematic or conceptual, that is, taking place at the semantic level alone. For instance, as in standard interior monologue, a thick blob of white and pink pigment on a painter's brush might suggest the gooey confections sold at outdoor fairs that are held during All Souls' Day. This in turn suggests the gloom surrounding that time of the year, the odor of acetylene lamps, and cheap baubles sold in fair booths, including porcelain statues of Buddha with white stomachs—which brings up the painter's model, half naked in her kimono, together with the realization that the aura of her love was the same as that of the fair, cheap and gaudy, that it reeked of "guilt and disaster." From there one is led to a remembrance of youth, of being so late coming home that no plausible lie could possibly account for it, and of the anguish that resulted (45-51).

There are several major narratives in *La Bataille de Pharsale.* One describes war episodes that could have been inserted in *Le Route des Flandres* without startling the reader. Another centers on an affair with a painter's model named Odette (the Proustian overtone is surely not accidental). A third tells of an auto trip to Greece and the site of the battle of Pharsalus. A fourth depicts a boy struggling with his Latin homework dealing with that same battle. A fifth involves a train trip through Italy. There are also detailed descriptions of lovemaking and battle scenes evidently based on sculptures and paintings. Narratives and descriptions are broken up and their frames juxtaposed, sometimes even interwoven. In the process, images of intense jealousy and death are set up against a foil of indifference on the part of those not directly involved. Various references, such as the one to "Uncle Charles," might lead one to assume that there is a narrator who is identical with the one in *Histoire,* but even more than in that work this text acquires an autonomy of its own and tends to push such an imagined narrator into the background if it does not destroy him utterly. He is no longer the actor; he is the stage upon which the action takes place. He is also the observer (of which there may well be more than one). As we learn in the last section of the second chapter, he is designated by the letter *O,* which is also the symbol for zero, that is, nonexistence, a blank. The initial *O* designates not only the observer but also the object being observed (a duality already hinted at in *Histoire*). In addition, *O* is the first letter of the name Odette, the model whose representation in the text could perhaps be seen as correlative to that of ancient Rome, for whom Caesar and Pompey were fighting (as two men appear to be currying favor with

Odette)—a struggle culminating in Pompey's defeat during the battle of Pharsalus.

If *Histoire* ends with a word that challenges the identity of the author of *Le Tricheur*, thus completing a rather wide circle, *La Bataille de Pharsale* achieves another kind of circularity, not unique in postwar fiction, by ending with the very sentence that set it in motion. This recalls a statement from the diary of Maurice Merleau-Ponty, in connection with the language of both Simon and Butor: "Such uses of language may be understood only if language is conceived as a being, a world, and if Speech [*la Parole*] is thought of as the circle."[11]

Les Corps conducteurs (1971) has a history that enables one to grasp in more concrete fashion the writing process characteristic of Simon's third manner. He had been asked to contribute a text to the Skira series called "The Paths of Creation." That text, published as *Orion aveugle* (1970; Blind Orion), came with a preface in which he explained how he writes. "From my point of view, there are no paths of creation other than those one clears step by step, that is, word after word, through the treading of the pen itself" (6). To which he added: "Before I start setting down signs on paper, there is nothing—aside from a formless mass of more or less confused sensations, of more or less precise memories; and a vague, a very vague project." A painting by Nicolas Poussin, *Paysage avec Orion aveugle*, serves as a metaphor for the writing activity, which has become, at this stage of Simon's evolution, nearly identical with the one described by Blanchot: "For everything begins again, starting from nothing . . . becoming aware that the work cannot be projected but only realized, that it bears value, truth, and reality only through those words that unfold it in time and inscribe it in space, he will then begin writing but will start from nothing and aim at nothing."[12] The writer is blind to the extent that, having nothing to communicate, driven by a need to say "something," he proceeds without knowing whither such a need might take him.

In the case of *Orion aveugle*, it began with the desire to put "something" together (*bricoler*), using as a point of departure a few paintings that he liked—in particular, *Charlene* by Robert Rauschenberg—which brought forth other images or representations of the American continent. Reference to the Poussin painting (which is at the Metropolitan Museum of Art, in New York) might have come either as the source or the aftermath of a sequence in *La Bataille de Pharsale*, the one I have mentioned in a different context, which describes the cavalryman gone berserk in "the barracks in the middle of which such a Goliath, or rather Orion, reeled about like a blind man" (140). It was then added, I suppose, to the construction being put together; the idea was to unify it within the theme suggested by the title of the Skira series. It must have seemed wondrously apposite, blindness having been, ever since Homer, a likely symbolic attribute of the writer. The text of *Orion aveugle* was then published, illustrated with reproductions of many of the generators that set it in motion, and itself standing as an illustration of a specific approach to fiction writing. The initial purpose having been fulfilled, Simon felt the need to pursue his work. "And it now seems as though the path cleared by *Orion aveugle* should lead somewhere" (13). That "somewhere," however, does not designate the traditional kind of ending one used to expect in a narration, for the emphasis is on the text rather than the anecdote. Consequently, the path followed by the writer "can have no other end than the exhaustion of a traveler exploring that inexhaustible landscape." The landscape he has in mind is that of man's language. At such a time of "exhaustion," a piece of fiction comes into being, "which will not tell the exemplary story of some hero or heroine, but that very different story constituted by the singular adventure of the narrator who never abandons his quest, discovering the world gropingly, in and through the written language" (14-15).

"Pottering" might be basic, but it is not sufficient for Claude Simon. He needs to weld things together within a unifying architecture. What Poussin's painting and the resulting symbolism did for *Orion aveugle* was not enough for the organization of the developing *Les Corps conducteurs*. The basic generative elements being linked with the American continent, it seemed natural enough to center the various textual products of such elements describing the brief stay of a traveler in a large American city. (Although unnamed, the city is easily identifiable as New York, in spite of the insertion of a number of European items that emerged out of the writer's consciousness.) The parallel between physical travel and a writer's "adventure" in language is obvious enough.

Plastic representations by Rauschenberg, Arman, George Brecht, Picasso, Brassaï, Jean Dubuffet, Poussin, Louise Nevelson, and Andy Warhol, photographs of the Amazon River and a public telephone, engravings and illustrations of various sorts pertaining to man's anatomy, a cigar box, Christopher Columbus in America, signs of the Zodiac, and an anarchist's bomb in the French parliament (all reproduced in *Orion aveugle* but omitted from *Les Corps conducteurs*) first produce a series of texts, which resemble descriptions, generated by those objects. The texts are then ordered into a sequence involving the consciousness of the traveler, who has attended a writers' conference in South America, has flown over the Amazon, becomes ill in New York, tries to phone a woman with whom he has had an affair, and so on. As far as the reader is concerned, the impression produced might well be that of a story centered in the consciousness of a main character. The circumstances and timing of his illness, acting upon his sensitivity, cause him to reflect on or to remember a series of incidents, which are then described. I believe it is an indication of Simon's success in giving *Les Corps conducteurs* an organic architecture that such a fable can arise. But from a textual point of view it is nonetheless apparent that the character has been created out of the sequence of textual descriptions (inscriptions might be a better term) generated by the objects I have enumerated. Indeed, the story of the traveler is neither particularly significant nor interesting. What is fascinating is the way things happen to him in the world of language.

All the generators for this text having been framed in one way or another (by the sides of the canvas, those of the cigar box, and the like), one begins to understand why an excerpt from this work, when it was published in *Tel Quel*, was entitled "Propriétés des rectangles,"[13] and why Simon thought a possible subtitle for the book might be "Propriétés de quelques figures géométriques ou non." The allusion is not only to the way paintings, engravings, or photographs usually appear, but also to the painter's awareness of the size and proportions of the canvas whenever a line is drawn or a colored surface inserted. Simon, having aspired to a painter's career before he became a writer, perhaps felt that awareness more acutely than other writers, with the possible exception of Michel Butor, and transposed it to his writing, where it becomes sensitivity to the demands of the fictional framework when organizing groups of those "signs on paper" that he has blindly set down. Thus the "conductive bodies" of the title are first and foremost the words in the text; they are also human bodies—those of the main character, of women, of crowds in the street, of the participants at the writers' gathering—all conductive of sexual impulses, emotions of various kinds, and political passion. Even at the high point of his convergence with Ricardou, Simon integrates sensual with textual activities.

Painting has never been far removed from his writing. Leaving aside *Femmes* (1966), a series of brief texts inspired by twenty-three paintings by Joan Miró, one notices that in *Le Tricheur* the protagonist is an unsuccessful painter and that works by Uccello and Poussin crop up in the text; in similar fashion, in *La Bataille de Pharsale*, for instance, the same picture by Utrillo resurfaces, and in *Orion aveugle*, Poussin's canvas plays a major part. Nor should one forget the altarpiece of *Le Vent*'s subtitle or *Triptyque* (1973), the basic connotation of that title being painterly. More complex than a single altarpiece, a triptych presents three paintings (or sometimes high reliefs), that is, three topics, which nevertheless are united by a given theme and interact with one another. One therefore expects and finds several narratives in Simon's transposition. This is not new, for at least five different narratives can be detected in *La Bataille de Pharsale*.

There are three in *Triptyque*, and the text is also divided into three parts—a longer central one of about ninety pages and two "lateral" ones of sixty pages each. The narratives, however, are not kept apart in the same fashion; they can be composed in the reader's mind, but only after the fact of the reading experience. One thus fantasizes the story of a young man arrested on drug charges and who will be released thanks to his connections, that of a bridegroom whose stag party gets out of hand, and that of a little girl who drowns as a consequence of several acts of carelessness. All three are intricately interwoven and could be seen as adding up to a pessimistic social commentary, something reinforced by the various incidents attached to the stories—the killing of a rabbit, for instance, which suggests a painting by Francis Bacon.

Visual elements are emphasized, although other sense impressions are not eliminated. As one reads, the text seems generated by a postcard of a Mediterranean resort, but the postcard soon disappears to make way for what appears to be "actual" description. I was reminded of Roussel's *La Vue*, but the process here is more subtle. Two movie posters, a large poster announcing a circus performance, eighteenth-century erotic engravings, movie film clippings, and so forth, soon replace the postcard and act as additional generators. Qualifiers used in their connection, such as "excessively blue," "garish green," "piercing," "bite into," "slashed," "cleavers," all on the first two pages, pave the way for scenes of violence, sex, and death that will eventually be inscribed in the text. Toward the end, as we see the conclusion of a movie, we also watch a large man working on a jigsaw puzzle; after he puts the last piece in place, he wearily relaxes for a moment and then violently sweeps the completed puzzle off the table. The puzzle is a representation: as the text is completed, the representation (or the reader's fantasy) should be destroyed. The process is the opposite of the one that gave unity to *Les Corps conducteurs*, which held together thanks to the anecdote, enhanced by the reader's fantasy: here, it is textual activity that welds the disseminated anecdotes into a single unit.

Leçon de choses (1975; *The World about Us*) actually started as a brief text commissioned by the Maeght Gallery and to be "illustrated" by the painter Alechinsky. Simon is said to have been "surprised" by the "distance" that separated the text from the painting.[14] At any rate, he was apparently intrigued by the possibilities of his own text and used it to generate a book-length product where three narratives are again intertwined, as in *Triptyque*. They find their source in the description of a room that is being renovated, the ordeal of a small military unit holding a house that is about to be attacked by the enemy, a story suggested by a painting by Renoir hanging on the wall. Various anecdotes grow here and there, determined both by the context and by Simon's preoccupation with death, time, and sex. In this connection, it should be noted that his erotic sequences are seldom if ever aphrodisiac; I rather see them as being matter-of-fact and bestial.

Les Géorgiques (1981), which may well be Claude Simon's major achievement, came out six years later, a time span even longer than that

which separated *Histoire* from *Le Palace*. The two works stand in a
similar relationship to the texts that preceded them. The chest of drawers,
the contents of which generated much of *Histoire*, is inscribed in the text;
the trunkful of letters and documents left by one of Simon's forebears is
not in the text, but we know about it because of what he has told several
interviewers after the book was published.[15] There is a similar relation to
Leçon de choses in that the connection between the preliminary pages of
that text and Alechinsky's painting is hidden, while *Les Géorgiques*
begins with a section describing an artist at work. What he is working on
is at first a drawing, which turns into a painting, and finally becomes a
scene in which the figures rise from the paper or canvas and actually
move, "for, as he continues to wave his hand, the seated man does not
raise his head" (17). The work of art says very little, the viewer gives it life
and meaning. The family documents that Simon found and read were
merely factual—like the accounts left by Marie, in *L'Herbe*. By inserting
them into a narrative and confronting them with other narratives he
interprets them and gives them meaning. His ancestor is thus brought
back to life, but it is a life that is other than the one he actually lived. All
the facts are there but he has become a fictional character, and so has
everyone else.

As in the two previous works there are three distinct narratives in *Les
Géorgiques* but the textual unifying force that was manifest in *Triptyque*
has been deemphasized. The stress is on collage, and this is made clear at
the beginning of the text proper as roman and italic passages alternate in
irregular fashion, marking transitions from one narrative to the other,
each one told in the third person. Roman or italic characters, however,
do not identify a specific narrative, as one sequence might be in italics in
one section of the book, in roman in another. Sometimes, as in the third
section of the first chapter, there is no typographical distinction between
different narratives. The persons in whom they are centered are not fully
named; one is designated by the letters L. S. M. (an artillery officer who
aided the revolutionaries, voted for the death of the king, was a general
under Napoleon, and died uneventfully on his own estate—also the
object of a passing reference in *Le Tricheur*); another by the letter O. (an
English writer who has much, but not everything, in common with
George Orwell); and the third, who is nameless, might still be called the
central intelligence, as he was in *La Route des Flandres* and *Histoire*—
two of the books that nourish this one. All three characters are immersed
in historical events that govern their lives and give the book significance
through their juxtaposition—the French Revolution and the wars it
provoked, the Spanish Civil War, and the French defeat of 1940. Underlying this, in a dialectical movement that affects everything, there is the
regular passing of time in the shape of seasons and the life of plants. This
is what produced the title and calls to mind the work of Virgil, as L. S. M.

displays a nearly obsessive preoccupation with seasonal caretaking, planting, and reaping on his estate. Also, the Latin poet had sought, in his own *Georgics,* to extol the virtues of an earlier Roman age (as had the eighteenth-century French revolutionaries). Simon maintains, in opposition to twentieth-century failures, the presence of earlier victories achieved against overwhelming odds.

But even the French Revolution, while retaining an aura of purity and righteousness, eventually turned sour as "the guillotine that served to behead a king was now used to chop off the heads of flower girls."[16] And in spite of the frustrations and suffering caused by the degradation of the revolutionary ideal, by the bickerings and shortsightedness of Spanish Republicans, by the fumblings and insanities of the military in 1940, all three figures remain faithful to their own instincts and continue the fight. In each instance, nature punctuates their struggle.

The text begins to function as words interact within each narrative and between the three sets. Several types of interaction are in evidence. For instance, the names of two strategically located rivers, the Sambre and the Meuse, are in one section drawn together to form a cultural unit. "Sambre et Meuse" evokes a striking military march, a former department extending over a part of what is now Belgium, and the site of a significant victory for the French revolutionary armies. The same rivers are mentioned in the narrative involving the 1940 disaster, but separately —and at the same time the reader is led to recall their conjunction and to contrast the spirit of 1939-40 with that of 1792. On another level, we encounter syntactic variations. At the beginning of chapter 2, simple statements pruned into short sentences follow one upon the other in monotonous fashion, providing spiritless, factual information. Gradually, however, as we witness the moral disintegration of a cavalry unit on a cold, snowy night during the winter of the so-called Phoney War, sentences become longer and more complex, the information is less certain, and as gloom and thoughts of death enter the picture the narrative begins to resemble that of other texts written by Simon. Something both analogous and different happens in chapter 4, where the main character is the Englishman, especially when the latter is faced with the problem of relating his experience to others. In each instance the very organization of language conveys as much as does the rational meaning of individual statements.

Like all writing, Simon's works are necessarily referential. In most of the major ones, however, the reference is to other texts and from that standpoint *Les Géorgiques* is exemplary. Those in which the reference is in large part to reality are *La Route des Flandres* and *Le Palace,* the reality of war and revolution. Curiously, though, the nature of the experience of reality is less determining than the condition of the writer's psyche and the distance separating reality from the writing process. Simon went to

Barcelona during the Spanish Civil War but did not publish *Le Palace* until twenty-five years had elapsed. In 1986, after receiving the Nobel Prize in literature for 1985, he was invited to a number of places in addition to Stockholm—New York, Finland, Moscow, and Central Asia. *L'Invitation* (1987) is a distillation of his visits to the last two locales. Although not labeled *roman*, it might well have been. On the one hand, it is vintage Simon, a work of high quality and strong evocative power; on the other, as the difference in time spans separating the writing from the experience would suggest, it is closer to the reality that provoked it than *Le Palace* is to the Spanish Civil War.

The narrative thread is spun around the invitation of fifteen personalities, each well known in his field and country, to visit Moscow and other cities in the Soviet Union. The group is, among various activities, taken to a ballet performance (whose star is old and emaciated, like the old ladies early in the text of *Histoire*), to the races (echoing numerous episodes in Simon's previous fiction), to a fourteenth-century monastery, and to receptions dulled by lengthy speeches. A pleasant, peaceful experience, one might think, especially when contrasted with that of a civil war. None of the fifteen guests is named; neither, in general, are the cities they visit, or their host, or other officials past and present (although readers who enjoy such games will be able to identify most of them, thanks to occasionally transparent circumlocutions such as "the seminarian gangster" or "the second husband of the most gorgeous woman on earth").

Among the few exceptions to anonymity is one that stands out, at the end of a paragraph, "streaking the darkness like black and gold lightning: Zagorsk" (86). One does not have to be French to feel the contrast inherent in a juxtaposition such as Avignon/Zagorsk, for instance. It opposes the familiar to the strange, the soft to the harsh, and that may well have been Simon's reason for singling it out. But the city of Zagorsk, located to the northeast of Moscow, is also the site of a famous monastery where the fifteen guests witness at least part of an Orthodox service. One supposes the point of the invitation was to illustrate the newly emphasized religious freedom, but what the narrator notices is an old woman slamming down against the stone pavement the head of a small boy who was trying to see what was going on while the congregation bowed low, their faces down to the floor.

What I have just mentioned subtends the entire text. On the surface the ceremonial visit to the Soviet Union is indeed peaceful and pleasant, although Simon's vocabulary, imagery, and style provide a large dose of irony and occasional sarcasm. The reader is not allowed to lose sight of past violence, and the possibility of present or future turbulence is suggested in a number of instances—and that gives the incident of the woman and child in Zagorsk an emblematic quality. The early reference to the host as "having just returned from a meeting with the other head of state who could also, by speaking one word, destroy a good half of the earth" has set the tone. The last lines of the text, which are preceded by a flashback to the aged ballerina who stands like a ruin at the center of the stage, ready to crumble into dust, evoke the images of dead revolutionary leaders at the Lenin mausoleum, "former rioters with professorial brows, their ties knotted any old way, their eyes closed behind a pince-nez, their faces serene at last, their lips forever sealed" (94). Images of blood and death, of a stillborn revolution, mark the final pages of *Le Palace*. *L'Invitation* is sealed with the fatalistic suggestion that all efforts to change the world are doomed to fail. As Simon told Jacqueline Piatier, "Literature, you know, keeps dealing with the same things—love, death, the passing of time, man's hope, disillusionment, and sorrow."[17]

Seemingly in contrast to such global preoccupations, at first glance at any rate, the more recent *L'Acacia* focuses on individual lives. But as with earlier works with a similar focus, *L'Herbe* for instance, wars and revolutions constitute a necessary background that (wars especially) generate the circumstances that gnaw at the characters' lives, when they do not destroy them. The book has much in common with *Histoire* and *Les Géorgiques*. Like the latter, it churns texts and documents—family documents and previous texts by Simon—in order to produce a new fiction, a new meaning. While in *Les Géorgiques* historical events and the forces of nature loomed large in their own right, they are now seen as obscure, overwhelming powers that crush the individual. The presence of such powers was not felt so strongly in *Histoire*, and the first-person narrator was obviously at center stage. Here, the story is told in the third person, although in at least one instance a relatively long quotation (without quotation marks) of the central character's thoughts, sprinkled with first-person pronouns, could unsettle the reader and lead him to conclude that this character is the hidden narrator (293-94). In its scope, *Les Géorgiques* included the French revolutionary wars and those of Napoleon, but *L'Acacia* goes no further back than 1880, a date that is significant only to the characters and includes merely those events in which they are directly involved—and since the highest rank any one of them achieves is that of captain, such events are insubstantial.

It is, however, a deeper and more personal examination of a man's recent background. In part, it tells the story of two sisters' abnegation, as they wanted to give their younger brother a chance to rise above the family condition. That was also a story told in *L'Herbe*, where they apparently succeed, but the brother lives on to reach a pitiful, despicable old age. In *L'Acacia* they fail in a way, and their brother dies "heroically" in one of the early battles of the First World War. In either case, the sum of suffering is about the same. The "hero" has a son who, through a stroke of luck, survives the 1940 defeat (*La Route des Flandres*): he is the central intelligence through whom the life of his parents is interpreted. There is a dialectic in the narrative that is reminiscent of *Le Sacre du printemps* as chapter topics alternate between the two World Wars, with two forays added, one going back to 1880 and the other forward to 1982, and the father's experience is filtered through the son's consciousness and confronted with his own. As in *Histoire*, there are twelve chapters, but they are numbered and titled with dates; in both narratives they lead up to a very specific point.

At the end of *Histoire* one is confronted with the physical birth of the puzzled narrator; at the end of *L'Acacia* one witnesses the birth of a writer, as the central character confronts a blank sheet of paper. Textually, the last page of *L'Acacia* leads straight to the first page of *Histoire:* nearly identical sentences describe the branches of an acacia tree (hence the novel's title) outside an open window; it is evening, light from a desk lamp shines on the leaves occasionally stirred by a breeze before returning to their immobility. The circular motion from the last page of *L'Acacia* to the initial one of *Histoire* is analogous to the repeated shift from rest to movement and back to a state of rest described in both novels—and also in *Le Palace*, where it involves the flight of pigeons in the park. Within the context of the entire work, this suggests a tension between the reassuring progression of the seasons with the promised return of spring, on the one hand, and the futility of human endeavors that cannot break the cycle of suffering and death. In such tension resides the essential appeal of Claude Simon's scription.

NOTES

1   See my article, "The 1985 Nobel Laureate: Claude Simon," in *World Literature Today* (Winter 1986): 5-8.
2   Claude Simon, *Le Tricheur* (Paris: Sagittaire, 1945), 236-37. Henceforth, all references to works by Simon will appear in the body of the text.
3   "Réponses de Claude Simon à quelques questions écrites de Ludovic Janvier,"in *Entretiens,* no. 31 (1972): 16-17.
4   Nathalie Sarraute, *L'Ere du soupçon* (Paris: Gallimard, 1956), 105.
5   Bernard Pingaud, "Sur la route des Flandres," *Temps Modernes,* no. 178 (February 1961): 1029.
6   Jean Ricardou, "Un Ordre dans la débacle," in *Problèmes du nouveau roman* (Paris: Seuil, 1967), 48.
7   The word *intertextuality* has its source in Julia Kristeva's *Le Texte du roman* (The Hague: Mouton, 1970), 12, where the notion of "text," which is close to that of "texture," was intended to replace that of "genre." The novel, for instance, is thus a text or texture that came into being through the interweaving of different strands borrowed from other texts (carnival, courtly poetry, scholastic discourse). "The term *intertextuality* denotes this transposition of

one (or several) sign systems into another, but since this term has often been understood in the banal sense of 'study of sources,' we prefer the term *transposition*" (Kristeva, *Revolution in Poetic Language*, trans. Margaret Waller [New York: Columbia University Press, 1984], 59-60). I was guilty of the same misunderstanding in the original version of *French Fiction Today* but have avoided the word since the mid-seventies.

8   Claude Lévi-Strauss, *La Pensée sauvage* (Paris: Plon, 1962), 43-44. Some twenty years ago Roman Jakobson confirmed to me that the term was used in discussions in Prague in the thirties, but he could not remember when or by whom it was launched.

9   Lévi-Strauss, 32.

10 Ricardou, "La Bataille de la phrase," in *Pour une théorie du nouveau roman* (Paris: Seuil, 1971), 118-58.

11 Maurice Merleau-Ponty, "Cinq Notes sur Claude Simon," *Médiations*, no. 4 (1961): 6.

12 Maurice Blanchot, "La Littérature et le droit à la mort," in *La Part du feu* (Paris: Gallimard, 1949), 308.

13 Simon, "Propriétés des rectangles," *Tel Quel*, no. 44 (Winter 1971): 3-16.

14 *Pierre Alechinsky*, by the artist (New York: Abrams, 1977), 237.

15 See Jacqueline Piatier, "Claude Simon ouvre *Les Géorgiques*," *Le Monde*, 4 September 1981, p. 11; Michel Muridsany, "Claude Simon: une maturité rayonnante," *Le Figaro*, 4 September 1981, p. 16.

16 Piatier, ibid.

17 Ibid.

6

Robert Pinget

Quelqu'un (*Someone*), the 1965 work by Robert Pinget, immediately invites comparison with Claude Simon's *Histoire* (1967). They both have roughly the same architecture, in that they are based on the activities of one man's life from morning till night on an ordinary day. In both, thoughts of the first-person narrator are stimulated by present actions and perceptions and directed elsewhere, in time or space. In the end, each one has unwittingly revealed a great deal about himself. In both, much is made about material possessions. In Pinget's book, however, objects and records, in addition to being clues or correlatives, are really the generators of the character's existence. Also, instead of being a receptacle of the past that determines his present (a major feature of some of Michel Butor's characters, too), that character is a voice that builds a facade of words, in which he represents himself. Such is also his present, one of his own manufacture.

The narrator of *Quelqu'un* may be the co-owner of a small rooming house in the outskirts of Agapa, in traditional Pinget country, where the Manu River flows. The way he tells his story, it all began some ten years earlier (Pinget characters have a tendency to think in terms of ten-year periods) when he ran into a friend he had not seen for a long time. Hoping to break away from their humdrum lives, the two decide to put their savings together and start afresh with a business of their own. As anyone might have guessed, they are now steeped in as much mediocrity as before, but that is merely a minor aspect of the tale. The narrator is an inveterate mythomaniac. Part of what he says is obviously false, and the rest is doubtful. On top of that he has a very poor memory, so that even when he is sincere he cannot be sure he has got the facts straight. On the day the text describes, he has lost a piece of paper he thinks important—although he later realizes that it is not. He says he is working on a

120

manuscript ("Anyway, what I call my manuscript"),[1] a treatise on botany, and the missing paper contains important observations. He starts searching for it, but he soon decides that the only way to find it is to pretend he is not looking for it. Consequently, he attempts to account for all his actions since he got up that morning. In order to make things clear (and this almost reads like a parody of Butor's *L'Emploi du temps*) he must throw in a bit of background. One item leads to another, and before one knows it his life is laid bare, all because of a lost scrap of paper. Or is he only pretending to look for his notes in an attempt to tell something about his life?

At any rate, he has a miserable day, fails to find anything, and is convinced he has flubbed the account of his life. For the reader, on the other hand, it is a moving and often hilarious experience. Gingerly treading his way among dangerous creatures—the maid (who doubles as cook during the summer), the co-owner, the two remaining spinster boarders (the others are away on vacation)—the narrator nearly always manages to say the wrong thing, arousing their ire or their scorn. Objects are untrustworthy. The one person more vulnerable than he is, a retarded boy who "helps" around the house, he cannot protect. There is also a neighbor whom he has never met. Something about the design of his weather vane convinces him that the two men could have nothing in common. But his need for someone (*quelqu'un*) is such that he keeps imagining his going over to the neighbor on some pretext or other and discovering that they do have a great deal in common after all. Even in those imaginary events he commits blunders. Finally, the only successful meeting they have is the one in which he imagines assisting his neighbor on his deathbed—then inheriting his manuscripts. Manuscripts and letters are recurrent motifs throughout Pinget's work, correlatives to the desire to communicate. The narrator of *Quelqu'un* says at one point, clarifying the title, "If only one would understand me, put himself in my place. I wonder if someone would want to. Someone" (52).

Pinget succeeds in transforming the reader into that "someone," and I, for one, was able to empathize with the poor wretch more than with Samuel Beckett's bums. I am inclined to accept the latter as images, located in a fantasy world truer than what we call reality—but still a world that is quite other. The horror world of Pinget's characters is much closer to the reader's. On occasion, though, its people reverberate faint echoes of Beckett. When the narrator of *Quelqu'un,* trying to remember whether or not he talked to anyone after breakfast and if so, to whom, suddenly exclaims, "But of course, it all comes back to me," one is reminded of Molloy's similar statement when he remembers his name at the police station. When Pinget's narrator expresses boredom with what he is relating, when he says "What rot!" (*misère*), one recalls Malone's boredom with the story of Sapo and his identical exclamation. To Beckett's crude bag or sack corresponds Pinget's more civilized valise: "One's existence in a valise, neatly packed, properly labeled, so as to have what might be needed, just in case. So, people are continuously preparing their valise, they are always in the midst of packing something. Even when they talk about the weather" (9). In *Fable* (1971), however, the valise becomes a knapsack.

While his fictional world partakes of Beckett's (and increasingly so in the more recent fiction), the material is at times, especially in his earlier works, similar to that found in books by Marcel Aymé or Raymond Queneau. It is, however, structured toward the achievement of effects like those of a Beckett whose pessimism had been tempered with a glimmer of faith. In one of his most widely read books, *L'Inquisitoire* (1962), he has also experimented with a device of his own, the questioning voice. Here, the main character is a lonely, deaf old man who is forced to submit to a lengthy, persistent interrogation. Who does the interrogating is never made clear, although there is enough in the text to allow one's imagination to picture a woman stenographer taking everything down, while sheets of paper keep piling up (as they do in *Molloy*). That all questions must be written out, because of the man's deafness, adds a touch of implausibility that enhances the unreality of the fiction and, as often happens, its effectiveness. At the beginning one might have the impression that a detective or some sort of police or government official is asking the questions and that one should concern oneself with the sudden disappearance of another individual. Long before the story is over, one begins to have doubts about the reality of the voice, or perhaps the whole affair could be taking place after death. Pinget himself explained the process as follows: "When I decided to write *L'Inquisitoire* I had nothing to say, I felt only a need to justify myself at length. I got down to work and wrote the sentence, *Answer me, yes or no*, which was meant for me alone and signified, *out with it.*"[2] The effect on the reader, however, can be very different from what the genesis implies.

The old man complains that to relate his life in such fashion "is like dying a second time," and he speaks of "all these dead people around us" (408, 435). On the other hand, he has been asked if "his case is incurable" (72), and he refers to the time he still has to live. Likewise, in *Passacaille* (1969), it is unclear whether anyone has died and if so who it is, or whether someone might be imagining his future death or someone is dying—perhaps even the text is a sort of *mémoire d'outre-tombe*. Such uncertainties are similar to those involving the reality or identity of Beckett's characters. In asking these questions, one gives evidence of having succumbed to the realistic fallacy, which contemporary texts implicitly denounce more and more vigorously. In the case of both Beckett and Pinget, no satisfactory answers can be given, and that matters very little. It is like the paper that may (or may not) have been

lost at the outset of *Quelqu'un.* As Northrop Frye remarked with reference
to the ghost in *Hamlet,* a literary text presents one with hypothesis or
postulate, which one accepts, and the imagination takes it from there—
otherwise, the reader has "no business in literature."[3] The hypothesis in
L'Inquisitoire is: let there be two voices, the one questioning and the
other answering. Gradually the text, aided by the reader's imagination,
causes the answering voice to materialize into a man of about sixty, who,
although deaf, is generally sound of mind and body. His memory seems
far from perfect at first, but one soon decides that he must be playing a
game of sorts: actually, he has a phenomenal memory. His questioner is
relentless, picking up every hesitation, every omission. In the end the old
man is forced to reveal all, or nearly all.

The first half of the book is replete with people and places of Pinget
country. Hundreds of characters appear fleetingly, many recurring out of
earlier works, filling the countryside, the woods, the estates, the hotels,
and the cafés in Fantoine, Sirancy, Agapa, and Douves. It is indeed the
most comprehensive repertory of that imaginary world. The main character (the answering voice) has been employed as a servant on the large
estate of two rich playboys, whose household includes a secretary, valet,
maid, cook, and gardener. All his identifications of people, descriptions
of places, and relations of events seem to have had one consequence,
probably not perceptible to the reader until the second half of the book is
under way: they have given the main character substance—created him,
so to speak. He was mere emptiness, a blank, but he now begins to
penetrate the book's substance, himself taking shape as it encloses what
he reveals. When one refers to his memory, to his descriptions, or even to
his existence as a character, it is because one tends to forget the original
postulate. There is no one there except an answering voice that, with the
reader's help, builds a "character" and his surroundings as it responds.
Still, for the sake of convenience, I shall keep on discussing him as a
character who fully existed at the beginning of the book rather than only
at the end.

A melancholy meditation (219-22) on the vanity and solitude of his life
marks a turning point (there are no formal subdivisions in the book).
Soon afterwards, the reader learns that the voice is that of someone who
has been married and has had a son. Both wife and son have died, under
circumstances that lead him to suspect foul play, on the order of witchcraft. A number of things hidden during the first two hundred pages
come to light, including a series of sadistic murders. The strangest revelation, though, has nothing to do with either crime or marriage. In spite of
his having already given an extremely detailed description of his
employers' estate, inside and out (he needs eleven pages to account for
the furniture in the salon alone), he is led to tell, because of a slip of the
tongue as the book is about over, that the mansion also comprises an

older section of historical interest, with official visiting hours. Furthermore, another slip makes him confess that a friend of his employers still
lives there, a gentleman named Pierre, an amateur astronomer who peers
at the heavens from the top floor of the dungeon. The old servant visited
him as often as he could, for being with Pierre brought him peace. He even
calls him a saint (448). If one thinks of the answering voice as a character,
the Freudian implications of such an oversight are obvious. Assuming
that the hero-victim of *L'Inquisitoire* reveals more and more of his inner
being as the interrogation progresses, or that the answering voice, who is
a kind of narrator (and how close is he to the author?), has to explore
further and further into the recesses of his imagination (or consciousness) in order to provide answers, the position of these last disclosures
gives them added significance. The implicit reference to the keeper of
the keys in the kingdom of heaven might well point to a transcendental
faith that tempers the pessimism of the narrative. The presence of
biblical motifs and texts will be more apparent with *Le Libera* and subsequent works. One might recall, in this connection, that an earlier book
by Pinget, *Le Fiston* (1959; *Monsieur Levert*), was a selection of the *Club
du Livre Chrétien*.

Pinget's universe was not created in a day. Its embryo may be found in
his first published work, a collection of short stories, *Entre Fantoine et
Agapa* (1951; *Between Fantoine and Agapa*). This stands in relation to
his later books very much as Nathalie Sarraute's *Tropismes* does to hers.
They are of course of a very different nature. To return to analogies I
suggested earlier, the fantasy of Pinget's brief sketches first reminds one
of Marcel Aymé; then important differences come to light. Whereas
Aymé draws out all the consequences of his outlandish premises and
exploits them for all they are worth, Pinget merely suggests, then lets the
reader take over. Once Aymé has set the stage, a rigorous, albeit mad,
logic determines the outcome. In Pinget's imaginary world, logic has
little place. In this respect, he is more like Raymond Queneau, who also
comes to mind because of the strange names given to characters. Somehow, Mahu Blimbraz and Polycarpe de Lanslebourg seem related to
Machut, Quéfasse, and Louis-Philippe des Cigalles. In addition to the
towns of the title, the tales also introduce fictional place-names such as
Sirancy-la-Louve, the Grance Forest, the Cygne Bar, and Gou Street,
which reappear in subsequent books. They are not, however, centered in
fictional territory: places like Paris, Saint-Cloud, London, and Murano
are also used as settings. The same holds true for Pinget's next three
works.

In *Mahu ou le matériau* (1952; *Mahu or the Material*), Fantoine and
Agapa are places one goes to. The former even needs to be identified:
"Fantoine, that's where I go on vacation" (28), says one character. They
are constantly present, but on the fringes of the narrative, which is clearly

set in Paris. In *Le Renard et la boussole* (1953; The Fox and the Compass), the story begins in Paris, moves to Israel, and returns to Fantoine as if to a new, mythical promised land. One might have expected Pinget's fiction to be anchored there from then on, and he possibly intended it so. Nevertheless, *Graal Flibuste* (1956) does not quite make it. Everything in that work belongs to the domain of fantasy, and there is probably too much reliance on the bizarre element. There are too many literary reminiscences for the fictional world to acquire the "reality" it later has. An early reference to a sultan and to palm trees inevitably carries the reader's imagination to the Near East, that is, to a stereotyped "reality"; subsequent references to Fantoine and Agapa do not restore a balance. It is only with *Baga* (1958) that a coherent atmosphere is established. The setting is still mythical, but there are no false notes to lead the reader astray. Once myth has been removed, as in all later works, Pinget's universe can be said to be firmly established, consistent, and as credible as it is imaginary. There is, especially in *L'Inquisitoire*, no lack of allusions to the outside world—to Amsterdam, Switzerland, or America—but those places are almost invariably foreign. Life, in the narrative, is found in Agapa and in Fantoine as transpositions of French towns. Versailles is only an architectural style (and perhaps an inadvertance). What we know as reality lies beyond the borders. Contrary to what took place in *Mahu*, people no longer go to Fantoine; they have their roots there.

The metaphor of Pinget's fictional universe was possibly stated in the story from *Entre Fantoine et Agapa* entitled "Firenze Delle Nevi." This tells how Lorenzo de' Medici, towards the end of his life, tired of the frequent uprisings that threatened Florence, decided to "compete with himself" (73). Climbing the southern slopes of Mont Blanc, he found a spot on which to erect a rival to his own city, at an altitude of some fifteen thousand feet. It required only two years to build, and in 1491 Botticelli put the finishing touches to his frescoes for the Municipio. Brilliant festivities celebrated the rebirth of Florence in the snow—and there may be significance in this happening just before the discovery of the New World. If you have never heard of Firenze Delle Nevi, it is because it was later destroyed in an avalanche. Pinget, as a new Lorenzo, somewhere in the heights of his mind has constructed a new world to rival the one in which he lives, and in its composition there must be beauty. As he himself has said, "For me, a book continues to be a work of art: I try to turn out a thing of beauty, one that pleases me."[4]

Basically, the texts of *Entre Fantoine et Agapa* are stories. Even the last section, entitled "Journal," could be viewed as a series of unrelated anecdotes, each one headed by an arbitrary date. That is an essential feature of Pinget's work. He and his characters have stories to tell (even though, at the outset, neither one knows what they are); they must find a way to tell them and someone to tell them to. His aesthetic problem is that he does not function in terms of one sustained major narrative: he would have been at home with the picaresque novel, and both *Le Renard et la boussole* and *Graal Flibuste* actually go far in that direction. That they are not as effective as later works follows not only from Pinget's failure to build a coherent world but also from another equally important fact: the anecdote matters less than the telling of it. Language and thought are one, and "one never thinks more than one says" (E 56). Everyone, therefore, has a story to relate and that story is himself. "As I proceed with my story, I have the impression of being what I tell" (B 126). Who, then, is that strange individual who calls himself a writer and tells the stories of others? hence the tale of *Mahu*.

Mahu ou le matériau is narrated in the first person by Mahu himself, presumably as Pinget's surrogate. But "there is also Latirail, he writes novels" (10), and a fellow named Sinture, the postmaster, who says, "I pull the strings, I pull the strings, I am the one who is writing the novel of your friend Latirail" (21). To complicate matters, Mlle Lorpailleur, also a novelist, "is writing the story of Latirail, the novelist" (42). Equally complicated and reality-stretching situations can be found in Flann O'Brien's *At Swim-Two-Birds* (1939) and Gilbert Sorrentino's *Mulligan Stew* (1979).[5] Nor should one forget the character in Raymond Queneau's *Le Vol d'Icare* (1968) who disappears from the papers of a novelist who then hires a detective to find him. Mahu, who thinks he, too, might be a character in his own novel, wants to help Latirail, whose "novel" has hit a snag. He suggests a development, introducing two new characters into his friend's story and locating the incident in Agapa. Latirail, however, rejects the idea. At this point, neither Mahu nor Latirail realizes that the new "characters" were conjured up by Sinture and sent to Agapa for the purpose of breaking into Latirail's novel. The next sequence displays them in Agapa as "real" characters in Pinget's book, amused by their mission, but embarrassed at having to tell Sinture that they have been rejected. Later, one of them will be forced into Mlle Lorpailleur's novel. It is all a grotesque illustration of a remark made in the narrative about "a fellow who thinks one cannot write novels. He says one cannot put oneself in someone else's place" (45). In other words, there are no char-acters; there are only parcels of a writer's imagination, something critics have been saying for some time, or words in his text, as one prefers to think of them today.

At any rate, Pinget was obviously enjoying his fantasy when writing *Mahu*, and it is great fun while it lasts. Unfortunately, he cannot sustain the merry pace. Towards the end of the first part (subtitled "The Novelist") each chapter stands as a semi-independent unit, almost like the anecdotes of *Entre Fantoine et Agapa*. Logically, it leads up to the second part, "Mahu Splutters," in which the narrator attempts to give his story. Again, what one has is really a sequence of stories, related by someone who is either a participant or a witness; they do not add up to one unified major story. Possibly, somewhat ahead of the times, Pinget was experimenting with fragmentation. One should perhaps also recall that passage from Sartre's *La Nausée*, to which I have alluded in earlier chapters, where Roquentin denies the possibility of what he calls "adventure"—something outstanding, with a beginning and an end, with an order in between. "When one lives, nothing happens. Settings change, people come in and go out, that's all. There are never any beginnings. Days are added to days without rhyme or reason, it's an endless, monotonous addition."[6] Adventures or unified stories can exist only in fiction, that is, as most contemporary commentators on that text would imply, in outdated forms of fiction. In a different kind of context, one might have been tempted to accuse Pinget of lacking imagination. What one should realize is that his activities are directed elsewhere. In harmony with a trend in twentieth-century fiction that antedates the concern with linguistic phenomena, his aim is more to create what André Malraux has termed "a universe, both particular and coherent."[7] It is also a necessary one, for, as Mahu says, "When someone has really invented something, he does not keep comparing it to the inventions of others, since his own has replaced everything else" (88).

Mahu's "spluttering" refers to the disjointed nature of the events he relates; what gives coherence to the universe Pinget presents here is Mahu's voice. The narrated events are not important, and Mahu even suggests that they cannot truly be narrated, basing his arguments mainly on problems of spatial and chronological points of view. The significant ingredients of his tale are to be found outside the story proper, in language and in style. The latter, as Roland Barthes has described it, in part, "is the decorative voice of an unknown and secret flesh, it operates as a Necessity."[8] The uniqueness, solitude, and compulsion implied in Barthes's study are indeed a capital feature of Pinget's works, and again one is reminded of Beckett. The first step is to express one's actual, uninhibited self, no matter what it is, and that is Mahu's concern: "What matters to me is not to sing well, but to hear my voice without bronchitis, you know, bronchitis, it's full of small wheezes" (212). The next step is to reach someone. A fairly obvious goal in *Quelqu'un*, it had already been expressed by the narrator of *Le Renard et la boussole:* "You at least know what I am thinking, and that is why we shall eventually meet. I have nothing to say to us, absolutely nothing, and you want to hear my voice, that's all" (10). The prologue of *Graal Flibuste* pessimistically alludes to letters that never reach their destination; the king, in *Baga*, writes for his hypothetical nephews. Levert, in *Le Fiston*, pretends to write a letter to his son; Clope, in *Clope au dossier* (1961; *Clope*), gathers evidence to prove his innocence, presumably for a judge; the inability to communicate with other people on the estate is what made life miserable for the old man of *L'Inquisitoire;* on the first page of *Cette voix* there is mention of "that letter, one forgets to whom it was addressed, drafts of which were found scattered all over"; and the much more recent *L'Ennemi* (1987) represents the flawed attempt of an old man to communicate who or what he is.

Before being able to express oneself, one should, from the standpoint of common sense, know precisely that; actually, it is very hard to dissociate one process from the other. Mahu, toward the end of his narrative, seems to have found his voice. But he protests when he meets a black who claims that his name is also Mahu: "I have never been black. That I am sure of." When the man remarks that Mahu still has a long road to walk, "he has a long life ahead of him," and advises him to "familiarize yourself with this black man that we are" (204), the implication is that Mahu has not really found out who he was because he had not yet said everything he had to say. It is hardly surprising that Robert Pinget's fiction is permeated with the theme of an inner quest, sometimes metaphorically transposed to the level of the narrative.

The narrator of *Le Renard et la boussole* bears the rather preposterous name of John Tintouin Porridge. *Tintouin* is slightly archaic and colloquial for "worry." In addition to the amusing clash between French and English components of the name, this pulls existential angst down to the comic level. Furthermore, the book is indeed a picaresque porridge or hodgepodge. A considerable amount of narrative confusion exists because, in part, the quest is conducted on a linguistic plane. One is not too far removed from the world of Raymond Roussel. Already in *Entre Fantoine et Agapa* Pinget had demonstrated his fondness for phonetic correspondences such as "Avec un zeste de citron / Avec un geste de siphon" (7)—which in English becomes nothing more than "with a twist of lemon" and "with a splash of soda"—and for puns of all descriptions. In *Mahu* Mlle Lorpailleur's name, since an *orpailleur* is one who pans for gold, suggests the phrase *chercheurs d'or* (gold diggers) to the novelist Latirail, who then decides to call his novel *Chercheurs de poux* (Lice Hunters), perhaps because one of his characters stumbles upon gold dishware at a flea market (he says lice can be trained the same as fleas)—but it is hard to figure out which came first!

The narrative begins with the narrator's name and a statement of his desire to write. A few chance encounters, such as the one with a Mary Stewart book in a store window, provoke a number of false starts, but when he recalls a biblical verse, which he misquotes as "Beware of the foxes, the little foxes" (21), it is as though he had hit upon a catalytic word. He accurately "takes" the fox, couples him with an old man who turns out to be the Wandering Jew, and packs them both off to Jerusalem. The Jew goes back to his origins, the fox, initially no more than a word out of the Bible, back to biblical lands. As each is a mere figment of Porridge's imagination, their trip is correlative to his own search for origins, a way of finding out who he is. Because the fox is referred to as Renard rather than *le renard*, thus suggesting Reynard the Fox, a medieval harmonic is added to the biblical tone. This helps to undermine conventional chronology, establishing analogies between a postwar journey to Israel and the Crusades. As a result, the quest motif is also clearly stated. Porridge, or Pinget, who on occasion experiences some difficulty in distinguishing between himself and the characters he has invented, meditates, improvises, and describes innumerable events. The book is something of an illustrated essay on life, art, and reality—with the reader's imagination picturing the "illustrations." Boredom is avoided through the variety and implausibility of incidents. Suleiman the Magnificent, Don Quixote, and Mary Magdalene are thrown in with refugees from Nazi concentration camps and citizens of Agapa.

One's head swirls by the time Porridge, David (the Wandering Jew), and Renard decide to take advantage of Louis IX's return to France and come home on the same ship, "what does it matter if it is powered by oil or by oars" (184). The fox and the Jew conveniently vanish, or rather they are absorbed back into the narrator's being. The picaresque aspect of the book is attenuated as Porridge comes back a changed man. Pinget expresses the transformation by having him show up not in the Paris he had left but in Fantoine, where he meets Sinture, Latirail, Mahu, and many others. Before his trip he had been employed in a hat factory; now he takes care of the gas pump in a service station. The turning point seems to have come toward the end of the stay in Israel, when Renard exclaims, after Mary Magdalene accuses him of being too logical: "No, no, we are not French, relax . . . I am from Fantoine" (176). Pinget himself exclaimed, during the course of a discussion at Cerisy-la-Salle, "I don't give a damn for logic!"[9] Porridge's true self has roots somewhere between Fantoine and Agapa, just as Pinget's distinctive voice is that which catches the language of his inner world. It required two more works, *Graal Flibuste* and *Baga* to sweep out the dross that is not his—the wheeze of his bronchitis.

Inevitably, the narrator's solitude is reemphasized. In *Baga*, the king speaks of "this prison I'm in" (110), and the metaphor is extended, the prison materializes, complete with walls, iron bars, and a guard. In *Le Fiston* (1959), Monsieur Levert repeats the king's identical statement (e.g., 34, 36, 43), but maintains it at the metaphorical level. What was a fantasy is now an obsession, that is, a psychological reality. Indeed, the entire narrative takes place on that plane. The setting is the fictional town of Fantoine, but the "reality" of fictional events is often in doubt, most statements being metaphorical. The story appears to deal with a Monsieur Levert and his letter or letters to his son, or to himself, and because of it or them, one learns who he is and of his relationships with the town and its people. In the long run, what happens on this or that occasion matters less than Levert's having chosen to write about them. As is the case with all of Pinget's subsequent books, there are a number of mundane questions that cannot be answered with any degree of certainty. In this instance the reader will never know if Levert was the real father of Marie, the cobbler's daughter, or where his son is (assuming that he does have a son, as the old man in *L'Inquisitoire* seems to believe), or the extent to which he himself actually exists. One probably should not even ask. A question, nevertheless, that surely haunts the reader is the one that was also put at the end of Butor's *Degrés:* "Who speaks?" There is throughout *Le Fiston* an uncertainty concerning the narrator similar to the one in *Clope au dossier.*

The narrative gets under way with what appears like an objective, flat, third-person account of Marie's funeral. It continues with a similar description of Monsieur Levert and his activities. Then there is a sudden switch to first-person narrative as Levert begins, "My dear son" (34); the ten pages that follow are utterly subjective. Here, however, tension begins to manifest itself, for the narrative voice switches half a dozen times from first to third person and back again—but without change of mood. Next, just as abruptly as before, the text becomes "objective" again and follows the actions of Marie's younger brother after the funeral. But as the young man begins to reminisce, illusions about the objectivity of this section begin to fade away. Much later, when similar reminiscences involving different characters are attributed to Levert himself, it becomes hard to reject the suspicion that the narrator, whoever he might be, is making up the whole thing. That, in a way, is rather obvious, since one knows that the narrator must eventually be recognized as Pinget's surrogate. The important point, nevertheless, is that those shenanigans result in a destruction of point of view. In other words, another literary convention is set aside, as it is later, in like fashion, in Jean Pierre Faye's fiction. Theoretically, *Mahu ou le matériau* contained similar implications, but the comic or fantastic nature of so many of its episodes helped to maintain literary definitions untouched as one was reluctant to take matters at their face value. More serious in tone, *Le Fiston* is naturally more disturbing. With *Mahu*, Pinget was very close to Aymé and Queneau; here, he is edging closer to Beckett's territory (one should not forget that it was Beckett's reading and appreciation of *Mahu* that led to a friendship between the two writers). When Levert, leaving no doubt as to the nature of his fiction, exclaims, "This lie bores me. Everything must be retold, and I don't feel like doing it. I go on, son" (130), he seems to echo lines from the last page of Beckett's *L'Innommable:* "You must go on, I can't go on, I'll go on."

As he "goes on" Monsieur Levert relates the events that constitute his being. The letters that he writes or pretends to write to his son amount to an attempted justification of his own existence. Part of the fiction may be that in giving an account of himself (consisting of a particular vision of people and events in the Fantoine area), he presents a mirror for his son to look at. Recognizing himself, his son will perhaps return home where he belongs. One knows, however, that "this letter will never be sent" (93, 158, 166). Behind the mask of fiction, Levert's justification must be intended for himself alone. Once that is accepted, the choice of events acquires new significance: death informs the narrative's entire structure.

Levert is approaching old age. His wife has died some time back; his housekeeper and his sister die between parts 1 and 2. Marie, who may be his daughter and whose funeral opens the book, is about the same age as his hypothetical son. Other deaths are mentioned, and as he attempts to establish the fact of his own existence, he is ironically led to present an eight-page description of the tombs in the Fantoine cemetery. It seems as though a magnet were drawing him toward the inevitable end. Shortly after the cemetery scene, language itself, which is the means of his justification, fails him and becomes dislocated (88-89). Something has gone wrong. As the second part begins, Levert realizes that he may have jeopardized his chance of success. He admits that those earlier "objective" accounts might not have been quite accurate. He proposes alternate or subsequent versions; he even transposes events into a different setting. He becomes desperate as a sense of failure overtakes him and he tries to put himself in his son's place. He imagines his son writing to him, "But the father has been dead for a long time" (161). It is hopeless; even through his son's eyes he cannot give himself substance. Possibly, he does not really exist. Having reached that stage, he or it or whatever produces the text can see no reason for going on. Hence the last sentence in the book: "Aside from what is written down, there is only death" (173). Matters may not be quite as hopeless as they seem, for a fair amount has been written, and in writing there lies salvation.

Clope au dossier (1961) also represents a justification, but it is directed outward. The third-person narrative form is sustained from the beginning to a few pages before the end, allowing shifts from one consciousness to the next without changes in tonality or style, a traditional technique. Pinget nevertheless achieves a tension analogous to the one he built up in *Le Fiston*, and he does this in two ways, first, as in Alain Robbe-Grillet's *La Maison de rendez-vous*, by means of explicit statement. Referring to the activity of a woman, Simone, in her kitchen, he writes, "She fills it again with the hot water remaining in the pan, if none is left she puts some on the stove again or has already done so" (51). There the reader has no way of knowing if there is any water in the pan or what Simone actually does. Second, through a shifting of tenses: as in the previous books, the reader is, at the beginning, lulled into taking the narrative for granted, shifts from present to past indefinite or imperfect being fairly commonplace in French fiction. But when a sequence in the conditional follows a matter-of-fact description in the present, the reader is alerted to the uncertain nature of the presentation (e.g., 60-66). In a later book, *Passacaille* (1969; *Passacaglia*), there are constant changes from present to past tense, to conditional, to future of probability. This again prompts the question, "Who speaks?" or, as Joyce phrased it in *Finnegans Wake*, "who in hallhagal wrote the durn thing anyhow?"[10] The omniscient author is ruled out by definition. Since in order to be less than omniscient about his own creation he must pretend to be someone else, one searches for a surrogate. One might first be led to surmise that it is the writer's consciousness in *Passacaille*, Clope's consciousness in the earlier work, that are being spread out on the pages of the book, even though Clope, like Monsieur Levert, refers to himself in the third person and is able to describe (or imagine) the dreams of Simone. In the final analysis, however, it is probably best to forget such individual consciousness, whether a character's or the writer's, and consider the text as an assemblage of words produced by a specific activity—the act of writing, or scription— which is governed as much by the laws of language as by the will of the conscious writer. I shall return to that in subsequent chapters.

Like Levert and several other Pinget protagonists, Clope is a solitary man. The book begins, "Being alone, that wasn't a position in life," and revolves about the conflict between the reality of each lone, isolated human being and the fables concocted by society. The rift is dramatized at the outset by Clope's unlawful shot that brings down a wild goose. In his supposed defense of himself, he keeps stumbling over that day "when everything might have begun" (124). Is Clope actually guilty of something more serious; has he committed a crime? A strong temptation arises to suppose that there is, as in Robbe-Grillet's *Le Voyeur*, a void in the novel, a blank in Clope's mind: a murder might conveniently fill it. In both works, however, it is the reader who is trapped into imagining the crime, as stereotyped forms of reasoning, so-called commonsense logic, and more generally speaking the fables of his society naturally lead him in that direction. Clope has done no more than his dossier contains, for outside the limits of the text he simply does not exist. The trivial shooting that reverberates throughout the book is a correlative to Clope's basic situation. He imagines himself indicted for antisocial behavior, and the reader unwittingly confirms this. Others consider him slightly mad when they speak as actors in the comedy of society. The narrative and its main character have been delivered to the reader in a malleable state, and in the interpretations the reader reveals himself or herself.

A welcome quality, absent in *Le Fiston*, that has been restored in *Clope au dossier*, is Pinget's humor—or what he prefers to call fantasy.[11] Accounts of Simone's early morning activities, her unsuccessful efforts to keep her child and kitchen clean, and the sputtering reminiscences of two old-timers on the village bridge are delightful as they lack mean or bitter overtones. The combination of laughter and seriousness, already present in earlier works, is now more fully integrated, as it is in *Quelqu'un.* In these works Pinget's attitude resembles that of Pierrot at the conclusion of Queneau's *Pierrot mon ami,* after all his efforts and hope had come to naught. Thinking of what might have been and of what actually happened, he simply burst out laughing and walked away.

Humor and ambiguity, as well as the theme of death and the quest motif, are concentrated in *Le Libera* (1968; *The Libera Me Domine*). The title is taken from the response sung during the absolution of the dead in Roman Catholic liturgy: "Libera me, Domine, de morte aeterna." A number of violent deaths, mostly of children, cast a pall over the narrative, and the description of a funeral constitutes its final episode. Again an unidentified voice is heard throughout, compulsively narrating, repeating, correcting, quoting, and surmising, alluding once more like *Baga*'s king and Monsieur Levert to "this prison I'm in" (216) and seeming to give testimony before some mysterious, unnamed judge— perhaps alluding to the Lord's judgment anticipated in the third verse of the response: "Dum veneris judicare saeculum per ignem." He refers to many characters of the previous books, but he is not as all-inclusive as the old man of *L'Inquisitoire,* nor is he as much interested in objects and places. Perhaps for that reason, he does not really materialize into a character. The villain of the narrative is Mlle Lorpailleur, who was a novelist in *Mahu* and in *Le Renard et la boussole.* She now reappears as a schoolteacher, a position she had already assumed in *L'Inquisitoire.* Actually, the narrator's point appears to be that she is still a novelist of sorts, that is, a fabricator of tales. She has spread a story implicating him in the murder of a young boy, ten years earlier (as usual), and he naturally insists that it is pure fiction. As things turn out, nearly everything is. There are few incidents in the book that are not told twice or more with considerable variants—an indication of Pinget's interest in musical composition. In some instances, one doubts that such incidents ever took place, and of course none of them did since we are dealing with fiction.

On the other hand, the general impression one derives, because of the usual suspension of disbelief, is that knowledge of others and of past events is practically impossible, which was already suggested as far back as *Mahu.* The solitude of the narrator is again obvious, and there is little or nothing to enable one to detect intimate relationships between him and the characters he talks about. It is the problem of communication, stated in earlier works, but endowed with a new dimension. Possibly, an answer is implied to the question put in *Quelqu'un:* the answer is no, not in this world.

Among the few episodes in *Le Libera* that are not questioned, that of the children's gala performance stands out. Often hilarious, it is also an exercise in futility that subtly blends traditional humor with the negative theme of the work as a whole. There is something about it that is emblematic of all of Pinget's fiction. The woman who is given credit for writing the poems recited by the children is using someone else's material. She is complimented for verse that she had acknowledged to have been written by Lamartine. Some children read parts that had originally been assigned to others, and one girl makes mistakes that no one notices. Life is a bumbling comedy of errors in which no one really understands anyone else.

But death, too, is a comedy of errors in which no one understands what is going on. Grim humor has perhaps induced Pinget to give the name of a most civilized, formal dance, the passacaglia, to his next fiction, *Passacaille* (1969), a text that comes close to being a verbal *danse macabre*. Actually, the description of the passacaglia (or the related chaconne), with its lack of complete tune, the theme consisting of "a short succession of harmonies to be repeated over and over again without interruption," could apply to this book once "linear narrative" is substituted for "tune" and "descriptive fragment" for "harmony."[12] Among other things, the work features a procession of cadavers, perhaps led or conjured up by a scarecrow. There is the corpse of the main character, a solitary man referred to as *maître*, sometimes as *Maître alchimiste*, who annotates a book and/or writes his memoirs and/or imagines the circumstances of his own death. Other corpses are of a retarded boy, who has been castrated by a farm implement, a mailman, who is also afflicted with a strange disease, a number of undetermined people, and, to add the indispensable element of the grotesque, a cow, a duck, and many dead animals in the woods. Many of the corpses end up on top of a compost pile, to which there are some thirty references. In other words, "The whole country is in a state of decomposition, dead bodies are strewn over meadows and roads" (93). Creation of present self, which I earlier suggested as being an object of Pinget's texts, becomes more and more questionable—partly because of the overwhelming threat of death, partly because the quest for identity appears hopeless (something one already suspected when reading *Le Fiston* and *Clope au dossier*). "Who speaks?" is once more a tantalizing question.

The narrative voice in *Passacaille* starts out in a very muted fashion. The first personal subject is "someone," tentatively governing a verb in the conditional, amid a number of verbless phrases or impersonal statements. A "man" appears next, and only on the third page does the regular pronoun "he" assume its role. More than halfway through the book, the third-person narrator steps into the text, interjecting a "Don't interrupt me" (86). One page later he produces the first "I," saying "I can still see it now," a statement that develops into a twenty-page first-person narrative (99-118), which reverts to isolated sentences, "I can still see him now,"

"I can still see the woman now," "I can still see the red piece of cloth (121, 123, 125), before dissolving completely. It appears again only in quotations from the *maître's* last will, at the very end of the book.

To return to the very beginning: "Calm. And gray. No sign of turbulence. Something must be broken in the machinery, but there is no outward sign of it. The clock is on the mantel. Its hands show the time." One is reminded of the "something there that isn't working" in Beckett's *Comment c'est.* One also thinks of the moment of literary creation, the more so when reading the very hesitant paragraphs that follow, with their verbs in the conditional. What is broken in the machinery appears to be a major generator of incidents that, somehow, an anonymous narrator attempts, without success, to fit into a narrative line. He first hits upon the machinery of life, hence illness and especially death as the major presence in the text; next, the clock is broken, and chronology is disturbed, then a farm tractor breaks down, requiring a mechanic to drive up in his pickup truck. That truck, or another one, lands in a ditch; a scarecrow needs repairs. Something in mind and reason goes awry, producing the retarded boy, drunkenness, and belief in witchcraft. The fabric of society cracks, producing war, exodus, lawlessness, and corruption in governments. A break in friendship occurs, caused by death—and one is back at the beginning. To think that it was such a calm opening, without turbulence. In the meantime, the narrative machinery has also broken down, a failure that produces a successful passacaglia, a beautiful dance of death, but the reader is left with a shattered text and a disembodied narrator—"Master alchemist of those trifles to which he owes his survival" (47, 59). Does such a master appear because human beings have lost their faith?

That Pinget consciously removed himself from the position of responsible writer is indicated by the date line appearing at the end of the text: "Sirancy, 1968." (He does this again at the end of *L'Ennemi* [1987].) *Passacaille* was not composed in Paris by the man with recognizable features known to many as Robert Pinget; it is a text that was generated in the imaginary country and ruled by the same language that has given shape to Pinget's mind, which he has been exploring since the days of *Mahu.* Call it a verbal country if you will, for *Passacaille* is a text that has been generated by a verbal context. One is within sight of Raymond Roussel, and life appears as a verbal whirlpool that sucks us into the sewers of death. As there is not much to be done about it, one might as well laugh.

Much of Pinget's work since the late sixties gives me the feeling that he is, in his own particular way, illustrating Pascal's phrase on the wretchedness of man when deprived of God. Sorry, comical substitutes for spiritual leaders or the divinity itself keep cropping up, as they had before, with *Baga* for instance, but in less fantastic fashion. I suspect the

Maître alchimiste of *Passacaille* is one such substitute, like the man who tells the protagonist of *Fable* (1971) the latter's eyes were closed the moment he knocked on his door (78). In this book the narrative begins with a situation analogous to the one on which *Passacaille* opens, where a man, watched by someone else, is soon found dead on a compost heap; in *Fable*, a man goes to sleep on a pile of hay—whether he dies or not is a moot question—and he is also watched by someone else who might also be himself, or his double. There are actually several variations on this beginning, scattered throughout the text (see 28, 35, 39, 47, 50, and 73), each one slightly more removed from the words of the first, and the last barely recognizable. Then a second (unnumbered) part of the book begins (80) with statements almost identical with those of the initial pages; some of the early ones are omitted and the protagonist who had first been called "Miaille ou autre" (10) and on page 79 uses his own knife to gouge out his eyes is then referred to as "Miaille ou Miette" (80), and the latter name, already present in *L'Inquisitoire*, is adopted to the end.

In French usage, *fables* were often contrasted with Christian legends, but here both classical myths and Christian references are intertwined so that it is hard to distinguish good from evil. Oedipus is alluded to, although not mentioned by name. Narcissus shows up rather frequently, in a complex manner: at first he is an unpleasant other, later he is multiplied into many dead corpses, and near the end Miette says, "my name is Narcissus, but this is a secret between you and me" (112)—but two pages later Narcissus dies once again. One page after the first "death" of Narcissus, there is mention of a "cross planted among the hills" on which "the blessed fruit" was nailed (62). Earlier, someone had said, "Show us the fruit of thy womb" (36), and a little later, "After this life's exile, show us Jesus, the blessed fruit of thy womb" (42). The two figures are complementary and mutually destructive. Narcissism is the only religion left for those who have been exiled from the kingdom of Christ. Indeed, *Fable* appears to deal with exiles and wanderers following what may have been a nuclear catastrophe—but that metaphor is not sustained very long (in Pinget's texts, metaphors are as uncertain as everything else). Exiles and strangers remain with us throughout and it is no accident that Miaille's (or Miette's) double is a Gypsy.

In *Cette voix* (1975; *That Voice*) the musical aspect of the composition is even more obvious. There are not only variations on the narrative of one or several murders or robberies but at least half a dozen phrases are repeated many times, like leitmotifs.[13] What starts out on the first page as *Manque un accord* ("A chord is missing") becomes on the next page *Manque un raccord* ("A link is missing"), which then recurs more than fifteen times; other leitmotifs are "the voice on the slate that is being erased," "the old myths reappear, chafers of despair," and so forth. The narrative is punctuated by a few religious holidays such as Good Friday,

All Saints' Day, and All Souls' Day, with considerable emphasis on the latter, and several of the anecdotes are centered on the town cemetery: "Thus I know that the action unfolds in the cemetery planned like a ballet or drama by some invisible big shot" (26-27). That same mysterious organizer has decided that the one who says "I" would settle in the cemetery in an abandoned vault, seat himself on its altar, find a slate and a piece of chalk, and take notes. Sometimes he sees nothing, but the slate records events just the same. "What a relief no longer to be the sole master of one's text" (29).

Again there is a *maître*, who may be the same Mortin who had appeared in Pinget's work before,[14] there are suitcases, a valise, a knapsack, filled with papers and letters. Mortin may have been swindled out of millions, perhaps killed, by one of his two nephews, who are both dead when the story of *Cette voix* is told. One of them, Alexandre, had inherited his uncle's house and papers, and is buried close to the abandoned vault. On All Souls' Day, the "I" who sits there sees a visitor to Alexandre's tomb, Theodore ("the gift of God"), a young protégé of Alexandre's, who has taken upon himself to classify the dead man's papers. Through his involvement with Theodore, the "I" in the cemetery becomes a reembodiment of Mortin, so to speak, through the letters and documents that are being read and sorted out—somewhat like the servant in *L'Inquisitoire* was "created" by the people he invented. (And what happens to Pinget's reader who assimilates all of this?) As someone is on his deathbed, assisted by his servant and his doctor, one reads, "As to the matter of who speaks the dying man said that's another story and I am delighted it is" (160). A little earlier the text itself seems to have spoken, "I somewhere in this unbearable night the recovery or reminiscence proves to be mortal and to what avail since the one who speaks but who no one as far as we know" (147). Night as metaphor is important to the contemporary writer who struggles in the dark, and we are spoken by others as much as by ourselves.

Punctuation in *Cette voix* is limited to periods at the end of paragraphs, and this gives the book a specific tonality. With *L'Apocryphe* (1980; *The Apocrypha*) Pinget returns to nearly conventional punctuation. The narrative is divided into two numbered parts and subdivided into 168 brief sections varying in length from nine or ten lines to a little over a page, also numbered, something he had not done since *Mahu*. (*Graal Flibuste* was divided into sections bearing subtitles but no numbers.) At the start, the effect is one of fragmentation; this, however, is attenuated after a while as a certain continuity becomes evident.

The reader who opens *L'Apocryphe* may well feel that he is gently being led into very familiar territory. The shepherd seated on a pile of stones, with his dog, seen by an observer from afar, could remind one of the early pages of Beckett's *Molloy* where a wanderer and his dog are being watched. The scene is uncertain: it could be a live description but it could also be a picture on a cup or vase—and that brings to mind the beginning of Claude Simon's *Géorgiques* (to be published a year later); references to and quotations from Virgil reinforce the familiarity (the quotations, however, are from the *Bucolics*, not the *Georgics*, and they are supplemented by biblical ones). The pile of stones is vaguely reminiscent of earlier piles of hay or compost. There is a master and his old servant living in a large mansion near a small town, and the servant gives detailed descriptions of the various rooms and their furnishings, as another servant had done in *L'Inquisitoire*. His master, often referred to as *le maître*, has a couple of nephews; he dies early in the narrative, of natural causes in the first version, but perhaps he has been murdered or committed suicide. All this is both familiar and expected, since apocryphal texts are of doubtful authority. As in *Fable*, the Christian and classical traditions are fused, but in gentler fashion; the Virgilian shepherd of the beginning merges with the Good Shepherd at the end. Likewise, the story is punctuated both by the natural seasons of the year (Virgil) and by Christian holidays.

Death is once more a persistent presence, maybe an obsessive one as the writer himself ages. "All these dead people around us" (A 54) is a statement that had already appeared in *L'Inquisitoire* and in *Cette voix*, and will be inscribed again in *L'Ennemi*—and all the dead speak to the lonely living. Even more so, they leave papers, documents, letters. Someone, later, will sort them out, transcribe them, make them into a beautiful book, like the one in *Cette voix*, bound in fine calfskin and chained to a desk in the public library, created out of Mortin's notes (CV 172-73). A new doubt is introduced, however, as the *maître*, working on the notes that are intended for his godson and out of which "a fine book can be extracted," stops and suddenly asks, "But what is a fine book" (A 51). Virgil's *Bucolics?* Later, the servant urges his master to stop reading: "Withering in one's room will not produce a fine book. Tomorrow is Whitsunday, one should think about that, inspiration might descend upon one" (154). The master (or the text) answers, "But what is a fine book." The Bible? Is anything worth doing or preserving? The text of *Cette voix* had once again sounded an echo of the final lines from Beckett's *L'Innommable:* "Impossible to finish impossible not to finish impossible to continue to stop to resume." It went on to state that it was impossible "To be anything but this piling up of drifting trivia" (CV 94-95). In *L'Apocryphe*, as the two nephews, now quite old in their turn, wander about the mansion's grounds, emptied of everything, each is an "identical hodgepodge of drifting trivia" (174), while in *Passacaille* there is an analogous statement that I have quoted above.

With *L'Ennemi* a new touch is added to the familiar. The wretchedness of this world, still present, is toned down, as is the evil of the various characters. The *maître* resembles the one who filled the pages of

L'Apocryphe; he has mediocre nephews, faithful servants, and he keeps a journal of sorts, but he has renewed an interest in alchemy and esoteric matters that characterized previous incarnations. He is, however, no longer the man who enjoys fooling his greedy heirs; he is one who suffers and who will die, not in several unverifiable manners throughout the narrative; rather, he will die as the text comes to an end. "The old seeker will disappear before completing the work, he will be fulfilled" (199). There is no mention of a "fine book." This new character may well have his source in the text of *L'Apocryphe* where the master awakens from a nightmare and says, "How many nameless things there are, buried in this head of mine, if I could sleep no more, no longer let the enemy have a hold over me, stay awake so that my tongue be loosened" (73). Though in *L'Ennemi* he complains of a flow of confused words, aimlessly transcribed, the source of the trouble is alike: "What spirit of darkness has produced them, the master's enemy" (38). The "fine book" has been replaced by "the crucible of fine work" (39): as in contemporary theory and practice, the process is more significant than the final product. And later he urges, "Withstand the enemy with the help of a friendly consciousness. / Where to find it? / Outside of sleep that weighs on the scriptor" (102).

The last words of the text, as the ancestor's portrait is described once more, its eyes seemingly staring at one, no matter where in the room that person stands, refer to the master as a "taciturn descendant." That may not be exactly the impression he (or previous protagonists) has given the reader. It could be, however, that the flow of words he had previously mentioned were the words that filled his dreams, his nightmares, hence the words of his unconscious. He believes those words are not really his own, they are those of his double. "That dream in which he is the double of himself. / The enemy, himself bent on his ruin. / One must get out of the dream" (193). The enemy is thus that other within the self, who prevents the true words from being uttered. It would seem that we have come full circle, the master's desire is the same as Mahu's. One might recall that Mahu did not want to sing well but to "hear [his] own voice without bronchitis." It is a quest that has been going on through many of Pinget's works, and the conclusion may well be that Mahu's wish can be fulfilled only in silence.

NOTES

1   Robert Pinget, *Quelqu'un* (Paris: Minuit, 1965), 11, and passim. Henceforth all references to Pinget's works will appear in the body of the text with the following abbreviations: *Entre Fantoine et Agapa,* E; *Baga,* B; *Cette Voix,* CV; *L'Apocryphe,* A.

2   Pinget, "Pseudo-principes d'esthétique," in *Nouveau Roman: hier, aujourd'hui,*

ed. Jean Ricardou and Francoise van Rossum-Guyon (Paris: 10/18, 1972), 315.

3   Northrop Frye, *Anatomy of Criticism* (Princeton: Princeton University Press, 1957), 76.

4   Pinget, "Pseudo-principes d'esthétique," 336.

5   Pinget could have been steered to *At Swim-Two-Birds* by Beckett, but this is a long shot. As to Gilbert Sorrentino, he is an admirer of Robert Pinget and paid him homage by appropriating several of his characters in *Odd Number* (San Francisco: North Point Press, 1985), *Rose Theatre* (Elmwood Park: Dalkey Archive Press, 1987), and *Misterioso* (Elmwood Park: Dalkey Archive Press, 1989); for games with "characters" see his *Mulligan Stew* (New York: Grove Press, 1979).

6   Jean-Paul Sartre, *La Nausée* (1938; rpt. Paris: Club du Meilleur Livre, 1954), 61.

7   Cf. Malraux's marginal annotations to Gaëtan Picon, *Malraux par lui-même* (Paris: Seuil, 1953), 38.

8   Roland Barthes, *Le Degré zéro de l'écriture* (Paris: Seuil, 1953), 20.

9   See note 4.

10   James Joyce, *Finnegans Wake* (1939; rpt. New York: Viking Press, 1965), 107-8.

11   Pinget, "Pseudo-principes d'esthétique," 332-33.

12   Willi Apel, *Harvard Dictionary of Music* (Cambridge: Harvard University Press, 1958).

13   See Pinget, "Address to the New York University Conference," *Review of Contemporary Fiction* 3, no. 2 (Summer 1983): 103.

14   See Pinget, *Autour de Mortin: Dialogues* (Paris: Minuit, 1965).

7

Alain Robbe-Grillet

In 1895 Paul Valéry, then a young man in his twenties, as much interested in the visual arts as in the functioning of the intellect, published his now-famous essay on Leonardo da Vinci. In a section dealing with the human tendency toward generalizations and preconceptions (at least in the Western world), he made an observation that is as pertinent to French fiction in the 1950s as it may have been to the paintings of his day: "Most people see reality with their minds much oftener than with their eyes. Instead of sensing space and color, they conceptualize. A cubic shape, whitish in color, rising from the ground, and peppered with reflecting glass panes immediately becomes a house; for them, it is the House. A complex thought, a merging of abstract features."[1] That and several subsequent paragraphs, along with marginal comments Valéry added in 1930, now read like the theoretical text that could have inspired the elaboration of Alain Robbe-Grillet's first published work, *Les Gommes* (1953; *The Erasers*). (His first work of fiction, *Un Régicide*, was not published until 1978, and I shall come to it later.) Had Valéry, instead of "mind" and "conceptualize," used "language" and "verbalize" his statement would have tallied with critical writings of the sixties. Robbe-Grillet's own statement, in a 1956 essay, concerning those shreds of our culture that keep clinging to objects and endowing them with a reassuring, human aspect, seems to echo Valéry's remark.[2] Whether or not there is influence is immaterial. The juxtaposition of texts separated by a sixty-year interval points to a deep-seated concern over people's relationship with the world about them.

There is a feeling that the accumulation of culture that is imposed upon succeeding generations has reached the point where one is being smothered by it and deprived of one's conceptual freedom. This is similar to what, in Marxist terminology, is seen as the effect of dominant ideology.

141

Everything one sees or hears is automatically related to something else, organized into preset patterns. That seems to happen periodically, whenever a culture becomes sclerotized. In the present instance at least, artists reacted early. Impressionism in painting, Schönberg's musical revolution, and Flaubert's *Bouvard et Pécuchet* may be taken as preliminary witnesses to a growing challenge to the world as it has been represented for too long. Because that challenge was recently extended to nearly all political and social institutions and has assumed worldwide proportions, one must take care not to exaggerate the significance of changed literary attitudes, contributory as they might have been. What matters is that they are not the gratuitous games of mandarins, the vocabulary of contemporary critics notwithstanding. They are necessary components of a broader picture. Related to Robbe-Grillet's early plea for a liberated vision are the concerns of Sarraute, Butor, and several writers of what was known as the *Tel Quel* group—more limited in the case of Nathalie Sarraute's struggle against characters and plots, broader with Michel Butor's indirect criticism of society, more radical in the activities of Philippe Sollers.

To the hurried reader *Les Gommes* resembles a mystery novel. But even a cursory perusal, aimed at discovering "who done it," uncovers some unusual features. A crime has been committed somewhere in the provinces. As the act appears to have important political ramifications, a detective is sent out from Paris to assist the obviously outclassed local police, and the customary search for a culprit is on. A slightly new twist is added as the reader, through a kind of dramatic irony, is given more vital information than the fumbling detective, and it is the local police official who, contrary to the stereotype of the genre, finally solves the mystery— too late, however, to prevent the detective from committing an ultimate blunder. The poor sleuth does not know that the victim, a man named Dupont, has not really been killed but only slightly wounded and is hiding for the sake of his own safety. His final error is to kill the man whose murder he was supposed to investigate, mistaking him for a member of the gang he thinks is responsible for the crime. Such an ironic yarn, it is true, might have come to the minds of a number of writers and spun for the mere fun of it. Yet it contains too many disturbing elements; there are too few things that come out the way one expects them to; the reader is bound to be unsettled or, at the very least, intrigued. And the manner in which pieces of the puzzle are put together point to Robbe-Grillet's denunciation of the humanistic fallacy that Valéry had unmasked.

All the major characters in the book are mythomaniacs of one sort or another, and, when it comes to solving the problem, all of them are wrong —except the local police official, who keeps his feet firmly on the ground. Ironically, when the latter discovers that the victim is not dead, the detective kills him, thus perfecting the crime that had been botched twenty-four hours previously. But at that moment also, the reason for many of the fancies elaborated by other characters disappears. All the nonsense generated by the strange interlude can be erased (*gommes* are erasers and, as Robbe-Grillet himself pointed out,[3] the title also refers to the gumma, a growth of syphilitic origin that affects one's ability to reason); the local police is in charge again; the detective is transferred to another division.

Events are presented by an omniscient narrator who writes as though he had selected a number of "takes," as a movie director might have done, and given them to us objectively (that is, without interference or explanation on his part), also adding impersonal statements on minor events or settings. In Hemingway-like fashion the narrator thus shows the reader what each of the major characters sees or imagines, as each one's subjectivity transforms reality and filters it through his mind, recalls it, or invents it to justify his actions. In addition, and independently of each character's consciousness, a number of hints have been inserted throughout the novel. Bruce Morrissette, the earliest of Robbe-Grillet's serious exegetes in this country, has carefully inventoried and analyzed the many references to the Oedipus myth and several to the tarot pack.[4] The assumption is that after all these have been put together and added up, it will be easier for the reader to get at the significance of the book. Perhaps so, and perhaps not. *Les Gommes,* as I see it, turns out to be a rather misleading work. Expert critics, such as Roland Barthes and Morrissette, disagree on basic aspects.[5] My own view, which I have developed elsewhere and in which I differ from Morrissette, is that the references to the Oedipus myth were inserted with the deliberate purpose of having the reader join the group of mythomaniacs in the text.[6] Such references constitute false clues that merely appear to fit together and point to an appropriate solution. But if one re-examines the evidence carefully, with both feet on the ground like the police commissioner, one sees that the relevance of the myth is nothing but a myth, so far as the detective-story plot is concerned. In the words of Olga Bernal, "Robbe-Grillet has retraced, step by step, the itinerary of Oedipus. At the end of that minutely reconstructed itinerary, the Oedipus myth collapses."[7] If the myth does indeed collapse, something else remains: the architecture of the fiction is based on that of Sophocles' play, *Oedipus Rex,* which acts as a vehicle for the reader's fancy. In contrast to Nathalie Sarraute's antagonistic attitude toward her readers, that constitutes a clever use of the tendency to appropriate the work in order to fit it into one's own worldview, at the same time giving one all the evidence to show that it does not work—the detective is simply no modern Oedipus.

Looking at *Les Gommes* with a cold, rational eye, one is almost obliged to call it a wildly improbable fancy. Most mystery stories do strain credibility to some extent, but this one goes much further. Unlikely events and strange coincidences abound, the most improbable being those about which the entire plot revolves. The detective's wristwatch stops unaccountably at 7:30 in the evening, exactly when the victim is first shot and wounded, and starts anew twenty-four hours later, again at 7:30, precisely when he perfects the crime. That in itself should be enough to indicate that Robbe-Grillet is not interested in realism as it is commonly conceived. He might actually be spoofing the realistic novel, which can be replete with unlikely, "unrealistic" occurrences, as Claude Simon noted in connection with Stendhal's *La Chartreuse de Parme*.[8]

There are two levels of events within *Les Gommes*, a realistic one and an imaginary one—even though both are obviously fictional. To the realistic side of the narrative belong two murders committed either by a small gang or several accomplices against two middle-class citizens in a small city; the two are killed on successive days at about the same time, early in the evening; the local police investigate. To the imaginary side belongs the narrator's hypothesis. Let us suppose that something went awry on the first day and the victim escaped with only a minor wound—it matters little, as the first crime was a routine affair that attracted no attention, acquired notoriety later only because of the repetition. Let us then imagine a set of circumstances that will enable someone to complete the first crime at the time the second one is perpetrated. An immense political plot involving a whole string of assassinations, shadowy connections between the two victims and high governmental circles is made up to provide the background for the events that fill those strange twenty-four hours separating the two crimes. The man who completes the unfinished murder, supposedly sent from Paris, does so as the narrator's agent, his wallah; he is the detective, "Wallas. / 'Special agent' " (30). He does not belong to the realistic world of the narrative. As the police commissioner correctly but inadvertently says, "The pistol shot that killed Daniel Dupont originated in another world!" (62).

I have not given what I call "the narrator's hypothesis" as an attempted decipherment of what went on in Robbe-Grillet's mind when he wrote the fiction. Rather, it constitutes a rational way of accounting for what is in the text and emphasizes its unrealistic aspects, which are present from the very beginning. Now everyone assumes in the presence of fiction that one is reading something unreal, even though there may have existed a pretense on the part of traditional writers to pass off the fiction as reality. Thus Conrad's device of having a "real" person, Marlow, give the "true" account of his search for Kurtz in *Heart of Darkness*. In *Les Gommes*, exactly the opposite takes place: there is a double affirmation of fiction as fiction, and that is something Robbe-Grillet will affirm more and more openly in his subsequent works—those, at least, that he labeled *romans*. Wallas drops a few hints in that direction as he keeps inventing stories to justify his questions or actions. Going beyond the limits of this particular book, one could view such behavior as the fictional correlative of a person's need to integrate his actions, no matter how original or strange, into a culturally acceptable pattern. On a more fundamental or primitive level it corresponds to the need to integrate the mysteries and horrors of the world into a reassuring or at least understandable myth.

In *Le Voyeur* (1955), the imaginary elements emerge perhaps a bit more clearly. As Mathias, a traveling salesman, is about to disembark on the island where he hopes to sell the watches he has in his case, several flashbacks (a term I use merely for the sake of convenience) help introduce him and prepare the reader for what is to follow. What happens is that the reader begins to construct a character that will fit the label "Mathias." He or she soon decides that this character has no distant memory, for the two stories from his childhood are each preceded by the sentence, "People had often told him this story" (9, 18). Mathias gradually takes shape. He was born on the island but remembers no one and no place. The day before coming, he has tried to learn as much as he could about topography and people, so that he could pretend to remember: "On this day, success seemed especially dependent upon imagination" (32). The same is true of the book, and the statement could be interpreted as a clue to the unrealism of *Le Voyeur*. Firing that imagination, Mathias starts telling himself about his childhood games and wanderings with other children on the island, of which he plans to remind them in turn. "People don't have that much memory; he would manufacture childhoods for their benefit, and that would lead them straight to the purchase of a watch" (32).

Getting off the steamer, he imagines his first sale, a successful one, of three watches to a woman and her two daughters; but after he has told the story to himself, he realizes that the scene has been ridiculously silent —not a sound was made, not a word exchanged. He tries again, starting this time with a resounding knock at the door. He is not very adept at dubbing the sound into his imaginary film and the story gets nowhere. His third try is off to a fumbling preamble as he makes up a connection with the woman's relatives. He gets out of it somehow, walks into the house, and opens his display case—but other images intrude, and the story dissolves into confusion (35-42).

After he has begun his door-to-door canvas he tells a couple of sado-erotic stories, vaguer in outline than his watch-selling one. He tells the first as he sits on the rocks by the water's edge waiting for the bicycle he has rented and the second as he is forced to wait while a woman gives him boring details about her children—trapped as he is by having told her he was a friend of the family. Each one is inserted in an idle period, if one considers things from the standpoint of his intended activities on the island. One hour elapses between parts 1 and 2 of *Le Voyeur*, and in part 2 Mathias's storytelling role increases. He is seen making attempts to account for the missing period of time. The reader, whose imagination has been primed by the sadoerotic material, soon suspects that Mathias is guilty of rape and murder, committed during that hour. The stories can now easily be interpreted as an effort to cover up the crime, an interpretation that helps them and the previous ones acquire psychological plausibility. In analogous fashion to the placing of Mathias's stories, the reader's sadoerotic vision inserts itself in the idle period not covered by the narrative. That interpretation of the book has been discussed at length and is only secondary in the present context, as it involves primarily the psychology of the reader.

Rhetorically speaking, there is no difference between the stories told by Mathias in the first part and those told in the second. They all correspond to the imaginary side of the narrative, as I defined it for *Les Gommes,* but more easily identifiable than in that earlier text. In both cases the narrative deals with an outsider who returns to a locale where he claims to have been before, and his actions have a superfluous quality about them. If Wallas belongs on the imaginary level of the fiction in which he appears, what that imaginary character does is clearly described in the text. What Mathias does during the missing hour, on the other hand, is left to the reader's imagination. Assuming, for one moment, that the latter's suspicions are correct, the "crime" either had been begun, perhaps even accomplished before he set foot on the island, or it would have been carried out anyway (Mathias's "victim" had a bad reputation, and when she disappeared another character says that, as most islanders see it, "It won't be much of a loss" [188]). Again, he is the narrator's agent, although he carries with him a much simpler fictional construct than Wallas did, a means to set fantasies in motion. At the end of *Le Voyeur,* he is able to leave the island as quietly as if nothing had happened. Actually nothing has, as far as verifiable textual elements are concerned.

Before the unaccounted-for hour that separates the two parts of the narrative, two of the stories he tells and many of the objects that attract his attention seem to presage the crime the reader thinks he will commit. While some critics have been inclined, in traditional fashion, to view such objects as symbols, Bruce Morrissette has more accurately referred to them as objective correlatives of the character's mental states. Perhaps a step further is indicated, for to the objects in *Le Voyeur* (cords, figure eights, chains, and the like) one must add premonitory stories and statements such as had also appeared in *Les Gommes.* Whatever their form, all such references might well be grouped under the heading of generative (rather than objective) correlatives because of their function in generating subsequent textual and extratextual fictional events. The principal domain of Robbe-Grillet's writing is not the domain of material facts but more properly that of the imagination. Wallas's victim shows up wearing tinted glasses, one lens darker than the other, because the police commissioner had previously asked about such glasses. It is not because Mathias will commit rape that the writer introduces suggestive references to such an act; rather it is as a consequence of his own fixations and of his relating them that he will either be led to his crime or be accused of it by the reader. Here, since there are no words to describe the crime on the realistic level of the narrative (or anywhere else for that matter), the only one who actually witnesses it is the reader, who thus becomes the voyeur of the title—a noun in which two letters of the word describing Mathias's activity are missing: *voy[ag]eur.*[9] What characterizes the missing hour, or the missing letters, from his viewpoint, is no longer traditional ambiguity but tension, as his growing certainty vies with the text's refusal to give direct evidence.

Robbe-Grillet used basically the same narrative technique in *Les Gommes* and *Le Voyeur.* In the latter, the narrator presents his "takes" from the mind of a single character, and outside, impersonal statements are more numerous. *La Jalousie* (1957; *Jealousy*) represents a more rigorous, exclusive use of one aspect of that technique, the transcription of interior "takes," which also characterizes his subsequent book, *Dans le labyrinthe.* The realistic level of the story has been all but eliminated, and nearly everything takes place on the imaginary level, a single character being involved. The "takes" are still offered objectively by the omniscient narrator, not distinguishing what the character sees from what he imagines or recalls; nor, in the latter case, is there any way of telling whether his memory is accurate or not, whether he is willfully or accidentally distorting things. In fact, the title suggests that some distortion is involved, for the secondary meaning of *jalousie* is "Venetian blinds," which do impede a person's vision—just as syphilitic gumma, in *Les Gommes,* impaired Wallas's judgment.

If the main character no longer can be considered a complete outsider from the point of view of the realistic part of the story (he is a Frenchman, perhaps living in the French West Indies, but localization is no more specific than in the earlier works), he remains one from the psychological standpoint. He is nameless, although we soon understand that he is the husband of A . . ., he gives little direct evidence of speaking or being spoken to, and whatever goes on between his wife and their neighbor, Franck, he cannot fathom its nature—whether there is sexual involvement, friendship, or casual relationship. All he can do is tell or invent the story of what may have happened on several recent occasions, when Franck came for dinner, when he was invited for lunch but did not show up, when he drove A . . . to the neighboring town to do some shopping, or when the husband just sat watching A . . . or gazing at his plantation.

As everything one reads has been "taped," so to speak, from the husband's mind, questions as to precisely which incidents are real, imagined, or distorted, or as to how many times Franck actually came to dinner, are somewhat irrelevant. There may be some value in attaching stylistic significance to the adverb *maintenant* (now) that begins five of the book's nine unnumbered sections and appears elsewhere within the text and in seeing it as a signal for a factual "take." It may well be that the counting of banana trees is factual, representing a form of therapy, a means to rid the husband's mind of obsessive jealousy. It is quite likely that the flaming crash of Franck's car into a tree is imaginary. But the reader is not asked to sit in judgment on the husband's truthfulness. The thing that really matters is that the reader is made to participate in the husband's own story, exactly as it is, with all its subjective deformation. One is not given an analysis of jealousy; one is not even told that the husband is jealous. One must create that feeling out of the raw materials of sense perception and mental images and experience it as it arises. There is tension between a seemingly dislocated text and the reader's effort to provide it with unity. The strength of such tension, hence the intensity of feeling, will then depend upon his or her sensitivity and imagination. It is even quite conceivable that some readers may stop short of jealousy, ascribing the images conjured up by the husband to excessive concern. In a way, each reader, through this and much other fiction, analyzes himself. As Gérard Genette observed, "All we see is a finicky, homely man, a fastidious observer."[10] The reader does the rest. In that light, the statement attributed to Franck, as he and A . . . play at changing the plot of a novel set in Africa that they are reading, seems ironic. "Things are what they are: one cannot change reality one bit" (83). For the husband, reality is incomprehensible; as for readers, they each imagine their own.

The liminary statement of *Dans le labyrinthe* (1959) openly warns the reader: "*The following narrative is a fiction.*" This might be interpreted as being no more than the usual disclaimer of intentional similarities, as the story is told against the background of military defeat and foreign occupation of an unnamed city. More likely, it affirms the preponderance of the imaginary level of the fiction, as I have defined it earlier. As in *La Jalousie*, the takes are exclusively from the mind of a single character. This time, however, narrator and main character are fused into one, and for the first time since the then-unpublished *Un Régicide* the narrator says "I"—although not often. His identity is not revealed; many have assumed he is a doctor, although he himself implies that he is not "a real doctor" (212). Very little belongs to the realistic level of the fiction: a room with its dusty furniture and drapes, a couple of objects on a dresser and a table, and an engraving on the wall. The narrator appears to be in the room, perhaps ill, or simply resting; perhaps he is even dying. One of the objects he sees is in the shape of a cross. In conjunction with the book's title, and remembering that some labyrinths were shaped like a cross (the allusion being to the inscrutable nature of the divinity), it suggests the idea that Robbe-Grillet is enjoying his role as inscrutable "author." Be that as it may, another object, a box on the dresser, and the engraving labeled *La Défaite de Reichenfels* are the generative correlatives that set the narrative in motion. Reichenfels, to the French reader, can only be a fuzzy reference; it is the name of an Austrian city that strikes no historical chord, but it is close enough to Reichshoffen, the site of an 1870 defeat, famous on account of a brilliant but useless French cavalry charge—the consequence of which was the loss of Alsace. The effect of such vagueness is to dehistoricize the text.

Rayner Heppenstall has suggested that of all the works of Raymond Roussel, *La Vue* was probably the most influential where Robbe-Grillet was concerned.[11] Indeed, the original title for *Le Voyeur* had been "La Vue," and as far as his fifth fictional work goes, the creative analogy between the miniature photograph in Roussel's pen (or the label on the bottle in *La Source*) and the Reichenfels engraving is hard to dismiss. That engraving also functions as a metaphor of the text in which it appears. It represents neither a battle scene nor the remnants of an army fleeing in defeat but shows the interior of a café, crowded with customers —bourgeois, workingmen, a young boy, and three soldiers. For the picture's caption to make sense, one must imagine events that are not depicted and create relationships linking them to the café scene. That is apparently what the narrator does or attempts to do in mentally isolating the box wrapped in brown paper and imagining a story to explain its presence in the room, using characters from the engraving, mainly a soldier and the boy (who holds a box similar to the one in the room), and assuming the contemporary reality of the defeat implied by the caption. This idea, the source of the story narrated in *Dans le labyrinthe*, is after all basic to the very concept of fiction or myth. It is an attempt to explain the existence or appearance of a phenomenon that the mind, at that moment, cannot rationally comprehend. Thus myths are born in early cultures to account for the sun's daily rising in the east, stories are told to children to explain how the leopard acquired its spots, and tales are elaborated to convince people that they must fight a war.

In this book, the reader is made to witness a mode of the creative process itself (which it would be better to call the productive process), of which the title also gives a representation. The writer is pictured as a man caught in the maze of a labyrinth and stubbornly attempting to find his way out. He tries one corridor, or one sentence, sees that it leads nowhere, discards it, tries another, and yet another, believes himself to be on the right path, then takes a wrong turn, is stuck again, experiments with several possibilities, stops to reflect every now and then, again finds himself making apparent progress for a while, runs smack into another dead end, and so on. Robbe-Grillet is not the first to have linked the concept of the labyrinth with a book, and it may well be that he was intrigued by one of Jorge Luis Borges's short stories, "El Jardín de Senderos que se bifurcan" (1941). In that story, however, Ts'ui Pên has written a book that is a labyrinth; that is, he has set forth and explored all the possibilities that could come out of a given situation. Obviously, Marguerite Duras, for instance, chose to have the narrator of *Le Marin de Gibraltar* abandon his mistress and follow Anna. Claude Simon chose to let the captain be killed in *La Route des Flandres*. Both must then abide by their choice, which determines what follows, but Ts'ui Pên refused to choose. He imagined that a man could be killed in battle and also come out of it alive, simultaneously, and his narrative would examine both outcomes. Naturally, subsequent actions were pregnant with a variety of consequences, all of which needed to be explored. The ramifications are infinite. The possibility of such a book's being in existence dazzles the mind. A fiction to end all fiction, it might be thought of in terms of an impossible ideal or of a temptation to be desperately resisted. In Borges's story, the labyrinth was meant for the reader; in Robbe-Grillet's fiction it is something from which the narrator must escape in order to make the work possible.

At the outset of *Dans le labyrinthe*, he tries several weather settings: "Outside it is raining . . . outside it is cold, the wind blows through black, leafless branches; the wind blows through the leaves. . . . Outside the sun is shining" (9). None of them seems adequate, and he muses a moment, letting his gaze wander over the furniture in the room, particularly over the dust that covers much of it (or the dust that he imagines) and the imprints left by objects that have been displaced. He is perhaps struck by the analogy between dust and snow, and he essays another setting: "Outside it is snowing" (11). That seems better, the story is off on the right track, generated by a speck of dust. Still, he is unsure of himself and allows the imaginary narrative to dissolve into the realistic fiction of the room once more. During this pause he realizes somehow that his narrative requires more snow than the beginning flurries he had envisioned: "Outside it is snowing. Outside it has been snowing, it was snowing, outside it is snowing. Thick flakes are coming down slowly, in a steady, uninterrupted fall" (14). Gradually, the pieces fit into place: the soldier waits in the snow, the package under his arm; the picture comes to life, and the boy talks to the soldier; they both walk in the snow-covered streets, all seemingly identical, seeking their way in a city that resembles a labyrinth; the soldier walks alone, he knows he is supposed to deliver the box to someone, somewhere.

As the story takes shape in the narrator's mind, it is not always apparent to the reader which sequence replaces a previously discarded one, which should be inserted earier in the series than where it appears, and which brings the narrative closer to its goal, that is, the arrival of the box in the narrator's room, thus closing the circle. Occasionally the writer is caught in a tighter maze and a number of false starts are punctuated by "No" (e.g., 96-97), but in most cases the reader is on his own and must use his imagination. Eventually, the soldier is wounded by machine-gun bullets fired by enemy patrols entering the city and is brought into a nearby building, where the narrator, unaccountably, gives some assistance. The soldier dies of his wounds, and the box is entrusted to the narrator, along with a bayonet that belonged to someone else. The narrator, perhaps, will see to having its contents delivered to the appropriate person: letters, an old watch with a chain, a ring, and another bayonet— that is, if one assumes that those objects are part of the realistic rather than the imaginary fiction, something readers must decide for themselves if they think it matters. Wherever it belongs, this is the third book in which a watch appears in a significant context, an interesting objective correlative to Robbe-Grillet's manipulation of chronology. (The watch comes with a chain, suggesting perhaps the way one's mind has been enslaved by clock time.) The book ends, in a manner reminiscent of Beckett's *Molloy*, with a denial of the fiction that has been elaborated, a reprise of a statement discarded on the first page: "Outside it is raining. Outside people are walking in the rain, heads bowed" (219).

One begins to sense, in *Dans le labyrinthe*, a slight shift of emphasis in Robbe-Grillet's fiction. With the generative correlatives more openly displayed, the focus is now increasingly set on the productive or generative process and consequently on the functioning of language. From now on I no longer believe that metaphors and myths will be dismissed or used negatively. Instead of criticizing them for their failure to reveal any depth or truth concerning "human nature," Robbe-Grillet or his texts will present them for what they are—surface elements that play a part in our culture. It may be that the unexpected and misdirected critical success of *Dans le labyrinthe*,[12] the ease with which it was appropriated by middle-class culture, the metaphysical interpretations it allowed, all convinced him that a change was in order, hence accelerating the evolution. If readers would not realize that they were injecting their own fantasies into the fiction, as they were somewhat ironically invited to do, that meant that the text was not functioning properly. From implications pointing to a sclerotized culture, which seemed to preoccupy Robbe-Grillet at the time of *Les Gommes*, it is a short step to being concerned over the social and political consequences of such sclerosis of mind and imagination. It is of course hard to even dissociate the one from the other, and I shall certainly draw no conclusions with respect to Robbe-Grillet's own political awareness. For those interested, he himself has commented on his family's and his own political attitudes in *Le Miroir qui revient;* I shall, however, concern myself only with some of the textual features of that book at the close of this chapter.

Two liminary statements, on successive pages, confront the reader of

La Maison de rendez-vous (1965). The first is much like the conventional disclaimer, denying any similarity between the fiction and actual life in Hong Kong. It corresponds to the realistic level. The second, claiming for the "author" a lifelong acquaintance with Hong Kong, affirms authenticity and suggests that skeptical readers might take another look, for things change fast in such climates. Ironically, the affirmation of authenticity corresponds to the imaginary (which might now be called mythical) level, the same on which the statement "Everyone knows Hong Kong" (13, 141) is made. Indeed, everyone today has "seen" Hong Kong and many other faraway places as well by means of photographs, films, TV news items, essays, and reporting. What they have seen, of course, is a distorted representation, a series of myths, and that distortion is conveyed by the interplay of the liminary statements. Even more than in *Dans le labyrinthe* the imaginary level predominates. The other level is glimpsed only through a few scattered references, the most extensive of which describes a visitor at the bed of a sick person, a Frenchwoman born in Belleville (traditionally a working-class section of Paris) who has never traveled to the Orient, but to whom stories about Hong Kong have been told—as they have been to most readers. While in the preceding work it was possible to establish a plausible link from one level of the fiction to the other, this is much more difficult here, and I doubt that it would be rewarding.

Again, there is a first-person narrator or there might possibly be three of them. The basic narrator, the one who says "I," is the visitor at the sickbed, and it is also he who, at first, seems to be telling the story that centers in the high-class brothel run by Lady Ava (or Bergman) in Hong Kong and the incidents that occurred during one (or several) parties followed by peculiar theatrical performances, which involve drug smuggling, prostitution, and shady political intrigue—all things one likes to contemplate and enjoy, provided they take place at a considerable remove from one's own life. Also at the party, which is part of the imaginary aspect of the fiction and as such not subject to the laws of contradiction and which might or might not have taken place in Hong Kong, there is a fat man who has lived in the British Crown Colony and talks about it a great deal. He is at one point called "the narrator" (106) and at another the person I have designated as the basic narrator implies, in an aside, that he is merely transcribing the narration. "The fat man with a ruddy complexion expatiates with self-indulgent precision on excesses committed under those circumstances, then he continues his tale" (168). He is apparently the "author" mentioned in the second liminary statement and also the one who has been telling stories to the sick woman.

Now things become a bit more complicated: the main character of the imaginary fiction could well be a man named Johnson (or is it Jonstone?), who is either Sir Ralph, known as "the American," or the American, known as "Sir Ralph." He has become infatuated with a girl named Loren, or Loraine, who is either a prostitute or the fiancée of one Marchat, or Marchand, whom she may or may not have abandoned in favor of Johnson, or Jonstone. He is about to leave for Macao and wants to take Loren with him, but she will consent only in exchange for a large sum of money, which he must put up before dawn, according to one version of the events, and the basic narrator appears to be describing his frantic efforts to do so. Soon after leaving Lady Ava's party he is stopped by the police because his behavior looks suspicious. Upon being asked to account for his actions that evening he explains, "I arrived at the Blue Villa by taxi at about ten after nine"—the identical words the basic narrator had used seventy-odd pages earlier (96, 23), and he repeats, verbatim, over half a page of that previous account, followed by "etc." Bruce Morrissette had, before *La Maison de rendez-vous* was written, brought up, in connection with *Les Gommes*, the ancient myth of the uroboros, the dragon or serpent that bites its own tail—and this suggests the ever-present theme of the circle. One is now confronted with a narrative that curls upon itself, bites its own tail, and even begins to swallow it. But who is the narrator? Who speaks? That question reverberates throughout much of contemporary fiction.

After being questioned by police, Johnson or the narrator takes the ferry to Kowloon, stops at his hotel, goes to visit someone else, takes the ferry back to Hong Kong, grabs a taxi and arrives at Lady Ava's Blue Villa at 9:10, just in time for the party he had already left some time ago. If we had previously witnessed the birth of fiction, we are now treated to the spectacle of fiction on the rampage. Actually, what takes place in this text is not so far removed from the uncensored workings of the inner mind and the peculiar logic of dreams. If Freud and Jacques Lacan are right, that is also the logic of language. The narrative of *La Maison de rendez-vous* is an avatar of surrealist texts—not automatic writing, but what I might call subconscious fiction, skillfully reorganized.[13] One comes ever closer to the concept of fiction held by those writers who, in the sixties and early seventies, flocked to the review *Tel Quel.* As Philippe Sollers had written in a 1962 essay on Robbe-Grillet, some time before *La Maison de rendez-vous* was published: "Only through composition does one avoid the absurd banality of description."[14] Representation of "reality" gives way before composition in language.

The Blue Villa is not the exclusive center of the fiction. It is the *maison de rendez-vous* of the title, a euphemism for brothel, but there is also a *maison du rendez-vous* (69), the shift from partitive to definite article restoring the phrase's literal meaning, "the house where the meeting takes place." It is the house where Edouard Manneret lives—a name close enough to that of Edouard Manet to make one take note. Perhaps the oblique reference is intended as homage to the painter's style. A general resemblance of the scene on Lady Ava's amateur stage that shows Manneret lying dead on the floor to Manet's *Le Torero mort* lends some justification to the idea. (Robbe-Grillet has told me that it was Manet's portrait of Mallarmé that he had in mind, rather than *Le Torero mort*. It might thus have generated some of the scenes in the *maison du rendez-vous* instead of those of Lady Ava's stage. He further pointed out that in using the name "Manneret," in which the second syllable would normally be elided when spoken, he also thought of the surrealist photographer Man Ray.) In general, however, allusions to paintings are few and subdued; they become more obvious in *Topologie d'une cité fantôme*. Photographic and sculptural correspondences are numerous, following a trend already begun with *Les Gommes* and *Le Voyeur*. Descriptions and actions in Robbe-Grillet's imaginary fiction often dissolve into or emerge from other representations. A magazine picked up by a street cleaner bears pictures of Lady Ava's party that come alive in the same manner the Reichenfels engraving did in *Dans le labyrinthe;* sculptures on the grounds of the Blue Villa represent scenes that take place at the party and elsewhere. Such scenes are apt to merge either with the garden sculptures or with porcelain likenesses found in a showcase in Lady Ava's salon or even with baroque sculptures in the Tiger Balm Garden of Hong Kong. Thanks to the stage in the Blue Villa, theatrical references are plentiful; some scenes are so depicted as to make it difficult to determine at once whether they take place on the stage, in a store window, or as part of the imaginary narrative. Clearly, Robbe-Grillet planned things that way, in order to lay stress on the predominant role of imagination and myth—both within the text and in life.

In spite of the shift in emphasis to which I have called attention, similarities with earlier works are numerous. The mystery plot involving the murder of Manneret (he is killed four separate times in at least three different fashions—strangled by a dog, shot by Johnson, stabbed by a detective, and assassinated by communists) recalls *Les Gommes*. Marchat is a name that comes out of that same novel. He had fled the city, fearing for his life, and four books and many thousands of miles later he meets with death in Hong Kong. He should have remembered the tale of the appointment in Samara and stayed put. There are several "frozen" scenes and a silent one like those in *Le Voyeur*. The sadoeroticism already present in that earlier book is carried much further; it is an aspect of Robbe-Grillet's work I find unappealing, but it is asserted more and more in subsequent volumes. In addition to many sexually oriented images or descriptions in *La Maison de rendez-vous*, it culminates in the story of the young Japanese prostitute Kito, who is both a new recruit at Lady Ava's brothel and one who must have been there a long time (if one insists upon chronological reality). She stands as a guinea pig for the strange experiments of Manneret and others, during one of which she dies or is killed, ending up with her flesh served to amateurs of exotic sensations in one of the floating restaurants in Aberdeen—all of that being somehow congruent with what the middle-class imagination sees behind the word *Orient.* A small alarm clock, heir to the watches that were important in three other narratives, plays a part in one of the murders of Manneret. A couple of times, a scene is interrupted with the exclamation, "*Mais non!*" (143, 177), similar to the interruptions of *Dans le labyrinthe* (and also to the more explicit ones of Beckett's *Malone meurt*). During one of his attempts to raise money, Johnson is mistaken for a doctor, as the narrator of the preceding book had been by readers. To the ironic statement of *La Jalousie,* "Things are what they are," Robbe-Grillet now provides the necessary complement: "Things are never definitively straightened out" (209). He joins the many other contemporary writers who keep affirming that the real is less important than the quasi-mythical order we impose upon it, which we commonly call reality; implicitly, all of us have the power to change that order.

In *La Maison de rendez-vous,* above the apartment of the woman from Belleville, there lived a man, perhaps a madman, who was called King Boris (the name first showed up in *Un Régicide*) and whose metal-studded cane could be heard through the ceiling. Those two people are the only remnants of the realistic side of the story. Toward the end of *Projet pour une révolution à New York* (1970), someone I shall call the narrator-interrogator asks concerning a rapping noise coming from above, "You are not really going to suggest that it is King Boris?"—thereby humorously and completely eradicating the realistic element. In *La Maison,* there is unresolved hesitation as to the identity of the narrator; in *Projet,* there is hardly any doubt as to his nonexistence. If characters were ambiguous then, it has now become irrelevant to discuss them as such. Everything is being carried one step further, although ingredients and technique are very similar to those used in *La Maison.*

Robbe-Grillet, on the surface, does not seem to have given up the narration. It would be possible to relate the story of *Projet*—actually one could relate several—even though that might involve a number of contradictions or implausibilities, but it would not reveal too much about the book. Narration is significant only because of Robbe-Grillet's concern with myths. Like the characters in *Les Gommes,* most people are mythomaniacs of one sort or another. They more or less unconsciously accept the myths of their society, of their class, the kind that Roland Barthes examined in *Mythologies,*[15] those that constitute the stuff of our daily lives. While in his earlier fiction Robbe-Grillet had seemed more intent on showing the workings of myth, the evolution I mentioned previously is now complete, and in *Projet pour une révolution à New York* he is simply working (or playing) with myths. As in the case of Hong Kong, everyone knows New York, especially those who have never been there, through a series of stereotyped myths transmitted by means of consumer books and consumer movies. Robbe-Grillet uses them in a similar manner, adding some American myths to those accepted by outsiders, especially as they imposed themselves on the minds of the middle class after the riots of the sixties in Watts, Detroit, and Newark. Those he has also supplemented with his own obsessions, and the previously mentioned sadoeroticism is with us again. A number of readers may well share those obsessions; while themes of such nature do blend remarkably well with other ingredients of the fiction, I still find them bothersome. In any case, the book need not be reduced to a display of sadistic acts; they are part of the functioning of the text, and their links with reality are tenuous at best.

As in *L'Inquisitoire* by Robert Pinget, what I have called the narrator-interrogator has a purely grammatical function; its operation is even more problematic than in Pinget's book. Early in *Projet* there appears to be a first-person narrative. A narrator is describing how he leaves his house, pausing at the door to look back, contemplating the imitation wood-grain on the door, and beginning to imagine things. The process is a familiar one for the reader who is acquainted with the previous books. Various narratives follow. Eventually, the original narrator walks along the street, then down a subway entrance, and returns. Later, the narrator is referred to in the third person; then a narrative involving a girl called JR (initials equally amusing to American TV viewers and to readers of William Gaddis) begins in the third person and switches to the first. In this instance the "I" is naturally feminine (the French rule for the agreement of past participles has some usefulness), but it suddenly becomes masculine again without any apparent change of character or locale. Finally, toward the end of the book, after many narrative shifts, the narrator is "identified" as one N. G. Brown, whom the reader remembers from his description as having been seen, on page 11, *by* the narrator as he looked at or through the door.

If the reader now thinks he can straighten that one out with a certain amount of careful rereading, he is in for another jolt. On the last page of the book, a character known as M, who was first shown as a hoodlum, then as the murderer who has been terrifying subway riders, and is now called "M the vampire," removes his rubber mask and is recognized as the narrator—whoever that is. In the meantime, some characters have been interrogating others, and soon enough an interrogative voice arises that challenges the text itself. Since the characters are no more amenable to positive identification than the narrator, it seems practical to refer to a narrator-interrogator as subject of the story, identifiable with whatever character each narrative segment deals with and serving to weld the text together.

Just as a magazine cover in *La Maison de rendez-vous* dissolved into a scene at Lady Ava's house, here the lurid paperback cover of a mystery novel, lighted in such a fashion as to deceive a man who is peeping through the keyhole, comes to life in the house behind the door. There are a number of such books lying around in the house that is central to the story. There is also a woman named Laura (there may even be three of them) who is perhaps sequestered there. The assumption the narrator-interrogator makes about the way she reads those novels appears like a clue to the arrangement of narratives in the book, a metaphor of its fictional architecture: "Laura read all those books at the same time, thus mingling, as she moved from room to room, the mystery adventures so meticulously calculated by the authors, therefore constantly modifying the composition of each volume, furthermore leaping a hundred times a day from one book to another, not fearing to go over the same passage several times, even though it be lacking in any apparent interest, while completely neglecting the essential chapter, the one containing the crux of an investigation and thus giving its meaning to the whole of the plot" (85). It is "the labyrinth of her diseased mind" that organizes the fiction of which she is a part—and this seems like an echo of the gumma and Venetian blinds of earlier books. It could also symbolize the diseased state of a class in society that is tortured by its own fears.

At a subversive underground meeting—which actually is held under-ground—it is explained that the color red provides the solution to the antagonism between black and white. The three main variations on the theme are rape, fire, and murder. Later, however, the narrator-inter-rogator explains that these are "metaphorical acts" and, anyway, a revolution thus brought about through selective violence will be far less costly in human lives than the standard indiscriminate variety. The quoted phrase, followed by such a preposterous but amusing argument, again emphasizes that we are dealing with fantasies and myth rather than with reality. Abundant contradictions in the text confirm this. Typical is the one involving JR, who is presented as "a gorgeous white girl, endowed with abundant red hair that was most effective in bedroom scenes" (57), and who proclaims, when the narrator-interrogator asks her if she is Jewish, "No, not at all; I am a black woman from Puerto Rico" (103). Robbe-Grillet is obviously enjoying himself.

At this point of his fictional production, he would appear to be on course—the one he was more or less consciously aiming for. The narra-tive of *Topologie d'une cité fantôme* (1976; *Topology of a Phantom City*) has no link to commonplace reality. It is once again ruled by fantasy and obsessions embodied in language. Divided into five "spaces" rather than "chapters" (the latter suggesting linear development, the former the somewhat Brownian movements of the imagination), the text is framed by an *Incipit* and a *Coda*. Its first section is entitled "Cellule génératrice," which provides a pun on the two meanings of the word *cell,* one referring to a biological cell, the other to a prison cell. The first proposes narrative development as being that of a living textual organism; the second alludes to one of the fantasies that inform the text: barely marriageable young women being held captive and subjected to sexual abuse. The sadoerotic aspect of the text, introduced in *Le Voyeur,* repressed in *La Jalousie* and *Dans le labyrinthe,* reaffirmed in *La Maison de rendez-vous* and *Projet,* can now be recognized as a permanent feature of Robbe-Grillet's work. (His films have been instrumental in this, but they are beyond the scope of my analysis.) To those who object to pornography because of its effect on readers' or viewers' minds, he has said, "We should never forget that Hitler and Stalin were above all virtuous," which may or may not be true, and virtue was "the justification of their massacres"; on the other hand, when the Marquis de Sade was called upon to sit on the bench of a revolutionary court, "he displayed so much leniency that he soon had to be removed."[16] The argument resembles the one offered in *Projet* in defense of "selective violence," which I quoted above, and cannot, in my opinion, be taken too seriously.

Leaving that aside, the most winning characteristic of *Topologie d'une cité fantôme* is its playfulness, independently of the matters that are being played with. As in *Projet,* the narrator has been sundered. He is the one who "stands just in front and whose thick, curly, black hair blurs the view" (36, obviously Robbe-Grillet himself!); he or rather she is also the female narrator in the fourth "space." Once more, the impression is that the text itself speaks—but silently, like the imaginary section of *Le Voyeur* mentioned above. There is indeed no conversation or monologue in this book; only a number of sounds are reported, among which the most notable are the splash of an object falling in the water (possibly an ironic echo of Albert Camus's *La Chute*), a woman's strident scream of pain, the screeching noise of an engraving stylet, and the peculiar insect-like, intermittent buzzing issuing from the mouth of a painter during the intermission of a play that serves as a *mise-en-abyme* of the book itself. In contrast to *Les Gommes,* where the well-known Oedipus myth, while undermined, was recognizably (and hazily) present, myths are here incongruous, unfamiliar, and distorted. The setting is clearly Mediterranean, the "ruined" temple that is being "built" in the first "space" (one is reminded of the sculptures of Anne and Patrick Poirier) is that of Vanadis, another name for Freya, the Scandinavian goddess of love and beauty and whose brother Frey is god of fertility. Here, however, Vanadis has a male "double" called David—an unlikely name for a Scandinavian deity. Vanadis is also the name of a convalescent young woman who lies recumbent, somewhere, sometime, and to whom a guidebook is being read. That book contains the description of a volcanic eruption during which the city of Vanadium (the phantom city of the title) was destroyed.

The city was also sacked and its population (exclusively female) exterminated at another time. There was also a destructive explosion of unspecified nature, but we are not told when this occurred. At the time of the narration, or one of them, a Mrs. Hamilton strolls about with her twin children, David and Diana, who once was Divina, after having been Vanadis, and who will become Deana and perhaps Vanessa. Deana is a name not to be confused with Danaë, and Robbe-Grillet adds in characteristic whimsical fashion that some writers claim Danaë is really the name of the ship that carried invaders to Vanadium; he does not add, but many French readers surely remember, that *"La Danaë"* is the title of a sea shanty about a frigate that sank during its maiden voyage, the lone survivor then encountering a beautiful, tearful woman on the beach, and so forth.

And so, thanks to the strolling woman, one meets David Hamilton, and this brings up something new in the works of Robbe-Grillet. The text of *Topologie* might be viewed as a collage of several separate texts published earlier with reproductions of pictorial works by several artists— the photographer David Hamilton and the painters Paul Delvaux, René Magritte, and Robert Rauschenberg. This process has been the object of an analysis by Bruce Morrissette, and I need not repeat the details here.[17] Actually, it is related to what Michel Butor had been doing previously, in a more elaborate fashion, involving the physical dimensions and aspects of the printed page; he began this practice when he published *Illustrations* in 1964 and has continued since.

Such a shattering of the text's unity, in which other fictional texts also assist (there are references to the Blue Villa of *La Maison de rendez-vous*, now located in Shanghai, the African novel of *La Jalousie*, the coffeepot from a short story in *Instantanés*, the bicycle used by Mathias in *Le Voyeur*), coincides with the growing interest in "fragments" shown by critics and theoreticians (e.g., Roland Barthes's *Fragments d'un discours amoureux* published a year later, in 1977). I submitted earlier that it would be possible, although not especially useful, to summarize the story line of *Projet;* that sort of enterprise has now become virtually impossible. After *Dans le labyrinthe* in particular, Robbe-Grillet's narratives have become increasingly fragmented and, just as painters have emphasized their work as an arrangement of shapes and colors, they stress the playful, pleasing arrangement of words and the images they conjure.

Fragmentation is also a prominent feature of the next fiction, *Souvenirs du triangle d'or* (1978), which reads, on the textual level (the only one that really matters), like a sequel. The jumbled stories in the two fictions, when they can be identified as such, have practically nothing in common beyond the mention of an earlier catastrophe that has left scars— "an ancient city after the downpour of searing ashes, a village square the day after the bombing, a seaside resort half destroyed by equinoctial hurricanes" (15). The setting is an imaginary South American country that has been at war with Uruguay, a war that has resulted in much destruction. Textually, the final section of the fifth space of *Topologie* is identical with the first section of *La Belle captive* (1975), where Robbe-Grillet's text accompanied reproductions of paintings by Magritte; early in *Souvenirs* one encounters the text of the second section from *La Belle captive* (a truly emblematic title). Later, one runs into the text of *Temple aux miroirs* (1977), which accompanied photographs by Irina Ionesco, and the preface to the Beaubourg catalog for the Jasper Johns exhibition of 1978. In other words, *Souvenirs du triangle d'or* is a sequel articulated on the text of *La Belle captive*, in which Irina Ionesco and Jasper Johns take over from Hamilton, Delvaux, and Rauschenberg as textual generators. Proper names also provide a connection between the two books: the goddess Vanadis and Vanessa as a butterfly genus; the person Vanessa, David's "false twin" in the first book, a medical student and part-time narrator in the second. Obviously, the bearers of such names play very different parts. As in *La Maison de rendez-vous* there is a space about which the text constantly revolves—the parody of a brothel where the people involved in supplying prostitutes are members of the "Triangle d'or" gang.

American readers might think of Pittsburgh's Golden Triangle when seeing the title, or possibly the Burma/Laos/Thailand drug route. Actually, the reference is to the female pubes ("The perfect triangle of a silky fleece as pale as straw" [60] or "The auburn tuft of the sacred triangle" [107]) whose symbolic presence is also manifested by the frequent stress on the letter "V"—e.g., Vanessa, Violet, Franck V. Francis (a narrator whose "real" name is Francis Lever ["le v"]), "verre de Venise," and so forth. Thus we return to the sadoerotic theme that appears so difficult to put aside. Both thematically and textually Robbe-Grillet may have felt that he had reached a dead end, for after the shattering of all fictional components and the explosion of pornography, what next? He was perhaps stung by those who complained about the disappearance of the narrative line in *Topologie*, and at the end of *Souvenirs* he has the interrogator demand that the narrator provide a "quick chronological summary" of what happened. He actually does so, in a dozen pages, but it is hardly satisfactory and the book ends with two questions: "What have I said? What have I done?" It is probably more than just a coincidence that he chose this moment to publish his first novel, *Un Régicide* (1978).

In his preface, Robbe-Grillet asserts that aside from a few pages at the beginning, rewritten in 1957, the text of the book published in 1978 is just about the same as the one he completed in 1949; he made only two or three "minute" corrections per page involving "punctuation, vocabulary, or syntax." The only important modification, he continued, was to change the "hero's" name from Philippe to Boris. If the change was indeed made in 1957, it would signal the first appearance of that name in Robbe-Grillet's oeuvre. The character thus named progresses from (imaginary) regicide to ruler: he is King Boris in *La Maison de rendez-vous,* Boris Godunov in the film *L'Homme qui ment,* and as King Charles-Boris, also known as Bluebeard Boris, he is ceremoniously assassinated in *Souvenirs du triangle d'or.* Again, a circle of sorts has been drawn.

The very publication of *Un Régicide* suggests another kind of circle: at the end of the journey one returns to the beginning. It may seem somewhat premature to refer to an "end" of Robbe-Grillet's fiction in 1978, and he could still surprise us all. The fact remains that the books he has published since then mark a change in perspective. *Djinn* (1981) is an entertaining tour-de-force, written in increasingly complex grammatical and syntactical structures that could be (and has been) used as a textbook for American students of French. The title refers both to the jinni of Muhammadan tales, popularized in France by a well-known Victor Hugo poem, and to the approximate French pronunciation of the English feminine name Jean. Eroticism is more subdued than in the books of the seventies, and the humor is more obvious; other features of the narrative convey the effect of clichés or parodies of a Robbe-Grillet text. The narrative is clearly entrusted to a narrator who does not know what is going to happen next, is known as Simon Lecoeur, calls himself Boris (there is also an Uncle Boris who may be a Soviet agent), writes alternately in the first and third person and once as a woman, and ends up exactly where he started and at the same time of day.

The following works, *Le Miroir qui revient* (1984; *Ghosts in the Mirror*) and *Angélique* (1988), have been placed in a separate category by Robbe-Grillet himself. They are not *"romans"* but *"romanesques."* As I see it, the *romans* had a fictional architecture built out of nonfictional materials; *romanesques* have a nonfictional, autobiographical (as it were) architecture filled with fictional ingredients. The initial statement of *Le Miroir,* written during the winter of 1976-77 and now appearing on page 10 of the book, surprised many. "I have never spoken of anything other than myself." There should have been no cause for surprise, provided one remembered the distinction posited by Proust between the superficial self and the true deep-seated self. Unfortunately, in addition to the childhood fears and nightmares that are discussed, a number of "personal" ingredients mentioned by Robbe-Grillet belong to the superficial self: the door of the house in Brest, which shows up in *Projet,* the German motorcycle and sidecar that arrived in the same city in 1940, which appear in *Dans le labyrinthe,* the factory where he was sent by the German occupation authorities in 1943, which is the model for the factory in *Un Régicide,* his own cranial measurements, which turn out to be those of Wallas in *Les Gommes,* the house where he lived in the French West

Indies, which is the husband's house in *La Jalousie*, and so forth. Sources
of that kind are both inevitable and irrelevant. The relationship of
Robbe-Grillet's writing to his deep, nonconscious, or unconscious self
are glimpsed, but he cannot explain them—in part because of what I
consider a misconception of the function of language. He writes in *Le
Miroir*, " 'Articulated' language . . . is structured like our clear-sighted
conscience, which is to say, according to the laws of meaning. It is thus, as
an immediate consequence, unable to account either for an exterior
world distinct from ourselves or for the interior ghosts that stir within our
body" (41). That is the representational fallacy. It is the way language
seems to function in everyday, superficial communication.

Nevertheless, Robbe-Grillet accepts Barthes's distinction between
écrivain and *écrivant*.[18] With that in mind, one can say that *romanesques*
have been, in part, written by an *écrivant* while the previously published
romans were the products of an *écrivain*'s work. I just suggested that the
autobiographical structure of *romanesques* was filled with fictional
elements. On account of their style, such elements become fused with
the autobiography, thus hardly distinguishable from it. This is perhaps
the way the mythical, enchanted folklore of Brittany (the land of his
birth) was long fused with the everyday lives of its people. The very titles
of the two books are most significant. *Le Miroir qui revient* alludes not to
any autobiographical incident but to a mythical element—one that runs
through this narrative and the next.

It is the story of Henri de Corinthe, someone who supposedly visited
Robbe-Grillet's father every now and then but whom he himself never
met. He gradually takes on reality as the writer builds him up from
variegated fragments that his imagination increasingly fleshes out. The
incident that corresponds to the title is told in the fantastic mode as
Henri de Corinthe rides his fine white horse along the Brittany coast. He
is puzzled by a strange noise, discovers it is made by a mirror in a large
wooden frame tossed by the waves not far from the shore. After a long
struggle he manages to drag the mirror to the beach and, looking into it,
sees not his own reflection but the likeness of his fiancée Marie-Ange, who
had drowned off the coast of Uruguay. Skipping a number of significant
details, I shall simply note that the narrator (sometimes it is Robbe-Grillet,
sometimes not) wonders whether he might be confusing Marie-Ange with
Angelica von Salomon, another very young, beautiful woman who had
also been quite close to Corinthe. Such, in extremely abbreviated form, is
the story of the mirror that returned from the other world—both South
America and the world of the dead. If Uruguay suggests *Souvenirs*, that
is fine, first because Angelica was mentioned several times in that book;
and Angélique, a similar name, also showed up, accompanied by a
veiled reference to an 1819 painting by Ingres entitled *Roger delivrant
Angélique*. Secondly, a Lord Corynth is also involved in that text; he has

been the victim of the "bloodthirsty, vampiric activities" of his fiancée, Marie-Ange Salomé (which is phonetically close to Salomon). In *Le Miroir*, however, her full name is given as Marie-Ange van de Reeves. Robbe-Grillet's narrators are clearly unreliable.

The name leads to *Angélique ou l'enchantement*, the subtitle again stressing the fantastic mode, which is much more developed in this book. The hesitation between Angélique and Angelica is given justification as the narrator, in spite of the title, states on the second page, "I now write Angelica's flickering name . . . Why does it still obsess me? . . . Why did you leave me. . . ?" Less than two pages later there is mention of Corinthe's heroic cavalry charge at Reichenfels in 1940—an absurdity, since the French army did not fight in Austria at that time. Nor could he have been involved in the 1870 Reichshoffen charge since he was born in 1889. We are definitely in the realm of myth. The wooded area of northeastern France where Corinthe (who is now said to be related to the German painter Lovis Corinth) supposedly meets, under strange circumstances, both Robbe-Grillet's father and one Frédéric de Boncourt (said to be a descendant of the German poet Adelbert von Chamisso) is much more akin to the forest of Brocéliande of Arthurian legend than to any "real" twentieth-century locale.

Angelica, who at one point is presented as Boncourt's niece (although their relationship may well have been less innocent), is also textually related to, if not identified with, Manrica, who shows up in the forest during the First World War. Her name is the feminine version of Manrico, who was brought up as a witch in Verdi's *Il Trovatore;* this suggests a touch of sorcery quite appropriate to the Brocéliande forest. She plays, or they play, a prominent part in *Angélique*, while Angélique herself is given less space—a space that is nevertheless quite significant, as it constitutes the final nine pages of the book. These pages had been heralded much earlier, after Robbe-Grillet stated that he saw "very little difference between my work as a novelist and that, more recent, as an autobiographer"; he then enumerated some of the "real life" ingredients that went into his fiction (which I mentioned above), ending with: "And this even includes the young girls I have loved, such as Violette in *Le Voyeur*, whose name was Angélique" (69).

The story of Angélique goes back to the time when the narrator was thirteen and she was twelve. A precocious, sexually provocative girl, she would tease him and play many far from innocent games with him— Roman soldier and Christian slave, for instance. After a particularly daring and, for him, traumatic episode, she disappeared. A few days later her body was found in a tidal pool, among the rocks and seaweed—as Angelica perhaps was found in *Souvenirs du triangle d'or*. The police decided it was an accident. After a brief description of her coffin and horse-driven hearse the book ends with a four-line paragraph in the style of *Dans le labyrinthe* (and Beckett): "As for myself, I have long since left my native house. Neither am I at Le Mesnil, I am in Greensboro, in the Carolinas. I live there alone. This is October 12, 1987. Outside, it is not snowing."

In reading most of Robbe-Grillet's fiction one becomes aware of a conflict between one's conventional reading habits (i.e., one's tendency to view the text as a representation of reality, one's prejudice in favor of linear narrative) and the actual functioning of the text, or a language where words play a more important part as signals than as conveyors of meaning. The tension one feels is between comfortable appearances one hates to give up and a disturbing reality one is reluctant to face. The clash is also between the "readable" and the "writable," to adopt Roland Barthes's terminology. Readable texts are those "caught within the Western system of closure, put together according to the aims of that system"; those that are "writable" endeavor "to make of the reader no longer a consumer but a producer of the text."[19] Faced with most of the *romans*, consumers are likely to sit back, commenting on the preposterous nature of the fiction, secretly enjoying what they think of as sexy descriptions, and perhaps reflecting on Robbe-Grillet's lack of seriousness. The producer, while agreeing that Robbe-Grillet is not afflicted with what Sartre has sarcastically called *esprit de sérieux*, will work on and with the language of the fiction, perhaps along the lines suggested by Ricardou in his essay on *Projet pour une révolution à New York*.[20]

The challenge to one's conventional reading habits is still present in the *romanesque* series but it has shifted to a different level. Not much more linear than before, the fragmented aspect of the narrative is at odds with the common notion of autobiography, which most people expect to be chronological. The frequency of essaylike sequences that are inserted into the narrative does not help; worse still, from the "consumer's" point of view, is the mixture of seemingly true or at least plausible accounts of the writer's life with stories that are clearly fictional. There are readers who must have been startled upon coming to the statement in *Le Miroir qui revient*, "The preceding passage must have been completely made up" (24), for an autobiography is supposed to be factual. The effect could be to make everything undecidable.

If the *romans* could well contribute to a change in readers' attitudes toward language, hence perhaps in their perception of reality, *romanesques* could prompt them to question the notion of literary genres, particularly the distinction between fiction and nonfiction, to examine themselves and their fantasies, wondering if they can ever perceive themselves and others without masks. In both series of texts there is a constant interplay between myth and reality, fiction and truth, but in the *romans* it strikes a more resonant intellectual chord.

NOTES

1   Paul Valéry, "Introduction à la méthode de Léonard de Vinci, "*Œuvres*, Bibliothèque de la Pléiade (Paris: Gallimard, 1957), 1: 1165.

2   Alain Robbe-Grillet, "Une Voie pour le roman futur," in *Pour un nouveau roman* (Paris: Minuit, 1963), 15-23. Henceforth all references to works by Robbe-Grillet will appear in the body of the text.

3   Jean Ricardou, ed., *Robbe-Grillet / Analyse. Théorie* (Paris: 10/18, 1976), 2: 421.

4   Bruce Morrissette, "Œdipe ou le cercle fermé: *Les Gommes*," in *Les Romans d'Alain Robbe-Grillet* (Paris: Minuit, 1963), 37-75. (A revised edition was published in translation as *The Novels of Robbe-Grillet* [Ithaca: Cornell University Press, 1975].)

5   Their disagreement actually extends beyond *Les Gommes*. See Roland Barthes's preface to the book by Morrissette.

6   See my essay "The Embattled Myths," in Frederic Will, ed., *Hereditas* (Austin: University of Texas Press, 1964), 77-94.

7   Olga Bernal, *Alain Robbe-Grillet ou le roman de l'absence* (Paris: Gallimard, 1964), 51.

8   See Jean Ricardou and Françoise van Rossum-Guyon, eds., *Nouveau Roman: hier, aujourd'hui* (Paris: 10/18, 1972), 2: 74-76.

9   Ibid., 136.

10 Gérard Genette, "Vertige fixé," in *Figures* (Paris: Seuil, 1966), 76.

11 Rayner Heppenstall, *Raymond Roussel: A Critical Study* (Berkeley: University of California Press, 1967), 25.

12 "*Dans le labyrinthe* then sold 15,000 copies the first year, and I was often much more taken aback by the praise bestowed on *Dans le labyrinthe* than by the objections to *La Jalousie*" —Robbe-Grillet in an interview with J. J. Brochier, "Robbe-Grillet: mes romans, mes films et mes ciné-romans," *Magazine littéraire*, no. 6 (April 1967): 12.

13 This formulation actually comes close to André Breton's pronouncement, "If the depths of our mind do harbor strange forces capable of increasing those at the surface, or countering them successfully, there is great profit in tapping them, tapping them first, before subsequently submitting them, if need be, to the control of our reason." In *Les Manifestes du surréalisme* (Paris: Pauvert, 1962), 23.

14 Philippe Sollers, "Sept propositions sur Alain Robbe-Grillet," in *L'Intermédiaire* (Paris: Seuil, 1963), 149.

15 Roland Barthes, *Mythologies* (Paris: Seuil, 1957).

16 Alain Robbe-Grillet, "Histoire de rats ou c'est la vertu qui mène au crime," in *Obliques*, no. 16-17 (1978): 170-71. The same arguments are repeated in *Angélique ou l'enchantement*, 195 ff.

17 Bruce Morrissette, *Intertextual Assemblage in Robbe-Grillet from "Topology" to "The Golden Triangle"* (Fredericton, New Brunswick: York Press, 1979).

18 Roland Barthes, "Ecrivains et écrivants," in *Essais critiques* (Paris: Seuil, 1964), 147-54.

19 Roland Barthes, *S/Z* (Paris: Seuil, 1970), 14, 10.

20 Jean Ricardou, "La Fiction flamboyante," in *Pour une théorie du nouveau roman* (Paris: Seuil, 1971), 211-33.

8

Claude Ollier

La Mise en scène (1958), Claude Ollier's first published fictional work, is set in the mountains of Morocco at a time when the French still ruled North Africa. This novel is remarkable on account of the stress that develops when latent aspects of the narrative begin to disturb the apparently plausible plot.[1] It does not take long for a reader to realize that two distinct narratives are involved. On the one hand there is the story of Lassalle's mission to the remote North African region of Imlil on behalf of a mining company, the purpose of which is to survey the most practical road to a mountain mine; on the other there is the account of the mysterious murder of a young native woman of the same area and the ensuing search for a culprit. The first narrative deals with a problem that will be resolved; the mystery underlying the second will not be—on the surface, at least.

There is danger ahead: with two independent narratives at work, the fiction is liable to fall apart, aesthetically speaking. Ollier copes with this, as other twentieth-century writers have, by devising a formal architecture, an arbitrary scheme, such as the twenty-four hours of a day (Joyce, Butor, Simon, et al.), that holds everything together. In *La Mise en scène* the architecture is based on the numbers three and seven. The book is divided into three parts; the first part comprises seven chapters, the second twenty-one (three times seven), and the third seven. In the first part the narrative covers the three days that it takes to reach Imlil from Assameur, the last outpost of "civilization"; there are nine (three times three) days in the second, while Lassalle looks for and discovers an access road to the mine, and three days again in the third as he returns to Assameur. More often than not, characters are presented in groups of three—when one is removed from the scene, another is likely to show up. On the return trip from Imlil, in part 3, when the three travelers cross a wadi in a storm, seven people assist them.

There are three representatives of the dominant class: the engineer Lassalle, Captain Weiss, and Lieutenant Waton—all three agents of the colonizing power (although published in 1958 the novel is set in the period preceding Morocco's gaining independence in 1956). Three languages are used in the area: French, Arabic, and Berber, which is referred to as "the dialect." The tribe living in the region near the mine is divided into three groups: the Baha, Ouguenoun, and Imlil *aïts* (families or clans), and the Imlil clan comprises three douars—Asguine, Zegda, and Ifechtalen. The Imlil basin is drained by three streams and surrounded by three mountains. The harmony implied by those numbers, whose presence it is not hard to detect, corresponds to the patent narrative, the outcome of which is successful.

The latent plot causes a play to develop between narrative and text, less obvious than the book's architecture but discernible just the same. There is play at the joints of the narrative, so to speak; this reveals the attempt at concealment and gives rise to meaning.

After the harrowing night described in the first chapter, when Lassalle is beset by fears of mosquitoes, spiders, snakes, and scorpions, the story proceeds without mishap and in roughly chronological order. Lassalle is briefed by Captain Weiss; the Imlil region is a blank on official maps (a cartographic lacuna), a region where neither French nor Arabic is spoken. Since Assameur is the small town where the engineer enters in and exits from the novel, one might say that he (and the reader) is about to enter an uncharted area of text where even language is an unknown quantity. In the third chapter Lassalle has reached an intersection in Assameur's souk; he has lost sight of the sergeant who was guiding him and waits for him to retrace his steps as he will certainly do as soon as he realizes Lassalle is no longer with him. Lassalle is calm, confident, and rational—we are clearly within what I shall call the surface or patent narrative. But this stopping at an intersection, which has been shaped like a circle, suggests that we may be at a crossroad in the text, that matters are perhaps to be centered on something else.

Indeed, even though the narrative might well proceed chronologically as soon as the sergeant shows up again, there is a flashback to the moment when Captain Weiss, who had driven Lassalle to the souk and taken him to his same intersection, finds the sergeant he had arranged to meet. "The captain . . . walked through the gateway [to the souk], paced briskly up the alley that led to the intersection, went to meet the sergeant, extended his hand."[2] Those words at once reactivate a section of the narrative that had been censored: "He walked through the portico . . . came forward briskly, extended his hand, took his place in the driver's seat," etc. This refers back to the moment when Captain Weiss and Lassalle leave headquarters to go to Assameur by car. The words just quoted trigger an account of that drive. During the short trip they stop at the infirmary where a small crowd had gathered; there they see a very young woman who is suffering from knife wounds, has been brought to the infirmary on a two-day mule trip from the direction of Imlil, and will die before nightfall. The censored narrative will end when they arrive at the intersection and the sergeant appears—and his appearance coincides, in dreamlike fashion, with his reappearance in the surface narrative: "The sergeant waves his hand as he spots him [the captain], lifts his cap, mops the back of his neck, takes a few steps forward . . . the sergeant emerges from the crowd, waves his hand, walks to the center of the intersection, lifts his cap, mops the back of his neck" (30). The censored text seems to rise through a rift in the surface narrative, a gap of only a few seconds. But why the censorship? Such a question prompts another— who is the censor, in other words, who is the narrator? The question becomes the more pertinent as one notices that the surface narrative is in the third person and Lassalle himself is frequently named; in the censored text Lassalle himself is a victim of censorship, he is designated neither by his name nor by a pronoun and his presence is manifested only numerically by means of statements such as "the three men standing around the bed" or "the two men who are walking away" (29). Nevertheless, the answer to the question must be postponed until further data can be extracted from the text.

Let us then return to the core of the censored narrative, to the infirmary scene where, in a small room with black and white tile flooring (like the room where Lassalle slept in chapter 1), the young woman, named Jamila, lies on a bed:

Her nape is slightly raised by the headrest. Her hair, very black, is parted in the middle and plaited into braids that, from behind the ears, come down on the shoulders on either side of a silver-coin necklace strung with a silk cord. Her forehead is wide and quite bare, the lower part of her face is very slender, her cheeks are hollow. Her lips, which are full and well shaped, quiver with minute tremors. Her eyes, unusually distant from one another, seem set on the edge of the temples, beyond the jutting of the cheekbones. Her eyelids are shut, her eyelashes absolutely motionless. (28)

This is a crucial section of the text. A few paragraphs later, some of its elements are taken up again, with minor variations; the headrest has become a pillow, the slenderness of the lower part of her face is expressed by the word *triangular,* paleness has been added, "the braids fall on either side of the necklace down to the start of her breasts. Her lips still tremble imperceptibly, but her eyelashes are raised, and her eyes, wide open, are now directed toward the door" (29).

Picking up again the thread of the surface narrative and following it to the evening of the second leg of the trip toward Imlil, I note that, during dinner with the influential Sheikh Agouram in Tisselli, Lassalle's attention is drawn, beyond the opening of the window, to the sight of two small girls; one is seated on a wall and holds a switch in her hand, the other is at her feet, squatting on the hard-packed soil (*terre battue*, literally beaten soil), and the switch swings between their two heads. Like portions of the narrative, her face is hidden. On account of the lighting, Lassalle is struck by "the braids on the shoulders" of the second girl (53). A little later, after a puzzling conversation with Ba Iken, whom he met during the day and who since acts as a peculiar sort of mentor, the talk adding a touch of mystery to the case of the young woman at the infirmary (the sheikh, who "is aware of everything that goes on . . . even at night," absolutely denies that anything resembling what Lassalle describes has taken place), the two girls are still outside; the second one "is leaning forward, her elbows on her knees, her head in her hands; her braids, flowing on either side of her shoulders, have come down on her breasts" (54). Words and phrases like *braids, shoulders, come down on,* and *on either side* refer to the description of Jamila in the censored text and introduce a sort of tremor into the surface narrative. At the infirmary, the lips of Jamila quivered; this, since the lips are one of the organs of speech, may be said to foreshadow the tremors of the narrative. The switch is a disquieting new presence.

Let us continue along the surface narrative until after Lassalle's arrival at Imlil, at the end of his second day, the third chapter of the second part, when he figuratively takes a bearing. He pulls out a notebook in which he had decided to set down the essential aspects of his daily activities—but he sees that he has written nothing since that morning before coming down to Assameur's souk. In order for Lassalle to make up for the lacunae chronology is interrupted and the text engages in a brief flashback. A skeleton account of what has taken place finds its way into the notebook; it isn't much, but it is exactly what he intended. At this point someone (Lassalle himself? the narrator?) intervenes, "Just the same, some of the lacunae are shocking" (80). And the text proceeds to enumerate some of the things that might have been accounted for; this goes on for some time until the surface narrative gives one the impression that Lassalle has fallen asleep and we are witnessing his dream—but that of course is a realistic fallacy. At any rate, the last lacuna the text mentions, hence, from one standpoint, the most strongly repressed, is the scene at the infirmary: "The young woman's head was upright on the pillow, her nape slightly raised by the headrest, her very dark hair, parted in the middle, was plaited into braids that came down on the shoulders . . . through the half-open door, her slender, triangular face, exceedingly pale, her quivering lips, her raised eyelashes, her wide-open eyes looking toward the door" (81).

Almost immediately after this description, what must be identified as another latent narrative comes to an end in a manner similar to the way the first one did. Here its oneiric or unconscious nature is clearly pointed out in the text: "Lassalle has just opened his eyes . . . perhaps he had had them open for several moments" (82). The mention of the proper name at the outset of the paragraph has the effect of making the reader aware of the censorship exercised against Lassalle's name in the immediately preceding narrative—as it had been in the first infirmary narrative. This will happen throughout the novel, affording one with a simple means of distinguishing surface narrative from repressed text.

Just before this, however, immediately following upon the end of the censored narrative, we come upon the description of a young woman, carrying a pitcher, who seems to be standing before Lassalle at Imlil. Repetitions from earlier ones are many and rather obvious. On the other hand there are new elements such as the bracelets and the "black and gold squares" modify the tiling of the infirmary. A further difference must be noted: the articulation between the first censored text and the surface narrative was effected, at the beginning and at the end, by means of the same characters—the captain and the sergeant. Here it would appear that, aside from Lassalle, we are dealing with different characters, distinct in both time and space, one of whom is dead when the second shows up. While this assertion might have to be modified later on, the surface discourse will state, seventeen pages later, through the voice of Ba Iken, that the second young woman's name is Yamina.

The following day, along the thread of the surface narrative, after nightfall, Lassalle is having trouble falling asleep; he goes out for some fresh air, and walks along a dry riverbed, hemmed in by two rocky barriers. It so happens that Yamina is there, too, and she is caught in the beam of Lassalle's electric flashlight. "A hand appears, pinned to the rock, next an arm, a fabric with red and white stripes"; then, "A braid flows down on the left shoulder; its tip joins the silver-coin necklace. Metal bracelets slide from the wrist to the elbow . . . 'Jamila . . . she's a cousin, a relative . . .' " Finally, "The light moves down the length of the skirt, along the legs to the knees, to the ankles and to the bare toes clenched on the pebbles" (119).

The striped dress and the metal bracelets would seem to indicate that this is Yamina, not Jamila; besides, the words within quotation marks are exactly the same, aside from the proper name, as those uttered by Ba Iken concerning Yamina. I am tempted to call this a Freudian slip, linked with the unconscious, hence with the censored text. In that case, who could the narrator be if not Lassalle himself? This seems confirmed when, the next day, in the surface narrative, Lassalle commits the same slip (125-26).

Later on, in what seems to be the latent text, we encounter the description of a young woman in a different position: "The young woman has hidden her face in her hands. . . . Then she lowers her head, backs up to the wall and remains resting on the hard-packed ground, her eyes vacant, her hands joined over her braids" (131). Words and phrases remind one of the scene with the small girls at Tisselli, the evening of the second stage of the journey toward Imlil. Here, however, the word *battue* in the French text is forced out of the idiom and regains its original strength, because the context shows that the young woman is in danger of being *battue,* i.e., beaten up. It may be possible to generalize and suggest that *terre battue* perhaps refers to the Moroccan land, the "beaten" land, the land trampled over by colonizers.

Some fifty pages later, Lassalle's attention will be attracted to two girls "who were filling their pitchers at the spring" (183). The subsequent description repeats a number of terms used to picture Yamina at Lassalle's awakening, thus effecting a kind of merger of four characters—Jamila, Yamina, and the two girls.

During the next to last night Lassalle is to spend at Imlil, the oneiric nature of the latent text is stated even more clearly than before, for it starts after the following statement: "Sleep, which had been so slow in coming, finally begins to take hold" (188). The dream narrative takes up again a part of the earlier night walk but leads to a sort of cavern that is perfectly spherical. (Previously, Yamina had led Lassalle to a cave where she wanted to hide from Sheikh Agouram who was coming to Imlil.) Now, "At the center of the cave stood Jamila, slim, slender, motionless, her arms lifted, her hands joined behind the nape, her head thrust backward. She wears a multicolored dress, very short, tightly drawn at the waist by a belt made of silver coins. Her bracelets slide one by one along her forearms. Her bare toes toy with the sand" (190).

A few terms are identical with those of the first description at the infirmary but their syntactical relationship is upset; others recall the description of Yamina at Lassalle's awakening. The latent text thus stresses the analogy Jamila/Yamina, which the sound of the names might already have implied and had been brought to the reader's notice by Lassalle's slip. The meanings of the two names are also related, "beautiful" on the one hand, "blessed" or "fortunate" on the other. Jamila's position at the center of a spherical cavern (etymologically, a hollow) echoes the metaphorical role I attributed to the Assameur intersection (one should recall that it has a circular shape) as well as the appearance of the first censored text in a lacuna (etymologically, also a hollow) of the narrative, and the central position of the description of Jamila in the infirmary narrative.

The latent text now continues the dream narrative, taking up again, with some changes, the theme of Yamina's flight. At one earlier point, Lassalle had "actually" seen a man treat Yamina harshly as she arrived home. In his dream, he is able to see the inside of the house. "The shape of a knife loomed above his [the man's] head. The young woman, on her knees, has hidden her face in her hands. Her braids come down over her breasts" (191). Several words recall the description of the little girls of Tisselli; furthermore, there could be a connection between the man's knife and the girl's switch.

The dream narrative ends shortly thereafter. Lassalle will see Yamina for the last time, within the surface discourse, at the time of leaving Imlil: "Kneeling on the flagstones, her chest motionless, Yamina holds the pitcher's neck under the stream of water running out of the hollowed tree trunk. She lowers her head, her braids come down over her breast. The coin necklace slides over the dark skin of her nape. Further down, her ankles show beyond the pleats of her dress, and her bare toes lie in the cold water" (207). The sight fascinates Lassalle to such an extent that he almost falls off his mule.

In its makeup this textual fragment is related to each of the previously quoted segments: "Kneeling" (the dream, Tisselli, and Yamina at night), "pitcher" (Yamina at awakening, the little girls at Imlil), "braids" (all segments except Jamila in the cave), "come down" (all segments), "coin" (infirmary, two descriptions of Yamina, and Jamila in the cave), "breast" (infirmary), "bare toes" (Yamina at night, Jamila in the cave), "ankles" (Yamina at night); identical with none, this fragment brings together elements that originate both in the surface narrative and in the censored text. Yamina's stance, as she fills the pitcher, reminds one of Jamila's at the end of the dream and of one of the little girls at Tisselli. Finally, I note the change that proceeds from the bare toes "clenched on the pebbles" (Yamina at night) to those that "toy with the sand" (the dream) and now "lie in the cold water." There is a kind of degradation, going from solid to liquid, of the matter on which the feet are resting; not only the feet but, through consecutive metonymies, the body, the character, and the narrative. Such a degradation, added to the textual correspondences just mentioned, all of which are independent of the characters' identity, allow me to posit that the girls and the two young women play the same part in the text. Now if I transpose that textual assertion to the domain of a possible reality to which it might refer, I am confronted with an obvious implausibility. The conclusion can only be that *La Mise en scène* is a productive fiction whose process is independent of the attributes of its referents in "reality." The main purpose of the anecdotes is to draw the reader into the text.

Ollier uses similar devices to identify Lassalle with Lessing, a geologist who had preceded him in the area. It becomes clear as one progresses through the book that scenes that are recollections of the past, products of the imagination, or dreams are part of the latent narrative and correspond to periods of concern or anxiety. Matter-of-fact descriptions of the present belong to the surface narrative and represent periods of calm and indifference, only occasionally disturbed by the appearance of brief segments from the latent texts. From a rhetorical point of view, the handling of descriptions resembles that of Robbe-Grillet. In *La Jalousie*, however, the concern could be readily interpreted (rightly or wrongly) as being of the nature of a pathological obsession. Lassalle's anxiety reflects an unspecified feeling of guilt, and his indifference is based on selfishness and ignorance—all of which can be found in the text as much as in the reader's imagination.

The appearance of the stabbed Moroccan girl early in the book represents not so much a threat against the innocent engineer in his present assignment as it does an opportunity to become aware of what is happening in the world, particularly in a country subjugated by a foreign power. In Morocco, Lassalle exists only as a Christian (i.e., a heathen), a representative of a foreign mining company, and a protégé of the French military. Like Revel in Michel Butor's *L'Emploi du temps*, he enters the locus of the story out of an unspecified past and environment, returning to the same unknown at the end. His experience might thus be viewed as a microcosm of a man's life, in this instance a man's life in a world dominated by colonialism. At the beginning, he is taken in hand by the authorities: official French military ones at first, then unofficial Moroccan ones in the person of Ba Iken, who speaks French because he has served in the French army and could be viewed as a "collaborationist" of sorts. He is an indispensable unit in the narrative as he knows everyone in the area, including *mogaddems* and *cheikhs*. The central chapters of the book see Lassalle through the completion of his engineering job. A shorter third part takes the engineer back to where he was on page 1, although by a different route, and this suggests a circle—decidedly a common figure in contemporary writing. Lassalle then experiences a metaphorical death.

The fate of the young Moroccan woman arouses his conscience in an uncomfortable way, as evidenced by the momentary suppression of the first-aid station episode, for he is the intelligence of the text. He tries to find out the circumstances of her stabbing, but he can do so only indirectly. His contact with others, after he has left the small French outpost, is through Ba Iken. His isolation is further emphasized when he does not stay in the village at Imlil but must pitch his tent at some distance. Natives are generally fearful of him or openly hostile. Eventually, it is a mute boy who presents him with material evidence linking the stabbing of Jamila to the murder of the geologist and points to the probable culprit.

Early in the book Lessing's name sounded obviously German to Lassalle, hence typically foreign. As he progresses through his narrative, Lassalle must become increasingly aware of his own situation as a foreigner (ironically, Lassalle is also the name of a nineteenth-century German socialist), and, as parallels between his own story and that of Lessing increase in number, the phonetic resemblance between the two names becomes more significant. Lassalle comes to realize that he is as much responsible for the death of Jamila as Lessing was. Like Lessing, he, too, must die. His identification with the dead Lessing at the end of the book signifies not only the end of his existence as a character in the narrative but the necessary death of a foreign presence in Morocco. He or the reader has come to this realization because the stage had already been set (*mise en scène*) by Lessing's dramatic journey—the latter was not named after a German playwright for nothing. The story operates as in Sartre's *Les Sequestrés d'Altona* (performed in the year following the publication of Ollier's book), where, through a representation of German behavior during the Second World War, French audiences were led to an awareness of their own responsibilities for what was taking place in Algeria. In Ollier's book, however, the operation is far more subtle.

Curiously, *La Mise en scène* is told in the third person, but Lassalle is so constantly its central intelligence as to seem a narrator in disguise. Perhaps Claude Ollier needed to maintain a certain distance between himself and his main character, a certain indifference that is heightened by the impersonal style of much of the narrative. Perhaps, more objectively speaking, there is evidence here of the slow emergence of the text itself as subject, while at the same time writer and narrator lose their autonomous existence.

In Ollier's second work of fiction, *Le Maintien de l'ordre* (1961; *Law and Order*), the point of view seems at first to be identical. The reader then receives something of a jolt when he encounters the first-person pronoun "I" at the end of the second chapter and realizes that he is dealing with a modified first-person narrative that allows the text's presence to be felt as such. The pronoun is used only about a dozen times throughout the book.

The precise locale and plot of this novel are very different, but theme and techniques are similar. We are still in Morocco, but instead of out-of-the-way, uncharted territory, a large seaport, presumably Casablanca, constitutes its setting. The unidentified narrator seems to be a minor official in the French civilian government of the protectorate. He has just uncovered some sort of torture chamber involving policemen as well as underworld extremists, but no one is eager to have a scandal break out openly. The narrator is caught between his conscience and his fear, his duty and his security. This time, contrary to what happened in the previous book, the dilemma is not resolved. That evolution is again symptomatic of the gradual change in aesthetics I have called attention to in other chapters. Ollier's concerns in the composition and architecture of *La Mise en scène* pointed toward an aesthetics in which responsibility for the creative act was firmly centered in the writer. The reader needs to play an active role, to be sure, but his is still a subordinate one. The writer has clearly suggested his value judgments.

In *Le Maintien de l'ordre* the burden has shifted more toward the reader. There is no mathematically rigorous architecture to strike one at the outset; a certain amount of symmetry is present, but its workings are more subtle. Also, the chronology of events is far less clear as the narrative swings back and forth between present and past, each time exploring a different level of the past. From that standpoint, the makings of a puzzle are certainly present, as they are in Robbe-Grillet's *La Jalousie;* but whereas Robbe-Grillet seems to have composed that work in such a way as to make a chronological reconstitution well-nigh impossible, Ollier gives the reader all the clues that are necessary for such a restoration. The reader must nevertheless take the initiative; he must make an effort that can be considered preliminary to, and also symbolic of, the true creative act. He can, for instance, feel the weight of the impersonal narrative segments, which tend to stifle the rare appearances of the personal "I," making him sense the shifting back and forth between the temptation to inaction and the weaker urge to moral action—without explicit comments by the writer. The last word of the narrative is *tomorrow.* While that might well allude to the impending liberation of Morocco from French rule, it is still up to the reader to decide what the narrator's tomorrow is made of—courage or indifference.

The oscillation also exists—one might even say that it is generated—on the textual level. First, one notices that verb tenses alternate between past and present,[3] the latter corresponding to the more intense moments of fear. Second, there are, as in *La Mise en scène*, descriptive segments of text that are repeated with modifications. The very first paragraph of the book, while describing what can be seen from a window overlooking the port, emphasizes the middle zone of the view, where it is hard to distinguish the sky from the sea, thus furnishing a correlative to the narrator's indecisive state of mind. It also establishes a kind of "vocabulary fund" to be drawn from in later descriptions, of which there are about seventeen. Two of these I am tempted to call focal points in the text. One is established when the narrator, who has been looking down toward the street to see if the two thugs (who had been shadowing him) are still there, jumps back to avoid being seen—and the open window then offers nothing but a "sudden vast glistening brightness" (49). The second is linked to his discovery of the torture chamber, when an outside door is opened, letting in "Raw, intense, blinding light" (200). The first segment is correlative to the narrator's fear, the second to the scandal he has uncovered. There is also a second series that undergoes a metamorphosis, beginning with a passage in the second chapter that starts, "The lighthouse illuminated the room" (27). It is taken up again about half a dozen times, ending with a mere flickering of the light. Here again the beams of light alternating with darkness represent the same psychological oscillation between fear (darkness) and scandal, that is, uncovering the truth (light). The two series, however, do not culminate in a specific message. The mere flickering of the light, in the last chapter, might seem pessimistic. On the other hand, the first series ends with "black" and "white" replacing the gray indistinctness of the initial paragraph, suggesting that a clear choice now exists.

Generally speaking, the setting for *Eté indien* (1963; Indian Summer) is a large city readily identifiable as New York. An introductory section takes place in the tropics, presumably the Yucatán Peninsula, and a concluding one is set on a plane headed for the same tropics. The protagonist, Morel, has been sent by a movie company to investigate the possibilities of making a film in Mexico. He has planned a two-day stay in New York. On the level of the anecdote, the book deals with Morel's activities in the city during the two days that become three because he misses his plane. A reader who is familiar with *La Mise en scène* notices a similar pattern. A man is sent to a foreign country on a technical mission; he does not know the language; before proceeding to a remote area, he is briefed by an "expert," here a professor of archeology. One then looks for hidden elements to emerge, but they do not. Nor is Morel presented with a choice or threatened in any way. He meets Cynthia, dates her, gets drunk, spends the night with her, oversleeps, and has to postpone his departure. That hardly upsets him; he just spends another day with Cynthia. The next thing one knows he is flying toward southern Mexico, and the narrative ends as the plane comes down close to its destination. Just before he had left New York it was beginning to snow—the brief Indian summer was over.

The book is puzzling: a more careful examination of the text is obviously called for. As one goes over the introductory pages a second time, they seem less "real" than before. Perhaps Morel is projecting ahead to the event that really matters—his arrival in the area of pre-Columbian pyramids. This seems all the more plausible as, later on, there are several more flights of the imagination. The opening pages may also be a clue in suggesting that all of Morel's subjective distortions are determined by his obsession with scenarios to be set in Mexico. In other words, if the pattern of Ollier's first work still holds and the protagonist's stated mission is only a pretext, one might look for significance in those events that resist Morel's flight into the future. The only trouble is that almost everything encourages such flights: his exhaustion after the transatlantic flight, his tendency to get carsick, a low resistance to drink, a poor memory. One eventually discovers that Ollier's character is little more than absence of character. Here again, the "blank" that has haunted so much contemporary fiction is revealed as soon as the veneer of appearances has been peeled off. Actually, Morel is no more negative than the characters in the previous fictions. The concern that informed *La Mise en scéne* and *Le Maintien de l'ordre* was communicated by the text much more than it was assumed by the characters.

Even Morel's name does not ring true: it bears an aura of fiction, bringing to mind, in addition to a character out of Marcel Proust's novel, the protagonists of Romain Gary's *Les Racines du ciel,* André Gorz's *Le Traître,* and Adolfo Bioy Casares's *The Invention of Morel.*[4] (Even the title of the book repeats that of an earlier work by Roger Vercel.) The people at the head office he seems responsible to are named Munch and Moritz. The identical initial letter recalls Samuel Beckett's parabolical naming of his personages. Moritz also rings another kind of bell: that was the name of the man who had gone to Imlil to make the initial survey two years before Lassalle, in *La Mise en scène.* This first clue to the unity of Ollier's fictional texts is given additional strength by Morel himself. When Cynthia shows him a number of personal snapshots, he can only offer her two in exchange. On the first he is seen on a mule against the background of a rocky mountain terrain, and on the second he is seen walking along a narrow street with the sun beating against windowless white walls (190-91). The allusion to the earlier works is transparent: one begins to suspect that the same protagonist is involved in all three.

I have indicated the role textual transformations play in the earliest fiction. Here the technique is similar, but it acquires greater significance as other elements lose theirs. The manner in which the introductory segment of the text undergoes a number of changes as it is disseminated throughout the pages of the book before being reassembled in different fashion in order to become its concluding section (once more, a circular motion) and a score of more or less distorted echoes that link other passages contribute to the assimilation of New York to the ruins of Mayan civilization, just as Lassalle had previously been assimilated to Lessing. The difference is that now the reader is on his own.

L'Echec de Nolan (1967; Nolan Is Lost) relates the attempts an investigator makes at clarifying the circumstances surrounding the disappearance of a fellow investigator named Nolan, who was reported missing in a plane crash. He travels all the way up to a small village in Norway, within the Arctic Circle, to talk to the only survivor of the catastrophe. What he learns or fails to learn leads him to seek out people who had been in contact with Nolan during earlier episodes of his life. This takes him to the Italian Alps, to southern Spain, and finally to some Atlantic islands, but it seems that the deeper he probes the less he discovers.

One common bond with the earlier fiction stands out at once: the main character is given an assignment in a foreign country (several countries in this instance), the language of which he does not know. He is given the assistance of guides or intercessors, but the amount of knowledge they impart is not in direct ratio to the ease of communication—quite the contrary. In a more complex fashion, it recalls the pattern of *La Mise en scène*, in which Lassalle had learned nothing from the French army officer in Assameur, had been only partly enlightened by Ba Iken, whose native language was not French, and had glimpsed the truth thanks to Ichou, who was mute. Negative properties of language, however, are not without positive values. As they block out external reality and confirm the difficulty there is in apprehending it, they create a new reality, which is not that of phenomena but of man's imagination. This should recall the myths Robbe-Grillet was concerned with, the "fantastic" aspects of works like *Le Maison de rendez-vous* or *Projet pour une révolution à New York*, and also the *préciosité* of Giraudoux. As the narrator of *L'Echec de Nolan* describes the Norwegian peninsula where he has arrived, with the hamlet of No located at its tip, he places the name of that hamlet at the very end of his descriptive paragraph. He then adds, to emphasize the linguistic nature of the topography, as a separate paragraph, "Isolated at the end of a sentence" (15). One is reminded of Giraudoux's sentence, which had been mistaken for a ship: "As I write these lines, we are off the coast of Timor Island. On an atoll, a Dutchman dressed in white stands at attention before what he thinks is a Dutch ship but is actually no more than a French sentence."[5]

A number of textual echoes soon convince the reader that Morel of *Eté indien* must be identified with Nolan. The latter, as the investigator points out, "never traveled under his real name. Each time there was a new one. A pseudonym" (104). Upon careful examination, *L'Echec de Nolan* can now be seen as working, in the parts entitled "First Report," "Second Report," and "Third Report," on the texts of Ollier's three previous works, but in reverse chronological order. The new text makes clear that Nolan is not only Morel but, as was suggested in *Eté indien*, he is therefore also Lassalle and the anonymous narrator of *Le Maintien de l'ordre*. One important clue furnished in *L'Echec de Nolan* has yet to be mentioned: three persons are listed as missing from the plane, and one of these is Nolan. In other words, three Nolans have disappeared. More important, they are not officially dead, they are missing. They have always been "missing," for that matter. This is one instance of the retro-active effect of this work on an earlier one, as it deprives Lassalle of whatever "flesh" the reader gave him when *La Mise en scène* stood alone. His metaphorical death at the end of the narrative now acquires even greater dimensions. He not only died as a character in that piece of fiction but his death becomes correlative to the death of the concept of character in fiction. The catastrophe that was vaguely suggested at the conclusion of *Eté indien* and affirmed in *L'Echec de Nolan* has a double effect, establishing the "missing" or "absent" nature of fictional charac-ters, a trait already noticed in Morel, and signifying that the only deaths connected with it were those of the realistic aspect of characters. What follows in *L'Echec de Nolan* is quite logical. When a fourth Nolan emerges as the investigator, he is also the nonexistent, impersonal narrator, having been absorbed by the text to the extent of being deprived of every last vestige of individuality. The narrator has given way to the text.

So far I have ignored the investigator's visit to those tropical islands in the Atlantic, supposedly the scene of Nolan's first mission. It is a baffling episode, for it does not correspond to any of Ollier's previously published fiction. One notes that at the time of that early assignment Nolan was possibly working for another company (220) and that the name "Nolan" is not original with Ollier, who discovered it in a text by Jorge Luis Borges (N 151 ff.). As Ollier himself has explained, the fourth section of *L'Echec de Nolan* refers to the texts of the first section of *Navettes,* which were written before *La Mise en scène* but not published in book form until 1967—and the tropical island setting was intended as a tribute to Robert Louis Stevenson, whom Ollier was reading at the time.

If one moves for a moment to Borges's short story "Theme of the Traitor and Hero," whence the character Nolan emerged, one may perhaps see things a little less darkly. A historian named Ryan, investigating the circumstances of an Irish patriot's assassination in the 1820s, unearths the fact that Nolan, a friend of the patriot, while himself investigating the failure of a number of uprisings, had found out that the patriot was a traitor. The latter is condemned to die, but the execution of the sentence is camouflaged in order to preserve the hero's image and indirectly serve the revolution.

What had struck Ryan in the first place were the similarities between the patriot's death and the deaths of Caesar and Macbeth. "These facets are of cyclic character; they seem to repeat or combine phenomena from remote regions, from remote ages."[6] That fits in very nicely with Ollier's Nolan being an echo of his previous creations—until one recalls that Borges's Nolan, a translator of Shakespeare into Gaelic, had engineered the fictitious plot and assassination, being undoubtedly inspired by the tragedies of *Macbeth* and *Julius Caesar.* A final twist provides yet another jolt: the traitor-hero was assassinated in a theater, prefiguring the murder of Abraham Lincoln. Ryan also realizes that Nolan had inserted in his plot a sufficient number of clues to enable an investigator such as himself to uncover its mechanism, thus including the historian in the plot. As a consequence, he decides to perpetuate the patriotic legend. As Ollier sees it, in his commentary on Borges's text, "Everyday reality, initially postulated as existing, finds itself gradually diluted, caught in a more and more perfect system of relationships that, finding support in one another, end up by constituting not a possible reality but *the only true reality*" (157). In such manner myths are born, as I suggested earlier. In a more limited fashion, that is how Ollier's Nolan imposes a new reality on Morel and Lassalle, not just his but the true reality of all four (if we include the anonymous narrator of *Le Maintien de l'ordre*). Or, to quote Ollier's

La Vie sur Epsilon: "Each one of his avatars is false, taken by itself. Taken together, they are true" (271). What Ollier has been doing is to suggest that the elements of reality can always be rearranged. "Beautiful setting, don't you think? ... Glimpses into the wilderness.... Backdrop of ruins.... The story hardly matters, in the end" (E 58).

His first four works of fiction having been reorganized and revitalized, Ollier began planning the next four. None of those, obviously, could stand independently now that textual reverberations were consciously assumed. *Le Vie sur Epsilon, Enigma,* and *Our ou vingt ans après* are thus related respectively to the first, second, and third texts; *Fuzzy Sets* is related both to the fourth and to the fifth, sixth, and seventh. Texts of the new series had already been adumbrated in the "Fourth Report" of *L'Echec de Nolan,* toward the end of which one finds a reference to a "homologue in a distant system" (228). This suggests that the anecdote of the forthcoming works will be set in a different planetary system, thus in the realm of science fiction.

Ollier's fifth novel (*epsilon* is the fifth letter of the Greek alphabet), *La Vie sur Epsilon* (1972), features an anecdote that covers a period of seven days, earth time, on the planet Epsilon located in a different solar system, where four suns make earth-time reckoning inapplicable. It involves four astronauts who have made a successful landing, after which an unspecified interference incapacitated all their machinery and communications equipment. Two of the men decided to go on an expedition. Weeks later a third undertook to find out what had happened to them. When the reader opens the book, the commander is alone in the silent spaceship. Soon, he, too, sets out in search of the other crew members. He finds them, one by one, and one by one they return to the ship as the interferences cease and communication is reestablished with their base. Such a brief outline brings out a familiar pattern: a man is sent to a distant land, he has an assignment to carry out, he does so successfully in spite of many difficulties, and he returns safely to his point of departure. *La Mise en scène* fits that pattern best.

When Lassalle, spending his first night in a strange country, thinks of the dangers that might threaten him, he remarks, "And yet he had been warned in several instances" (MS 11). At the outset of *La Vie sur Epsilon* the commander, thinking of the awesome phenomena that are manifested on the planet, recalls that "He had been instructed at length, during the training years" (V 9) about such matters. Other textual echoes soon reverberate. For instance, "the line of demarcation between light and dark" (MS 10) brings forth "a fluctuating state of relationships between light and dark" (V 9). The "slats" and "hinges" of shutters in the room at Assameur (MS 11) produce "slats" that are "hinged" (V 9, 10, 22, and passim) in descriptions of a peculiar atmospheric disturbance, which, like shutters in the room, produce darkness when it engulfs the spaceship

(69ff.). The "slats" are seen as "sliding, crisscrossing, and permuting" (9), while on the wall of his room Lassalle sees threadlike shadows "undulating . . . interweaving, unraveling" (MS 13). He soon realizes that the shadows are caused by leaves on a palm tree; in French, dropping the initial letter, *lame* (slat) is an anagram of *(p)alme.* Thematic details also reappear, like the moving geometric visions in both the introductory and closing sections of *La Mise en scène* that become "natural" visions of the strange slats or images on television screens. The memory of crouching behind a bush of mountain laurel (V 183) suggests the ravine where Lassalle hid, near the spot where there were also bushes of mountain laurel (MS 138, 146). The last image on the screen of the spaceship is a five-pointed star (V 272), which is also the emblem on the Moroccan flag, and *La Mise en scène* was set in Morocco. Many more examples could be given.

Heretofore the protagonists of Ollier's fiction did not know the language of the countries to which they were sent, nor did they bother to learn once they arrived there. But on the planet Epsilon there is no animal or plant life; there are no human beings. Even the four astronauts hardly qualify. In their case, we can readily discard the "living" or "human" attributes of traditional fictional characters. They are successors to Ollier's previous ones, in alphabetical order. After L(assalle), (. . .), M(orel), and N(olan) we now have O., P(erros), Q(uilby), and R(ossen). The extraordinary phenomena that are found on Epsilon, of which the enveloping "slats" constitute only one, cause those who are caught in them to lose present consciousness and to relive other episodes—not necessarily of their own lives. Furthermore, two different "individuals" may relive exactly the same episode. That, on the level of the anecdote, thoroughly destroys the characters' individuality.

Initial letters might have been enough to designate all of them, except for emphasizing that the commander in the anecdote, protagonist in the fiction, reduced to the initial "O." amounts to a mere cipher in the text. As that letter is also the initial of Ollier's name, this might be interpreted as pointing to the reduced significance of the concept of "author." The analogy with the earlier fiction is reaffirmed: rather than O., it is the text that has been given the assignment on Epsilon, and it is linguistic in nature. Its task is to explore Epsilon as a foreign text, for almost anything can be considered as a text or hieroglyphics to be deciphered. Such an enterprise is clearly stated here as a result of the now familiar process of inscribing key segments of relatively short length into the narrative and then repeating them with significant variations. The one that immediately concerns the reader is the very first sentence of the book: "At the beginning, he does not attach essential importance to such metamorphoses: it is an attribute of this land, he says to himself, of this sand, of this land of snow and sand, an aspect of its climate, perhaps seasonal, a fluctuating state of relationship between light and dark." In one of its early repetitions, the word *metamorphoses* is replaced with *metaphors, land* with *language, light and dark* with *images and words* (V 21). When all instances of the repeated segment are compared, it is easy to form two clusters that may be said to be in a dialectical situation: light, source of light, sun, image, space, and lines on the one hand; darkness, materials, shadows, words, narrative, and colors on the other.

While the text, or the language, of Epsilon is unknown, Ollier's own text must use known words in its exploration of it—just as the reader constantly does, using words that apply to past experiences (not even his or her own) to account for the new situations that are encountered. A difficult task, seldom met with success. At one point Ollier's text admonishes, "One must describe everything, even at the risk of inventing everything" (77). Words are obviously inadequate but, "It is better to say 'sand' and 'snow' for the while. Keep on saying: air, light and water, lavender, yellow, and white. Green. Wind (there is no wind). Black (but black can be seen nowhere)" (101), even though the substances they designate do not correspond to what they commonly stand for. It is perhaps not possible to see things as they "really" are. One might as well accept "as a practical compromise and basis for future calculations that everything actually happened as he imagines that it did" (124). That may be the failure that undermines the seemingly successful mission of O., one that is implied in the final pages of the book when the five-pointed star appears on the screen and Rossen admits he does not know what the symbol stands for: "It does not figure in the code!" (272). *La Vie sur Epsilon* is indeed to be read as a study in and of language, but its science-fiction anecdote allows one to enjoy it as an adventure in language.

Enigma followed in 1973, and I think I have sufficiently explained the textual processes that produce meaning in Ollier's works and link them with one another—and other works as well, in this instance Villiers de L'Isle-Adam's *L'Eve future* (1886), a fantastic science-fiction tale featuring a mythical Thomas A. Edison. The book is divided into two parts of nine chapters each, like the first and third part of *Le Maintien de l'ordre*. Each chapter comprises five texts that have distinct grammatical and syntactical features; they are more rigorously handled than in *Le Maintien de l'ordre* as those traits are repeated from chapter to chapter, in the same order. The narrative begins as a sort of science-fiction spy story, and one might say that, from a thematic standpoint, a certain order must be maintained.

Something happens, however, that upsets the plan foretold in *L'Echec de Nolan.* Part 1 is entitled "Iota," after the planet where the action takes place—but this is the ninth letter of the Greek alphabet, not the sixth as one might have expected. The second part is called "Ezzala," not a distant planet but a holy city in the Sudan. People are often sent there for vacations or periods of rest, and O., the protagonist of *La Vie sur Epsilon*, who has been under investigation and made to undergo a peculiar form of psychoanalysis, has been sent there to recuperate. The point is that the narrative leaves "the distant system" in midcourse. It returns not only to earth but to Africa and more specifically to the land of Islam. Textual processes are the same as before but the setting being so different the reader cannot help experiencing different sensations. One is taken from abstract, intellectual episodes to concrete, sensual ones. Typical of the shifts that take place is the one leading from Naima, the feminine name for a psychoanalytical computer on Iota, to Nejma, the woman in Ezzala to whom O. is attracted and with whom he has a positive erotic experience. She is a textual avatar of both Jamila and Yamina of *La Mise en scène*, and she is also related to Naima (the link with a machine is made possible by Villiers de L'Isle-Adam's story) as well as to Tiamat who appears in the book that follows. O. is then sent on another assignment and "given cryptically the names of the seven lands he is to visit" (*Our* 19), that is, the seven previous texts.

Our ou vingt ans après (1974; Ur, or Twenty Years Later) relates what happens on this new mission, as O. is instructed to proceed to the ancient Sumerian city of Ur, where he is taken in hand by Mardouk (the Marduk of Babylonian epic lore, patron deity of Babylon). Ironically, a beautiful woman named Tiamat is placed at his service; in the Babylonian epic of Creation, she was a dragon who symbolized chaos. The protagonist, however, is now totally anonymous and loses even the initial letter of his (former) name. Metaphorically, the writer as "author" has now fully disappeared. As Michel Butor has said, "a work is *always* a collective work. . . . Anyway, one always writes with words one has not invented."[7] Claude Ollier's eighth book is a very conscious manifestation of that fact. There are, as one might have foreseen, references and paraphrases from the seven previous ones; there are also many more allusions, quotations, and modified quotations from other writers' works than before. Thus the title itself is not only an allusion to the twenty years Ollier had been working on language since his writing the early texts of *Navettes* (dated 1950-1954), it is also a reference to Alexandre Dumas's *Vingt ans après*, the sequel to the adventures of the three musketeers. Scholars have already identified "sources" of *Our* in Greek and Babylonian epics, the Bible and the Koran, the *Book of the Thousand Nights and a Night* and fairy tales, and many more recent writers: the Marquis de Sade, Bernardin de Saint-Pierre, Jean Jacques Rousseau, François René de Châteaubriand, Arthur Rimbaud, Edgar Allan Poe, Charles Baudelaire, Stéphane Mallarmé, Lautréamont, Gustave Flaubert, Jules Verne, Maurice Leblanc, and Gaston Leroux (the last two are popular mystery writers).[8]

One might legitimately ask why the protagonist, this collector of texts, has been sent to Ur, the ruins of which lie in Iraq. One reason, as I see it, is that Sumer produced one of the "seven original and fully developed systems of writing,"[9] beginning some time around 3100 B.C. Toward the end of the narrative, Tiamat, with whom the traveler, the "chosen one" (as he is now called), has a sexual experience similar to the one O. had with Nejma, steals four crucial tablets in cuneiform writing and disappears (as did Sumerian culture). Another reason may be that Sumer was the place where Sumerian and Semitic civilizations came together (with poetic license, where east and west did meet) and that Ur was inhabited by Arabs during the fourth century B.C. In spite of history and many specific details of the anecdote, however, the latter's presence is the one most pervasively felt in *Our*, as a backdrop, with the "Islamic crescent" hovering above (44), thus manifesting Ollier's fascination with Islam— one that had begun also some twenty years earlier when he was sent to Morocco as a civil servant in the French colonial administration. Islam was then discovered as the Other, but not one to be studied from a distance as an anthropologist or sociologist might do, not enjoyed, also at a distance, as an exotic (hence inferior, even though picturesque) culture. Rather, he would try to understand it, to learn from it, and (something his fictional characters did not do) learn as much of the language as he could (although he claims he is not gifted).

Much of that encounter is inscribed in a later work, *Marrakch medine* (1979), where the unusual spelling of the city's name attempts to bring it closer to the native pronunciation (especially for a Frenchman accustomed to placing the stress on the last syllable). Since there were two "encounters," as Ollier returned to Morocco and spent a couple of years in Marrakech in 1973–1975, this book should be considered as a text rather than an "autobiographical" or historical record, for memory is not very efficient at reconstructing the subjective past; in many respects, it reads like a prose poem. It is not, however, the lyrical description of an exotic land and culture. It conveys in a "grave and soft" voice, an abolishing of the "racial, cultural, and social barriers" accompanied by a "tension of the Recognition of the Other. Recognition not only in the sense of apprehension, discovery, travel, but also in the sense of gratitude, of 'indebtedness' to the Other for being what he is, for constituting, simply by his 'being there,' a lesson of difference ... that finally permits a correct self-questioning of identity and its fractures."[10] This places Ollier's textual investigation at odds with that of the "Orientalist," as defined by Edward W. Said, for whom "Islam remained forever the ... idea (or type) of *original* cultural effrontery."[11] Ollier does not deny the shock: "Islam is experienced as a full slap across the lips" (MM 34). But the resulting trauma leads neither to condemnation nor to idealization; rather, it provokes an exploration. It is a quest, and it is significant that there is so much wandering in *Marrakch medine*, as there is in Ezzala, in the second part of *Enigma*, as there is in so many of Ollier's and other contemporary novels where the narrative constitutes a form of wandering,[12] and is for that reason discontinuous. "This thread of the discontinuous includes within it the labyrinth of the medina, so that the notion of the labyrinth is internal to the law of the narrative, to the energy of the discontinuous, to the rebuses of the unconscious."[13] *Marrakch medine* thus points to the significance of *La Mise en scène* as the first major trace of that traumatic experience, one which informs Ollier's entire work and justifies the return from Iota to Ezzala.

Now to proceed to the final volume of the series adumbrated in *L'Echec de Nolan* and which, early in 1975, he decided retrospectively to call "Le Jeu d'enfant" (child's play, or game): *Fuzzy Sets* (1975). The title refers to the mathematical theory of sets and more particularly to Lofti A. Zadeh's notion of fuzzy sets.[14] The sets could be the two cycles of texts now being brought to their end (or back to their beginning), they might also be sets of texts defined by genres (starting with *L'Echec de Nolan* the word *roman* no longer appears on the cover of Ollier's texts) or by "authors." The latter is a fuzzy set indeed when one considers the borrowings noted in *Our ou vingt ans après*. The very notion of text might plausibly, too, constitute a fuzzy set.

References to other texts are equally abundant in *Fuzzy Sets*, a book in which the narrative takes us away from the earth but not too far. The anecdote is situated in a space station orbiting our planet, manned by two teams, and the names of the crew members point to some of those other texts.[15] The first team (team "B") includes Gosseyn, newly arrived in the space station (he is the protagonist of a popular science-fiction novel, *The World of A*, published by A. E. Van Vogt in the 1940s; like Ollier's characters, although in a very different fashion, he is able successively to live a similar life in different bodies), Spender (is he the historian or the poet—or both?), Cyrano (the one who wrote one of the first texts of science fiction, *L'Autre Monde ou les Etats et Empires de la Lune* [1657] and also the romantic, swashbuckling character in Edmond Rostand's play), and Noah, here called *l'Ancien*, "the elder" (who saved samples of all living things). Those of the other team, team "A," comprise Gagarin, the first cosmonaut (the prototype of actual and fictional manned space-exploration heroes), Sindbad (who opens up the collection of Arabic travel-romances that have correspondences in and from Homeric, Indian, and Persian texts), de Crac (an eighteenth-century fictional character who has been compared to Munchhausen), and Nemo, "Nobody" (a name claimed by Odysseus, and the captain of Jules Verne's *Nautilus* [Ollier's craft is named the *Octopus*, as it rests on his eight texts]). They conjure a wonderful hodgepodge of unrelated and even contrary texts. Nevertheless, due to an obvious harmony between team members in team "A" and their counterparts in team "B" (real and fictional space traveler, de Crac and Rostand's Cyrano, poet and romance

character, captain of the *Nautilus* and builder of the Ark), and because of
the fuzziness of all categories, they manage to blend into Ollier's work. As
the narrative gets under way, the spaceship is over what were once
Sumerian cities; very soon it is over Baghdad, then Shanghai. After that
there are practically no references to the outside world: the emphasis is
on the text itself.

The first sentence of *Fuzzy Sets* is a question: "Am I in the book?" The
person who asks it is presumably the narrator, O., but it could also be the
reader, for it is repeated on page 23, standing alone in the middle of that
page, as "Are you in the book?" De Crac answers the question on page
97, "You are in the book, yes," and probably nowhere else. This is almost
self-evident as far as the narrator is concerned and it is again true of the
readers. While not "produced" by this text they have at least been
"activated" by it, as they have been by all the other narratives of their
culture. Awareness of the role of narratives in the shaping of one's consciousness is probably what convinced Ollier and others that they must
reject the harness of the accepted narratives of the past. In Ollier's case,
the discovery of Islamic narratives and their specific grammar and syntax
clearly was an adjuvant.

One fully sensitive to the text's impact might well decide that the latter
points to "Octave" as being O.'s name (15), which he would thus recover
in this final volume. It is a possible name, one originally given to the
eighth born; it is also a musical term designating the eighth tone of the
diatonic scale. Thus, complicating things a bit, the protagonist of *Fuzzy
Sets* could be seen both as Ollier's eighth born and the seventh modulation (in keys solely based on the natural scale) of Lassalle/Lessing. The
ever-present quest is narrated in a different mode (or key) as the various
efforts of previous characters are subsumed in the quest for the essence
of writing. O., who is actually a stowaway on the *Octopus*, is pursuing
Tiamat and the stolen tablets of cuneiform writing, who is now presented
as the "winged Queen" whom he "believes he has been hunting down
and catching up with through narrative tricks from volume to volume"
(51). The awareness of the quest was a fuzzy one in *La Mise en scène*,
clear only in the final volumes of the series. He now plans his moves very
carefully although drowsily (has he been drugged?) as in a chess game
(one is "described" in the text but does not make sense) and discovers
Tiamat in a hidden room of the spaceship, where she is a prisoner: "She
was in the Book, yes" (159). An erotic scene follows, at the end of which
Tiamat leans over O. and addresses him, "Traitor to Wise Men, fantasiz-
ing, bookish hero, myth filcher, false Chosen one!" (163). At the end, a
theatrical "debriefing" takes place during which it appears that O. has
acted as expected of him, as he had been programmed to do, in short that
he has failed and will now be turned back out of the book; he is taken
back to the Île-de-France region where he was born "and rushed toward

the white vehicle" (189)—an ambulance, perhaps? In the meantime the text has been materially disintegrating. At first, there is no more than an unusual spacing of the text, as in Mallarmé's *Un coup de dés*, or geometric patterns appearing on the page (as with some poems by Dylan Thomas), and in each case the text survives. Soon, however, the text is eaten away by the figure (69 ff.), and toward the end there are truncated columns of text that appear on the page as if they were the result of a careless collage. The essence of writing is as elusive as ever.

A little over ten years went by before Claude Ollier returned to the same topic, but he presented it from a very different point of view. *Une Histoire illisible* (1986) is a text that attempts to make sense out of a person's relationship with writing, or, to put it another way, the link between the body and scription. Given the role of narrative I alluded to above, this involves making sense out of one's life in the light of the way it can be narrated. The title suggests, however, that the closer one gets to that sense, the more unreadable the narrative becomes. The book begins with an introductory text, what might be called the description of a house and of the people who live in it during a short period of time. The word *seroual* that appears on the first page regarding the clothes a gardener is wearing tells us that we are in Morocco, eleven or twelve years earlier, when Ollier was there completing *Fuzzy Sets*. It begins, "The house had a body. It had hands and eyes. / It breathed." Soon a man settles in the house, then a woman and a child. A certain congruity is established between it and the people. Something happens, however, and the spell is broken. "The woman was the first to leave the house. One morning she was no longer there" (13), the man and the child left in turn. The house died and was demolished. After this introduction the phrase "Many years later" appears at the center of a blank page, and the text proper then begins.

It is tempting to see the house as standing for a set of narratives; the house in Morocco, the "summerhouse" as it is called, representing the series Ollier has called "child's play," which is now done with. The protagonist (this is a third-person narrative) lives alone in a house near Paris. There are portions of it he would like to describe, but he does not know how to do it. "Paul would have described the wall but Paul is not there, he is traveling" (18). Paul is an obsessive absence and eventually a strange presence; his name is that of the main character in *Mon Double à Malacca* (1982), a fantasy inspired by comic strips and mystery novels set in the Far East and featuring characters very much like the writer and his daughter. When Paul first shows up in *Une Histoire illisible* he has just returned from the Far East and he is indeed Bruno's "double" of sorts—Bruno being the name chosen by the writer in this section of the text (a name that crops up as that of a "real" person in the third volume of Ollier's notebooks, *Liens d'espace*). Now that Paul is in the house, Bruno is able to write both the description of the "summerhouse" (which we have read at the beginning) and that of the present one. Paul also persuades Bruno to go on a trip with him, and they devise a game to let chance decide where they will go: it turns out to be a place not too far from Dar el Hamra, in other words Marrakech, the setting that produced *La Mise en scène*. They go, and in a small abandoned village they meet Schlomo, the old Jew who in that earlier novel had been in charge of the Jewish quarter of Imlil. He and Bruno talk and drink a great deal, and this somehow causes the narrative to switch tracks. Bruno, who had been traveling on a donkey, now rides a horse, while nearly all the people he had been with disappear, including Paul, and new ones take their place.

Time has been pushed back a number of years, for the Moroccan and French flags both fly over official buildings. We soon learn that Bruno's name was then Denis. The different name corresponds to the different character one creates when narrating different episodes of one's life, set in different places, among different people. Nevertheless, in the case of Bruno/Denis there is one constant: the women who enter his life fleetingly keep disappearing. The mysterious princess he sees before the meeting with Schlomo and who might, in one's imagination, be connected with Tiamat, Jenna in Paris ("He never saw Jenna again" [175]), Kay in the suburbs ("Kay never reappeared" [194]), Leni in Dar el Hamra ("she left the day before, she took the bus" [222]), and finally Mae, who may well be the unnamed woman of the introductory section. Denis has returned to France after he was "created" in Morocco, lived in several places, and seen Paul show up again as strangely as he did earlier in Bruno's house. Paul, whom Denis used to call his "alter ego" (200), finds that his friend "is no longer the same" (218). On a whim, Paul decides they will go to Morocco (where there is now only one flag on government buildings), and instead of traveling by foot or by donkey they rent a car. They return to France, Paul goes off on another of his long journeys. Denis, after a period of aimless wanderings, both metaphysical and actual, meets Mae. He experiences what he sees as a steady, definitive romance: "You are the woman of my life" (240), but the cliché may be destructive. They have a child, and eventually Mae is offered a job in Dar el Hamra. He will go ahead of her, find a place where the three of them can live, get everything ready—and the book ends with a description of the "summerhouse" of the introductory pages, with a number of variations, and ends on an ominous note as "his shadow against the wall is broken where there are windows." Textually, one keeps coming back to *La Mise en scène*, thematically one returns to Islam again and again, psychologically one cannot escape the figure of the circle, of uroboros, the dragon biting its own tail.

Two years later, with *Déconnection* (1988; *Disconnection*), Ollier made his contribution to a theme that has preoccupied a number of writers of his generation as well as younger ones. I have called it the return of the repressed, and it involves giving expression to experiences of the time of the German occupation (see my chapter on Perec and the conclusion). In *Déconnection* the narrative at first gives the appearance of a continuous series of brief fragments; upon reading, however, it is soon evident that two distinct, alternating narrations are involved, distinguishable as the initial third-person narrative switches to the first person on page 11, back to the third person on page 16, and so forth. One series of sequences is set in a forced-labor camp in Germany toward the end of the Second World War, the other in a small French village at the end of the century—and perhaps of the world. The narrator of the second series is identical with, but older than and distant from the protagonist of the first—who is called Martin.

It seems as though the horrors of the war have simply undergone a temporary interruption of fifty years. They are now, in the near future that is, resuming under a different guise. If it is the end of the world it is a silent end and no one seems to care. The commodities and services one had been accustomed to slowly disappear. "Who would have imagined this? Public transportation at a standstill, machines out of order, power out, postal and phone service not available—all that was unexpected and already mind-boggling. What is more serious is this resignation, this latent as if unconscious acceptance, this absence of reaction" (119-20). T. S. Eliot had put it succinctly, *"This is the way the world ends / Not with a bang but a whimper."* Somewhat as in the case of Claude Simon, but not so strongly, a vague faith in life persists as the narrator, alone, contemplates nature. The last line of the text reads, "Something else has begun, perhaps."

NOTES

1   For a slightly more detailed study of *La Mise en scène,* see my "Concealed Production in Ollier's First Novel," *Review of Contemporary Fiction* 8, no. 2 (Summer 1988): 57-72.

2   Claude Ollier, *La Mise en scène* (Paris: Minuit, 1958), 26. Henceforth all references to Ollier's works will appear in the body of the text with the following abbreviations: *La Mise en scène,* MS; *Eté indien,* E; *L'Echec de Nolan,* EN; *Navettes,* N; *La Vie sur Epsilon,* V; *Marrakch Medine,* MM.

3   I have analyzed a number of textual operations effected in Ollier's first three fictions in an essay entitled "Le Jeu du texte et du récit chez Claude Ollier," *Le Nouveau Roman: hier, aujourd'hui,* eds. Jean Ricardou and Francoise van Rossum-Guyon (Paris: 10/18, 1972), 177-98.

4   Respectively published as follows: Paris: Gallimard, 1956; Paris: Seuil, 1958; Austin: University of Texas Press, 1964. Vercel's *Eté indien* was brought out by Albin Michel. Bioy Casares's Morel invented a machine analogous to some

of those described by Raymond Roussel in *Locus Solus*. It "films" the totality of a person, and when reprojected he or she appears in three-dimensional totality—body and soul—but the person dies after the film has been taken. Morel, on a tropical island with friends, decides to relive forever a seven-day sequence. They die, and the "film" is replayed again and again, Morel, as I see it, having become like an actor in a continuously performed play, or a fictional character in the minds of readers who read and reread the book where his name is inscribed. Originally issued in Buenos Aires in 1940, it was available in French translation in 1955 (published by Laffont).

5   Jean Giraudoux, *Choix des élues* (Paris: Grasset, 1939), 155.

6   Jorge Luis Borges, "Theme of the Traitor and Hero," in *Ficciones* (New York: Grove Press, 1962), 124.

7   Michel Butor, *L'Arc*, no. 39 (1969): 2.

8   See Madeleine Van Strien-Chardonneau, "Pratiques intertextuelles dans *Our ou vingt ans après*," in *Recherches sur l'œuvre de Claude Ollier*, ed. Sjef Houppermans (Groningen: Cahiers de Recherches des Instituts Néerlandais de Langue et Littérature Françaises, 1985), 93-119. For further insight into the writing of *Our* see the third volume of Ollier's notebooks, *Les Liens d'espace* (Paris: Flammarion, 1989), 76-79, 88-91, 93-94, 101-3, 109.

9   I. J. Gelb, *A Study of Writing* (Chicago: University of Chicago Press, 1963), 60 ff.

10 Abdellatif Laabi, "Claude Ollier and the Death of 'The Orient' in *Marrakch medine*," *Review of Contemporary Fiction* 8, no. 2 (Summer 1988): 117.

11 Edward W. Said, *Orientalism* (New York: Pantheon, 1978), 260.

12 Olivier de Magny had pointed this out in 1958. The prototype, as he saw it, would have been Leopold Bloom's wanderings through Dublin in *Ulysses*, and it inspired, directly or indirectly Robbe-Grillet's *Les Gommes* and *Le Voyeur*, Beckett's *Molloy*, Simon's *Le Vent*, Pinget's *Graal Flibuste* and Butor's *L'Emploi du temps* (among those texts then published). See his "Panorama d'une nouvelle littérature romanesque," *Esprit*, July-August 1958, 8.

13 Abdelkehi Khatabi, "Traces of a Trauma: On *Marrakch medine*," *Review of Contemporary Fiction* 8, no. 2 (Summer 1988): 108.

14 See Zadeh et al., eds., *Fuzzy Sets and Their Applications to Cognitive and Decision Processes* (New York: Academic Press, 1975). For the reasons that Ollier chose "Child's Play" as a collective title for his eight works of fiction see *Les Liens d'espace*, 197-99. For instance, "If, as a child, I had not played, or so little that nothing brings back any memory of it, it is between the age of thirty and fifty that I at last devoted my whole being to play, to the play of one who does not know how to speak—to *child's play*. . ." (198).

15 See Sjef Houppermans, "Mille-pertuis," in *Recherches sur l'œuvre de Claude Ollier*, 120-47.

9

Michel Butor

In Michel Butor's first work of fiction, *Passage de Milan* (1954; Milan Mews), there lies a wealth of signs pointing in several directions: into the past, into the future, and into the writer—as scriptor rather than as ordinary person. Keeping strictly to the literary domain, one encounters ironic allusions to older writers such as André Gide and François Mauriac as well as specific references to Charles-Bernard Renouvier's *Uchronie*, all remnants of the past. Foreshadowing future works, a certain amount of fire imagery prefigures the conflagrations of *L'Emploi du temps* (1956; *Passing Time*) while a burning piece of paper damages Martin de Vere's painting, which had previously been compared to an "emploi du temps" and was divided into twelve squares, just as the city of Bleston, whose map Revel later burns, comprises twelve precincts. The apostasy of Father Jean Ralon has its counterpart in *La Modification* (1957; *A Change of Heart*) through the figure of Julian the Apostate, a correlative of Leon Delmont's interior change. The transformation in relationship that takes place between Louis Lécuyer and his first cousin, Father Alexis Ralon, the one a student, the other a chaplain in the same lycée, and the fiction one of the characters is writing, in which he seeks to "put the simplest human relationships to a test, and, with that in mind, he modifies family ties,"[1] both adumbrate a major theme of *Degrés* (1960). The attention given to the dreams of Felix, Jean, and Alexis anticipates the role dreams play in *Histoire extraordinaire* (1961), *Mobile* (1962), and the five volumes of *Matière de rêves* (1975-85; The Stuff of Dreams) among others. From the standpoint of technique, the discontinuous architecture of this first book, in which the reader is confronted with a very large number of juxtaposed sequences, each dealing with a different set of characters or actions, points, beyond the narrative continuity stressed in *L'Emploi du temps* and *La Modification*, to the more deliberate rhetoric

191

of discontinuity that characterizes *Degrés* and is fully developed in *Mobile* and a number of works that follow.

As to the third area of resonance in *Passage de Milan*, it emerges most clearly from a confrontation with one of Butor's subsequent works, *Portrait de l'artiste en jeune singe* (1967; Portrait of the Artist as a Young Ape). Called a "capriccio," this portrait might well be termed autobiographical fiction, if all fiction were not, to some extent, autobiographical and all autobiography fictional.[2] The salience of patently biographical elements is due, in part at least, to the shift in rhetoric that I have just alluded to, and which is linked to the realization that the elements of a work of art are less important in themselves than the order in which they are assembled.

The central feminine figure in *Passage de Milan* is Angèle Vertigues, whose name suggests "angel of the heights," for whom a party is given. Among those dazzled by her charms is Louis Lécuyer. She is also one of the queens of the standard pack of cards, of which Martin de Vere is trying to give a representation in the twelve areas of his painting. The characters are manipulated as by the player of a game of solitaire or as by the painter in his complex construction. When the corresponding queen is accidentally destroyed by fire on de Vere's canvas, Angèle dies because of Louis's well-meant but clumsy interference. The link between the two events was established earlier when the narrator warned that Angèle might be displaying seductiveness in vain: "Into pitiful ashes might you find your fine flames resolved" (215). In the end Louis is about to leave for Egypt, where he could well experience a spiritual rebirth.

Portrait de l'artiste en jeune singe is narrated on two separate levels— dream and reality—in alternating chapters. The realistic side gives an account of the visit paid by the narrator (specifically identified with a youthful Butor) to a German nobleman shortly after the end of the Second World War, during which he explores his host's priceless library and teaches him new games of solitaire. To the other side of the narrative belong his nights. He imagines a serialized dream that is adapted from the tale of the second Kalandar, begun by Scheherazade on the twelfth of her thousand and one nights. In that tale, the Kalandar, who has been changed into an ape, is unwittingly responsible for the death of not one but two women—and the second one is literally turned into those ashes that were metaphorically introduced in *Passage de Milan*. In *Portrait*, the Kalandar becomes a visitor to the German castle narrating a dream. While its basic features have been retained, the Arabian tale has been shortened and modified in several respects. Particularly pertinent here is the episode in which the dreamer, still in the guise of an ape, engages the king in a contest. As Scheherazade told it, they matched their skills in games of chess, which the king loses, but in Butor's dream the king is bested in his knowledge of solitaire. The shift is significant in that solitaire manifests the prophetic qualities of cardplaying. Although there is no mention of solitaire as such in the text of *Passage de Milan* (the previous reference was my own metaphor), cards play a similar prophetic role in de Vere's painting.

In both narratives a young man's future is at stake, and chance is instrumental in shaping it. A propitious outcome is intimated by the recurrent number twelve, a symbol of salvation. Chance, however, is normally surrounded with an aura of mystery and obscurity. Father Jean Ralon muses at the outset of *Passage de Milan*, "Wasn't there a path opening there, the path into nightfall, which, invariably too soon, one ceased pursuing, which one would never find the courage to follow down to its major turning points?" (9). Ralon is an Egyptologist, and Egypt, one of the main sources of Gnostic lore, is also thought by some to have been the birthplace of playing cards. While Angèle's party, which bears the earmarks of a modern initiation, moves on toward its fatal climax, Jean Ralon has an extraordinary dream, resembling a more arcane initiation, inspired by the Egyptian *Book of the Dead*,[3] which confirms his estrangement from the Church. In *Portrait* the narrator is intellectually initiated to the writings of Athanasius Kircher, who, as the first serious student of Egyptian hieroglyphics, might be called a prototype of Father Ralon, of alchemists like Nicholas Flamel and Basil Valentine, of the Protestant mystic Jakob Böhme, and of others, even more obscure. Note that I said "writings" rather than "thought." What matters here is the language of the texts, particularly those pertaining to alchemy, its array of symbols, which illumine areas of consciousness that have been darkened by rationalism.

As Butor explained in an essay written about the same time as *Passage de Milan*, "The language of alchemy is an instrument of considerable pliability that allows one to describe a process with precision, relating it to a general concept of reality."[4] In *Portrait* the narrator does not discuss those writers (who are not all alchemists); he quotes them. That explains why the playing cards of neither book can be assimilated to the tarot pack. Butor needs to remain outside of its closed system of symbolism as much as he must stay at one remove from alchemy and Gnosticism. His viewpoint recalls that of André Breton toward the dark, subsurface forces in the mind: "It is of the utmost interest that we gather them, gather them first, and later submit them, if need be, to the control of our reason."[5] As objective correlatives of such depths, the German castle contains a collection of precious stones, rare minerals extracted from the bowels of the earth (one recalls that a character in *Passage de Milan* had shown much interest in a newspaper article on mines). After the relation of his trip to Germany has come to an end, the narrator of *Portrait* concludes, "How could I not, after that, at the earliest opportunity that presented itself, how could I not have sailed for Egypt?" (231)—echoing the outcome of *Passage de Milan*.

The selection for the dream sequence of *Portrait de l'artiste en jeune singe* of a passage from *The Book of a Thousand Nights and a Night* is extremely suggestive. In the central chapters of *Passage de Milan* (and on the central floor of the apartment building as well), concurrently with other events, a group of intellectuals discuss a work on which they might possibly collaborate and other works that they have individually written. One of them, who has published a book called *Les Faubourgs de Trieste*, is quoted as having said, in answer to a question pertaining to his writing method, "I imagine myself after my own death . . . attempting to see what is going on in those places where I have lived" (138). That statement, also referred to by Georges Charbonnier in the course of an interview with Butor, transforms the removal of the writer from his "creation" and his topic into a distance between the writer and the world expressed through the metaphor of death. During the same Charbonnier interview, Butor himself developed it into a myth, that of the writer as Scheherazade. Ill at ease in a society that he cannot accept, in a universe that he does not fully understand or approve of, dissatisfied with his own being, the writer, at the same time as he removes himself from the stage, re-enters the world by means of his literary work. In so doing, he transforms the outside world for his own use; he also provides others with a vision of reality that can help them effect a transformation of their own. In related fashion, Scheherazade, through the telling of her tales, manages to postpone her own death and also to remove the threat of death that was hanging over the women of Baghdad. "Every writer is Scheherazade, every writer harbors within himself a threat of death . . . both within himself and about himself. The threat that lies outside of him corrodes him, so to speak, internally. . . . The writer, in speaking, will at once remove the threat of death that weighs upon him, and, of course, also weighs on the entire future of society."[6] It is obviously no more than a coincidence that Butor's name is a near anagram of Burton's, the translator of the Arabian tales, which is also the name of the mystery story writer in *L'Emploi du temps*. But the coincidence could not be more suggestive.

Scheherazade's role is congruent with the impression one derives from the main characters of Butor's first four works of fiction, who are also the writer's surrogates. Louis Lécuyer, Jacques Revel, Leon Delmont, and Pierre Vernier are strangers who appear out of nowhere to disappear into the unknown at the end of each book. That impression is greater than in the works of several other writers I have discussed, Robbe-Grillet for instance, because of the weight given to linear narrative in this group of novels. Where there is similar stress, as in Ollier's *La Mise en scène*, the same effect prevails. The protagonist's alien status is clearly stated in *L'Emploi du temps*, where it is an integral part of the anecdote. It is implied elsewhere by various means that isolate the character from his family and his environment. Louis Lécuyer does not belong in the apartment house of *Passage de Milan* in the same manner as others of his generation, who all live with their parents (even Henriette lives with her father, although she does not know it). The only one in a situation vaguely resembling that of Louis is Ahmed, the Egyptian boy, who is literally a foreigner. Nor has Louis been invited to the party in his own right: it is Henriette who is invited and who has asked him to escort her. He is in love with Angèle, but she does not even know his name. His aunt, who has practically adopted him, implies that because his father had died and his mother was worthless he has had no real upbringing: "We nicknamed him Puss the evening he landed in our home . . . he looked like a wet kitten" (28).

Louis bears a large part of the text's burden of significance, but to think of him as a main character in the usual sense of the term is to betray the work of which he is a part. *Passage de Milan* stands halfway between the next two books, where there is greater emphasis on the principal character (even though, in each succeeding one, the common concept of character tends to disintegrate further),[7] and the following ones, where the emphasis lies elsewhere. All are related, and a key to the concern that informs the aggregate of Butor's works can perhaps be found in the final chapter of his first book: "Every apartment building is a warehouse.... As every mind is a warehouse . . . of which an inventory is never taken" (281). The reader has been presented with a partial inventory of the building and the minds of individuals as incomplete as the map of Bleston in *L'Emploi du temps* or as the list of objects and cities in *Mobile*. It is one possible view of a Paris apartment building, but even though it is a distorted one it makes a significant statement about its values. As Jacques Revel exclaims in *L'Emploi du temps,* "How precious was such a distortion!" (122). That selective process serves to emphasize human solitude, within and in spite of certain social structures, because of certain others. The two brothers of the second floor, who are pointedly brothers in Christ since both are priests, are complete strangers to each other. The numerous members of the Mogne family who are crowded into the third-floor apartment are solitary human beings, avoiding one another as much as possible. The intellectuals gathered on the fourth floor fail to respond to their host's call for collaboration. The party that is given on the fifth floor is the very symbol of separation and failure. When Virginie Ralon opens the door to her son, Father Alexis Ralon, as he returns from his lycée, he goes into his room without speaking a word. When Frédéric Mogne gets home from a day at the office, opening the door to the apartment with his key, no one bothers to greet him, and he goes alone into his room to put on his slippers. Mogne's father and mother-in-law, who also live in the apartment, are even more isolated than he is, having been cast aside by those who are younger. Young people, too, bear the heavy weight of solitude, and theirs is essential to the meaning of *Passage de Milan*, but detailed expression of isolation among older people tends to remain in the reader's mind because of an imagistic link with the theme of deterioration that also runs through Butor's work.

Decay is quite naturally associated with death; solitude fits the idea of an inventory of discrete things or beings. All four are stated on the opening pages of *Passage de Milan*. The lonely priest contemplates a vacant lot in which a complement of discarded, useless objects slowly deteriorates while a bird of prey ominously hovers above. Those are correlatives of the evils of the world, against which the writer battles. Paradoxically, he must make common cause with evil in order to vanquish it—remove himself from life in order to sustain it, represent reality in order to change it, choose solitude in order to communicate, produce a series of functioning texts that are in constant danger of becoming mummified. It is a paradox that was already present in the legend of Scheherazade, who, in order to live, had condemned herself to a form of death, existing only through the stories she told.

The writer's situation is more ambiguous than hers, for he agrees with King Shahryar, who cried out, "Only in utter solitude can man be safe from the doings of this vile world! By Allah, life is naught but one great wrong."[8] In essence, that is similar to the remark made by Albert Camus's Caligula—"Men die and they are not happy"—and in both instances the reaction led to additional wrongdoings and death. In the end, the king praises Scheherazade for having been "the means of my repentance from slaying the daughters of folk,"[9] and Caligula is forced to admit: "I did not follow the right path, I have come to nothing." Both, out of different forms of despair, like those responsible for the Santa Barbara bombing that I shall again refer to later in this chapter, were driven to violent action. Scheherazade, on the contrary, was moved by compassion, and her means was to change the king's outlook. So the writer, knowing he cannot change the world through direct action or even propaganda, attempts to change his reader's conception of the world.

Such a change, if effected in one's reading of Butor's fiction, may be the cumulative result of statements and images, none of which is shocking by itself. In that, he differs from those writers who, instead of relying on the scandal caused by conflicting representations, seek to dismantle, so to speak, the very process of linguistic representation in order to show how one such process (that of bourgeois society) can produce a "great wrong." Butor accepts the means of representation of his society, but he keeps changing his angle. What he has said of Raymond Roussel could, with a slight alteration, be applied to himself: he wonders, in the presence of any sort of event, if it could not be represented in a different light or from a different standpoint. In his four novels that difference is insidiously suggested to the reader in statements such as are made by Jenkins, who is a kind of host to Revel, concerning the city of Bleston in *L'Emploi du temps:* "You have mainly seen the fine sections until now, those avenues and gardens where the trees protect us, but someday you will necessarily go forth into those nearly deserted streets where one gets lost" (91). Just as the theme of solitude and the imagery of decay oriented the reader of *Passage de Milan* toward a rejection, or at least a questioning, of a behavior that he, as a Frenchman, recognizes as his own, the same factors, intensified in *L'Emploi du temps,* imply a broader challenge of urban life in Western Europe.

Images of decay and disease are supplemented by others that suggest basic structural flaws. Typical of such is the fissure that has long existed in the tower of the Old Cathedral, preventing the bells, of which the city was proud, from being rung on festive occasions. The correlation is obvious between that image and the writer's inability to find happiness because life is "one great wrong." In this book, everything crumbles except the text itself. Even fire, of which there are many manifestations, loses part of its dual symbolism, and its purifying and regenerative virtues give way before a vision of annihilation. Tinged with a kind of death wish, apprehension rather than hope dominates the narrative. When Jacques Revel, the narrator, who has already lost his first love, Rose, learns of her sister Ann's engagement, he pictures himself as thoroughly vanquished, with no hope of revenge, "As if I were already dead" (252), and during his last few days in Bleston he behaves like a specter: "Ghostlike, Saturday, in the house of All Saints Garden.... Ghostlike during the afternoon, on Sunday.... Ghostlike each evening" (296). When Jenkins expresses his own anxiety, telling Revel that "the desire swells within me more and more to see all those calamities break out, in order to bring the suspense to an end"—that part of the statement is more likely to remain in the reader's mind than its less discouraging sequel: "and enable us to walk at last, speak at last, breathe" (92). Jenkins, of course, whose family is from Bleston and who himself has never left the city, is close to being the warden of established order that Burton, the mystery-novel writer, talks about. As such, he has reasons for being fearful of the future. Revel, on the other hand, resembles the detective whose aim is to "shake up, disturb, ransack, lay bare, and change" (147). He does little of that in Bleston, but he is only Butor's agent and his presence is that of a passive consciousness, which, as it acquires deeper awareness, tends to prod the reader into active consciousness. Bleston is eventually a representation of the reader's reality, and what Revel does not do in his fictional existence, the writer's text may well effect within the reader.

If *La Modification,* which also carried forward the same themes and imagery, is the instance of the greatest emphasis on a single character, who is this time pointedly assimilated to the reader by means of the second-person narrative, *Degrés* marks a return to the multiplicity of characters and stress on relationships that distinguished *Passage de Milan*. *Degrés* also relies less on relatively conventional plot and fictional continuity than *L'Emploi du temps* and *La Modification* and points in the direction of Butor's later texts with their emphasis on discrete textual elements. The unsettling effect of *Passage de Milan*, both within the text and within the reader, was obtained by confronting sixty-odd solitary characters with one another within two separate frameworks—a family unit and a social event. Basically, the same holds true for *Degrés*, with the lycée, "that building for dreary initiations" (241), taking the place of Angèle's party. In addition, outside factors are given a greater role. I refer not only to the presence of a foreigner from black Africa, Maurice Tangala, a student who expands the part of Ahmed (as Horace Buck, who is also African, had done in *L'Emploi du temps*), or to family events that are allowed to intrude upon the activities of the lycée but also to the quotations. These, although an integral component of the teacher–student complex, represent an intervention from outside the time–space limits of this book, a manifestation of the reverberations from one book to another that reinforce their functioning and significance.

Even more than previously, all components of the fiction are commonplace. This applies to the realistic elements as well as to the imaginary ones. It includes characters' impressions, dreams, and fantasies, although the latter are far less frequent than before. To French readers who have had a secondary education (Butor himself has admitted that under present conditions that is the only audience he can hope for), every detail of the book was a familiar one: the behavior of students in and out of the classroom, their teachers' appearances and attitudes, family life with its concomitant pleasures and sorrows, the various courses in the curriculum, the types of homework, literary excerpts to be memorized, classroom procedures, tests, and the classic writers that are read—and it remained so until the French lycée curriculum recently started to change. Of course, not everyone has experienced within his or her own family the complete assortment of adultery, divorce, and deaths that plagues families in *Degrés*, and today not too many take Greek, Latin, Italian, and English in school; but even though some of the experiences may have been vicarious, they are all related to commonplace events. All those who have attended a lycée have in all likelihood read selections from Clément Marot, Rabelais, Montaigne, Bossuet, Boileau, Racine, Saint-Simon, and other French writers, perhaps those precise texts that are quoted. Likewise, those who took Greek read Homer; those who took Latin studied Virgil and Livy; those who selected Italian read Dante; and the many who enrolled in English courses know *Macbeth*, *Julius Caesar*, Keats, and Coleridge. They have been confronted with similar experiments in physics, the same exercises in algebra, the same illustrations of the way the earth's surface is projected on a map. But no one, surely, has

had anything comparable to the experience provoked by a reading of
Degrés. To repeat what I said earlier in this chapter, the order in which
the elements of the text are put together is what matters. Within such an
order, interactions between contiguous elements acquire importance as
chronology and ordinary time intervals are eliminated.

During an interview given in Buffalo in 1964, Karlheinz Stockhausen
said that to compose was to relate. That is essentially what Michel Butor
has done in *Degrés*. The originality of this work, when contrasted with
L'Emploi du temps and *La Modification*, lies in the importance given to
the newly created relationships and in their direct contribution to
meaning. The story line has its importance, but it is less a means to signify
than a framework within which signifying elements are located. In *La
Modification*, the contiguity in Delmont's wallet of an expired member-
ship card in the Louvre Museum and a valid one for the Dante Society
has meaning only as a correlative to the complex feelings he has toward
Paris, Rome, his wife, and his mistress. In *Degrés*, the teacher of Italian
returns home to his wife, who is critically ill. When she asks what happened in class, he begins, "Well, it was the usual routine stuff" (51).
Before he can finish, his sister brings the routine afternoon tea. The next
sequence shows a student watching his physics teacher "go through the
same gestures he had made one year ago, at the same moment of the solar
cycle." That page conveys much concerning death and its inability to
disturb the habits of life and, conversely, the failure of dull, deadly teaching to spark intellectual life. That is closely related to the narrative thread
along which Pierre Vernier proceeds, but it reaches the reader independently of it. The story line is so intimately fused with the architecture of
the novel that it tends to recede into the background while one reads,
coming to the fore again during reflective periods after the book has
been read and helping to unify its many components.

Degrés is about relationships or, as the title suggests in part, about
degrees and qualities in relationships; it also effects a removal of masks.
The twenty-one characters who are introduced in the first part of the
book are presented in seven groups of triads, ranging from the very tight
to the extremely loose. The tightest is formed by the three main characters, narrators, or pseudonarrators: Pierre Vernier, his nephew Pierre
Eller, and the latter's other uncle, Henri Jouret. The loosest is comprised
of the African student, the physical education instructor, and the Catholic
chaplain; within the historical past, there is no possible way in which they
could be kindred. As they stand, these triads might also be seen as ranging
from the social (or contrived) to the purely human (or true). In this
instance, the most human triad is also the loosest. The initiation at the
lycée consists in introducing its participants into the basic community of
people, and the process is made possible by the complex web of relationships Butor has devised, that is, by the book's architecture. That initiation

is what a lycée should provide in actual life but does not. By presenting, as a backdrop to the drama that unfolds, the reality of the lycée, its failure to educate truly, Butor leads the reader through a more effective form of education or initiation. But, as in all such rituals, the reader's active participation is required if the process is to be fruitful.

While one focus of *Degrés* is on relationships, a second is on the courses that are taught, especially what is called the pivotal lesson on Columbus's landing in America (pivotal both in the book and in history) and others on aspects of the Renaissance. They were obviously chosen because they correspond to an age when so many things were being seen in a new light. As one of the students expresses it in class, it was a time when "people have been compelled to admit that the world was not what it had been thought to be" (34). They were also chosen because of a number of parallels that could be suggested between the Renaissance and present times. To the Europeans' physical discovery of America would perhaps correspond a spiritual one, that of a new concept of the brotherhood of men, to which America is not completely foreign and which is symbolized by the group formed by Tangala, the priest, and the instructor. It is signified in negative fashion by the interest Tangala shows in "everything that can take away from Europe, from whites . . . that exclusiveness of civilization they continue to claim for themselves, in spite of all the evidence they have themselves unearthed, which they themselves continue to search for and bring forth, fostering that contradiction, that great cleavage, that great lie that undermines them" (91). The fissure of Bleston's Old Cathedral reappears, running through the length of Europe.

The Renaissance is linked not only to a general attitude existent in this century but more specifically to the lycée as well when the students are asked to read what Rabelais and Montaigne wrote concerning education. Explaining that a changed view of the world entailed a corresponding change in the educational system, the narrator adds, "an educational reform that took a long time getting under way, that is perhaps no more than roughed out even today" (34). Pierre Eller has been undergoing the inadequate initiation provided by the lycée when he is suddenly confronted with his Uncle Henri wearing the mask of a teacher: "You didn't get over that tremendous change . . . for the man who was so gentle, so whimsical, so playful, whom you knew so well . . . suddenly has become someone else, tough, curt, somewhat sarcastic" (23). As a result, both the former mask of uncle and the present one of teacher are destroyed, leaving Pierre Eller with the sense of a new relationship that he does not quite understand, the strangeness of which causes him to blush. A similar doffing of masks, although for different reasons, occurs when the teacher of Italian, after the death of his wife, can no longer hold back his tears in front of his class.

Pierre Vernier undertakes to write his book for his nephew and, indirectly, for all those who, like him, have been through the grades in a lycée, in order to correct the "great wrong" that is embodied in the present system. The compelling force that drives him and Butor even more so is implicitly mentioned when students are translating "The Rime of the Ancient Mariner," and he quotes one of Coleridge's marginal commentaries, "And ever and anon throughout his future life an agony constraineth him to travel from land to land." This calls attention to the unquoted lines, "And till my ghastly tale is told, / This heart within me burns"—a perfect example of the reverberations I mentioned above, as unwritten words are nevertheless inscribed in the text. His is a dangerous project, and as his friend Micheline warns, "You will lose your own life at this" (320). He is willing to risk death in order to save his nephew and countless others, just as Scheherazade was willing to face the same danger when she asked her father to take her to the king, and she persisted in spite of his exhortations: "I shall never desist, O my father."[10] Pierre Vernier's answer to Micheline is that of a lover: "Fortunately you are with me." She remains with him to the last paragraph of the book, when he lies on a hospital bed, long since unable to continue his work. The narrative has managed to progress without his help. That is one indication that *Degrés* does not represent a step backwards (in the direction of *Passage de Milan*) from the standpoint of narrative technique. Vernier's withdrawal does not merely reveal the failure and death of a character, it signifies the death of the narrator as the subject of fiction. Revel and Delmont do tend to disintegrate, but it is left for Vernier to demonstrate that the narrative can continue even though he, the narrator, remains silent (he has been silent for two-thirds of the novel). "Who speaks?" is the anguished question that closes the book.

The narrator, thus having been exposed as a dispensable device, no longer needs to be present. Yet it is characteristic of Butor that he does not allow himself to be constricted by any rhetorical principle. In works that follow *Degrés* the narrator is either present or absent, textual matters are dominant or subordinate, according to the specific needs of a particular undertaking. In *Mobile* (1962), subtitled "Etude pour une représentation des Etats-Unis," an appropriate sequel to the discovery of America that was featured in the previous work, the narrator has vanished and, as in the first and fourth "novels," commonplace elements are carefully rearranged in order to produce an uncommon impression, more valuable, nevertheless, than the conventional one. The rhetorical shift already in evidence in *Degrés* is now fully effected. Plot and the narrative continuity one associates with it, which had made a comeback of sorts in *L'Emploi du temps* and *La Modification* only to decline again in *Degrés*, have now been discarded and are thus no longer available as a vehicle for meaning. A textual interplay, already present in *Degrés* in the shape of allusions, references, or quoted texts, is given considerable emphasis. One is tempted to say that fictional elements have, like plot, completely disappeared—but such a statement would be meaningless. Representational fiction, after all, is no more than a rearrangement of "reality"; every minute element in the wildest of fantasies possesses a specific referent in that "reality."

In *Mobile*, textual elements are not fused into a narrative having the continuity one is conditioned to impose upon events. They have been welded into an architectual continuum that is aesthetically unfamiliar, thus giving the impression of discontinuity. The process could be more effective in disturbing the reader's prejudices to the extent that one is aware of its arbitrariness. His or her sensitivity produces meaning more freely than within a narrative sequence. In *L'Emploi du temps*, when Revel fails to note Horace Buck's address at the time of his first visit, making it impossible for him to return as he promised, even though he makes a foredoomed effort to do so, the reader is almost inevitably led to pass judgment on his character. When in *Mobile* a mention of the Southern Ute Reservation is placed alongside a quotation from Dodge and Zim's *The American Southwest* describing Indian culture of about 400 A.D., the reader is free to consider the juxtaposition as irrelevant, or interesting, or shocking.

By selecting a relatively long quotation (from Jefferson's *Notes on the State of Virginia*, for instance), provided it is unified by a strong theme or subject matter (such as racism) and, after breaking it up in such a way as to preserve the theme in each fragment and distributing it throughout the book, Butor eschews the dullness of repetition and contributes to architectual cohesiveness. Since there is, within the quoted text, narrative progression from one fragment to the next, that contributes to the motion or "mobility" of the whole. Using a number of quotations taken from a variety of outside texts enhances such results. To anyone interested in the United States—and it is hard to imagine *Mobile* as being read by a Frenchman who is not—the quotations do not usually offer new knowledge. The basic referents of the text, being theoretically factual, are also familiar to many. The small fictional components, such as "An apricot-colored Nash driven by an old black" (83), are little more than accentuations (rather than distortions) of factual elements. In short, with the possible exception of a few dream sequences, every detail of *Mobile* is a familiar one, in most cases with a factual referent, but the aggregate is fictional because of the unusual relations that are suggested and the unconventional view that is conveyed.

As a prospective reader approaches this book, two outside sets prepare his or her reading experience: Alexander Calder's "mobiles" because of the title, Jackson Pollock's paintings because of the dedication. (Not far into the text, the collection of patchwork quilts in Shelburne, Vermont, introduces a third set, or guide.) Calder allows for a twofold mobility, the reader's, as he or she moves around the text, and that of the text itself, in which the various components act upon one another. As the lines, with Pollock, instead of combining to form a representational drawing, proliferate in their own right, the sentences in *Mobile*, instead of adding up to a continuous, linear narrative, tend to remain isolated and clash with other isolated sentences or relatively short sequences.

What is important about those sets is that they are respectively sculptural, painterly, and artisanal—in other words, visual as well as material. This implies that the physical features of the book can play a part in the production of meaning; it is a notion that crops up now and then over the centuries, then fades away, and was most brilliantly rekindled by Mallarmé in his *Un Coup de dés jamais n'abolira le hasard.*[11] As a result of Butor's interest in putting such considerations into practice, format and typographical disposition distinguish *Mobile* from everything that precedes. Unlike what Ollier would do a decade later in *Fuzzy Sets*, where the process suggests a sort of disintegration, Butor uses visibility and materiality to enhance the productivity of the text. Instead of rushing through words in order to reach their semantic facet, the reader can, is actually invited to, stay with the physical presence of words or groups of words on the page.

The few words isolated at the center of the first page, which is relatively very large (more noticeably so in the original French version) and almost completely blank, or white, assert the opposite of whiteness: *nuit noire* ("black night," or, more idiomatically, "pitch-dark"). Through printer's ink and meaning they convey simultaneously the darkness of the night and the dark skin of a large part of the population of Alabama, the first of the states examined in this étude. They also point to the moral darkness of those who are called whites, to the disproportionate amount of space whiteness occupies on the page. Theirs is a deep darkness that invades their entire being, effecting a synthesis of the two phrases of the text— "black night" and "Deep South." The assertion of blackness in the middle of a large white page is correlative to the nonviolent affirmation of civil rights made by Martin Luther King a few years earlier, precisely in Alabama.

The word *ALABAMA*, printed in capital letters and separating the two phrases just mentioned, allows such a correlation. Nevertheless, the mention of the specific place-name, "Cordova, Alabama," comes as a surprise. One might have expected Birmingham or Montgomery, or even more so Mobile, which the book's title seemed to call for. Mobile and Alabama were probably considered as being too much in harmony, as both words are derived from the names of Indian tribes. Cordova, on the other hand, is a small, little-known town in Alabama; the name almost inevitably suggests the famous Spanish city, hence a foreign intrusion.

The word thus stresses the foreign, colonial origin of the white population of the United States, which imposed its materialistic civilization (the wealth of Cordova, Spain, during the Moorish occupation is proverbial) on Indian territories.

The antithetical juxtaposition of Alabama and Cordova is typical of the rhetoric at work throughout *Mobile*. Cities as opposed to the countryside with its plants and animals, whites as opposed to blacks and Indians, European culture as opposed to the attempt to forge a new, American culture, various nationalities retaining their features as opposed to the dream of the melting pot, and so forth. The word *Cordova* vibrates like a chord and because of the Spanish city's material wealth foreshadows a proliferation of objects: automobiles painted in outlandish colors, clothing, trinkets, numerous flavors of ice cream . . .

The words *black night* and *Cordova* appear again on the next page, now linked to the word *Alaska* and a phrase, the "extreme north," that stands in antithesis to the "Deep South." It also introduces "the extreme proximity" (an antithesis in itself) of the "dreadful, the abominable, the unimaginable country" that has caused Americans to have so many "nightmares." The Soviet Union is not mentioned nor will it be anywhere else in the text. Nightmares will reappear, all of them linked to the fear felt by many whites with respect to blacks. It is the fear of the other, and the way in which the text assimilates the two others, the position in which the patchwork technique places them, tend to emphasize their irrational foundation.

At this point, and without even exhausting the meaning produced by those first two pages, it should be obvious that the text does not primarily refer to the reality of the states that are "represented." Cordova exists, but is of no consequence to the history or economy of Alabama; the same could be said of Douglas, Alaska, the second city of the text. Alabama is a southern state, but there are others, and one might say that Mississippi is even "deeper." Closeness to Siberia is not the most important element of Alaska's objective reality, in spite of army bases and military personnel; the latter are there because of a myth and they serve to perpetuate it. The text, however, does not refer to army bases; it utters the myth that brought them into being, a myth emanating from the "temples" of what will later be described as the "sacred city of Washington" (131). It is also significant that historical clichés such as gold diggers in Alaska or Alabama's role in the Civil War are ignored. The "representation" promised by the subtitle of *Mobile* is therefore not a mimesis but, as in one common meaning of the French term, a show or a performance based on words and on myths. The musical meaning of the word *étude* might also be kept in mind. Just as a sonata is composed in a given key, in B flat for instance, the architecture of *Mobile* is based on the order of the alphabet. That is why Alabama comes before Alaska, Cordova before

Douglas, Buick before Cadillac, apricot flavor before banana, and so forth. But since the text must also be productive, *Mobile* might be seen as an exercise in walking a linguistic tightrope, in seeing how far the alphabet can be taken before it must be modified lest it hamper the production of meaning. Another constraint, for which musical analogies could be found (in twelve-tone techniques, for instance), is that the name of a city can be mentioned only if it has a homonym in a geographically or alphabetically contiguous state. Such constraints are not new to literature, and in the past they have mostly affected poetry; more recently they were emphasized in the practice of the Oulipo, founded by Raymond Queneau (see my chapter on Georges Perec). To return to painterly echoes, one might imagine drawing lines on a map of the United States that would link all homonymous city names: the result would call to mind, in very general fashion, a painting by Pollock.

The United States has been subjected to an interpretation similar to the one applied to the lycée in *Degrés*. In the process, both shortcomings in the present or past and opportunities for the future have been disclosed. In each instance, the revelation has come out of the reader's experience with the text rather than because of a demonstration by the writer. When Sartre, in *Le Sursis*, confronts the situation of Mathieu in southern France with that of Milan Hlinka in Central Europe, he explains: "At 3:30 in the afternoon, Mathieu was still waiting, on the threshold of a frightful future; at the same instant, at 4:30, Milan has no more future."[13] In *La Peste*, before describing Paneloux's first sermon, Camus warns: "Long before that sermon, people were already talking about it in town, and it constituted, in its own way, an important date in the history of that period."[14] Interpretation, in traditional fiction, is often added to the narration as an integral part of the text. Interpretative statements were present in *Degrés*, as when Pierre Vernier pretends to read Tangala's thoughts but actually gives Butor's own indictment of Western civilization. Nor are they totally absent from *Mobile*. Toward the end of the forty-ninth sequence ("Wisconsin") the exclamation, "How eagerly we await you, America!" along with several others in that and in the final sequence are attributable to Butor, thus testifying to the difficulty writers have in leaving the reader alone.

Although *Description de San Marco* (1963) reminds one of *Mobile* in several respects, it signals the reappearance of the narrator. That is less a reversal of a rhetorical trend than a necessity brought about by the nature of the text. Clearly, neither the alphabet nor homonymy could provide a satisfactory basis for an interpretation of San Marco in Venice. Quotations remained a possibility, and Butor might have used works by Ruskin, Proust, and many others. But the basilica provided its own text, the numerous inscriptions taken from the Latin Vulgate translation of the Bible serving as captions to the mosaics of the church. Mosaics and captions provided the means to translate spatial architecture into the sequential features of a book. Since San Marco is a major tourist attraction, a distinction that tends to eclipse its existence as a place of worship, the narrative account of a visit, more aesthetic than touristic, is a logical device to give effective unity. It could also be one through which a form of irony is introduced, for had not the basilica been degraded from its original state, its true narrator might have been an officiating priest. Also, because of the fixed, monumental nature of its object, as opposed to the motion that characterized so many referents in *Mobile*, the narrative line adds an indispensable minimum of movement to the text. The result is a work of fiction, for obviously a description of San Marco either narrated by a priest or centered in the consciousness of a person attending Mass would have been an utterly different one, as it would have been had Butor chosen to emphasize statuary and architectural lines rather than mosaics. To paraphrase Jean Ricardou, the most objective description of the basilica would be limited to those two words, San Marco.[15]

Detailed description, because it is both incomplete and linear, marks the birth of fiction. Rather than a true description, it at once becomes a "precious distortion," to adapt a phrase from *L'Emploi du temps*—provided the writer is able to endow it with that quality. Here, it is inevitably a worldly representation; the visit begins on the piazza in the midst of tourists from all nations, buying souvenirs and consuming coffee, fruit juices, and *gelati*. They are present throughout the visit, as indispensable to San Marco today as were the merchants, butchers, *condottieri*, and pillaging crusaders of earlier times. Tourists' conversations, echoes from the past, descriptions of mosaics, and Latin inscriptions are the basic elements that are played against one another as others are in *Mobile*. All are familiar to anyone who has visited Venice, most are familiar even to those who have merely read about that city. As in previous works, their selection and ordering determine the meaning that a reader will extract from the text.

The typography and format of *6 810 000 litres d'eau par seconde* (1965; *Niagara*) recall those of the two works just discussed. Two texts from Châteaubriand's works, depicting Niagara Falls, play a role similar to that of biblical inscriptions in *Description de San Marco* or to the varied quotations in *Mobile*. The motifs of tourists visiting a famous monument and of the interaction between visitors and monument are taken up again with different emphases. The technique of using a multiplicity of couples as visitors stems from the honeymoon tradition associated with the Falls, and disintegrating relationships make one think of *Degrés*. A complex architecture based on numbers and units of time is common to this and nearly all other previous works.

6 810 000 litres d'eau par seconde is divided into twelve sections corresponding to months of the year, from April to March. On another level, the book encompasses a continuous time sequence of some seventy-six hours. Those, however, are not evenly spaced among the twelve sections. As the waters of the Niagara seem to increase their speed on approaching the precipice before the final downward rush, the hours appear to slip by faster and faster in Butor's text, their number being regularly augmented until the final section includes twelve. Throughout the book, an "announcer," who recalls in a depersonalized fashion the narrator of *Description de San Marco*, whose voice predominates, provides a descriptive and thematic narrative.

After Niagara Falls has been presented, mostly by means of Château-briand's words, two couples arrive at the site. One shares their expectations, their hopes, their reactions, and their memories. The hint of deterioration voiced in the initial section ("it goes without saying that the scene has changed considerably" [14]) becomes a major theme in the third and later it gradually permeates all relationships. Toward the center of the volume, a "Bachelor's Invocation" expresses the lament of the contemporary individual, alienated from so many things, especially from love. The theme of love (which a mere mention of Niagara Falls is bound to evoke), that of its decline, and the pageant of seasons from spring to winter might conjure up in the mind ancient myths of death and resurrection. Intimation of rebirth, however, such as could be detected in *Passage de Milan* or *Mobile*, is lacking here. The mood is more in keeping with that of *L'Emploi du temps*. Unlike what takes place during the American Indian Shalako ritual that occupies a crucial space in *Où*, there is no promise of a vernal return. Finally, the "announcer" speaks of tears and blood; the newlyweds fail to communicate; the older couple echo the words of the opening section, "We have changed." The text closes with Châteaubriand's description of badgers attempting to fish out of the whirlpool the broken remains of other animals. At the end, the concluding words are taken from the subtitle of *Atala:* "The Loves of Two Savages in the Desert."

Once more, one has witnessed the same process in its operation. Niagara Falls does not belong to the American folklore alone, it is as internationally famous in its own way as San Marco is. Most of the details presented in *6 810 000 litres d'eau par seconde*, with the exception of such precise data as are given in the title or here and there in the text, are familiar to Europeans and Americans alike, but the total impression is unlike anything the words *Niagara Falls* could have suggested before. Once more the writer has seen that life was "one great wrong" and, like Scheherazade, has described it in his tale, hoping to change the reader-king before he does additional wrong.

Portrait de l'artiste en jeune singe, with its undisguised biographical elements and interplay of two series of fragmented narratives, heralds a third aspect of Butor's fictional production. It is one in which textual interplay has a dominant role. He has been conscious of the process before, as I have shown, and as a 1964 text suggests: "A book must be a mobile awakening the mobility of other books, a flame rekindling their fire."[16] As with Jean Pierre Faye's *Analogues* and Claude Ollier's *L'Echec de Nolan*, the primary purposeful work is done with his own texts, but the process is altogether different. Many of his works of the seventies and eighties give evidence of that phenomenon, but for the purposes of this presentation I shall limit myself to examining *Illustrations II* (1960), *Où* (1971), and *Boomerang* (1978).[17]

At the source of *Illustrations II* lie nine texts that had originally been generated by photographs, engravings, watercolors, paintings, music, and "logograms," the latter being a special form of poetry invented by Christian Dotremont—one might also say, a special form of painting with words. Dotremont's presence here furnishes a key, as it implies that his work and, say, André Masson's are basically of the same nature. In other words, Butor's concept of "text" is a very broad one. To him, paintings and other works in the plastic arts are texts; landscapes are texts; the city of Bleston, in *L'Emploi du temps*, is a text that Revel needs to decipher. Seen in that light, those nine elements are themselves conscious absorptions, transformations, and representations of other texts. They are then transformed a second time, recast into a new shape.

Sometimes an intermediate step is involved. To elucidate this, a specific example should prove helpful. Out of the nine texts that eventually produced *Illustrations II*, I have chosen the one based on engravings by Jacques Hérold. First, fifteen plates were published under the title *Dialogue des règnes* (1967; Dialogue between the Kingdoms), each one displaying an embossed engraving by Hérold and a text by Butor. The plates are boxed but neither bound nor numbered so no definite sequence has been imposed upon the series. On each plate, arrangement and length of text differ according to the shape and mass of the engraved surface. Sometimes the text appears to rush in and fill all available non-engraved space; sometimes there is a mirrorlike effect between engraving and text. In all cases, perhaps because of the contagious effect of the title, a dialogue seems to develop between the free, rather dynamic abstract shapes and colors of Hérold's work on the one hand, and Butor's verbal inscriptions on the other. Lesser masses of text, usually vertical in shape, tend to be enumerative and devoid of syntax. Larger masses, often but not always horizontal, are made up of one or more complete sentences. In nearly all instances, each textual mass begins and ends with one of a series of key words: *sommeil, murmure, poussière, brume,* and *ombre*. On each plate, the word that ends one mass usually begins the next one. Days of the week, months, and seasons also provide recurrent words for the texts, as do names of countries and continents. The "reigns" of the title are those of the animal, vegetal, and mineral kingdoms. From the actual dialogues that have been imagined within the texts, there arise familiar themes, common to much of Butor's fiction and none the less serious for being stated by lesser creatures. Those dialogues merge into a lament conveying feelings of solitude and separation, exile and imprisonment. One is reminded of Revel's exile and imprisonment in Bleston, the bachelor's solitude as expressed at Niagara Falls, or the falling out between Vernier and his nephew.

The intermediate step was taken when Butor's text alone was published in a conventionally bound book.[18] As a first consequence, an unchangeable order for the text had to be established. It turns out that the bound version begins with what was the ninth plate of the original collection as it came from the publisher: "Shadows of pine trees stretch out over the water on a Monday dawn." The selection may have been made because the references to dawn and to the beginning of the week seemed appropriate in such a position. What was originally the first plate now constitutes the last sequence, with references to sleep, November, night, and midnight. To avoid the too obvious coming together of identical words at the end of one paragraph and the beginning of the next, more noticeable now that masses of text have been changed into linear sequences, one or several of the original series of key words have been inserted as separate paragraphs. Later, a full phrase or sentence, containing one of the same words, is placed in a similar position. So that there would not be too great a difference in length between sequences (several of Hérold's engravings left little room for the text), the total number has been reduced from fifteen to ten. While the mobility of the original plates has been lost, Butor has tried to prevent the order from becoming too rigid by separating them with the phrases *Ou bien* and *Ou encore;* both imply the possibility of permutation.

The final transformation occurs when the text of *Dialogue des règnes* is absorbed, along with others, into *Illustrations II.* A number of changes were made in preparation for the insertion. For instance, some of the longer run-in paragraphs have been pruned of many phrases or clauses that accented their lyrical quality. They are now set in lines of unequal length, and the resulting general appearance of "verse" compensates for the loss of a more obvious lyrical effect. Key words, groups of words, or statements that served as articulations between paragraphs have generally disappeared, since the linear nature of sequences, which gave them birth, has also vanished. The text is now composed to function on the page, each page existing as a unit, with the size and shape of the masses of print again being taken into consideration. On occasion, the former articulations have been replaced with vertical series of words taken from a larger vocabulary store in the text; the series plays the part of thematic echoes.

Since the text has been inserted into *Illustrations II* among others emanating from different sources, the textual interplay now begins to function. What preceded is not very different from what a writer might do when preparing previously published short pieces for inclusion in a collective volume. It would clearly be impossible to go into all the details of actual and possible interactions between the nine texts (or seven texts and two vignettes, as Butor refers to them) inasmuch as they depend in large part on qualities of the reader's imagination. I shall therefore attempt to give only a general idea of the placing of sequences from *Dialogue des règnes*. The ten have been reduced to five groups. Disjunctive phrases like *Ou bien* have been maintained, but the unity of the ten earlier sequences has been abolished. The table of contents of *Illustrations II* permits one to identify precisely the page on which each group begins and where it ends, but what happens in between is less obvious. Yet one perceives at once that since the text of *Dialogue des règnes* is disseminated between pages 40 and 157 of a 262-page book, it will interact more strongly with some texts, less with others. Since those having their source in a painting by Irving Petlin or in photographs by Bill Brandt do not appear before pages 184 and 226 respectively, they will presumably have only a secondary effect. On the contrary, the presence of texts based on watercolors by Ruth Franken, *Dans les flammes*, and on music by Henri Pousseur, *Paysage de répons* (Landscape of Responsories), will be felt at once, the more so, I believe, because of the contrasts that exist between these three. As befits the title, there is something allegorical and archaic about *Paysage de répons*, and that in itself acts as a setoff. *Dans les flammes*, on the other hand, has its original source in Ruth Franken's reaction to the self-immolation of Buddhist monks in Vietnam. Butor's accompanying text is entitled "Song of the Monk, addressed to Mme Nhu" (Mme Ngo Dinh Nhu was the sister-in-law of Ngo Dinh Diem, who died in the 1963 coup). Its opening lines, appearing on a left-hand page, "Lips of fire. / Nostrils of black fire / in a castle of balks" (50), confront a segment from *Dialogue des règnes* on the right. "February sleep in Piedmont at dawn, / come, beautiful still waters, said the spark, / come into this modest hearth, come and glow, / slowly burn in the center of this core of fervent porphyry" (51). The corresponding nouns "fire" and "spark" serve as catalysts for the interaction, also recalling and revitalizing an earlier association between "spark," "burning," and "blood" within the text of *Dialogue des règnes* (42).

The death of a watchman in Santa Barbara, following the explosion of a bomb at a university faculty club, in *Où* (1971; Where/Or), corresponds thematically to the fiery suicide of an Indo-Chinese monk in *Illustrations II*. In *Où* there are seven texts (or, in the same manner as before, five and two, the latter called "poles" rather than vignettes).[19] Their "autobiographical" nature is what one notices at first, out of habit, I suppose, and a bad one at that. Indeed, those of *Illustrations II* are just as "autobiograph-ical," for they represent the result of a writer's personal confrontation with a newly discovered "text" in the plastic arts. The basic sequences of *Où* are the outcome of the same writer's confrontation with another kind of "text": a place or event to which he has come or which he has experi-enced for the first time. In either case, the problem is to find a linguistic text that will adequately account for the experience, and I do not see that there is any essential difference either in the experience or in the process of representing it. Actually stressing the similarity, there is mention very early in the book of "the rectangle of my window" (11), by means of which the scenery is framed very much as a painting is (the very word *rectangle* is disseminated throughout the text). The possessive in that quoted phrase pinpoints the major distinction between *Où* and *Illustrations II:* here a narrator reappears, as he did in *Description de San Marco* following the more neutral *Mobile.*

The presence of a narrator constitutes one of two unifying factors, the other being a thematic use of climatic phenomena, mud, rain, fog, snow, and cold, in the five texts: "Le Boue à Séoul," "La Pluie à Angkor," "La Brume à Santa Barbara," "La Neige entre Bloomfield et Bernalillo," "Le Froid à Zuni." The two "poles" about which those texts revolve are Paris and Sandia Mountain in New Mexico. "J'ai fui Paris" opens the book; its corollary "Je hais Paris" is near the center. Both reverberate throughout the book while on the two closing pages are statements such as "I am coming back," "I shall have to flee again," and "But I shall come back" (391-92). Sandia Mountain also gives birth to two sequences, "35 vues du mont Sandia le soir l'hiver" and "Neuf autres vues du mont Sandia," that are similarly fragmented. Bringing the two together—thirty-five and nine views of Sandia Mountain—calls attention to another textual inter-play, in addition to the sort that was found in *Illustrations II.* In one of his volumes of collected essays, *Répertoire III,* Butor had entitled "Trente-six et dix vues du Fuji" his commentary on Hokusai's prints, *The Thirty-six Views of Mount Fuji.*[20] That suggests an analogy between Sandia Mountain and Fuji-san, the sacred mountain of Japan, the diminished number of "views" implying a hierarchy between the two. But Sandia is no sacred mountain. The sacred abode of the Taos Pueblo Indians, in the Blue Lake area, lies to the north. Sandia's first syllable repeats Fuji's honorific suffix, emphasizing that it is sacred only as a textual echo; it is a sacred word in the text.

In his essay on Hokusai Butor also drew an analogy between the Japanese artist and Claude Monet, who, in 1862, painted twenty views of the Rouen Cathedral as seen from the same window (Hokusai's prints each show Mount Fuji from a different vantage point). That, in turn, permits me to propose a further analogy, this time between Monet looking at his cathedral always from the same spot, and Michel Butor observing Sandia through the rectangle of his window always from the same angle, bemused by changing shapes and light patterns as the sun goes down. I intimated earlier that for Butor a painting was a text; the equivalence is now complete as his text becomes a counterpart of Monet's paintings. In the same essay he pointed out that "for Monet, the cathedral of Rouen is a pretext."[21] The word *pretext* is perhaps a bit strong where Butor's use of Sandia is concerned, but with that qualification it helps to understand what is involved in his "representation" of reality. His work is, without question, a textual representation, as the subtitle of *Mobile*, "Study for a Representation of the United States," already indicated; and I noted earlier that even the "description" of San Marco constituted a distortion of the basilica. One should, as I suggested earlier, keep in mind that the French phrase *représentation théâtrale* corresponds to our "theatrical performance." In the word *performance* the idea of mimesis is no longer present. Putting it differently, in a *représentation* the performance is more important than its object—which has almost become a mere pretext. As if to justify such an interpretation, Butor himself has written: "I feel more and more like organizing visual images, sounds, with words. In that respect, anyway, one can view a book as a small 'theater.' "[22] The narrator of *Où* also casts some doubt on the appropriateness of the word *description*—"My description (is it a description?)" (390)—and he exclaims several times as he attempts to inscribe on paper his "view" of Sandia, "any mountain is indescribable" (19, 110, 124).

Motion is an important theme in *Où*, for which one translation of the title might be "(T)here." Written with a grave accent *où* is a pronoun meaning "where"; without it *ou* is a conjunction meaning "or." While no equivalent device can be found in English, my suggestion does maintain the alternative between Paris (there) and Albuquerque (here). The notion of travel is implied in the five basic component texts. The manner in which Paris penetrates the text suggests both an attraction and a repulsion, translated into references to flight from and return to the French city. Sandia Mountain, seemingly the most stationary fixture in the book, is itself constantly changing as sunlight hits it at different angles, bringing out its different facets. The Indian Zuñi ritual of the Shalako, taking place at the time of the winter solstice, evokes the passing of the seasons and the years, the motion of the sun, its fading away coupled with a promise of return, animates many pages of the book. The presence of a narrative, which winds its way in and out of typographical devices similar to those in *Mobile*, also contributes to the feeling of movement. An even more eloquent manifestation of that theme is the way in which the act of writing has maintained its dynamism on the printed page. Far from becoming frozen into a rigid text, it preserves an atmosphere of constant struggle as the narrator attempts to give a textual representation of what he experiences. "I endeavor to cast my very small net over that enormous prey" (15). He frequently explains that he might have written or should have written something else, that he is tempted to erase or strike out what he has written, or that he has just torn up a page. In the end, he is forced to admit that what he has written is not what he thought he was going to write: the experience is common to most writers, but there are few who are inclined to reveal it.

As previous works do, *Où* gives evidence of the writer's sharing with King Shahryar a revulsion at the "great wrong" that permeates the world. Here it is the wrong perpetrated against the Indians by the whites who came to America (the book is dedicated "to all the Indians of New Mexico"); the wrong done by idealists, driven to despair, who resort to terrorist bombs; finally, the ever-present wrong of war. "*A pool of blood from distant not-so-distant wars present and close spatters you*" (252). And everyone else.

Like the preceding books, *Boomerang* displays a distinctive typography; like *Où*, it suggests a back-and-forth motion. As *Où* took the reader to various locations but emphasized the United States and its Indian population, *Boomerang* does the same while stressing the Australian aborigines. Differences, however, are even more notable. The first thing a reader notices is that inks of three different colors are used— black, red, and blue; one suspects that if the publisher had not worried over his profit margin Butor would have liked to have seven, one for each of the seven texts that interacts within the book (seven texts as before, but no "vignettes" or "poles"). Naturally, the texts are broken up, and colors serve to identify the text to which a sequence belongs. Thus "Jungle" is always printed in black, "La Fête en mon absence" (The Ceremony I Missed) in either red or black, "Courrier des antipodes" (Letters from the Antipodes) always in red, "Nouvelles Indes galantes" in either blue or red, "Bicentenaire kit" in blue, "Carnaval transatlantique" in blue, red, or black, and "Archipel Shopping" in blue or black. This entailed the requirement that no contiguous sequences of the last two texts, for instance, could be printed in the same color (with the exception of brief two-page sequences, for special effect: pp. 5-6, 24-25, 40-41, 54-55, and so forth). An additional constraint, obviously due to the economics of publishing, is that each sequence must have sixteen pages, no more, no less. While the color thus helps in identifying the text to which a sequence belongs, it is not enough: a blue sequence might belong to any of three texts. Words and symbols in the running heads complete the identification, as does their position at the top, middle, or bottom of the page. The sequences themselves are printed as masses of nonindented paragraphs, one or two per page, at the top, middle, or bottom of the page. The running heads also tell one whether one is in the northern (top of the page) or southern hemisphere (bottom).

As in previous texts, there are quotations from many sources, including Butor's own writings. He has read accounts of the voyages of Captain Cook and Bougainville, myths and legends of Australian aborigines as well as those of Northwest Coast Indians, novels by Jules Verne, Buffon's *Histoire naturelle*, the libretto of Rameau's *Iles galantes*, and he makes reference to the writings of Barthes, Bataille, Breton, Butler, Châteaubriand, Claudel, Diderot, Duchamp, Lautréamont, Melville, Roussel, Ségalen, and others, not to mention newspapers, brochures, and catalogs. He also quotes himself, one might say, using fragments of texts such as *Mobile* and *Bicentenaire kit* (1976), the latter being an homage to Marcel Duchamp and his green box, enclosed in a blue one, a celebration of the French mythical view of the United States, on the occasion of the bicentennial. A scholar has taken the trouble to compare the texts quoted in *Boomerang* with the originals.[23] He has discovered that often the "quotations" are more like paraphrases or adaptations; often, too, the "quotations" from Butor's own texts are "so substantially reworked as to constitute virtually new texts."[24] This establishes the primacy of the new text, as the earlier ones are subordinated to the role they play in the one that calls them forth. Nevertheless a distinction probably needs to be made between texts that were originally intended for insertion into *Boomerang* and those that were brought in as the book was being composed. The letters he wrote to his wife and in which the "Courrier des antipodes" is centered belong in a special category. He knew beforehand that he would put a lot of information in those letters, kept carbon copies for reference, and used some of the information in the book. As biography crept into the text, as it had in *Où*, more mundane sections of the letters were excerpted (e.g., problems with airline tickets, quality of the food on board, etc.), but the extent to which they were rewritten or partially invented cannot be determined at the moment, nor is it particularly important. What is significant is the emphasis they place on the architectural role of biography in the composition of *Boomerang*. In contrast with what happens in *Où*, it tends to textualize the narrator who, in most cases, belongs to an outside narrative—the one that is being quoted.

The title of this work also means more than a repetition of one of the thematics of *Où*. In both instances, of course, the writer is propelled out of his own country by a need to confront other cultures with his own and after a curved trajectory he is, like the actual boomerang, returned to his point of departure. He told one of his interviewers that he had been made aware, long before writing this series of books, of certain similarities between Egyptian art and the art of the Northwest Coast Indians; he also learned that the boomerang was known in the first dynasties of Egypt, and later forgotten.[25] On a metaphorical level, the boomerang of desire that took him to the Northwest Coast Indians and then to Australia landed him back in Egypt where the protagonist of *Passage de Milan* and the narrator of *Portrait de l'artiste en jeune singe* ached to go. Furthermore there is an analogy with the works of several other writers (Claude Ollier in particular) that appear to be haunted by earlier ones, which are like boomerangs that return to the place of writing. The situation is different with the several volumes of *Illustrations*, for instance; except in the case of the very first one, Butor knew when he was writing texts based on paintings that he would eventually recast them into books from which the original artworks would be absent. It is most unlikely that, in the early sixties, when writing *Mobile*, he planned to use portions of it in a new book to be published sixteen years later. Here, not only the texts return but also a portion of what Proust called the "deep self," which is naturally present in all of Butor's texts, one might say by definition, but is not easy to detect. With *Boomerang*, it could manifest itself a little less darkly.

Over a ten-year period, between 1975 and 1985, Butor published a series of five volumes under the general rubric *Matière de rêves* (The Stuff of Dreams). The first one was called by its generic title; the second was *Second Sous-sol* (1976; Second Basement); the third *Troisieme Dessous* (1977; Third Basement); the fourth, *Quadruple Fond* (1981; False Bottoms), was followed by the final *Mille et un plis* (1985; A Thousand and One Folds). He tends to group his books by five: there have been five volumes of criticism, *Répertoire* (1960-82); there are to be five of *Illustrations* (the first came out in 1964, the fourth in 1976), of *Envois* (1980 and 1983), and so forth. The stuff of dreams is both experiment and practice in the narrative form. It has nothing to do with dreams as such, and at the same time it has everything to do with them. As everyone knows from personal experience, dreams are like the real: they are knowable only in vague, fragmentary fashion. Psychoanalysts have never analyzed a dream, for all they have at their disposal are narratives of dreams. If the patient is honest, he may tell all he remembers, which might not be much, and his memory might be unfaithful; otherwise, he consciously omits, adds, or modifies. The ordinary narrative bears the same relation to the real as a dream narrative does to the dream; it is the product of journalists and historians. The literary or poetic narrative has a more problematic link to the real but it is not essentially different, for the two are subject to the laws, conventions, and stereotypes of language.

I have previously alluded to the importance and frequency of dreams in Butor's narratives, beginning with *Passage de Milan*. In those texts that could, without provoking too many objections, be called "novels," dreams were inserted as they had been in any number of different nineteenth- and twentieth-century novels, different from one another as Sartre's are from Proust's. In *Mobile* and *Portrait de l'artiste en jeune singe*, as well as in his essay on Baudelaire, *Histoire extraordinaire* (1969), dreams are more fully welded into the text. The novelty now is that instead of having an actual or fictitious dream narrative inserted into another narrative, the entire fictional text is composed along lines that are commonly featured in dream narratives. Among these I might mention abrupt and seemingly unmotivated changes, sudden appearances and disappearances, inability to see or to act. For instance, "We recognize a sign but cannot decipher what it says"; or, "Unfortunately unable to speak a single word, to utter the slightest sound. I would gladly tell them anything they want, but I am not able." In similar fashion, "In which direction should I crawl, for I can only crawl," and also, "I am paralyzed, the knees held tight between my arms." In one of the "dreams" the narrator is a Frenchman on a lecture tour in the United States. During a cocktail party that follows the lecture, he slips out via the back door, walks toward a beach, has a number of mishaps and eventually gets lost, sees a shack in the woods where he is greeted by a shaggy-haired man who says he used to be a French professor on a lecture tour and whose name is Bernard; he is taken in charge by several men whose name is also Bernard and who call him Bernard, and his skin soon turns black. The villa where the dinner in honor of the lecturer was to be given disintegrates because of a fire, but four pages later the setting for the dinner party is reconstituted on a barge. Toward the end of this narrative the narrator's size increases tremendously, and time, which had been stretched, now suddenly shrinks: the statement, "the sun is rising," is followed, a mere five lines later, by "It is already nightfall."

Other examples could easily be found. The point is that they are narrative devices, analogous to those of dream narratives, but functioning in conjunction with other devices. One such is what I might call the integrated quotation; when it appears in the first three volumes of *Matière de rêves* it foreshadows or is roughly contemporary with the practice already noted in connection with *Boomerang*. Outside texts are usually not set off by quotation marks, as they were in *Degrés* and as is common practice. In addition, many quotations are taken from different pages of the same text or series, providing them with a textual leitmotiv. Most of the "outside" quotations are from different works by Butor, others are reduced to single words—the names of characters out of well-known novels. For the French reader (who has had a secondary education) identifications may be easier than with an ordinary quotation: Mathilde de la Mole, Mme de Nucingen, Esmeralda unfailingly point to Stendhal, Balzac, and Hugo. The leitmotivs have a unifying effect, and one set of internal quotations results in wrapping up the series very neatly: the last dream of the fifth volume, "Le Rêve de la signature qui disparait," quotes rather abundantly from the first dream of the initial one. The result is to place considerable stress on one of the themes that runs through not only this set but through much of Butor's work, the problem of identity. It could also point to a conflict between the culturally induced desire for identity (with its concomitant originality) and the rational observation that one can invent little and that all works of art and literature are collaborative.

I have noted that the "quotations" in *Boomerang* are occasionally paraphrases. A third narrative device used in *Matière de rêves* is the paraphrase of a work of art; neither art criticism nor description, it comes close to a meditation. As a matter of fact, a text Butor wrote using paintings by Soulages as a starting point was, when cast into *Illustrations III*, called "Méditation explosée." A number of the texts I am now considering have their source in art works, thus establishing a continuity between the two series in spite of many differences. Graphics by Alechinsky, Peverelli, Kolár, Delvaux, and others lurk in the background of these texts. "Le Rêve de Vénus," for instance, was set in motion by eighteen paintings by Paul Delvaux; it was originally published in 1975 along with reproductions of the paintings,[27] then adapted with a number of textual additions for inclusion in the second volume of the *Matière de rêves, Second Sous-sol,* the following year. The process is very similar to the one undergone by "La Conversation," a text based on several paintings by Alessandro Magnasco that finds its way into the first volume of *Illustrations,* and already exhibits some of the features of the dream narrative. While tracing the steps that lead from an accurate description of some aspects of the paintings to a form of fiction triggered by those same paintings is fascinating for the scholar, such an analysis is hardly necessary for the cultured reader's enjoyment. What is required of him or her is a general acquaintance with the literary, artistic, and musical background of the time.

This leads to the final narrative device I want to mention here—adopting some of the procedures of musical composition. Butor, as well as other contemporary writers like Philippe Sollers or Maurice Roche, is quite knowledgeable about music.[28] He has used musical forms, the canon, for instance, in *L'Emploi du temps,* in order to strengthen the architecture of his novels. What one encounters in *Matière de rêves* are reprises, counterpoint, and some of the features of serial music.[29] Reprises involve both the literal repetition of brief sentences and repetitions, with variations, of slightly longer statements. One humorous version of the latter occurs in "Le Rêve des pommes" and has its obvious source in the traveler's anxiety when going through customs at a foreign airport. The statements are syntactically identical but nouns and qualifiers vary as the narrator assures the "Jailer," "Controller," "Adapter," or other official that he did not even bring this or that for his work or problems, he is so law-abiding, respectful, and so forth, the very idea of smuggling anything makes him blush, really, all he carries is a small bomb, qualified in various ways. Syntax is in this instance the framework within which an almost infinite series of variations could take place. While not identical, the process is not far removed from serial composition, if one can imagine grammatical categories taking the place of musical notes. There are actually texts by Butor in which the device is used exclusively, such as the various *Chansons pour Don Juan*, which are literally inexhaustible and any reader could continue to produce (more or less successfully).[30]

Counterpoint has been mentioned before in literature, and the names of Dos Passos, Huxley, and Gide come to mind in that connection. The use of the term, however, was purely metaphorical and one might well argue that counterpoint is impossible in writing. If one grants the correspondence between melodic line and narrative, two different narratives would have to be superimposed and perceived simultaneously. There are, nevertheless, in *Matière de rêves*, passages that come quite close. In one instance words or phrases from three different statements alternate, and the three statements can just about be read simultaneously—provided one does not read too slowly. It is then possible to identify the description of a peculiar operating room, a reference to the nature of the text itself, and the narrator declaring his love.[31] A truer form of counterpoint is theoretically not impossible; an elementary model is provided by Ferdinand de Saussure's anagrams.[32] What Butor is practicing in this series, and in so many other works as well, is precisely what he advocated in his essay *Les Mots dans la peinture* (1969), breaking down the aberrant barriers that separate literature from the other arts.

Ever since 1962, beginning with *Rencontre* (Encounter), a set of "meditations" on five etchings by Enrique Zañartu, but especially in the seventies and eighties, Butor has been composing texts in collaboration with graphic artists. These were first published in limited editions and then reworked for publication in trade editions such as *Illustrations*, *Matière de rêves*, *Envois* (1980 and 1983), or *Avant-Goût* (1984, 1987, and 1989; Foretaste), and I have briefly discussed the recasting process involving one of the texts of *Illustrations II*. Literally hundreds of titles for the original editions are in existence, some handwritten and handmade in fewer than ten copies each.[33] There is no practical way to give a critical account of them all in such restricted space as the chapter of a book. As to the "final" texts, I believe they all exhibit characteristics that are similar to those I discussed in the second half of this chapter. They bear witness to Michel Butor having created a new kind of fiction that transcends previous categories and for which there is presently no name. These texts not only tear down walls between writing and painting and the other graphic arts, they also dissolve the distinctions that were drawn between so-called literary genres—fiction, nonfiction, autobiography, poetry, prose. They represent an attempt by the "real" of personal experience to overcome the binding "reality" of culture and tradition. One might recall Jacques Lacan's statement, "Reality is the ready-made of fantasy, the real is when one gets bruised."[34]

NOTES

1   Michel Butor, *Passage de Milan* (Paris: Minuit, 1954), 152. Henceforth all references to works by Butor will appear in the body of the text.

2   Butor himself has written that Beethoven's Variations on a Theme by Diabelli was also an autobiography: see *Dialogue avec 33 variations de Ludwig van Beethoven sur une valse de Diabelli* (Paris: Gallimard, 1971), 237.

3   See Jennifer Walters's essay, "Symbolism in *Passage de Milan*," *French Review* 42, no. 2 (December 1968): 223-32.

4   Butor, "L'Alchimie et son langage," in *Répertoire* (Paris: Minuit, 1960), 19.

5   André Breton, *Manifeste du Surréalisme* (1924; rpt. Paris: Pauvert, 1962), 23.

6   Georges Charbonnier, *Entretiens avec Michel Butor* (Paris: Gallimard, 1967), 41-42.

7   I have developed this point in an essay entitled "The Problem of Point of View in the Early Fiction of Michel Butor," *Kentucky Romance Quarterly* 28, no. 2 (1971): 145-59.

8   Richard F. Burton, trans., *The Book of the Thousand Nights and a Night*, Medina Edition (printed by the Burton Club, n.d.), 1:9.

9   Burton, 10:55.

10 Burton, 1:23.

11 See my essay, "Readable / Writable / Visible" in *Visible Language* 12, no. 3 (Summer 1978): 231-44.

12 For a more detailed analysis, see my "Gloses sur les premières pages de *Mobile* de Michel Butor," *Modern Language Notes* 87, no. 6 (November 1972): 83-95.

13 Jean-Paul Sartre, *Le Sursis* (Paris: Gallimard, 1947), 7.

14 Albert Camus, *La Peste* (Paris: Gallimard, 1947), 109.

15 Jean Ricardou, *Problèmes du nouveau roman* (Paris: Seuil, 1967), 18-19.

16 Butor, "Victor Hugo romancier," in *Répertoire II* (Paris: Minuit, 1964), 240.

17 *Illustrations* (1964), in my opinion, does not quite belong to this group. It does share a similar origin with the other volumes having the same title, and changes to the original texts were made when they were collected in this edition. They were not fused together, however, and their individuality remains intact. The textual interplay involved is of a more common kind.

18 Butor, *"Paysage de répons" suivi de "Dialogue des règnes"* (Paris: Castella, 1968).

19 See also Butor, "Comment se sont écrits certains de mes livres," in *Le Nouveau Roman: hier, aujourd'hui* (Paris: 10/18, 1972), 2: 243-54.

20 Honolulu: East-West Center Press, 1966.

21 Butor, "Trente-six et dix vues du Fuji," in *Répertoire III* (Paris: Minuit, 1968), 163.

22 Butor, "Réponses à *Tel Quel*," in *Répertoire II*, 297.

23 See Michael Spencer, "Introduction" and "Afterword" to his translation *Letters from the Antipodes* (St. Lucia, Queensland: University of Queensland Press, 1981), a partial translation of *Boomerang.*.

24 Spencer, 163.

25   Jennifer Walters, "Michel Butor: An Interview," in *Malahat Review*, no. 60 (October 1981): 126-38.

26   See Michel Butor's *Le Retour du Boomerang* (Paris: PUF, 1988).

27   See *Delvaux* (Lausanne-Paris: Bibliothèque des Arts, 1975). For a more detailed analysis of this process, see my essay, "Un Texte perturbé: *Matière de rêves* de Michel Butor," *Romanic Review* 75, no. 2 (March 1984): 242-55.

28   See "Dossier Butor," in *Musique en Jeu*, no. 4 (1971): 63-111.

29   See Elinor Miller, "Critical Commentary II: Butor's *Quadruple Fond* as Serial Music," *Romance Notes* 24, no. 2 (1984): 1-9.

30   See the review *Degrés*, no. 1 (January 1973), for one version of these *Chansons*, together with instructions for composing other variations.

31   The texts read as follows: Une peinture où je vois mon visage. Leur hôpital. Textes éffilés. Qui flotte. Cécile. Sur un lac. Je t'aime. Dans la salle. Agnès. D'operations. Textes laminés. C'est la même lampe. Irène. Bleue, éblouissante. Je t'aime. Mais il n'y a pas. Mathilde. De table. Je t'aime. Ils m'étendent. Textes tréfilés. Sur le sol carrelé. Et s'accroupissent. Textes serpentins. Autour de moi (*Matière de rêves*, 16). The three individual strands that compose it are the following:

    a) Une peinture où je vois mon visage: textes éffilés, textes laminés, textes tréfilés, textes serpentins.

    b) Cécile, je t'aime; Agnès, Irène, je t'aime; Mathilde, je t'aime.

    c) Leur hôpital qui flotte sur un lac: dans la salle d'opération, c'est la même lampe bleue éblouissante, mais il n'y a pas de table, ils m'étendent sur le sol carrelé et s'accroupissent autour de moi.

32   For Saussure's anagrams, see Jean Starobinsky, *Les Mots sous les mots* (Paris: Gallimard, 1971).

33   See F. C. St. Aubyn, "Butor's Rare and Limited Editions: 1956-1983," *Review of Contemporary Fiction* 5, no. 3 (Fall 1985): 176-83.

34   As quoted by Jean-Francois de Sauverzac, "Au-delà de la psychologie," *Les Nouvelles littéraires*, 17-24 September 1981, 32.

10

Jean Pierre Faye

The first book by Jean Pierre Faye, *Entre les rues* (Back Alleys), made a rather quiet appearance in 1958, at a time when the notorious special issue of the review *Esprit* was publicizing the fact that something was astir in the world of fiction.[1] Belonging to the same generation as Robbe-Grillet and Butor, he waited longer than they did before writing his first work. A poet like Butor, he published poetry when he was twenty—much earlier than the latter. Indeed, strands of poetry run through Faye's early work, and he often daubs objects with an aura of significance quite different from the correlative status to which they appeared limited in Robbe-Grillet's early prose.

Entre les rues exhibits neither the rigorous architecture of Ollier's *La Mise en scène*, for instance, nor the technical and theoretical preoccupations of Robbe-Grillet's *Les Gommes*. At first glance, the formal divisions of the book seem haphazard: there are two parts numbering 71 and 136 pages, with seven unnumbered chapters in the first part and eleven in the second. Chapters are of uneven length, and four chapters in the second part, not always the longer ones, are subdivided into two or three sections. It would also seem that the world of appearances is respected. The events of the narration follow in conventional chronology, taking place in easily identifiable locations. Of course it does not take long to discover a simple pattern in the organization. The shorter chapters describe actions or events, the longer ones are made up of reflections or discussions of those events and are located close to the beginning and end of each part. Two short chapters precede the first long one (obviously something must happen before it can be discussed), two short ones follow the last long one—and they suggest the consequences of a failure. While chronology is respected, not a single date is given, nor is it possible to determine precisely how much time elapses between the beginning and end of the narration—certainly several weeks, perhaps a number of months. At any rate, it is the reader who assumes chronology (since nothing in the book denies it) or even creates it. A geographical reference to Cicero on the third page unmistakably places the setting in Chicago, and later the scene shifts to Nevada and to Los Angeles. Chicago, however, is not mentioned by name. I assume the presence of Las Vegas because it is a gambling town reached while driving in a northeasterly direction, with the Mojave Mountains visible in the rearview mirror, and I take Los Angeles for granted because there is little else west of Las Vegas that might fit Faye's evocation. The French reader, for whom the book was intended, could possibly not reach such conclusions, but it hardly matters. The point is that Faye is not concerned with reproducing everyday reality; he suggests it, as a matter of course, or even plays with it, something that is quite evident in his treatment of detail.

Occasionally, as with several other writers, one is reminded of Giraudoux—a Giraudoux who would have read Henry George, the nineteenth-century journalist and social reformer, rather than La Motte Fouqué. There are in *Entre les rues* narrative ellipses of a sort that Giraudoux might have committed, as when the narrator, who is guiding a policeman to the body of a dead man at the end of one chapter, appears on a Nevada highway at the beginning of the next. Sometimes the ellipsis takes place within one sentence: "We were riding along without a word, and she was waving to me from the car window as she drove away."[2] What clearly has been left out, immediately following the comma, is something like "and then she let me off in front of my place; I watched her leave . . ." Faye's statement manages to convey more effectively the narrator's impression and state of mind. *Entre les rues* also contains Giraudoux-like images, those resulting from an unexpected and suggestive association of words that carry the statement far beyond what the immediate context would have suggested. The opening paragraph of the novel presents an expressionist view of a barber shop, with a row of customers facing a row of containers of shaving cream, hair lotions, and the like on a shelf along the mirror. "One must read them differently, objects from left to right, men from right to left from professional to conjugal hand." Giraudoux's tone was different, and he was much more verbose, but the stylistic approach was very similar. "She had written to Houbigant, to the tailor, to *Old England* for sweaters, to the other tradesmen for socks, to all such addresses as Jérôme had imposed upon her like holy scriptures and which were now the frightful tags of Bardini's life."[3] When Faye comments, still in that same first paragraph, "The ivory object . . . encloses this empty section of the mirror where a face was nodding, he was sleeping ironically, but it was no longer true, because faces are stated in the imperfect amidst things in the present," he reminds one of Giraudoux's remark about the Germans "Who have invented, just to pass life and time away, beer, war, the ocarina, and such a large number of irregular verbs."[4] None of this is meant to imply that Jean Pierre Faye was influenced by Giraudoux; rather it suggests a more general kinship, a metaphysical anxiety masked by wordplay, analogous to that which allowed Claude-Edmonde Magny to draw a parallel or two between Giraudoux and Maurice Blanchot. It also identifies one of the poetic strands I have referred to.

A European immigrant or visitor, Verdier, stumbles upon two seemingly unrelated events one evening in Chicago: a conversation overheard in a cafeteria and the floor plan of an apartment inadvertently left on the table on the one hand, and on the other an unidentified dead man lying in the apartment of a girl named Mona, where Verdier was supposed to obtain an address. Partly by chance and partly because he is curious by nature, he finds himself trapped in a series of interlocking circles, all circumscribing the victim whose body he had discovered. They include militants of the Left, intellectuals, blacks, labor union groups, artists, and a few who have made a political switch to the Right. In his stumbling fashion, he comes close to solving the murder, which, with the uncertainty common in this work, appears to have been both political and fortuitous —unless a woman was the pretext. Be that as it may, someone decides that Verdier has become too inquisitive. As he walks along a quiet street a car stops beside him, three men jump out and push him inside. He is driven out of town to an abandoned quarry or tunnel or perhaps a cave, and the reader is left in doubt as to his ultimate fate.

A critic has said that "*Entre les rues* makes us participate in the obstinate, hesitant walk of a man trying to orient himself."[5] Verdier, who tells his story in the first person, does wander a great deal, but his obstinacy makes one think of a quest and brings to mind some of the other quest-oriented fiction of twentieth-century French literature. Comparisons and contrasts, enlightening as they may be, would take one too far afield. I shall simply mention Gide's *Faux-monnayeurs* (1925), Giraudoux's *Aventures de Jérôme Bardini* (1930), Aragon's *Les Voyageurs de l'impériale* (1947), Giono's *Le Hussard sur le toit* (1951), Beckett's *Molloy* (1951), several works by writers discussed in this volume, and draw a few analogies with Céline's *Voyage au bout de la nuit* (1932). Like Bardamu, the narrator of *Entre les rues* turns out to be a former medical student; like him, he has undergone brain surgery and appears recurrently afflicted by it. In both instances there is a wandering that is brought into focus through an agency that is independent of the narrator—the existence of Robinson and his determined presence in Céline's novel, a murder in Faye's. Both protagonists go to the United States, one briefly holding a job at the Ford plant in Detroit, the other working in a steel mill in Gary, and both fail in their undertakings. In both instances the text ends with a lyrical statement conveying at least pessimism and perhaps despair. The effect of each work is very different of course, and Faye's ellipses contrast most obviously with Céline's dynamic profusion. But lest such analogies lead one to the wrong conclusions, the initial reaction of the critic cited above is worth recalling: "[It is] the most unusual, most baffling, and perhaps most original novel that has been published in a long time."[6]

Entre les rues is told exclusively from the point of view of a first-person narrator, even though, from the standpoint of the reader, some uncertainty on that score pervades the first few pages. In effect, the text conveys a discontinuous series of immediate sense perceptions. In his second work of fiction, *La Cassure* (1961; The Break), Faye exploits the ambiguity of the narrative point of view, thus pointing to what is surely his major preoccupation as a writer: the meaning of narrative. As in the previous work, the main character appears to be drifting among members of several circles, but this time the locale is France. The book derives its unity not from a murder but from something more intrinsic to that character's being—it is not something he stumbles upon by chance, it is something within himself that produces a break with his wife. To the previous question, can the murder be solved? now corresponds a new one, can the marriage be repaired? There is tighter integration of the various components of the book when the medical problem, for again there is one affecting the main character, is used as a correlative of much of what takes place. It is also reflected in the book's title.

Simon Roncal, the protagonist of *La Cassure*, wanders from woman to woman (his wife, Guiza, walks out on him several times), and is more or less loosely tied to three separate social or political groups. At one point he briefly attends an informal lecture and discussion on the subject of hebephrenia, which is a chronic form of schizophrenia. Important as the reference is, however, I do not believe we need be concerned with precise clinical manifestation of such a psychosis. The allusion helps to enlarge upon the meaning of the title and to structure a number of features or events in the direction of a single center. Justification for tying hebephrenia to Simon is provided in the text, when he is introduced to those attending the lecture: "He is interested in what you are doing now" (78). Many things then fall into place. When Simon is asked if he is married, he answers, "Partly" (34). He is an elementary-school teacher conducting a series of examinations in the north of France when the book opens, but although the month is June (not yet summer vacation in France) the text gives no sign of any pupils, and when he is asked about his friends he replies, "Here I don't have so many friends" (29). In the fall he is transferred to Paris, without a regular teaching assignment—he says he is *détaché*, and that appropriate administrative term acquires suggestive connotations (133). His situation is similar to that before: "Do you have any friends here?—Hardly anybody" (73-74). Having drawn on the wall of a phone booth a symbolic design (a diamond inscribed in a rectangle) that clarifies for himself his relationship with other characters in the fiction, he feels he cannot relate his discovery to anyone else, that is, transform a spatial network into linear, narrative terms. "What in space constitutes a single chord cannot be translated into a sequence without falling to pieces" (172). The narrative is linear, of course, but flashbacks begin to undermine it, and the sort of ellipses already noted in *Entre les rues* acquire even greater relevance here. In that earlier work I tended to think of Giraudoux rather than mental illness. When the latter was noticed it seemed an isolated character's illness, one which did not affect the core of the work. In *La Cassure*, such ellipses echo the break between Simon and Guiza, as well as the disturbances that affect each one individually, the gaps that separate the groups (teachers and labor unions) that Simon is working with, and finally the split within France that nearly exploded in full-fledged revolution—the narrative ends in May 1958, when the Fourth Republic collapsed under the pressure of French army generals in Algeria.

Actually, to speak of discontinuity in the narrative line is not enough. There are six different narrative lines in this work, each one identified by the person of the subject pronouns. The third-person narrative accounts for an overwhelming majority of the statements in the text. On the second page, however, one encounters the first of nearly a dozen shifts to the second-person singular, generally of short duration. At the outset of the second chapter, there are shifts to the first-person singular as well as less frequent instances of the first-person plural. That plural person varies in designation and must therefore be considered as making up two separate narrative lines. In chapter 2, *nous* designates Simon and his wife Guiza; in chapter 8, Simon and Liana, the woman who looms more and more importantly in his life. Finally, there are two instances, one in chapter 3 and one in chapter 4, where the first-person pronoun quite obviously refers to Liana and not to Simon. With the latter two exceptions, one might be tempted to assume that it is Simon who is speaking throughout, whether he speaks of himself in the third person, or whether he uses the first and directs his words at Guiza as *tu* (this invariably happens in her absence). In a different context Emile Benveniste, taking Arab grammarians as a point of departure, has said that the third-person pronoun is used to designate the one who is absent; it represents "a non-personal invariant and nothing else." He is led to the observation that "the statement 'I is an other' in Rimbaud furnishes a typical expression of what is, properly speaking, mental 'alienation,' in which the 'I' is deprived of its essential identity."[7]

One might say that when Simon refers to himself in the third person he proclaims a distance between his two selves, mirroring his schizophrenic condition. A clue to that, as well as to the likelihood that the first-person narrative corresponds to a higher degree of consciousness, occurs when Simon settles down for the night in an armchair: "He touched the arm of the chair, and he searched beyond as he turned on his side; the distance would awaken him, again he was saying I" (160). The split within Simon goes far back, and he tells a personal myth to explain it. Born on the French side of the Pyrenees, he bears the name of a small town, Roncal, that lies on the Spanish side—perhaps because of the indiscreet behavior of one of his female ancestors who returned pregnant from a festive trip across the border. Nevertheless, one should keep in mind that Simon is the focus of the narration, whatever complexity might have been engendered by a multiplicity of pronouns. He is the intelligence through which nearly all that happens is conveyed to the reader. It is not so much that he is mentally ill; rather, conditions are such as to be amenable to significant statement only in terms of mental illness and its linguistic correlatives. If the blurb on the back cover of the book is any indication of Faye's intentions, the *cassure* is to be found first in Guiza and not at all in Simon. Apparently his correlatives got out of hand, or, perhaps, the statement should be taken ironically (and this implies a more subtle form of *cassure*). The initial break that exists within Guiza, although a minor one, enables both characters and readers to become fully conscious of the more important ones that exist within themselves and within their society.

Seemingly casual references to the town of Cicero, to Henry George, and others in *Entre les rues* are echoed in *La Cassure* by the mention of Guernica, Jules Guesde (the French socialist), La Bourse du Travail, La Libre Pensée. They should serve to establish within the reader's consciousness the network of a canvas upon which a dialectical text can be woven—one that possesses a definite political orientation. For a number of readers, however, this did not happen. French reviewers of those two works made no mention of any political overtones. This seems hard to account for, even if one grants that the American setting of the first text might have made political references more obscure. One possible explanation is that those who read Faye in 1958 and 1961 were prejudiced by the label of poetry pasted on his previous publications and by the affinity they detected with other young writers whose absence of overt political statements in their fiction they had misinterpreted. Be that as it may, it became impossible to ignore the political context of *Battement* (1962; Throbbing).

At this point, the extent to which basic patterns are repeated becomes particularly striking. Again the main character is alienated; he is a stranger, as was Verdier in *Entre les rues*, and is designated by the same initial letter as that of the earlier protagonist, V. It appears that he worked in a pharmaceutical laboratory in France, but the job has become unbearable. He has been given a temporary position, selling medical encyclopedias. At the outset of the narrative he is in Munich, where he is to spend a few months. His wife has stayed behind, in Paris, thus completing his estrangement. Actually, she believes he has come to Munich because a former mistress, who has since married, lives there—but he does not even know her married name. As with the earlier Verdier, much happens to V. by chance, and he soon stumbles upon the woman, now married to a Bulgarian doctor. That is important, as much because of the stumbling as of the actual meeting. It suggests, beyond the nature of the role of reality that I have already mentioned, the role the anecdote plays in Faye's fiction—something I shall make clear presently.

The word of the title, *battement,* refers to a throbbing or a pulsation, which is translated into every aspect of the text. Thematically, it imposes itself in the very first pages, as sounds and lights from the city break like waves, rhythmically, into the hotel room where the main character is staying. The rhythm is not only temporal but spatial, for zones of light and darkness hit him from several directions, creating stripelike patterns on the walls (also providing a title for the first of the book's three sections—*Bandes*). Such thematic manifestations are present throughout. In addition, some of the correlatives of the constantly present pulsations are linked, imagistically, to narrated events. For instance, the pulsating sound that emanates from crowds in the city is, on several occasions, translated as *abois* or *aboiements* (barkings), which echoes the sound of barking dogs V. remembers hearing outside the mental hospital where he had been treated earlier (his symptoms are similar to those of Verdier and Roncal). Another sort of oscillation develops, mental rather than physical, between city and hospital. But the phenomenon also takes place on the level of the narration.

At this point it will be helpful to remember that, during a symposium held under the aegis of *Tel Quel* and presided over by Michel Foucault, Jean Pierre Faye stated his conception of the present moment as divided between an actual present and an immediate past, as a person is both receptive to impressions from the outside and productive of verbal statements (interior or spoken).[8] At any given moment, one of the two usually predominates. It constitutes the person's actual present, and the other is relegated to the immediate past. Sometimes inner consciousness pushes the outer world aside, sometimes outer consciousness obliterates thought. Faye expresses such alternations, in the text of *Battement,* through shifts from present to past imperfect tense and, seemingly to add a further disruptive element, from first- to third-person subject. Consequently, what according to Benveniste is the "absent" subject commands a verb in the present while the first person (expressed or implied) is tied to the (immediate) past. The text might be said to be throbbing internally as its verbs oscillate. Each succeeding brief chapter, of which there are about a hundred and twenty, some of them flashbacks, alternately

presents the main character from the inside (*je*) and from the outside (*il*).
Yet in spite of that there remains the impression of a single narrator—a
word used by as knowledgeable a reviewer as Philippe Sollers.[9] Obviously
there is no one else, aside from the writer, to whom the sections written
in the third person could be ascribed. One is allowed to penetrate no
other consciousness, and since V. is continuously present throughout,
one might say that everything, regardless of pronouns, is described from
his point of view.

In the early sixties it had not yet become the practice to speak of the
text as a somewhat autonomous, generative assemblage of signs. Books
like *Battement* soon made a new terminology indispensable. As in the
case of some of Ollier's protagonists, calling V. a "narrator" raises a
number of irrelevant questions having to do with realism and plausibility
(which was not so obviously the case in *Entre les rues*). Referring to V. as
the central intelligence is not particularly adequate, for there is nothing
to be filtered through his consciousness aside from the events that affect
him directly; besides, the impersonal style of much of the text often
conveys the impression that he is not really involved. He seems as much
detached from the events in Munich as personal pronouns referring to
him are scarce, whether *il* or *je*. There are chapters where the first-
person pronoun is avoided throughout, even though, according to the
pattern of alternations, those pages should present a first-person narrative
with verbs in the imperfect. Personal pronouns appear more frequently
when V.'s individual problems come to the fore. That might be considered to conform with the behavior of a schizophrenic person, who has
difficulty in maintaining an interest in the world. Yet I do not see *Battement*, any more than the two preceding books, as a study in mental illness.

Just as the plague in Maurice Blanchot's *Le Très-haut* was metaphorical, schizophrenia in Faye's fiction appears to correlate to the
plight of the uncommitted. V. seems as much lacking in political or social
awareness as he is incapable of true emotional involvement. He goes to
Munich for purely selfish reasons. Once there, he makes some half-
hearted attempts to locate his former mistress, Mérie. But everything
that happens to him is accidental. It simply turns out that the woman who
occupies the room next to his and with whom he strikes up an acquaintance is connected with the National Liberation Front of Algeria (FLN).
It is by sheer coincidence that he meets Mérie again, who is also working
for the FLN and gives him a copy of a book directed against French
colonialism—which he does not refuse. It is merely by accident that he
later drops the book in the street, thus allowing it to be identified by
members of La Main Rouge, a rightist group, who are following him
because of his meetings with FLN sympathizers. The rightists quite
logically (and wrongly) conclude that his encyclopedia business is
merely a cover for distributing FLN propaganda, and, on the last page of

the book, they kill him. There is, however, no overt statement in the text that specifically justifies any of the points I have just made, nor is it even stated that the action takes place in Munich. Rather, the work is so structured as to make such conclusions, in my opinion, inescapable.

The story in *Battement* functions as a kind of lens through which verbal and thematic elements are refracted, converging on its focal point, which is the meaning of the narrative. The protagonist of Camus's *L'Etranger* has no socially accepted scale of values and he is, by chance, trapped by a series of events that eventually lead, after he kills a man, to his execution. It was accordingly quite appropriate for Philippe Sollers to entitle his review of Faye's book "Un Nouvel etranger." But while Camus could not hide a certain amount of feeling for Meursault and endowed him with a peculiar aura of innocence, V. benefits from no such treatment. He is not innocent but ill, and to Meursault's moments of happiness correspond V.'s moments of suffering. Meursault's innocence might be said to signify either his estrangement from a society in which a man may be condemned to death because he failed to cry at his mother's funeral or a refusal to accept the guilt of colonialism. In the final analysis, as all elements of *Battement* converge, they point to V.'s illness being not so much schizophrenia as alienation. It is a total alienation, beginning with the Marxist connotations of the word (and that is probably why Verdier, Roncal, and V. reveal so little of professional activities that are, in such a sense, alien to them) and broadening to include the self. As V. says, after he remembers seeing the faces of the two men who followed him reflected in a store window, "As if I had seen them without knowing it, as if they had been seen without my being involved by the one who watches everything without thinking about it" (64). Such a person, in the presence of a danger that he does not comprehend, can only behave like a trapped animal: "This might precisely be, perhaps, the time to recognize that an animal has fallen precipitously and flutters or stays trapped indefinitely, or remains petrified in a showcase in an unspecified location" (111).

Those three works of fiction have displayed the growing involvement of Jean Pierre Faye with narrative technique, not so much on account of the techniques themselves, but because of the meanings the various forms of narrative can generate. I have alluded to the interplay between the several pronouns, *je, il,* and *nous,* and also between verb tenses, and to the assault made on narrative linearity. I have also mentioned a similarity in the pattern of events, which mirrors the narrative techniques. The question now raised by *Analogues* (1964) is whether those fragmentary narratives are truly independent or constitute fragments of a larger narrative.

Labeled *récit autocritique,* implying, as did Ollier's *L'Echec de Nolan,* a reworking of the former narratives, *Analogues* begins with an *Hors-texte,* which might have been called a "preface," in which Faye brings up the issue of the narratable and the nature of the narration. Putting aside all questions related to ethics, the question of what is aesthetically narratable has received varying answers over the centuries, and concern over the effect of narrative over narration has probably increased of late, concomitantly with that of point of view. That there might be a correlation with the historical evolution of musical composition is also suggested: "It cannot be purely a matter of chance if the first romances in prose are contemporary with *ars antiqua* and the first examples of polyphony, and if so-called classical narration is an outgrowth of the Renaissance as much as Florentine and Venetian recitatives" (12). The evolution from tonal to serial composition has a counterpart in the development of contemporary narrative techniques. (Faye's interest in music, which he shares with other contemporary writers, was already in evidence in *La Cassure*, where he compared spatial representation to a musical chord; his knowledge is not as extensive as that of Maurice Roche, to whom *Analogues* is dedicated, and who explained aspects of musical composition to him.)[10] If broadening the concept of the narratable and multiplying points of view actually enrich the narrative, increasing its signifying possibilities, a writer might achieve similar results by filling in gaps, so to speak, and having earlier narrative segments proliferate. And that is precisely the function of *Analogues*.

As I understand it, the title refers to the relationships between events in narration and the narratives (when there is more than one point of view) and between different characters and events in separate narratives. At first sight, the book would seem to presuppose the reality of the characters in the three earlier works of fiction, the writer now deciding to reveal details, antecedents, or developments that he could not, for one reason or another, mention before—somewhat as François Mauriac revealed what happened to Thérèse after she disappeared into the crowd in Paris at the end of *Thérèse Desqueyroux*. But that is the kind of realistic fallacy that needs to be guarded against. There are indeed "characters" in Faye's fiction, and they are "credible" to the extent that a French critic, in reviewing *Battement*, found himself puzzling over what could have made the narrator's former mistress so attractive to him.[11] There are also, as I have pointed out, recognizable settings. In either case, however, belief and recognition are subjective and incidental, taking place in the reader's mind rather than in the text. There is such a place as Roncal, in the Spanish Pyrenees, but had Faye invented it the effect in *La Cassure* would have been the same. A young woman named Dow-Jones, in *Entre les rues*, says she is the grandniece of the corporation's founder, and it matters little that the actual founders, Charles H. Dow and Edward D. Jones, were separate persons, for the name is needed on account of its suggestive value; it gives rise to the burlesque incident in which she marries a stranger in order to get rid of such a compromising surname. The setting of *Battement* is clearly Munich, but all it needs to be is a large foreign city. More important than links with commonplace reality is the interplay between pronouns, verbs, places, and circumstances, for what this ultimately involves are fundamental relationships between human beings, both as individuals and as groups. Hence, in large part, the inevitable political overtones of Faye's fiction.

The main setting for *Analogues* is the city of Basel, through which the Rhine flows, describing a curve in the reverse image of the one traced by the Seine in Paris and dividing the city into unequal parts. The correspondence recalls the title of Faye's collection of poems, *Fleuve renversé.*[12] The mirror image could suggest the distortion imposed upon a narration by a new narrative. The city stands at the intersection of three countries, France, Germany, and Switzerland. It is thus analogous to the book, which is born out of the confrontation and proliferation of three earlier works of fiction. It is a multilingual city, just as the book is written in a number of narrative styles.

There are two parts to *Analogues.* One might say that these are articulated by means of *La Cassure,* the "break" having become a hinge. The name of Guiza is used in section headings exclusively in the first, that of Simon almost exclusively in the second. The section concluding part 1 is indeed like a hinge that allows the second part to unfold. The major domain of Mona, a name from *Entre les rues,* is part 2; and El., from *Battement,* while dominating part 1, cannot be ignored in part 2. For me, at least, El. dominates *Analogues*—poetic justice after having been practically suppressed by the main character of *Battement.* Each part, in turn, is divided into "Genesis," where the emphasis is on narrative, and "Counterpoint," where it is on characters, all of which are now described in the third person. The effect is one of a gigantic collage (there actually is a sequence entitled "Collages" with excerpts taken from texts ranging from the *Iliad* to *Finnegans Wake*) and held together in the reader's mind by the very analogies that exist between *Entre les rues, La Cassure,* and *Battement.* A new character, Imra, who acts as a sort of mirror, is introduced to provide an anecdotal link with Mona, Guiza, and El., feminine characters of previous works. What she reflects is not reality, for she operates within the fiction only, serving to generate analogies. The male characters are obviously linked through their mental illnesses and surgery and additionally through the new connections established between feminine characters. Another new character, this one masculine, an Algerian who remains nameless, emerges in order to give El. the possibility of engaging in a self-searching dialogue that runs through a large portion of *Analogues.*

As narratives, dialogues, and statements are played against one another, as characters grope their ways often in languages not their own, one gets the impression that all this is a struggle to become integrated in a universal human narrative that would transcend the various languages that men speak and that, if attained, would speak the truth about the human condition. There seems to be a vague mystical aura about *Analogues.*

The same year as *Analogues* and two years after *Battement, L'Ecluse* (1964; The Sluice) brought Faye general recognition, as the result of a literary prize. Many elements of this fourth work of fiction (actually his fifth but I am placing *Analogues* on a separate plane) are similar to those of the previous ones, which Faye had earlier described as forming a trilogy. Perhaps, even though the blurb for this one speaks of *le carré du récit,* they could be viewed as constituting something like a tripod, a base from which this new work has been launched. *L'Ecluse,* while it does not enter into the narrative complex of *Analogues,* shows the same allusive treatment of reality and plot. It presents an estranged main character, handles the narrative line by means of shifts from first- to second- and third-person pronouns, and develops the theme of illness—just as the previous works did.

The initial letter of the main character's name is again V. But this time it is a woman, and that letter links her to the protagonists of *Entre les rues* and *Battement* only through an artifice: her name was Jane, but an Italian friend changed it to Gianna and later to Vanna. That is the phonetic equivalent of the French word *vanne,* meaning a sluice, which makes of her a correlative of the book's title. Verbal echoes then reverberate in several directions. Most of the setting for *L'Ecluse* (three out of four parts) is Berlin, and that city's network of canals brings to mind the necessary sluice gates. The same word, *sluice,* is used to refer to a checkpoint between East and West Berlin, where currencies and language were commuted (118). Vanna herself, at one point, because she cannot, on account of special circumstances, outwardly express thoughts or emotions, is described as being imprisoned within herself—a condition linked to the title by way of the book's epigraph, *exclusa aqua, eau enfermée.* Many other references might be adduced, but the last one mentioned reinforces the analogy between Vanna and earlier characters. I should emphasize, however, that Vanna differs from them in one important respect: in spite of her being manipulated by powerful forces, she appears much more aware and concerned than they were.

Cleavages similar to those affecting Roncal and V. are shown to be present in Vanna. Her mother was English, her father was a French general. She still loves a man, Alexandre (known to some as Alé, to others as Sandro), who has left her to marry another woman and possibly sleep with a third, but she has successive affairs with other men. She resides in the then divided city of Berlin (a character in *Entre les rues* says, "When I hear people talk about leukotomy I think of Berlin" [75]). Though she works in the West she is much intrigued by what goes on in the East. She fantasizes a great deal, but not all her daydreams are exclusively self-centered. In the end she survives, and it is Alé who is killed, presumably by the mysterious organization whose presence is felt throughout most of the book.

Vanna is not pictured as being ill, although she does become so at the end of the second part. Indirectly, her sickness results in her inability to return to East Berlin, and that could be symbolic. Other characters are ill or they have head scars similar to those of Liane in *La Cassure*. All that should be familiar material to a reader acquainted with Faye's previous books, especially as the most significant use of illness transcends individual instances. Vanna recalls that earlier she had to explain the Berlin situation to Alé by equating Nazism to a disease: "The city had suffered a long and violent illness, and no one had known how to treat it; and by chance, or for want of something better, not knowing anything better to do, they had cut it in half" (38-39). That, in fact, is the only specific reference to a generalized pathological state, a presentation quite in keeping with Faye's allusive technique. It suffices nevertheless to raise the significance of illness as symbol beyond what it had previously seemed to imply. At times *L'Ecluse* comes close to being hallucinatory. A member of the international subversive organization to whom Vanna has been introduced describes to her a developing situation that may possibly lead, and therefore will lead, inevitably and by chance, to the destruction of Jerusalem (a divided city when Faye was writing and therefore similar to Berlin), without anyone's being able to blame anyone else for it—the perfect international crime. One implication is that it could only be conceived by madmen. A subtle basis for one's acceptance of that wild scheme is established by suggesting an analogy between the present and the early Middle Ages, when Christianity was supposedly united in a holy war against the "infidels." Vanna's fantasies, in which she imagines first Alé and then others as Ogier the Dane, a reference to Galahad, and the introduction of a character named Gavin, which, to a French reader's ear, might suggest Gawain, all help to create an atmosphere that is congenial to the spirit of a modern, paranoid crusade.

Les Troyens (1970) is subtitled *Hexagramme ou roman*. Allusion is thus made to the existence of six narratives—the six books of fiction published by Faye, including the present one—and to the manner in which they are related. Early in the book there are descriptions of cloud patterns over a city and light patterns on the ceiling of a room, both gradually changing shape, into which the word *hexagram* is inserted. Within the last twenty-five pages of *Les Troyens* there are several instances of diagrams and *calligrammes* that either suggest or clearly depict a specific geometric figure. Examining their design and further prodded by medieval references similar to those just noted in *L'Ecluse*, one might

easily think of the *hexagrammum mysticum* of those times, later system-
atically studied by Pascal. But I am less impressed with the hexagram's
geometric properties as demonstrated by Pascal than with its "mystic"
modifier, since it confirms the impression made by *Analogues* concerning
the direction Faye's narratives appear to be taking. I have already noted
the extent to which, from the very beginning, links between narration
and reality were inessential to the significance of the narrative. At best,
reality was a prop for the narration.

Already in *L'Ecluse* there were hints of its being pushed even farther
into the background, some passages making me wonder if Faye was not
about to rocket into a form of science fiction (there were already other
coincidental analogies with the work of Claude Ollier). "To this purpose,
powerful reflectors have been set up and, in effect, turned back inward
and aimed at the city; they register an image of the city; they emit a
violent radiation that takes the city's cast, so to speak, removing it
completely, and then they flash in order to reflect it several times before
it is finally sent back by transmitters, and finally stabilized and con-
densed in a special way" (129-30). In that book, there was perhaps a
hiatus between such statements and those that clearly referred to the
actual city of Berlin, with the wall that divided it between 1961 and 1989,
its canals, subways, and airport. In *Les Troyens*, on the other hand, there
is greater homogeneity in the narrative; reality is mainly in the text itself.
Not only is the reader drawn into its verbal functioning, but even the
"characters" are engaged in linguistic activities. One could possibly say
that Faye is, for the reader's benefit, attempting to create or to convey
the experience of a mystical awareness, no longer of God but of human
reality as language—as a web of narratives.

A noticeable architecture, which I had found lacking in *Entre les rues*,
has gradually been imposed on his texts through the interplay of narratives, beginning with the alternating *je* and *il* of *Battement*. Now the
number six presides over the organization of *Les Troyens*. There are six
chapters, entitled "Walls," "Night," "Sea," "Wave," "Siege," and "Body."
There are six "characters" or functions, three of them masculine, often
referred to as narrator (who is called Nar, obviously because he narrates,
but also because he is *narus*, the one who knows,[13] and the name could
also be the beginning of the German *Narr*, the madman), witness, and
participant (*interlocuteur*), and the three others feminine. And there is,
of course, the hexagram.

As in previous works of fiction, the setting of *Les Troyens* is an
unnamed city; in this case its inhabitants are known as *Troyens*. Now
there is a French city named Troyes, in the Champagne province, and it
played a role in *Battement*. It has been laid siege to many times in history
(a useful correlative for chapter 5, "Siege"); it is divided into high and
low sections—a feature mentioned in the text, and any such division is

important to Faye. It would seem to be a good city for his purposes, but I do not think it looms as large in the consciousness of someone reading the book as did, for readers of previous books, the other cities he had then selected: Chicago, Paris, Munich, Basel, and Berlin. The cultural presence of Homer's Troy is quite strong, especially when assisted by statements such as, "No longer the Trojans, *but Hector is being pursued*" (241), preventing an unquestioned identification with the French city. One might recall that the number six has long been a symbol of ambiguity.

The narrator has come to the city in search of a lost narrative continuity. In a series of leather-bound volumes, presumably the complete works of a writer whose name is missing, a ribald narrative is suddenly, at the beginning of a subsequent volume, replaced with a prudish one, while nothing in the appearance or presentation of the volumes has changed. In a manner slightly reminiscent of Kafka, Nar seems to depend for his subsistence and also his assignment to the city upon a vast, mysterious bureaucracy. Thinking that he has come to the wrong place to search for his lost narrative he requests a transfer, but the delays involved make it seem hopeless. When he is asked about his job, he does not immediately talk about the book; he answers that he works in textiles (*je travaille dans le fil* [48]). If there is again ambiguity there is no real contradiction, for cotton thread and narrative thread are analogous for the purpose of this text. In addition, and perhaps in opposition, to the bureaucracy upon which the narrator depends, there is another vast, secret organization with which he comes into contact. There are amusing references to specialists in romance philology and to the Old-French mafia. It is clear that, like Faye and others, this worldwide subversive association knows the power of language.

Nar, especially in his dialogues with a feminine function again named El., plays a part that is similar to that of the nameless Algerian in *Analogues*, who had made El.'s acquaintance because of a cinder in her eye. In *Les Troyens*, Nar meets El. on account of an injured kitten (39). Much later, over the phone, she makes the connection: "It's true, I answer anybody's call. Even if all he does is to bring me a tuft of cat fur, or a speck of dust in the eye" (312). Even more than functioning as a narrator, Nar seems to act as prompter for narratives, and that explains statements such as these: "a mute narrator"; "on his part, he questions; he is a narrator who tells no story"; or "the wordless narrator" (164, 178, 72). As a surrogate for the contemporary writer who needs a reader in order to complete his work and give it meaning, the often silent narrator utters his call for assistance. In correlative fashion, within the text, someone issues a call of distress. An Algerian in *Analogues*, a Puerto Rican in *Les Troyens* (Nar says he was born in Guayama), in either case a member of a non-white population, appeals to a Western conscience. (As this is the first time Faye's text openly suggests such a specific interpretation, I might note that the number six was also considered a symbol of the human soul.)

The general pattern is not new. In each instance, as in Maurice Blanchot's narratives, the call has gone from man to woman (beginning with Verdier and Mona). Before *Analogues* the nature and purpose of such calls were not clear. As they are made explicit in the sixth book they also become involved in the other set of analogies I have just alluded to—that pertaining to the relationship between writer, reader, and text. As implied in Blanchot's reading of the Orpheus myth and also affirmed by Philippe Sollers, the relationship between a writer and his writing can be interpreted in erotic terms; so can the interaction of text and reader. In Faye's fiction the appeal made from man to woman becomes more and more patently erotic. The narrator experiences intense desire for three women—the three feminine functions of the text. One he knows only through her picture. She is Vanna or Joanina, and he writes to her presumably in Berlin, although he associates her name with the besieged city of Ioannina, Ali Pasha's stronghold in Greek Epirus. The other, El., is directly linked to the hexagram in that the geometric design the narrator sees on his ceiling comes from her room across the courtyard. To him, she seems a figure that can be drawn within the framework of her window, and it is his drawing her that arouses his desire. The third is Linda Lee or Lé Lin, depending on where she happens to be. The split that existed in earlier characters shows up again, but it is first expressed in linguistic terms, on the level of words, rather than in rational terms, on the semantic level. The duality of her name is translated into a physical event: she often dreams of violence and blood, and at the end she is seriously wounded, dismembered (*écartelée*) as had been the woman in her dreams, under circumstances that are left to the reader's imagination. On the last page, the narrator purposely breaks the glass pane of a door behind which Lé Lin is lying and repeatedly slashes his hand.

If there is more sexuality there is also more violence in *Les Troyens* than in the previous works of fiction. There is a riot, which reminds one of the student riots of May 1968; this prompted Faye to specify that the book was completely written by February of 1968. Actually, as the description of the riot is interspersed with many brief quotations from what might be *La Chevalerie Ogier de Dannemarche*, it is relatively easy not to succumb to the realistic fallacy. The generalized violence, nevertheless, might be interpreted as a sign of Faye's moving in the direction of a deeper realism that, as opposed to the superficial realism of verisimilitude, reflects the dangerous and potentially violent conditions of human relations today. Seen from that standpoint, *Les Troyens* is both disturbing and challenging.

It also displays a form of poetry that I might call abstract, and this is accentuated in *Inferno, versions* (1975). I already noted the abstract quality in some of Nathalie Sarraute's work; Faye, however, goes much farther in that direction. Furthermore, he creates an uneasy tension between abstraction and precise references to the human body. He had previously used bodily impairments as metaphors, but they were not precisely described. While the poetry of the first books reminded me slightly of Giraudoux, Faye has been steadily moving away from lyricism toward a more esoteric form of allusiveness, which makes the reader feel he or she has to be intellectually in tune with the writer.

The unspecified setting of *Inferno, versions* is Jerusalem; it is also Paris, and shifts between the two often take the reader by surprise. If the city is not identified by name, allusions, in the vein of Faye's practice since *Entre les rues,* such as those to the Gate of Jaffa, the King David Hotel, and the Hill of Sion help situate the narration. The river that divides the city is perhaps more reminiscent of the Seine in Paris than of the Kidron in its valley, but there is no question that Jerusalem is split along a number of planes: physical and cultural, spatial and chronological. Nor is there any doubt of the violence that embroils it and the surrounding lands, thus matching the increased violence already noted in Faye's texts. Such violence, as noted above, had already been "foreseen," so to speak, by a statement in *L'Ecluse,* which went so far as to announce the city's destruction.

The title refers to Dante's *Divine Comedy* and more particularly to the concentric circles of hell, which correspond to the whirlpool at the center of which the narrative is located. The *versions* refer to the various narratives that claim to render the reality of the Middle East situation. There are four versions of reality that claim to speak the truth; the Old City was divided into four sections—Armenian, Greek, Jewish, and Moslem; and four languages are spoken. But the geographic, cultural, and linguistic categories no longer correspond. One is never sure of a person's loyalty to this or that cause. As one "character" says to another in the middle of a heated discussion, "Okay, so we are all Arabic Jews, that's obvious" (26).

The architecture of *Inferno* is rather subtle and complex. Where one might have expected a division into four parts, there are only three, perhaps because of the destruction of the Jewish sector of the Old City. The first part is divided into eleven unnumbered and untitled sections of twelve numbered subsections, except for the first, which comprises thirteen subsections (maybe corresponding to the twelve tribes of Israel and the thirteenth "lost" tribe). Part 2 appears to have shed all regularity. Thus, on the first page, there is an expository set of statements about a coming insurrection; this is followed by three pages divided into two columns in which the text alternates between left and right columns and constitute three sets, each numbered 1 to 4, except that the last set is numbered 1, 3, 2, 4, 1. The following page again harbors an expository text on the same topic as the first. The next three pages are divided into two columns of alternating texts but the numbering seems haphazard and the texts themselves show signs of excisions and interruptions. On the tenth page, numerals appear on the left-hand margin, but they are not followed by text. After the eighteenth page (102), numerals disappear completely, but similar, irregular alternations continue to the end of part 2. The apparent disorder mirrors the confusion on the level of the narration: "Don't get involved here, this is the essence of confusion, such confusion can be dangerous for you, and even if it were harmless for you, it carries with it a danger effect, and an intolerable possibility of any kind of reversal" (117). Part 3, in which the plans made in part 2 are carried out, shows a similar sort of disorganization. There are accounts of fighting, interspersed with peculiar bits of conversation, and some of the fighting takes place in what could well be the equivalent of nineteenth-century Parisian catacombs and sewers. Violence increases as one comes closer to the end of the book and finally, in allegorical but nonetheless horrible fashion, that violence is concentrated in one of the feminine characters. Like all others, she has been a function throughout the narrative, but precise bodily references transform her into a "character" in a few isolated spots, illustrating the kind of tension I mentioned above.

In the same year that *Inferno* was published Faye brought out *L'Ovale (détail)* (1975) and characterized it, in the back-cover blurb, as "the page that was missing from *Inferno*." There are fairly obvious thematic links between the two books, but what I find particularly striking is that, on the one hand, the narrative functions of *L'Ovale* appear to be "characters" much more so than they did in *Inferno;* and on the other, the importance of eroticism is also emphasized more. Not only does eroticism, as I mentioned earlier, preside over the relationship between the writer and his writing, it also underlies most human activities—especially political and revolutionary ones. Descriptions of public events (meetings, demonstrations, jailings) are larded with erotic references, while overtly sexual scenes allow political references to interfere only exceptionally: eroticism is clearly the dominant element. Both major masculine and feminine characters make this identical statement on separate occasions: "I have problems with desire, generally speaking" (65, 91). Part of these problems involves language, as one might expect, and the difficulty there is in talking or writing about sexual matters directly or "crudely."

The title of the book sounds like the caption for an enlarged reproduction of part of a painting—and on one level it is indeed an enlargement of a detail out of *Inferno,* but one that could not be seen in the other text. This would be like Georgia O'Keeffe deciding to produce a painting that would show, say, the inside of *Cebolla Church.* On another level, the title works as do O'Keeffe's large paintings of shells with their erotic implications. The "oval" refers to the mouth or to the female sex organ. At first, it is the mouth that is overtly designated ("the oval that speaks and says"

[52]). Finally, because of the other words with which it is listed ("You know very well that one can't do without those words and what they lay bare even more than the very things they talk about: cunt, slit, vulva, weft, oval" [81]), it obviously points to sex.

The text suggests a further contrast between the two "ovals": there is "what she says [*dit*] between her lips and what is forbidden [*interdit*] between the legs" (14)—with the ban being essentially linguistic. Female sex is protected by a prohibition against naming, an inter-diction. "It is, as the word says, a diction, a diction that speaks between the things it says" (80). What started as a cultural problem, however, spills over into the act of scription. Geometrically speaking, an oval is an ellipse, and in French that word is identical with the one for ellipsis; *Ovale* is replete with uncompleted sentences and missing words. Thus the problem is with language in general and eroticism is its privileged exemplar.

There has been in Faye's work up to this point a gradual shift from subtle political allusions to an inescapable political meaning. And yet what he has written, especially the early texts, might be termed ironical since the main characters are politically uncommitted and fail to make the necessary choices that the writer, who invented these characters, would himself have advocated. Such a failure, as I have pointed out, becomes translated into the metaphor of illness. Concomitantly, Faye's own interests may have evolved: while he appeared at first to be concerned mainly with the meaning of narrative, he now seems more interested in its effect. In 1966, several years before *Les Troyens* appeared, he published an essay called "Le Récit hunique,"[14] which might be translated either as "The Unique Narrative" or "The Hunnish Narrative." In it he recalls one of the preposterous stories of G. Bonnot de Mably, the eighteenth-century "historian." As his story goes, after the Huns reached the shores of the shallow Sea of Azov, some of their hunters, after pursuing a deer across the marshes, were so impressed by what they saw on the other side, they described it in glowing terms to all and sundry. The consequence of that narrative was that the Huns crossed the Sea of Azov, and this eventually changed the face of Europe and the course of Western history. Faye, of course, considers Mably not as a writer of history but of apologues: what caught his attention was the urge to spin a narrative and the consequences thereof. Thus, the Middle East conflict that constitutes the background of *Inferno* (and to a lesser extent, *Ovale*) is posited as consequence of conflicting Israeli, Palestinian, and other narratives.

One should therefore not be surprised by the splitting of his subsequent writing into several kinds of texts. There are first what I would call narrative commentaries. *Les Portes des villes du monde* (1977) goes back over the books I have described and explains how they came into being. He tells "what was not written but implied *in between* the written" (13), thus suggesting that, even though he had made the same point in *Ovale*, his narratives had not had the full intended effect—and this is hardly surprising, considering the way most people have been taught to read. The title explains in part why each of his fictions is centered in a city: there are "many possibilities for allowing us into the narrative [of history] or, more precisely, we have a series of such possibilities—the monumental doors constituted by the cities of the world. The cities of the world are the doors into the human narrative" (20). The book is subtitled "Roman des récits," which enables one to place it in a category that does not point to a factual, accurate accounting of the genesis of the other narratives but rather a musing on what Faye had in mind when and after composing them. *Commencement d'une figure en mouvement* (1980) is of a similar kind. Written in the form of a dialogue with Philippe Boyer, it goes over Faye's literary and political activities, in more prosaic fashion, which include the founding of what he called the *Change* "collective," which included a review, a group of writers, and a series of publications. It was started in 1968 as a challenge to *Tel Quel* after Faye broke with Philippe Sollers and lasted until 1983 when he replaced it with *Change International*, which lasted only two years; at the time the "collective" included, among others, Maurice Roche (who was gone in 1970) and Jacques Roubaud (who stayed until the end came in 1985).

Like *Tel Quel*, *Change* refused to be confined to belles-lettres and took sides in all political issues of the time, French and worldwide (in a 1971 issue the "collective" published an essay by Angela Davis). Faye brought out a number of books that are basically political as well as theoretical texts, such as *Théorie du récit* (1972), from which political considerations are not absent, and a 771-page doctoral dissertation, *Langages totalitaires* (1972), an examination of how language practice and devices made Nazi ideology acceptable to Germans in the twenties and thirties. The practice of scription, however, no longer seems to lie at the center of Jean Pierre Faye's concern.

NOTES

1   "Le 'Nouveau Roman,'" *Esprit*, no. 7-8 (July-August 1958): 1-111.

2   Jean Pierre Faye, *Entre les rues* (Paris: Seuil, 1958), 171. Henceforth all references to works by Jean Pierre Faye will appear in the body of the text.

3   Jean Giraudoux, *Les Aventures de Jérôme Bardini* (Paris: Emile-Paul, 1930), 27-28.

4   Giraudoux, *Siegfried et le Limousin* (Paris: Grasset, 1922), 83.

5   Olivier de Magny, "*Entre les rues*, par Jean Pierre Faye," *Les Lettres nouvelles*, no. 65 (November 1958): 607.

6   Magny, 605.

7   Emile Benveniste, "Structure des relations de personne dans le verbe," in

Problèmes de linguistique générale (Paris: Gallimard, 1966), 231 and 230.

8   "Débat sur le roman," *Tel Quel*, no. 17 (Spring 1964): 23.

9   Philippe Sollers, "Un Nouvel etranger," *Nouvelle Revue française*, no. 121 (January 1963): 115.

10 See David Hayman, "An Interview with Maurice Roche," *SubStance*, no. 17 (1977): 5.

11 André Marrissel, "Jean Pierre Faye: *Battement*," *Esprit*, no. 59 (December 1962): 1068.

12 Paris: GLM, 1960.

13 Faye, "L'Idéologie littéraire (changement matériel et changement de forme)," in *Littérature et idéologies* (Paris: Editions de la Nouvelle Critique, 1971), 191.

14 *Tel Quel*, no. 27 (Fall 1966): 9-16. It was reprinted as the lead essay in a collection bearing the same title (thus stressing its importance), *Le Récit hunique* (Paris: Seuil, 1967).

11

Philippe Sollers

Philippe Sollers is the driving force that made the review *Tel Quel* and the group of writers and critics associated with it the most challenging and controversial enterprises in French intellectual history of the sixties and seventies. He and his friends have questioned most concepts previously associated with literature, belles lettres, humanism, and the like. It was a different young man who founded the review in the spring of 1960 (and he is a different man today). The title brings to mind that of a work by Paul Valéry, and indeed in his presentation of the new quarterly Sollers quoted approvingly Valéry's image assimilating the work of art to an "enchanted structure." He implicitly rejected *littérature engagée* (in the vulgar sense of the phrase), denounced the sway of ideology over literature, and placed poetry, "in the broadest sense of the term," on the highest plane.[1] The five other members of the editorial committee of *Tel Quel* were little known, with the possible exception of Jean-René Huguenin, who shortly afterwards was killed in an automobile accident. None remained with the review to the end. When the review was launched, Sollers himself, then in his early twenties, had published two works of fiction, *Le Défi* (1957; The Challenge) and *Une Curieuse solitude* (1958; *A Strange Solitude*), the first of which was less than forty pages in length. Such works and the dozen or so that followed, will concern me here much more than his performance on the Paris intellectual stage.

If any evidence were needed to point to the vitality of surrealism after the Second World War, those two texts by Sollers, who was born twelve years after the publication of the surrealist manifesto, would provide convincing pieces. *Le Défi*, written in 1956 when he was barely twenty and published the following year, carries an epigraph taken from André Breton's *Nadja:* "A few very exceptional human beings, who can expect and fear everything from one another, will always recognize each other thanks to their extreme propensity for challenge." A self-centered tale of love and death, told in the setting of a seaside resort town, its mood and style bring Julien Gracq to mind. Occasionally, a touch of youthful cynicism reminds one of Radiguet—"Youth is the art of wasting time within the family circle."[2] Affirmations couched in a sort of abstract lyricism are evocative of Camus—"The insoluble and the contradictory were indeed my kingdoms" (7). There is one sentence in *Le Défi* that reads almost as if it had been lifted out of a text by Breton, which it evokes even in its syntactic pattern: "And what can we expect, anyway, out of life, if not, on the occasion of an apparently commonplace event, furtive glimpses of the supernatural [*merveilleux*]?" (9). Sollers has also confessed to having been influenced by Châteaubriand. Imitation and pastiche are natural in the first writings of youth. Echoes from Camus and Radiguet, even those of Gracq, will soon fade away. Surrealism, although it is not a tradition one would detect in Sollers's later texts, will not be so easily dismissed.

When his first full-length work of fiction, *Une Curieuse solitude*, appeared in 1958, one could see that it did not betray the "literary promise" evidenced by *Le Défi*. Textual reverberations are still noticeable, those from Radiguet in particular, and, to me at least, overtones from Stendhal are more in evidence than those from Chateaubriand. A ten-line quotation from Proust (119) records his own affinities. In this book Sollers tells the story of a young man's experiences in sexual desire, told in the first person (as had been *Le Défi*), full of innocent cruelty and deceit with a concomitant mixture of suffering and joy. The narrator is as egocentric as before, but as he discovers himself he also becomes conscious of the world and his role in it. In *Le Défi*, the girl who gets involved with the narrator and whose suicide he is responsible for was hardly more than a fantasy ("I relished my own self under the name of Claire" [12]). Now, the young Spanish woman, Concha, is clearly the Other. Actually it is he, not she, who tends toward nonexistence. Concha calls him Felipe, and since he is French his name can only be Philippe, the same as the writer's, but nowhere is that name mentioned. The situation is one of the narrator's accepting the mask imposed upon him by the Other, just as the writer seems to accept his role within a given cultural tradition and adopted what Roland Barthes called the scription (*écriture*) of the French twentieth-century "novel." Written in an impeccably controlled style, *Une Curieuse solitude* was welcomed into the bosom of belles lettres by Aragon (*Le Défi* had been praised by François Mauriac) —but it was no revelation. Sollers later dismissed that work as having been written not so much by himself as "by a specific social group (the bourgeoisie), whose spokesman I happened to be at a given moment because of my class origins."[3]

Still, with the benefit of hindsight, it is possible to detect several signs pointing to his subsequent works. Perhaps that book was indeed written by a young bourgeois eager to adopt the aesthetics of his class, but he also happened to be Philippe Sollers—that is, a person who received a specific intellectual formation and was developing a given awareness. While *Le Défi* contained the seed of a well-rounded plot, *Une Curieuse solitude* shifted the emphasis to the narrator's interpreting a problematic relationship, for which no resolution is provided. His words matter more than what they refer to. Even in the case of Concha her name is as important as her being: "The woman whose name it was seemed to me so perfectly wedded to it that I could not separate the one from the other, and I only possessed her through its intermediary" (69-70). Along similar lines, an awareness of the determining role of language crops up in a number of instances. Some of these merely reflect traditional attitudes, such as this distant echo from La Rochefoucauld: "But desire consists mainly in the vocabulary of desire" (38). A few others give a more compelling ring: "There might, however, be something quite healthy . . . for those who, at times, become tired of language to an extreme degree, in suddenly changing it, speaking only in borrowed phrases, creating for themselves a new, restricted world, without connections with that of their childhood and their weariness" (24). One might even suggest that the sexual encounter between Felipe and Concha constitutes but an extended metaphor for the erotic experience Philippe Sollers, as writer, has with language as he gives shape to the text. The role her name plays in Felipe's possession of her would then be correlative to the role language plays for the narrator in coming to terms with the world. Such remarks, however, to which I might add an interesting mirror metaphor—"that mirror of my awakening, capable of ordering the strangest elements that become caught in it" (83)—acquire significance only in retrospect.

With his next work, *Le Parc* (1961), it could be said that a new writer was born. Very different resonances could be detected. Even more so than in the early fiction of Claude Ollier, the narrative seems to develop along the pattern of Robbe-Grillet's first books. A narrator transcribes a series of visual impressions, first provoked by "reality" and then by memory and imagination, all blending in such fashion as to make it difficult to distinguish the one from the other. He lives in a corner apartment, with balcony, on the sixth floor of a building in a large city. The location affords a privileged view in several directions, enabling him, for instance, to look into a number of apartments across the way, peer back into his own room, or watch the street scene below. The reader is with him from dusk to dawn on a night when he can hardly sleep, partly because of asthma, partly because of a sequence of obsessive thoughts, and again throughout a day that may or may not be the following one. A man and a woman, who are strangers to him and are seen to move about in the living room of another apartment he had been watching, gradually fade away, being replaced by acute remembrances of a different man and woman. Later, the figure of a child is woven in. The child is probably himself and he may have had a love affair with the woman. The man, whose friend he was and with whom he occasionally identifies, is now dead.

That much I think we can reasonably be sure of, although the web of relationships that links those three roles to the narrator is not clearly defined. Reminiscent of Robbe-Grillet's handling of the engraving in *Dans le labyrinthe* is Sollers's introduction of a painting in the apartment bedroom. It represents a fishing port teeming with the activities of sailing vessels, while on land, "right here, two men and a woman, all three impassive, appear to pursue a conversation or to make parallel statements without connection with what is taking place behind them" (16). These could be the three main characters of *Le Parc*, whose involvements are equally ambiguous or enigmatic. But in contrast to what happens in Robbe-Grillet's book, the characters (if the word is still appropriate; Jean Ricardou calls them "pronominal characters," and I have suggested the phrase "grammatical functions" in another chapter of this study) do not emerge out of the painting in order to participate in the narrator's fantasies. Rather, the painting seems to draw them like a magnet to the other side of visible reality. Very near the end of the text, the narrator describes himself and the woman in a setting that is precisely that of the painting—one implication being that they have removed themselves from the "reality" of the fiction. In other words, they are no longer characters in the traditional sense of the word.

It should be noted that references to painting are relatively infrequent in Sollers's works (especially when confronted with what happens in Claude Simon's texts, for instance), and the picture just mentioned is a fictional one. While they increase in the more recent books (there are references to Tiepolo toward the end of *Femmes* and to Manet in *Les Folies françaises*) they are never as striking as the musical references are. This may be an indication that he writes more for the ear than for the eye. His interest in painting, however, is considerable, as two book-length essays evidence: *Les Surprises de Fragonard* (1987) and *De Kooning, vite* (1988).

A public park serves as the setting for some of the incidents and gives the book its title. Also, as defined in the epigraph by means of a quotation from Rousseau, it provides the text with its own metaphor: "It is a mixture of sites that are very beautiful, whose contributing parts have been chosen in different countries, and where everything appears natural except the aggregate." Slightly transposed, that could also have been applied to those works by Claude Simon in which every detail seems realistic but the entire work does not. To the various spots in Sollers's

park correspond, in one set of analogies, the separate elements of the
narrative, and in another, the several grammatical functions involved.
Robbe-Grillet, in the final analysis, may well have been more of a challenge than a model, and Sollers's ties to surrealism remain unbroken at
this stage. As he himself explains on the back cover, its sentences and
paragraphs proceed "like the imagination," by means of analogies. The
epigraph also suggests a bringing together of several distant elements of
reality. It is out of similar confrontations that, according to André Breton,
surrealist images are born. One might thus go to the surrealist manifesto
to find an aesthetic justification for the enigmatic quality of Le Parc:
"The two parts of the image have not been deduced from each other by
the mind with the intent of producing a given spark";[4] rather, the elements
are placed in juxtaposition, and then one records and appreciates the
"luminous phenomenon." Such a phenomenon can only take place in the
reader's imagination.

In addition to exhibiting a tension between reality and imagination,
between persons seen and persons imagined, the narrative gravitates
about different texts. Various colors of ink and kinds of paper distinguish
those written by the child, the woman, the man, and finally the narrator
himself. Eventually, just as the "characters" were drafted away from
reality, the whole narrative is drawn to the words of one text. The last
sentence of the volume refers to "the orange-colored notebook, patiently
filled, overladen with an even handwriting that has been led to this page,
this sentence, this period, by the old fountain pen often and automatically
dipped into blue-black ink" (155). Again it turns out that what the
narrator has been writing becomes the book one is reading. The time has
perhaps come, however, to ask whether such a statement of the process,
culminating with the book and its implication of finality, is the most fruitful one. It might indeed be better to reverse the terms and think of the
book that is being read as a text that is being written. In addition to
placing emphasis on its generative aspects, that further suggests that the
book the writer proposes is still lacking something essential when purchased by a prospective reader. "A work exists by itself only potentially,
and its actualization (or production) depends on its readings and on the
moments at which these readings actively take place."[5]

The part played by elements of the narrative should now become more
apparent. Little need be said about the part assigned to the woman and
the man in developing themes such as love and friendship or of the contributions those concepts make toward an understanding of oneself. The
balcony enables the narrator not only to see his room as an outsider might
(or, symbolically, to see himself in the same fashion), it places it (and his
existence) at a spatial distance from himself. A temporal distance is then
provided by childhood memories (the distance is increased by the use of
words like "the child" instead of first-person pronouns). That, along with

illness and preoccupation with mirrors, which Pierre Mabille called "the most commonplace and at the same time the most extraordinary of magical devices,"[6] a statement with which any reader of Lewis Carroll would agree, insinuates the theme of death. Its presence can be felt long before the death of the narrator's friend is recorded on the last page of the first part of the book, without any appearance of the word *death*.

Near the end of the narrative, as the narrator once more faces his mirror, he concentrates less on the material self that confronts his gaze than on some intangible, imperceptible gap that might be detected between existence and its reflection. That enables the reader, I believe, to point to a preoccupation that affirms itself more and more in the subsequent texts by Sollers, namely, the fusion of problems of meaning and existence with those of writing—or, as that word is inadequate for conveying the special connotations that accompany the word *écriture* (as it has been used by Barthes, Derrida, and others), meaning both the work with language performed by a writer and the interplay of words (as signs and signals) in the text, I shall use the term "scription." Derrida, in his attempt to define the science of scription, which he called "grammatology" and in which he would include word as well as script, was led to generalize from a concept introduced by Ferdinand de Saussure— that of the difference (with other words) that enables us to distinguish any one particular word. At the source, "the concept of script [*graphie*] implies, as a possibility common to all systems of meaning, the process of *instituted marking* [*trace instituée*],"[7] meaning an unmotivated but distinctive marking, a reference by means of which a "difference appears *as such.*" The conceptual and purely hypothetical "arch-marking" is then defined, in order to express the notion of movement implicitly contained in the idea of difference: "*The (pure) marking is a deferring.*"[8] Hence the preoccupation with the gap that separates the markings in the mirror from what they designate and the difference it refers to—himself.

To those looking for realistic, linear narrative, Sollers's third full-length fiction, *Drame* (1965; *Event*), must have seemed even more esoteric than the second. What removes it from convention is that, even more so than in *Le Parc*, anecdotal elements have faded far into the background. The quality of "abstract lyricism" detectable in the early narratives has been transformed into a more concrete kind of scription. In *Drame*, one is constantly confronted with particulars, with tangible aspects of reality, even when they are molded into rather unusual images and metaphors. The title itself owes something to Mallarmé. In a talk given in 1965 (the same year as *Drame* appeared), and first published in *Tel Quel* the following year, Sollers remarked that, for Mallarmé, when writing the Great Book, "the fundamental problem is . . . the theater, that is, the three-dimensional book."[9] He then added, after several developments, "We must therefore realize the possibility of the text as theater along with that

of the theater and of life as text."[10] References to the stage abound in
Drame, but the link between the idea of theater and the action of the text
on the reader is more organically integrated into Sollers's next book.

In *Drame* he is again attempting to explore an individual consciousness—his own, naturally. But he generalizes the experience by projecting
it in two directions: first, that of a community of beings, thereby enabling
the reader to participate in the exploration; second, that of the writer,
again bringing in the reader, this time by means of the concept of double
creation—which we are now familiar with. The text itself oscillates
between two points of view, that of a seemingly omniscient narrator who
describes the quest and that of someone or something writing about his
or its quest—the latter sections (or cantos) readily identifiable by being
set within quotation marks and preceded by the statement, "He writes."
There are also other pronouns or grammatical functions, a feminine one
with whom the subject is involved but who does not ever become a
subject, and a second-person pronoun whose referent may vary. A child
makes a most fleeting appearance.

There are two settings, each appearing to correspond to one of the
projections I have mentioned: a large city by the ocean, with its port,
streets, buildings, and beaches, and a library, perhaps a private one, with
its world of books. Giving the fiction unity, one is clearly the correlative
of the other. Travel is alluded to a number of times, by car, by train, or by
plane (only once by ship), but no destination is involved. There is an
accident or two, perhaps even three, but no possibility of establishing
realistic logical links or anecdotal continuity. The "story" has a beginning
of sorts that is established by the words "At the outset," "first," and
"beginning"—all on the initial page. The brief second sentence, "Swiftly,
he conducts the investigation," evidently proposes a quest, possibly of his
own (our own?) identity. A few pages before the end, at first reading, one
is hard put to imagine why or how the narrative would come to a close.
Indeed the first-person subject explains in the final paragraph: "One
might as well imagine that the book founders [*échoue*] here" (159)—a
situation similar to that in *Le Parc*, where the text ended because the last
page of a notebook had been reached. In French, *échouer* commonly
means to fail; when speaking of a ship, it means to run aground. The main
ship in the book is the book itself, which now lies on the beaches of the
reader's mind.

In large part, once more, we are dealing with the account of a book
being written in the active presence of the reader. Such an account
might be termed ironic in that it also describes the failure attendant upon
the conventional process of (successful) fiction-writing, based on the
assumption that once a writer has a story to tell, he will readily find the
words needed to relate it—"He thought that at the required moment
[the French phrase *au moment voulu* recalls the title of one of Blanchot's

books] the true story would allow itself to be told" (11)—and eventually results in a novel sort of text that draws its strength from its inability to become a "novel." Toward the beginning, the word *manqué* (missed) signals a few false starts, recalling Beckett's "what tedium" in *Malone meurt* as well as Robbe-Grillet's "No" in *Dans le labyrinthe.* Irony and that sort of reminiscence soon fade away before a more positive textual experience.

Night is of considerable value to Sollers. More recently, when asked to contribute something to a series called "*carnets*" he entitled his text *Carnet de nuit* (1989). The connotations of the word strike a familiar chord in contemporary fiction and thought, and in the text of one of his essays Sollers linked his concept of darkness to Joyce's: "In the night that Joyce entered through his writing, tongues are unknotted and come to life, revealing their ambiguity, their multiplicity, of which we are the daylight reflections—reflections, images believing themselves to be clear and protected."[11] By means of that statement he deprives language of its commonplace function. No longer a convenient tool for conveying thoughts, a means by which people express themselves, it becomes a reality that is a constitutive element of our consciousness. In *Drame,* a book is opened in the hope that it might prove of assistance in writing the text, the drama of which unfolds. That book, however, was not written by a Proust, or a Joyce, or a Blanchot, and it is of no avail. It is replete with characters who indulge in much activity without realizing that they accomplish nothing. Of them we are told that they sleep, eat, read, write, and so forth, "Without realizing that they have not progressed beyond a single page, a single word, they are still and ever on the same side." In other words, they have not taken that step through the looking glass. Furthermore, "They have not for a single moment experienced the night when they talk about night" (92). This comes close to the question Michel Butor attributed to one of his characters: "Wasn't there a path here, the path into nightfall, which one abandoned always too soon?"[12] It is also related to what Kafka noted in a letter: "When one writes, the night is yet not night enough."[13] The metaphor seems compelling.

Mirrors were significant in *Le Parc;* their presence, by implication at least, in the previous statement concerning Joyce and their continuing role in *Drame* is an indication that they belong to Sollers's store of fundamental imagery. In *Drame,* however, the nature of mirrors varies. They can be like a looking glass; they can gain transparency and become an ordinary pane of glass; or they can lose all but their reflective qualities, and the reflection then is synesthetically transformed into an echo. (A similar play with the notion of mirror, with different variations, can be found in Butor's *L'Emploi du temps.*) In all three cases, there is some form of interference between the object perceived and the perceiver, and it is hardly surprising at this point of the analysis to discover that in many of those images words are the tenor. They are the looking glass through which the writer attempts to push the reader. If the latter persists in considering them as signs that point to referents in "reality," he is apt to remain mired on the near side, where meanings are imposed on him and creativity is lacking. In one instance the writer appears to be luring the reader, as he imagines him on the other side. "I sometimes imagine your being beyond the line that the sky reaches by means of a single black curtain riddled with stars: there, again close by, you come and go in a boundless land . . . I wonder if you know that power" (33). He sees him on the other side of words, on another shore. That statement, in the same passage, suggests to him the image of a wall at the far end of an estate (again the idea of interference), with games being played on the near side and only silence on the far one. Silence has evocative powers similar to those of darkness; it is a word "toward which other words proceed and vibrate" (65). In an essay on fiction and, more specifically, the act of writing, Sollers has said that "One writes in order gradually to silence oneself, to attain the written silence of memory that paradoxically translates the world in its ciphered movement, this world of which each one of us is the dissimulated and irreducible cipher."[14] Beyond the wall of *Drame* lies authentic matter (the "real" as distinct from "reality"), here specifically the earth with its hills, vegetation, rocks, animals, and so forth. All these, in the aggregate, make up "the necessary coating for the mirror of words" (34). It is the same mirror that, in the very next sentence, turns words back into silence.

Drame is, like any fiction or poem, an assemblage of words. Hyperconscious of that fact, the writer does not, however, allow it to degenerate into mere rhetorical exercise. From the epigraph ("The blood that permeates the heart is thought") to the final sentence ("Thought . . . that is nimblest and swiftest of all and rests upon the heart"), it is firmly rooted in materiality.

In the fall of 1960, Sollers recalled the enthusiasm with which, at eighteen, he had read E. M. Cioran's *Précis de décomposition*, in large part because of its appeal to what he called the "corrupting exuberance of life." He was also struck by a statement "that seemed to me, that seems to me still one of the most appropriate maxims, almost a slogan, of the new spirit: 'One does not discuss the universe, one expresses it.' Wonderful, I thought. We have come a long way. All we need do is begin."[15] He has traveled yet a longer way to gain the practice that underlies the composition of *Nombres* (1968; Numbers), as they underlie, though to a lesser degree, *Le Parc* and *Drame*.

"I imagine," he wrote in 1962, "the beginning of a book; its sentences, asserting their presence in an unusual way, surprise the most sophisticated reader."[16] Such a reader, he continued, vainly seeks the writer's usual qualities, his themes, his obsessions, nor does he discover references to fiction passed off as reality. Instead of entering a different kind of world, organized by someone else, instead of confronting a specific object existing outside of himself, "he is, on the contrary, thrown back to his own personal situation."[17] Rather than a representation that he could appreciate, accept, or reject, the text facing him "has both the opaqueness of a facade and the limpidity of a mirror."[18] The image is a familiar one; the rejection it implies is not only that of literature conceived as a representation of "reality"—he has called that an absurdly naive preconception[19]—but also literature as an expression of a particular thought or feeling. As in the case of several other contemporary writers, his point of departure lies in the works of Mallarmé. The idea of considering the outside world as a text (I also noted this where Butor is concerned), of asking oneself how it can be written, of a writer's removing his presence from the text—those now familiar notions are stressed again. "In short, a book is the locus of a double movement: on the one hand, a suppression of the author (Mallarmé frequently compares the book to a *tomb*), who abandons speech for writing and thereby lends himself to the transformation of time into space ... and on the other, the enhancement of the reader."[20]

The matter of the author's disappearance needs some elaboration. There is no question that a specific writer is involved in the making of a text. The common error has been to view the "author" as "creator" of and "authority" on the text. "An author is not truly the cause of what he writes, but rather its product."[21] Roland Barthes, in an essay written in 1960, had previously come to the conclusion that the traditional view of the relationship between the writer and the work seemed "less and less defensible." He also asked, "What if the work were precisely what the author does not know, what he does not live?"[22] It remained for Sollers to give the statement a rigorous justification based on contemporary linguistic theory.

According to Emile Benveniste, "the possibility of thought is tied to the properties of language, for language is a structure endowed with significance, and to think is to handle the signs of language."[23] One should not deduce from such an affirmation that a specific language might prevent a given intellectual development from taking place. To use Benveniste's own example, the structure of Chinese was no obstacle to the assimilation in China of dialectical materialism. What it does suggest is that language structure can determine the direction one's thought will take, unless one is actively aware of that structure and of its operation. To deal with specific points, French society today "needs the myth of the 'novel' " (as undoubtedly American society does, too), the reason being that "The novel is the way this society utters itself, the way the individual must live himself in order to be accepted there."[24] Fiction in literature reproduces whatever myths are imposed on a people, and people then reproduce the myths (and the characters) of literature. When art imitates "reality," reality in turn imitates "art"—and neither is true. What we know as "reality" is no more than a convention. "Declared real, in given historical circumstances, is that which the greatest number of those in power are obliged, for precise economic reasons, to hold as real. The real, moreover, is manifested nowhere else but in language, and society's language and myths are what it decides to take as reality."[25] Each person's options are either to accept what society guarantees as reality, at the same time foregoing the possibility of making any fundamental challenge or change, or else dismantle the myth from the inside, that is, within the functioning of language. The process begins with the realization "that we are signs among other signs, signs producing signs."[26] Precisely because the fiction he wrote until the early seventies no longer resembled the traditional novel, Sollers maintained the word *roman* on the cover of his books, thereby attempting to dismantle the literary concept of genre, again from the inside. His definition, "We shall call a *novel* the incessant, unconscious, mythical discourse of individuals,"[27] aims at debunking the notions of "creative genius" and "originality." "Authors" and their "masterpieces" or "works of art" give way before scription and reading.

While he was elaborating a literary theory, Sollers continued working in fiction. In 1968, the same year as *Logiques*, the collection of essays from which the previous theoretical comments have been extracted, he published *Nombres* (the echo from the fourth book of the Pentateuch is not fortuitous). The reader, perhaps a bit awed by the essays, may well approach this book with fear and trembling, wondering what he or she is supposed to do. The answer is simple—read. *Nombres* is not a difficult book once one has discarded a few bad reading habits. It should be read deliberately, as one might read poetry, absorbing each word, allowing connotations and resonances to develop. One should not, of course, try to extract characters and anecdotes from the text. At the end, the reader might emerge a changed person.

Architecturally, the book is made up of twenty-five sections of four sequences each, for a total of one hundred sequences—which amounts to the square of the sum of the first four numbers (the title defines the architecture). Each sequence is numbered in the margin, identifying its place both in the book as a whole and within a given section. Within each section, the first three sequences are written in the imperfect tense, the fourth in the present; all are narrated in the first person (singular or plural), but the fourth sequences show a preponderance of second-person pronouns, a means of drawing the reader into the text. Diagrams printed in the book suggest that sequences one, two, and three may be thought of as developing on the three sides of something that vaguely resembles a stage. The fourth side, opening out on an assumed audience, is where the fourth sequence takes shape—a sequence more clearly directed at the reader. That side is made of thin air, or seems to be, but this is merely an illusion: it is a "distorting panel," an "invisible, opaque veil," a "mirror or reflector" (22)—whence arise a number of illusions for the spectator. The reader should not be taken in, for the page on which the text is printed is seen as "wrapped" around both stage and house, and it gives the only truthful account.

If pressed to say what *Nombres* is about, I could not answer that it deals with any one topic or that it is specifically one thing or another. It refuses to become the object of "literary" chitchat. Yet it is possible to enumerate several domains one is conscious of exploring when reading the book. There is the writer's own experience in and through language; there is the situation of the reader with reference to the language of his culture; there is the functioning of the text itself, correlated with sexual acts; there is the existence of a worldwide revolutionary situation; there is the confrontation between the two diametrically opposed cultures of east and west; and there is the increasingly encompassing manifestation of Marxist thought. All of these take place successively and concurrently, separately and homogeneously. Jacques Derrida, in a seventy-five page essay (Sollers's text is 112 pages long), has attempted to convey that complex process, and he has succeeded to a degree made possible only by the intricacies of his own scription, more baffling in some ways than the text it describes.[28]

One of the more striking features of *Nombres*, noticeable even if one merely flips through its pages, is the presence of over forty Chinese ideograms disseminated through the text. Obviously, they mean nothing to the majority of readers. They produce a certain amount of tension on the pages where they appear, but as far as immediate effect goes, Sollers could have tossed in ideograms culled at random from Chinese prints. Nevertheless, he chose them carefully, for their meaning is always relevant to the context—sometimes simply translating a preceding word or phrase, sometimes summing up a statement. For instance, the quotation from Lao-tzu, "To produce without acquiring, to act without gaining self-assurance, to help develop without imposing one's will" (95), is followed by the character transliterated as *tsu*, meaning "sufficiency."[29] For one who understands the Chinese elements, their role could be purely thematic. Yet I suspect Sollers put them there less as thematic symbols than as indication of the growing presence of an alien thought and culture, that of the Orient—and also as provocation.

With the publication of *Lois* (1972; *Laws*) it became clear that Sollers was unpredictable. When a few pages of the forthcoming book appeared in the summer 1971 issue of *Tel Quel*, they seemed to follow the general pattern set by *Nombres*, Chinese ideograms included. They were, however, considerably revised for the final version. Most of the ideograms disappeared (although direct and indirect references to Mao actually increased), punctuation and syntax were modified in the direction of spoken, slangy French, and, most noticeably, many neologisms were introduced. Sexual allusions became much more explicit and, so to speak, more materialistic than they had been in his earlier fiction. It may well be that, spurred in part by the student uprising of 1968, Sollers's intent was one of general demythification—of ideologies, literary language and genres, romantic love, and humanism among others. Nevertheless, in the process of working on the language of his text, he found himself favoring ten-syllable clauses or sentences, which happens to be the rhythms of the old French epic poems known as *chansons de geste.* This must have pleased him, for he did not censor such lines; their relatively frequent appearance, especially when rhymed, have a humorous effect, usually intentional (e.g., "Et le souvenir de p'tit poléon sur son cheval d'arcon avec ses grognons" [93]), sometimes perhaps not—although Sollers did say, "I wrote this very cheerful book in a state of permanent laughter."[30] While the decasyllabic line harks back to a literary tradition, it is one no longer upheld by the contemporary French establishment. Likewise, neologisms and portmanteau words may well have been inspired by Lewis Carroll and James Joyce, but they are not fancied by French writers—with a few exceptions such as Raymond Queneau. I did not find *Lois* particularly appealing, but others have been impressed by the vigor, one might say the gutsiness, of the writing. As Sollers himself put it, "It was a sort of taboo-breaker, a rather strange book which almost got away from me."[31]

Lois may have marked a turn into a dead end, an attempt to carry fiction writing to an explosive point out of which something new and valid might develop. As I see it, instead of exploding it fizzled; consequently, Sollers made a new departure, as different from *Nombres* and *Lois* as *Nombres* had been from *Drame.* One should keep in mind, however, that from the writer's standpoint every book is somewhat unsatisfactory, for if it were fully successful there would be no need to write another. Complete success being elusive one must go on trying, and the publication of *H* (1973) heralded what I consider a third stage in Sollers's continual evolution or quest.

The category *roman* is maintained on the title page but is absent from the cover, where it has been replaced with a graphic by Giordano Bruno, *Figura Intellectus.* The Renaissance philosopher who was excommunicated and burned at the stake in 1600 thus provides the book with a fitting emblem. It also provides us with one possible interpretation of its title: H for heresy. But there are a number of other interesting words beginning with that letter. *Hermeticism,* for instance, or *hallucination,* which appears on the first page of the text; if this leads one to think of drugs, words like *hashish* or *heroin* crop up. (Sollers told an interviewer,

"But to read my texts you should be in a state something like a drug high."[32]) And why not *history*, perhaps even *H-bomb* since the word *bomb* also appears on the first page and *hydrogen* on the last. The title, however, is not only written, it is pronounced. In French, the pronunciation of the letter *H* is the same as that of the word meaning "ax" (*hache*), an instrument as old as language and as ambivalent as writing—practical and constructive as when it is used for shaping wood, destructive and ceremonial when used as an instrument of war or punishment. At one time in history, beheading with an ax was reserved for criminals of high rank. One might think of the book as an instrument intended for the elimination of a certain concept of man (*homme* in French, of course), which has dominated Western culture since the days of Giordano Bruno.

Such musings upon the title are an indication of what can happen throughout one's reading of *H*. The text is neither punctuated nor divided into paragraphs; no capital letters are used. Words seem to have been poured on the page until it was full. As a result there is often indetermination of meaning, as the reader cannot be sure that a qualifier modifies the noun that follows rather than the one that precedes, or that a pronoun is relative rather than interrogative. Those hesitations, however, affect only matters of detail, and the context usually straightens them out as one is carried along by the torrent of words. Indeed, the absence of punctuation makes it difficult to stop anywhere, just as it is difficult to quote a coherent sequence since it is hard to identify the beginning of a sentence. But the reading process is not impeded, for there is much less damage to conventional syntax than there was in *Lois*. What does happen is that a definite meaning is not imposed by visible punctuation and sentence structure on the one hand, and on the other the imagination is not allowed to run completely wild because that structure is implicitly present.[33]

If *Lois* was a mock epic dealing with the Western concept of man personalized, after a fashion, as *l'homo*, sometimes called *huma* [*nité*], *H* is a personal odyssey in which Sollers continues to explore his own consciousness beginning with the name of the father and his own birth in language when he chose his own (pen)name; he experiences much of modern literature and philosophy, and contemporary history as well, while discovering his body and his sex. At the end of his back-cover presentation (which begins "To state the reasons why this book cannot have a presentation would undoubtedly take up as much space as the book does") he writes: "There are two people, here, in the night." The image of darkness once more is an essential one. Also, while the narrative is told in the first person and includes an unobtrusive number of third-person pronouns, the second person in the form of *tu* is relatively frequent. As such, it often implies the reader's presence (e.g., "a ta santé, lecteur" [157]), who is thus one of the two people in the night.

The writer's experience is somewhat similar to what transpired in the earlier books but the scription is different. Working in language brings slang and neologisms into the picture, as in *Lois* but in a more subdued fashion; it also features wordplay. In *Lois* this tended to be punctual as well as less frequent, calling attention to a single item in the text; or else, the pun acted as a "structural metaphor" the way it did on occasion in Claude Simon's scription, for instance: "en défunts d'occis! Occident sans fard" ("as dead people, murdered! Outspoken Western world" [41]). After Pynchon writes, "So as the mustache waxes, Slothrop waxes the mustache,"[34] he lets the matter drop—and most writers do the same. This is fine, for even punning just for the fleeting fun of it does represent a challenge to the symbolic system of language. Opening *H* at random, however, I find that when Sollers writes "pourquoi minerve toujours avec la chouette pourquoi pas mouette blanche posée sur le sel," something more takes place. The common (and Hegelian) linking of Minerva with the owl (*chouette*) is modified, perhaps under the influence of the initial letter in the goddess's name, and produces a sea gull (*mouette*). The whiteness of the gull calls forth the whiteness of salt basins at low tide on which one imagines it resting—the friable *sel* both calling to mind and contrasting with the firmer *sol* (ground). But that is only a beginning and in subsequent lines the dynamic implication of the Atlantic ocean's tides is distinguished from the absence of tides in the Mediterranean—an absence reflected in the static nature of Greek philosophy: "there's need of an ocean around here too much of a siesta atmosphere I feel like throwing in the moon the tides that stagnant state must have influenced them" (126). Thus the writing subject removes himself culturally from the classical sea; a while later the removal becomes physical as well as he settles down in the Pacific on a homeward-bound ship also carrying *White-Jacket* —"chapter on the way to have poems published on a ship of the line song of the sirens signed virgil the public the people I agree let us hate the one and unite with the other." These lines include a Mediterranean resonance in keeping with the initial motion that linked owl and sea gull and ends with a nearly literal rendition of the last two lines of Melville's forty-fifth chapter: "The public and the people! Ay, ay, my lads, let us hate the one and cleave to the other." A shift in the initial consonant sound of a word has energized a portion of the text, so to speak, and located the act of scription as well not within the framework of one writing for a literary audience he might seek to please but within the movement of history and its concomitant class struggle. One might recall that in Melville's account the *Song of the Sirens* was published, as it were, by being shot out of a cannon: "That's the way to publish . . . fire it right into 'em; every canto a twenty-four-pound shot; *hull* the blockheads, whether they will or no." An uncanny presage of the occasional violence of Sollers's text.

Seven years later the first volume of *Paradis* (1981) appeared; installments had come out regularly in *Tel Quel* since the fall of 1976, continuing after 1981 and into a couple of issues of *L'Infini* (a name change that was mandated by a change of publisher). *Paradis II* was published in 1986. Merely looking at titles, one senses a shift from what Baudelaire called *paradis artificiels* to Dante's *Paradiso*, implying a more Catholic, or mock Catholic, approach. Sollers himself linked Baudelaire to Dante when he wrote, "*Les Fleurs du mal* constitutes a postscript of the broadest scope to the *Divine Comedy*."[35] Such a shift, however, important as it may be, is a surface modification, for what strikes me at this point and makes the work of Philippe Sollers fascinating is that he has been writing the same book over and over again (he is not the first to have done so)—trying to find the most effective scription, the most appropriate point of view in order to fulfill his quest for social and psychic identity. The unpredictable feature in Sollers's work, to which I referred earlier, has to do with scription (and opinions) rather than the nature of the quest. From the start, each one of his fictional works has been a bio-graphy, that is, a scription of the self, in which the self is a perpetual question mark.

Like *H*, *Paradis* is an unpunctuated, page-saturated book. Even more so than with *H* one is tempted to read aloud, as one might read poetry (a reference that continually comes to mind when confronting Sollers's texts), for even though this is scription it is intended for the ear much more than the eye—and this is quite the opposite of the *Calligrammes* of Apollinaire and Mallarmé's *Un Coup de dés*. He himself said it was an "Ode to Voice."[36] It is probably no coincidence that the first word of the text is indeed *voice*—the first of the short series "voice flower light echo of the lights," which reappears several times at irregular intervals. The word *echo*, with its primary link to sound, emphasizes the importance of the ear, and in its final occurrence the series is modified to make it even more important: "voice flower voice echo of the lights" (244). The word *flower*, with its suggestion of eroticism and death, has a thematic rather than scriptural value. Thematically, of course, all the senses are involved, including sight, and at the very end the narrator, relaxed, tilts his head back and appreciates the sun. Appropriately enough, *Paradis II* begins, "sun voice light echo of the lights sun heart light scroll of the lights."

Few words in the text are univocal. The light in this recurrent series is not only the light of the sun, or the light that radiates from paintings such as Tintoretto's great *Paradise* (1588) in the Scuola della Misericordia in Venice (one of Sollers's favorite cities), it is also that of intellectual enlightenment. The scroll (*rouleau*) that appears in the second line of *Paradis II* is, among other things, the scroll of the Torah, that is, another text. The practice that began with *Nombres* is continued here—quoting without acknowledging the source or, at best, merely alluding to it. Michel Butor, as I have had occasion to note, has pointed out that "a [literary] work is *always* a collective work" because the individual writer always emerges out of a cultural fabric; and the very words he uses are words that he has not invented.[37] Hence, perhaps, the contemporary writer's propensity for neologisms, partly to stamp his or her personality upon the text, partly to provoke the reader. And if one borrows words, why not extract whole sentences from other books, especially if this runs counter to accepted practice. Michel Butor and Georges Perec were moving in the same direction about the same time. In *Paradis* quite a few borrowed phrases or sentences are in Latin, and this can pose a problem for younger readers, even in France, who have neither studied it in class nor been subjected to it at Catholic mass. Thus strengthening the theme of light, the following appears on the first page of the book: "325 *lumen de lumine.*" A number of readers will perhaps identify the Latin as coming from the Apostles' Creed, but fewer will remember that A.D. 325 is the year of the first Council of Nicaea, which formulated the version of the Creed generally accepted by Catholics in the West. Close to the end of *Paradis* one encounters the final Latin quotation: "*introibo ad altare dei . . . qui laetificat juventutem meam*" (253). The resonance is both Catholic and Joycean (the first four words are uttered by Buck Mulligan on the initial page of *Ulysses*), and the narrator comments that the two men who uttered the Latin words smiled as if alluding to something they alone knew. Many readers would probably agree. As to the dates scattered throughout the book, they function somewhat like the Chinese ideograms of *Nombres*, but instead of suggesting an alien thought and way of life, they manifest the theme of time that permeates much of those works.

Simultaneously with the composition of *Paradis* Sollers engaged in a very different kind of scription, which some have termed "realistic." The intent may well have been to emphasize what had apparently not been clear in the evolution of his writing: he has been, as I said earlier, experimenting with different approaches to the same essential topic. Now, instead of using such diversified scriptions diachronically, he does so synchronically—although not within the same book.

Interjected between *Paradis* and *Paradis II*, he published *Femmes* (1983) and *Portrait du joueur* (1984; Portrait of the Gambler); *Paradis II* was then followed by *Le Cœur absolu* (1987; The Absolute Heart), *Les Folies françaises* (1988; The French Folies), and *Le Lys d'or* (1980; The Gilded Lily). Punctuation, division into paragraphs, sections, and chapters, along with linear narrative have returned; the first three, especially *Femmes*, are far more voluminous than anything he had previously written—but we are again faced with the same topics, the same quest, although we are not so much experiencing a quest in process as we are reading its log.

On the concluding pages of *Paradis* a traveler (*voyageur; The Divine Comedy* is the account of a journey) brings a book (perhaps a copy of *Paradis*) to a cathedral where a priest, who is a friend, helps him place it in a hole in the wall from which a stone had been removed and will be replaced and sealed. At the beginning of *Femmes* the narrator states that he is writing the "Memoirs of an unprecedented seafarer [*navigateur*]." (Later, he has his guardian angel address him as "traveler": "Voyageur, resumez-moi vos impressions de la terre" [309].) In both instances the quest theme is implied, and it is suggested that the quest is over—its record is enshrined in the stones of a cathedral or inscribed in the seafarer's log. At one point in *Femmes*, the narrator discusses the book's title (supposedly still undecided) with the Devil, who happens to be the ghost of Laurence Sterne (who furnishes the epigraph for *Le Cœur absolu* and with whom Sollers might be said to have a few affinities); among the possibilities that are mentioned are "The End of the World" and "The Second Book of Revelations," both suggesting not a quest but an apocalypse. Nevertheless the present title stands because, as the narrator explains on the first page, "The world belongs to women. / This means that it belongs to death. / On this matter, everybody tells lies."

The narrator of *Femmes* is an American newspaper writer, a Southerner (the French often prefer Southerners to Yankees), who has talked Sollers into signing his book, perhaps to emphasize the difference between narrator and subject of writing. He works in Paris, is married, travels much (New York, Israel, Italy, Spain), and enjoys many affairs with various women. Eroticism is explicit to the point of pornography, and this has bothered a number of readers. Curiously, it had not been a point of contention in previous works even though the erotic features were equally present, a fact I have already mentioned; as early as pages 19 and 20 in *Paradis*, for instance, peculiar sexual incidents are precisely described. It would appear that the formal "abnormality" of the text (lack of punctuation, and so forth) was more offensive, or perhaps it prevented some readers from entering the text at all. In contrast with the eroticism that permeates the books of Alain Robbe-Grillet, Sollers's version does not include what is commonly associated with sadism. (It should be noted, on the other hand, that he has written a number of positive essays on the Marquis de Sade himself.) No harm is done, no wound inflicted; the emphasis is on pleasure given and pleasure received, without any romantic notions added. Love is not denied but placed on a different register. As the narrator says, about his wife, "As time goes by I admire her more and more . . . I wonder how she manages. . . . What madness, really, not simply to stay with [her], peacefully . . . not fully to accept that sort of death" (180). Who knows? Sexuality might, in the final analysis, be a disability (317).

Twenty-five years earlier, in *Une Curieuse solitude*, the narrator noted, "I did not differentiate—I have never done so—the experience of being alive from the feeling of pleasure" (48). Such is indeed the constant feature of Sollers's work. In the 1958 novel, however, the narrator keeps looking beyond pleasure; he thinks that, in his feelings, "there was some truth or other to be discovered," and he refers to "our need of the unknown" (110, 89). His affair with Concha is embellished with the ideology of romantic love, which is in large part what he later rejected along with the bourgeois, belletristic ideology of style.

It would seem that the rejection of this particular ideology preceded what could be termed disillusionment with all ideologies—or what he perceived as such: everything that molded people into a group and imposed upon members of the group a certain view of life. This of course included fascism and communism, but also Marxism and Maoism, and, among others, feminism. The narrator of *Le Cœur absolu* reminds us that Robespierre and Saint-Just sent many to the guillotine but Sade and Fragonard are responsible for the death of no one. In the context of *Femmes*, his antifeminist position has caused much confusion. Instead of glorifying male eroticism (and even though the narrative is androcratic) his purpose, as I see it, is to strip sexual pleasure of what he sees as oppressive mythology. His narrator even writes, "Let me clarify my aim: what I am writing here is in praise of women" (257). The women he has in mind are those who have discovered or recovered their singularity, their separate bodies, their independence vis-à-vis the mythical concept of Woman—the Woman who marries, has children, brings them up, manages a household, plays the part assigned to her by society, thus perpetuating that society's myths, contributing to its deadly sclerosis. In a way, however, keeping in mind several of the previous quotations, one might detect in *Femmes* an occasional display of vulnerability to the death drive that questions the pleasure principle. Although in a different fashion, that is Pascal's challenge to Montaigne, the Catholic challenge to the spirit of Bordeaux (the latter being shared by Montaigne and Sollers).

Disillusionment is indeed the key notion that characterizes Sollers's texts of the eighties. He himself has described his "realistic" novels as follows: "My narrator is always a complete sexual atheist. He takes note of the aberration [of the times], consents to it, shies away from it, writes down his observations. . . . *Femmes* was an inventory of present-day attitudes and behaviors."[38] The inventory even included transparent references to a number of contemporary intellectual and political figures, and an obviously fictitious interview with the pope. As a result, many readers stressed the roman-à-clef aspect of the book, as others had done in 1954 with Simone de Beauvoir's *Les Mandarins*, eager to sniff out scandalous bits of gossip. But it is a fictional text, and one critic has pointed out that its "characters" do not reveal the true identity of this or that "real" person but "what has caused such flesh and blood beings to drift toward their fictionality. . . . Such beings could only become the fiction of their being."[39]

To continue Sollers's own account: "*Portrait du joueur* [is] the description of a hypersophisticated affair accompanied by ritual (one of the solutions of the day). *Le Cœur absolu* [is] a set of suggestions for the new underground (establishment of networks, as in a secret society). *Les Folies françaises* [is] a barely veiled apology of a discreet, reasoned incest between father and daughter. In all those books, what was essential was to devise a strong, flexible nervous system in order to survive in the midst of contemporary closure and collapse." One need not agree with Sollers's interpretation of his own works, but it is at least as valid as (although no more so than) anyone else's. There is no question that their scription brings them together, with the exception of the last (and also *Le Lys d'or*, which had not yet been written).

The "underground" of *Le Cœur absolu*, known as the Society of the Absolute Heart, is dedicated to pleasure and knowledge and was founded in Venice at the close of a beautiful day. There are five members, three women and two men, including the narrator, and their sexual activities are unrestrained—within and without the society. Sex is the metaphor for all pleasure. Their anthem is Mozart's Clarinet Quintet in A, "the absolute heart of his work" (195), which is then performed in Venice in the presence of the pope, about midway through the narrative. Such a musical undercurrent is hardly surprising: Webern's *Das Augenlicht* was in the background of *H*. Other Mozart works are mentioned here, such as *Così fan tutte*, the Clarinet Concerto and *The Magic Flute*, but to me Bach's *Saint John Passion* is the most memorable reference, in part because its opening notes dominate Sollers's first pages and are taken up again later, but also because of the ironic counterpoint it adds to the narrator's discourse. On the one hand, we hear him reject the part of the sickly, suffering writer, we listen to his insistence on happiness, witness his carefree acquiescence to numerous whims, and on the other we see the metaphor of the Passion continuously cropping up. Death looms large, especially in the second and fourth of the book's seven parts. Cancer, AIDS, and suicide wreak havoc among the narrator's acquaintances, and he is led to fashion a black-humor reference to Georges Perec, "suicide, mode d'emploi" (67). Those deaths reverberate throughout the text: "The number of shades keeps increasing . . .Their drawn faces, their smothered voices . . . They are the ones that keep pulling you back . . . Can't do anything about it, we have known them, we must accept their weight" (186).

As in English, the French word *cœur* refers not only to a body organ but also to the "heart" of the escutcheon; in French, however, the word *abime* is often used to designate such a "heart" (hence the fashionable literary phrase of some years ago, *mise-en-abime*), as the narrator is careful to explain (188). Since the heraldic meaning is not the most common one, the chances are that it will be pushed aside, in the reader's imagination, by what corresponds to the English words *abysm* or *abyss*. The absolute heart could then join the absolute abyss—the absolute infernal pit. This fits in with the narrator's interest in Dante's *Divine Comedy* (he is, off and on, working on an adaptation of it for television!). But while there are many references to the *Inferno*, beginning with "the absolute image of fraud," Geryon, "at the heart of corruption" (22), matters are never simple nor univocal in a text by Sollers; near the end, conversing with a cardinal who happens to be a Dante scholar, the narrator states that *Paradise* is his favorite part of the poem (411). Actually, the secret society is probably no more than a pretext, a device that gives *Le Cœur absolu* some sort of unity, like freemasonry in Mozart's *Magic Flute*, according to the narrator. What matters much more are the variations on the themes of pleasure and death, reality and ideology, set against a background of contemporary terrorism and mediocrity, developed with the help of texts by Casanova, Dante, and others.

　　Les Folies françaises is indeed a story of incest. The narrator has had a brief affair with a woman he calls Madame, eighteen years before the narrative begins. They had a child, whom they called France (a name perhaps generated by the title), Madame left for New York, got married a couple of times, and now suddenly reappears, accompanied by her daughter, "this lively young marvel with brown eyes." The latter knows the narrator is her father; she has already had several lovers, one of them older than he is. The rest follows, very naturally, and in another commentary Sollers called this novel an "example of what can be done with what is ultrapositive, in terms of liberty, in our culture."[40] Incest, like sexual casualness, is stripped of all perversity and is symbolically set against terrorist repression. This particular affair lasts three years until she marries her steady boyfriend (of whom the narrator approves), a medical student who has been offered a position in Australia; she leaves, the affair ends, they know they will never see each other again. And that is it, there are no erotic details, little slang, and more understatement than provocation. There is much talk about literature and art, and the narrator is working on a new version of Don Juan (one recalls that the narrator of *Le Cœur absolu* had been working on an adaptation of Dante for television). There is something neoclassical about the narrative, and when one remembers that Sollers loves music and is knowledgeable about it, the fact that François Couperin wrote a chaconne entitled "Les Folies françaises" causes a number of things to fall into place. Not that Sollers patterned his narrative on the dozen couplets by Couperin, but several aspects of the latter adumbrate features of Sollers's text(s). The detached style of *Les Folies françaises*, for instance, seems to parallel the distance there is, to a twentieth-century listener, between the harpsichord variations and their sensuous theme. Couperin's piece is subtitled "les dominos" (in the sense of "masks"; see p. 58) and this suggests the numerous masks assumed by Sollers's narrators. It has been said that the quality of Couperin's music sometimes "springs from an apprehension of transience; from a recognition that all this graciousness and beauty must pass, perhaps quite soon."[41] As the narrator of Sollers's book puts it, "You know that time does go by and also does not; that we are outside of time behind our masks. . . . I kiss your eyes, which are destined for darkness a little later than mine" (123).

The narrator of *Le Lys d'or* wears yet another mask; he is a professor of Chinese philosophy and religion in Paris. The Chinese aura that surrounded *Nombres* thus reappears—but in a very different guise. While Lao-tzu is present in both books, the spirit of Mao is more noticeable in the 1968 text; in the more recent one it is detachment that dominates, as exemplified in the following quotation from the Chinese: "I pity him who has gone astray, I pity the one who pities him, I pity the one who pities the complainer, and thus I become more and more detached from the world" (152). The narrator's casual sexual relationship with women (along with a persistent query as to the nature of woman, one that comes close to concluding, as did one of Malraux's characters in *La Condition humaine*, that man and woman belong to two different species) provides a thematic thread, and references to death are again unmistakable. Like some of his earlier avatars, he is married and seems fond of his wife and son, but these two constitute no more than an unproblematic background. There is a difference, however, in that he has fallen in love, something unexpected in recent Sollers texts, with a woman who bears the improbable name of Reine de Laume—an echo of Proust's Princesse des Laumes (Oriane de Guermantes) and of a seventeenth-century Cardinal de Laume "who appears briefly" in Saint-Simon's *Mémoires* (102). (Interestingly enough, the narrator, Simon Rouvray, shares quite a few letters of his name with Louis de Rouvroy, duc de Saint-Simon.) They enter into a peculiar compact whereby she provides him with a monthly salary for two years during which he must write a book about himself, of at least a hundred pages, in which he will disclose his ideas, his fantasies, as freely as he wishes—again, a bio-graphy. This of course turns out to be the book we are reading (although it was stipulated that the text would be Reine's property and should not be published). Actually the love story is that of a failure, and the narrative is unfinished.

There may be two aspects of this text that shed light on Sollers's other writings. The first concerns the relationship between the narrator and what is traditionally called the "author," especially in the case of a first-person narrative. Readers are too often prone to confuse the two, perhaps forgetting Rimbaud's assertion that the "I" is "another person" (better stated as "the 'I' is an other," as reaffirmed and interpreted by Lacan),[42] or Proust's distinction between the superficial and the deep-seated "I." Over the years, Sollers's treatment of the matter has been somewhat uncertain. Giving a Spanish name to the first-person narrator of *Une Curieuse solitude* was an ambiguous gesture since the name was a literal rendition of his own; the nature of the subsequent texts, with the narrative being somewhat removed from a clear referent, pushed the problem into the background as the reader was increasingly confronted with a sort of abstract scription. Then, *H*, with a seeming or possible identification of narrator with writer, again brought the issue to the fore. I have already mentioned the conceit that presents *Femmes* as having been written by an American journalist and merely signed by Sollers. *Portrait du joueur*, on the other hand, begins with the narrator's nostalgic return to the landscapes of his youth—mental, physical, and fictional—which coincide with Sollers's own, to the point of resurrecting Concha and calling her Asuncion.

The character who says "I" in *Le Cœur absolu* is not given a precise identity, but the first letter of his name is "S" and he is said to be the "author" of the two previous novels, but this does not fit in with what we have been told. In *Carnet de nuit* Sollers assures us that the narrators of his last five novels are all different: he is working with what he calls "close multiple identities" (126). Perplexing as this may be to the naive reader, other "characters" in *Le Cœur absolu* appear to be annoyed: "Is that S. truly the initial letter of your name, says Carl. S. as in what? As in Stinker? Scholar? Stealthy?" To which the narrator counters, "Sévigné, Saint-Simon, Sade, Seingalt, Stendhal" (375). It does not help much but aside from affirming a literary tradition it adds a note of humor to the text (and there are quite a few such notes).

As for the narrator of *Les Folies françaises*, all we know is that he is a writer about whom an American student is writing a biography that will be "teeming with erroneous interpretations" (128). The agreement that gives a fictional birth to *Le Lys d'or* could be seen as an ironic spoof on the legend of the poet and his muse; its effect, however, is to throw additional confusion into a problematic relationship, and this may well have been Sollers's more or less conscious intent. The quest I referred to in connection with his earlier novels was, in part, related to what people have, somewhat misleadingly, called a search for identity; it is more properly a search for the answer to the question that keeps cropping up —who speaks? The confusion that Sollers seems to introduce could be his way of recognizing, to use Julia Kristeva's terminology, the heterogeneity of the split subject.

The second aspect of *Le Lys d'or* that I want to stress stems from the title's connotations, which are reinforced by the text itself. The "golden lily" is in all likelihood a Madonna or Annunciation lily; it occasioned the meeting of Reine and the narrator. (According to the narrator of *Le Cœur absolu*, the lily is an "accursed flower" [273].) Both were struck by the object, seen in an antique dealer's window in Paris; she bought it and, on the last page of the text, on what is left of the aborted sixth section of the manuscript, it is specified that she gave it to the narrator. The lily was originally described as dating back to the seventeenth century and having been part of an Annunciation sculpture probably located in a church. Following this through, it would seem that Reine played the part of the angel and the narrator that of the Virgin. The day when they were to meet, at her invitation, at her château in the Touraine region, was the fifteenth of August, the feast of the Virgin Mary's Assumption, the day one supposes the narrator was to reach an erotic heaven. He arrived on the thirteenth, as planned, but it does not work out as expected, he leaves on the fourteenth. They made love, but nothing happened. The Catholic notion of the Virgin Mary, and other aspects of Catholicism as well, have constantly fascinated Sollers. He has absorbed Catholic culture because, like most Frenchmen, he was brought up in the context of that religion, but instead of rejecting it outright, as many have done, he appears to be both intellectually detached and emotionally involved (and the reverse might be said of his considerable interest in the Bible). The Touraine episode might well be emblematic of the tension that exists within the subject of writing between love and sex, virility and femininity, life and death, and which has permeated Sollers's work so far. *Le Lys d'or* ends with a quotation from the *Tao Te Ching:* "Retire your body when the work has been accomplished, such is the Way of Heaven." And the narrator adds, "That is all" (251). But who speaks?

NOTES

1 "Présentation," *Tel Quel,* no. 1 (Spring 1960): 3.
2 Philippe Sollers, *Le Défi,* in *Ecrire 3* (Paris: Seuil, 1957), 5. Henceforth all references to Sollers's works will appear in the text.
3 Sollers, "Réponses," *Tel Quel,* no. 43 (Fall 1970): 71.
4 André Breton, *Manifeste du surréalisme* (1924; rpt. Paris: Pauvert, 1962), 53.
5 Sollers, "The Novel and the Experience of Limits," in *Writing and the Experience of Limits,* trans. by Philip Barnard with David Hayman (New York: Columbia University Press, 1983), 193. This is a selective translation of *Logiques.*
6 Pierre Mabille, *Le Miroir du merveilleux* (1940; rpt. Paris: Minuit, 1962), 22.
7 Jacques Derrida, *De la grammatologie* (Paris: Seuil, 1967), 68.
8 Derrida, 92.
9 Sollers, "Literature and Totality," 80.
10 Ibid., 82.
11 Sollers, "The Novel . . .," 197.
12 Michel Butor, *Passage de Milan* (Paris: Minuit, 1954), 9.
13 Franz Kafka, *Briefe an Felice* (S. Fischer Verlag, 1967), 250.
14 Sollers, "The Novel . . .," 195.
15 Sollers, "Choisir son style," *Tel Quel,* no. 3 (Fall 1960): 43.
16 Sollers, "Logique de la fiction" (1962), in *Logiques* (Paris: Seuil, 1968), 15.
17 Ibid., 16.

18   Ibid.
19   Sollers, "The Novel . . .," 201.
20   Sollers, "Literature . . .," 75-76.
21   Sollers, "The Novel . . .," 193.
22   Roland Barthes, "Histoire ou littérature" (1960), in *Sur Racine* (Paris: Seuil, 1963), 157, 164.
23   Emile Benveniste, "Catégories de pensée et catégories de langue" (1958), in *Problèmes de linguistique générale* (Paris: Gallimard, 1966), 74.
24   Sollers, "The Novel . . .," 186-87.
25   Ibid., 194.
26   Ibid.
27   Sollers, "The Novel . . .," 191.
28   Jacques Derrida, "La Dissémination," in *La Dissémination* (Paris: Seuil, 1972), 319-407.
29   Thanks are due Professor Goren Malmquist of the University of Stockholm, who was visiting professor at Columbia during the summer of 1968 when I was reading *Nombres* and who translated the ideograms for me.
30   Shuhsi Kao, "Paradise Lost? An Interview with Philippe Sollers," *SubStance*, no. 30 (1981): 47.
31   David Hayman, "An Interview with Philippe Sollers," *TriQuarterly*, no. 38 (Winter 1977): 125-26.
32   Ibid., 129.
33   This has been analyzed in detail by Julia Kristeva in "The Novel as Polylogue," *Desire in Language* (New York: Columbia University Press, 1980), 159-209.
34   Thomas Pynchon, *Gravity's Rainbow* (New York: Viking, 1973), 211.
35   Sollers, "Je sais pourquoi je jouis," *Tel Quel*, no. 90 (Winter 1981): 12.
36   See Jean-Paul Enthoven, "Aller-Retour dans le système Sollers," *Le Nouvel observateur*, 19 January 1981, p. 86.
37   Michel Butor, in *L'Arc*, no. 39 (1969): 2.
38   Sollers, "Journal du joueur II," *L'Infini*, no. 23 (Fall 1988): 51.
39   Jean-Luc Steinmetz, "A propos de *Femmes* de Sollers," *Quinzaine littéraire*, no. 390 (1983): 29.
40   Sollers, "Pour célébrer la vraie révolution française," *L'Infini*, no. 25 (Spring 1989): 165.
41   See Wilfred Mellers, *François Couperin and the French Classical Tradition* (London: Faber & Faber, 1987), 37.
42   Jacques Lacan, "Psychologie et métapsychologie," in *Le Séminaire*, Livre II (Paris: Seuil, 1978), 15 ff.

12

Maurice Roche

Of about a dozen books published by Maurice Roche, six bear the imprint of Philippe Sollers's series "Tel Quel," at Le Seuil; it was Jean Pierre Faye, however, who, after reading the manuscript of *Compact* in 1964 (it had been completed in 1956, four years before the first issue of *Tel Quel* appeared), recommended it to his fellow members of the *Tel Quel* board. Sollers published an extract in the sixteenth issue of *Tel Quel* (Winter 1964), and the book came out in 1966, dedicated to Jean Pierre Faye, with a preface by Sollers. When Faye left *Tel Quel* to found his *Change* "collective," Roche went with him but did not stay very long. Like Ricardou and many other French intellectuals, he was briefly with the Communist party—but he was obviously not regimentable. Perhaps just as important as that ideological background is that the first text published by Roche was not *Compact* but a book on Monteverdi in 1960. (An earlier, lengthy work of fiction, "Bazar de haute lune," remains unpublished as of this writing.)[1]

Noting that there exists no portrait of Monteverdi's wife Claudia Cattaneo (who died after only twelve years of marriage), he suggested that "her likeness emerges out of all the melodic sequences that Monteverdi has imprinted in us, and thus we know her immortal profile." He added that there is no reason why we should not imagine Claudia's features to be similar to those of Simonetta Vespucci, as painted by Piero di Cosimo and reproduced on the cover of Roche's *Monteverdi*.[2] Simonetta appeared again, some twenty years later, toward the end of his *Camar(a)de* (1981, 144), facing a reproduction of Van Gogh's painting, *Squelette fumant une cigarette*—and at the same time this page echoes the book's cover, which reproduces Antoine Wiertz's *La Belle Rosine*, in which a nude Rosine contemplates a full-size skeleton.

Those seemingly superficial details nevertheless point to key aspects

267

aspects of Roche's work. Like Michel Butor, he would break down the artificial barriers dividing one form of art from another, specifically writing, music, and painting. Although he published relatively late, he started writing early; he has also composed music, perhaps even earlier, and he has an undeniable gift for drawing. It goes without saying that his practice is very different from that of Butor, as merely leafing through their books would show at once. While dates of publication suggest that Roche's work is an outcome of the various intellectual and literary movements of the fifties and sixties, the fact remains that his actual practice preceded them. He harks back directly to Mallarmé, Joyce, and even Rabelais, and his leap forward has landed him in a rather different spot from theirs.

The illustrations I mentioned point to his fascination with death and the beauty of women. One could perhaps say that the mask of death is the hallmark of his entire work, beginning, in obvious fashion, with the picture appearing on the back cover of *Circus* (1972)—a photo by Ivankow showing Roche fondly holding a skull against his cheek, as if it were a loved child or woman. The best-known of those skulls is the one appearing on the antepunultimate page of *CodeX* (1974). It reminds me of Apollinaire's calligrams rather than Mallarmé's *Un Coup de dés* as curved musical staffs, the word *peace* written in many languages, and exclamation marks are disposed on the page in such fashion as to convey the likeness of a skull. The interesting thing here is that the reader is able at the same time to see the skull and go beyond it to the meaning of the words, and that is not always the case with the calligrams of Apollinaire. In the latter's "Il pleut," for example, one either visualizes a downpour or slants the page slightly in order to read the text. What is possible in the instance of the *CodeX* skull is due in large part to the various words all having the same meaning, but the variety of languages suggests the universality of the desire for peace without obliterating the mask of death. The exclamation marks could be seen as an ironic commentary on the contradiction between man's yearning for peace while threatening the world with (atomic) death, and also as a representation of falling bombs.[3]

As summed up by Philippe Sollers, *Compact* is "the 'story' of a dying blind man who, in some imaginary metropolis, like a latter-day Faust, haggles over his tattooed skin with a Japanese doctor Mephisto assisted by a transvestite, and happens to be at the same time the focus of noises, languages, literatures, and mythologies, the deepest of which appear to be orchestrated around his father's death."[4] The "story," a word Sollers carefully places within quotation marks, is a text made up of a number of strands, each identifiable by means of typography: roman, boldface roman, italics, boldface italics, small roman capitals, small italic capitals, large capitals, and so forth. This in itself calls attention to the physical appearance of words on the page, to the materiality of the text, which is emphasized by the irregular aspect of the typography, the many blank spaces, a number of wordplays, and the occasional splitting of the page into two columns when a sentence goes into two different directions at the same time; after eight or ten lines the two strands merge back into one.

There are perhaps thirty sequences (there could be more or less, depending on one's interpretation of the blank spaces separating blocks of print); in most, two or more strands are woven into the text. The book begins with what I identify as a sequence that includes a boldface italic strand, written in the second-person singular, and a boldface roman strand in which the subject of the verb is the impersonal "one" (15-21). The italic strand has a lyrical, quasi-biblical tone that tempts one to render the "tu" with the English "thou": "Thou shalt lose sleep as thou shalt lose your eyesight. While thou shalt enter into the night, thou shalt penetrate a deeper and deeper darkness; thy memory, already failing, diminishing as—coming out of a long lethargy—thou shalt become conscious of thy condition." Such initial style, however, is soon shattered by the interaction of the numerous narrative strands; it sticks in the mind in large part because of the contrast. It does set a certain tone, just the same, as do the opening chords of a musical composition, leading listeners and readers to the final notes or words that are determined at the start, no matter how many incidents or distractions intervene in between. The last pages of *Compact* display two characters, the one who says "I" and his companion (he had first appeared in the second sequence and his strand is printed in ordinary roman type) who on New Year's Eve are sitting in a nightclub located on a dead-end street called Alley of the Catacombs, and when he describes their appearance as seen in a mirror this provides the reader with a representation of a skull—"our image reduced to the size of a skull (and we are inside)." The scene is reprinted white on black, with the skull made visible, on page 68 of *Circus;* it is interpreted in a drawing by Francoise Rojare on page 127 of *CodeX;* it is repeated in English translation on page 105 of *Opéra bouffe;* and reappears in the original French on page 75 of *Camar(a)de.* In the meantime the reader has been treated to many fanciful, frightening, erotic, and comical sideshows.

Even though I have just used the word *character* (for convenience's sake), what characters there are in *Compact* are not really "people." They are what I have called the strands of the narrative; they are like the melodic lines in an opera that are assigned to a variety of voices— soprano, tenor, baritone, and so forth. Just as the combination and interaction of such voices gives the opera aesthetic quality and meaning, the interplay of the narrative strands give Roche's text its significance. Thus, while no explicit statement is made, one is led to link the Japanese doctor's quest for tattooed skins that would become art objects with Nazi concentration camps in which human skin was made into lampshades; and because that same doctor has been interested in the skins of the victims of the Hiroshima bombing, along with the presence of an American floozy, the threat of worldwide atomic death must not have been far from the mind of the writer in the fifties and his first readers in the sixties.

Compact is clearly not a "structuralist" novel as a well-known French critic, Maurice Nadeau, had mistakenly claimed.[5] While *Circus* (1972) first surprises the reader because of the unusual aspect of its pages, where typographical experimentation is taken several steps further (on occasion one might be reminded of concrete poetry), this second fiction, too, is strongly committed (*engagé*). It is committed less because of the obvious political references such as I have noted in *Compact* than by reason of its attack on the narrative and on the conventional way of using language—the latter being the main organizer of social, cultural, and political reality. The premise is that if we would only learn to read differently we would better be able to resist what the dominant narratives of the ideology attempt to impose upon us. Such a proposition is also advanced in the writings of Jean Pierre Faye and specifically acknowledged by both writers. The typographical disposition on the page is thus not aesthetic but functional: the purpose is to discourage the habit of reading each line sequentially from left to right, or worse, reading diagonally down the page. One is forced to read chaotically, as it were, some paragraphs being amenable to conventional reading, others requiring each phrase or word to be deciphered, while yet others are splintered and require creative interpretation. There are statements in German, Italian, Latin, Spanish, English, and other languages, as well as pictographs and musical staffs with notes and lyrics. To the puns of *Compact Circus* adds what I might call creative typos—sham typos that have been "corrected" to suggest another meaning. In other words, everything calls attention to the material presence of signs on the page and opposes their transparency.

The seventh page of *Circus* begins with the line, "Lost Inferno (¿le gusta este jardin?)." The question refers one to Malcolm Lowry's *Under the Volcano*, in which it appears on a sign in the Consul's garden and is strikingly repeated on the book's last page. In its full form it reads, in Lowry's text, "¿Le Gusta este jardin que es suyo? ¡Evite que sus hijos lo destruyan!"[6] It is an admonition that Roche would surely endorse, assuming the world to be our "garden." The split paragraph that follows, in *Circus*, could, in both of its statements, be interpreted as a thematic reference to Lowry's novel. Reading a book that leads one to a sense of "powerlessness," and seeing in another man's drunkenness a "precedent" (Roche told Anne Fabre-Luce that *Circus* was a "comedy of intoxication") might nevertheless enable one to be rid of the "self's frightful tyranny." The page concludes with, on the right side, in the same italic typeface as the statement that ends with the word *powerlessness,* the stereotyped words that follow each section of a serial publication, "*(to be continued),*" and on the left, in roman, "Titulus tumuli"—inscription on a tomb. Like the statements they conclude, they are contradictory, or perhaps dialectical, thus emphasizing the notion of struggle, with writing and with life. They also hark back to the first phrase, "Lost Inferno": it is the Mexico of Malcolm Lowry and of his Consul (which led to the latter's death), Dante's *Inferno,* which was the first part of a journey in the direction of Beatrice, and, indirectly, Milton's *Paradise Lost,* which is the account of Lucifer's downfall. A wealth of interpretive possibilities thus arise out of one of the more straightforward pages of *Circus.*

The book's title bears the connotations of the English word and those of the French "*cirque*" as well. About two-thirds of the way through the book American Indians begin seeping through the text, then briefly followed by blacks. Baiting Americans for what we have done to both groups is a favorite pastime for French intellectuals; here, however, they stand not only for all oppressed people but for all human beings, and the white oppressors, too, potentially stand for all human beings. Mark Polizzotti has remarked on "Roche's ethnic heritage, an unlikely mix of French, Jewish, Irish, and Cheyenne,"[7] and the latter strand perhaps justifies his stance. America's civilization, having gotten where it is ahead of other Western nations (for better or for worse), is also an attractive symbol for the excesses of Western civilization as a whole. Nevertheless, the point of view is not that of a Cheyenne, or of anyone else for that matter, for there is no more point of view than there are characters. We thus have the image of someone, locked in a rectangle of sorts, who is condemned to run around in circles, has to pretend he is attempting to escape, either on foot, or "on horseback—in the ring of a traveling 'Circus,' describing a spiral and raising a cloud of dust" (86). Perhaps a dismal view of the human condition, but on the next to last page whoever dies is said to be "dead because he closed his eyes on a dream" (128). Things are therefore not so bleak after all, and if only human beings would keep up the struggle... But the text of *Circus* does not allow me to complete the sentence and deliver a clear, unambiguous message. Few works of art permit one to do that; what is frustrating here, however, is due to the knowledge that Roche is a committed writer.

To complicate matters, a contradictory statement appears in the body of the subsequent *CodeX* (1974)—"dead because he looked life straight in the face" (111). In both cases, however, the metaphor that is conjured up involves sight; one might recall that the text of *Compact* featured a blind man and that *Circus* teems with visual tropes. (These, to me, are more striking, but Roche's imagery calls on the other senses as well.) That was to be expected, since much of the texts' concern is with reading and, inevitably, writing, activities that entail the use of sight and call forth the complementary metaphors of blindness and night (one recalls other writers' concern with night). Marx had criticized classical economists such as Smith and Ricardo for not seeing what was in front of their eyes. As the saying goes, it stared them in the face, for which the French equivalent, literally rendered, is, "it gouged their eyes out" ("*cela leur crevait les yeux*"). As I pointed out earlier, Roche is concerned with people's inability to read, that is, to see what is actually taking place in the text: they are taken in by the ideology. One tries to do something about it but, "since it stares you in the face [i.e., gouges your eyes out, blinds you] you don't see much of it" (*Circus*, 108).

When *CodeX* was completed it was apparently viewed by Roche as the final volume of a trilogy and its two epigraphic pages display five quotations from the previous volumes. Three of them seem to point forward to his later works, a reflection of the change that is slowly taking place as his obsessions shift from the social to the personal. The fate of the world and the threat of atomic annihilation is ever present, but his own health intrudes more and more. The text proper begins, "I am a sick man and my father knows it" (11). One of the epigraphs, printed white on black, reads, "Life is there, merely for the record," and another, the simple phrase "Jivaro or the lost paradigm," refers to the headshrinking Indians of South America. The context of the latter makes it clear that Roche had psychoanalysis in mind—and what he considers its failure—but it seems hard to dismiss what used to be those Indians' actual practice with the heads of their dead enemies, hence the thought of what happens to oneself after death. The text is permeated by death in various forms, and it includes a parodic "Funeral Cantata" (103-21) followed by an equally parodic *danse macabre* entitled "Get ready for the stiffs' hop." The fear and horror associated with both life and death are thus alleviated by humor, which is produced by a sort of overemphasis either through wordplay ("He looks quite awful. Wounded in the face . . . Loss of eyesight. / Being rather blind, he is not aware of it" [*CodeX*, 17]) or through imagery ("the enchantress drinking ambrosia or mead from the cranium, scraped clean of its grub, of her lover whose corpse still smells good" [*CodeX*, 55]).

The typography of *CodeX* recalls that of *Circus* but in a more subdued manner, and in most cases the text functions as it did in the earlier books rather than in linear fashion. Roche's own back-cover blurb calls it a "Text about the burying of the text and the updating (revelation) of the book—which is never the same, each reading changing it. / An archeology of fiction. A collection of laws, of remedies: medesinful recipes. Advice on how to 'die cured' of life—and rest in peace!" The first part would appear to correspond to Roche's intentions, some of which are realized, the second to his practice. Two pages before the end the reader is faced with the calligram of skull and bombs, which I have already discussed; on the next page comes the explosion, and on the final page we have nothing but this brief exchange, in English: "—Mama! oh, mama! . . . / — Shut up! will you . . ."

The title of *Opéra bouffe* (1975) is a reminder that Roche thought of calling his works, collectively, "An Operatic Novel." His musical background again comes to the fore. Here the emphasis is on humor—black humor as usual. The architecture recalls that of the Italian opera buffa with its division in two acts, each called intermezzo, framed by an introduction, intermission, and finale. The humor is often self-directed, and the tone is set by the one-line "introduction," "They had given away my toys I had so few," leading to the last line of the "finale," "He's dead, the old jerk." As a correlative to the increasing intrusion of the subject of writing, I would mention the appearance of the cat, Roche's favorite animal: "The kleine Nachtmusik box that had been promised me . comfort me after the loss of my cat . Not given !" (25). The animal shows up a number of times, and on page 67 as he signs his name on a mirror with a piece of soap the initial "M" of Maurice is modified to look like the head of a cat—a graphism he has used again and again, both privately and publicly.

Interesting, humorous, and moving as his subsequent books may be, my sense is that his major contribution to the art and practice of writing lies in his first three, the fourth serving as a hinge between them and his more recent works. The ten sections of *Mémoire* (1976) are recollections, improvisations, or fictions based on such themes as the exploitation of workers, illness, doctors, cats, and death. Some are quite amusing, others depressing or bitter; the following excerpt of an imaginary last will is typical of the latter: I bequeath "my eyes beyond sleep and dream (neither dreams nor death can be inherited!) to a needy living being steeped in darkness and who, having recovered his sight, shall be able to appreciate with his own eyes the surrounding ugliness and filth, and the nastiness of human beings" (55).

Macabré (1979) is, once more, a parodic *danse macabre* with many illustrations by Roche himself. *Maladie mélodie* (1980) is presented mostly in dramatic form, that is, as a number of dialogues with scenic indications. The mainly theatrical portion is divided into nine sections that alternate with six divertimentos, one intermezzo, and one interlude —an architecture related to that of *Opéra bouffe*. It is a fantasy on his own death, and it includes the last will that appeared in *Mémoire*. Perhaps because religious funeral rites, especially in the Catholic church, include a considerable amount of music, quotations from many composers from Couperin to Koering appear on nearly every page. As the title almost suggests, deadly illness is changed into heavenly music, and as the text actually says, "Dying, you know, is nothing to be in a terrible state about;

in a pinch, you might call it a love song, a funeral march, a requiem, a song
. . . you know, a beautiful melodic line!" (130). As a coda, Roche imagines
himself awakening from his fantasy, and on the last line of the book he
asks, "Is it the pain that goes away or am I getting used to it?"

Camar(a)de (1981), which introduces something akin to the creative
typo into its very title (comrade/death), is a series of meditations on over
sixty paintings, photographs, and sculptures, nearly all involving death,
skulls, and skeletons. Except for the theme, the process is akin to some of
Michel Butor's own meditations on paintings. *Ecritures* (1985) is a
delightful collection of aphoristic quotations from the works of Maurice
Roche, each one on a page facing an equally remarkable drawing by him.

He has called his *Je ne vais pas bien mais il faut que j'y aille* (1987) a
"short stories novel." It consists of seven texts organized into four
unequal sections. The title might be translated as "I am not feeling well
and yet I must go on feeling" and it emphasizes the kind of punning
aphorisms that have always been present in his work but are especially
characteristic of his more recent books. The typography is almost conventional, the various "short stories" can be read in linear fashion, and
the writer's *persona* is close to the surface; what links it to the other works
are the themes we are now familiar with. The first sentence of the initial
short story (which makes up the entire first section), "Ahead of his time,
he had gone too far," has the ring of an autobiographical statement. The
person it refers to, however, is an efficiency-minded bicycle racer who is
not sure his performances have any meaning (a faint echo of Raymond
Queneau may be detected here) but just the same gives himself body and
soul to his work. And it all ends up in failure—and in a fatal heart attack as
he is taking an electrocardiogram in his doctor's office.

In the second text, a narrator goes at dusk to his mistress' apartment,
knowing full well that she is not there; the place is empty except for a cat,
covered with eczema, and he claims his fondness for the animal is the
secret reason for his coming—to keep it company and feed it. He reminisces in morbid fashion and then walks away knowing he will never
return. In the third, we are treated to a description of the narrator's
dilapidated apartment, encumbered with broken-down furniture and
objects of various kinds and purposes, among which he navigates with
difficulty, partly because of poor eyesight, partly due to the effect of
alcohol. He is "a writer because he is unhappy, unhappy since he is a
writer"; among other aphorisms he suggests that "One should die first in
order to live afterward. But what for?" (57). He is referred to a psychiatrist
who lives near Bordeaux and owns a vineyard. There is something wrong
with the doctor, too, for he thought he could be a successful writer;
unfortunately, in spite of a preface by François Mauriac no publisher
would take his book, which he then had printed at his own expense, sold
not a single copy, and stored them all throughout his house. The book is

entitled *What's the Use?* Then there is the story of a painter who, unable to afford a model, dredges up memories of the women he has known, but without avail: he cannot transfer them to his canvas. Finally he decides to do a self-portrait and the end result resembles the now familiar skull. His counterpart appears in the next narrative: a composer has seemingly succeeded in writing "the partition of his life's work" (88)—but it is called *Totenbuch.* As he describes one of its sequences to the narrator the latter wonders if its performance (for which the French term is *execution* and includes the same deathly connotation as its English cognate [102]) might not cause a heart attack in the performers or listeners. The final text is more meditation than short story; women, alcohol, and music are absent from the surface of the text, which is permeated with the drudgery of life and the thought of death. "I experience death at every moment. I have the feeling that I came into this world with death in my skull" (116).

A fragmentary "novel" like the previous ones in the sense that there is no anecdotal link between the seven texts, its pieces fuse together because of the tone, the themes, and the textual repetitions: sentences that are often cast in the form of aphorisms are the leitmotivs that signal the writer's unifying presence and personality. The question that comes up at this point is whether or not any combination of fragments might not have the same effect. In other words, any combination of extracts of his works can be identified as a text by Maurice Roche, with the writer's persona being in every instance the sole unifying factor.

During the course of an interview, Roche explained among other things that *Circus* was begun with his making a general, elaborate outline. The latter was then modified as he proceeded with the actual writing; in any case, however, the text "could not have been written in the order in which its pages would be published." Its first publication was disordered as various sequences came out in at least half a dozen periodicals, in no particular order. Possibly, an arrangement different from the one adopted for the volume might have been chosen—but not just any order: "One cannot shuffle the book's pages like a deck of cards."[8]

The means of testing that statement has actually been provided by an anthology recently published that includes sizable extracts from six books by Maurice Roche.[9] As I went through the volume, I felt that it unquestionably read like the anthology it was supposed to be. It thus demonstrated, if that were still necessary, that linearity, a particular anecdote, and a cohesive plot are not the indispensable element of a written work of art. Verbal, musical, and visual factors also play an important role. In other words, there is a way of welding fragments together that endows them with significance and distinguishes them from a random set of fragments.

NOTES

1   These details have been culled from various interviews given by Roche to
    David Hayman (*SubStance*, no. 17 [1977]: 5-11), George Charbonnier
    (*Maurice Roche par les autres* [Paris: L'Athanor, 1978], 9-16), Jacques Henric
    (ibid., 99-108), and Eva Corredor (*French Review* 54, no. 4 [March 1981]:
    538-50). See also Anne Fabre-Luce, "Maurice Roche: réunir le monde en un
    texte" (*Quinzaine Littéraire*, 16-30 April 1972, pp. 3-4).
2   Maurice Roche, *Monteverdi* (Paris: Seuil, 1960).
3   For further considerations on such matters see my essay, "Readable /
    Writable / Visible," in *Visible Language* 12, no. 3 (Summer 1978): 231-44.
4   Philippe Sollers, "Preface" to *Compact* (Paris: Seuil, 1966), 10.
5   That is, if one gives "structuralism" the somewhat perverted meaning a
    number of French critics have ascribed to it (with the notable exception of
    Lucien Goldmann) and in which the nonsubjective, stable (if not static),
    univocal, autoreferential aspects of writing are overemphasized.
6   Malcolm Lowry, *Under the Volcano* (1947; rpt. Philadelphia & New York: J. B.
    Lippincott, 1965), 128, 377.
7   Mark Polizzotti, "Introduction" to his translation of *Compact* (Elmwood Park:
    Dalkey Archive Press, 1988), ii.
8   Both quotations are from Georges Charbonnier, "Entretien avec Maurice
    Roche," in *Maurice Roche par les autres*, 14-15.
9   Jean Paris, *Maurice Roche* (Paris: Seghers, 1989). This is a 69-page essay by
    Paris followed by a 102-page "Choix de textes."

13

Jean Ricardou

In July 1971, at the Centre Culturel International in Cerisy-la-Salle,[1] a
ten-day conference brought together fiction writers, critics, and university professors from all over the world. The object was to examine the
state of such fiction as had been heralded as "new" fifteen years earlier
and attempt to determine where it was headed. All the writers who came
to speak or sent a paper to be read (Sarraute, Simon, Robbe-Grillet,
Butor, Pinget, and Ollier) had once been included in the so-called
nouveau roman confederation but the turn their fiction was taking led
people to talk of a *nouveau nouveau roman*—a phrase that was as misleading as the first. Forgetting the label, if possible, the truth remains that
what prompted its coinage was the most significant conclusion to be
drawn from the meetings of that Cerisy decade. Indeed, it was possible to
detect a break in the work of almost all writers who were discussed, after
which the fiction they published showed a different orientation. What
may be even more significant, no matter how uniquely distinctive the fiction of each writer might have been before the change, the orientation it
assumed afterward was similar—although it retained distinguishing traits.
Invariably, their work was directed toward a subversion of literary and
social structures by means of textual procedures. One exception is Nathalie
Sarraute, who has always been independent and in some respects ahead
of the times. My own examination in previous chapters of several of those
writers leads to the same conclusion: something happened during the
sixties that made it difficult for them to write as they had before. I hope I
have also shown that the seed of discontent was present earlier and that
the change was not due to a sudden illumination.

The "discovery" of Raymond Roussel in the fifties was an omen of
things to come—certainly not a cause. Actually, a truer predecessor was
Blanchot, who quietly effected his own break in 1948 with *L'Arrêt de*

277

mort. Beckett's *Comment c'est* and Sollers's *Le Parc*, both published in 1961, register the new mode, although Beckett's presence in French fiction, in contrast to his theater, will never again be what it was in the fifties. Butor's *Mobile*, early in 1962, was not only a break but a scandal, leading some to question the writer's sanity. A few months later, Faye's *Battement* accentuated a development already visible in his work. Then came Duras's *Le Ravissement de Lol V. Stein* (1964), Robbe-Grillet's *La Maison de rendez-vous* (1965), and Ollier's *L'Echec de Nolan* (1967); those were followed, almost simultaneously, by Pinget's *Passacaille* and Simon's *La Bataille de Pharsale* in 1969.

One might always point out, of course, that the sixties were likely years for changes in writing to take place. After all, nearly everything else had been shaken. Those were the years of worldwide student upheavals, of the rise to consciousness and militancy of blacks, women (although in France this occurred later than in the U.S.), Algerians, and other oppressed groups, of the Chinese cultural revolution, of the "conquest" of space, of war in the Middle East, of the sex and drug "revolutions," of the Russian-American confrontation over Cuba, of the Czech revolt, and of the spectacle of the most powerful nation on earth showering a record tonnage of bombs over one of the weakest in a vain attempt to subdue it. In such times, a revolution in writing is plausible—but why this particular one? There must have been a connection, but I am not sure those events alone could have been determining. Writing practices will bear watching in order to see if the worldwide changes that began about 1989 will have any significant effect on the scription of those writers I survey in my conclusion. While these upheavals affected the communist regimes as opposed to the challenges to capitalism evidenced in the 1960s, the two are in some ways related as they were, in the final analysis, triggered by abuses—perversions of the communist and capitalist systems.

Some of those present at Cerisy in 1971 may have suspected a lesser cause and identified it with Jean Ricardou, one of the organizers of the colloquium, who chaired many of its sessions. They were mistaken, of course, and yet here, too, there was a connection. One should remember that he was for nine years on the editorial board of *Tel Quel*, from the spring of 1962 to the fall of 1971, and a contributor beginning with the second issue (Summer 1960). In my opinion, whatever influence he may have had is inseparable from that of the review and the group to which he belonged in the sixties.[2] Not that I consider *Tel Quel*, any more than either Ricardou or Sollers alone, as the exclusive cause of the change in fiction writing or in writing in general during the sixties and seventies. What I am suggesting is that a scanning of the texts published either in the review itself or under the group's aegis would permit one to identify what lines of thought might have converged toward textuality.

Ricardou's critical and theoretical essays attracted considerable attention when they were published in book form throughout the seventies; his contributions to the various conferences that he directed have also been influential because of the intellectual rigor they evidenced. Nevertheless, he has preferred to think of fiction as being the locus of his major activity. To be more precise, he has downgraded the distinction between theory and practice, asserting that the writing of fiction could also be a theoretical activity. He now has seven volumes of fiction to his credit, beginning with *L'Observatoire de Cannes* (1961; The Observation Tower in Cannes), which is roughly contemporary with those books marking the new direction taken by the writings of Sollers and Butor among others. Ricardou's work has no main character, no narrator, no definite point of view. The concept of "omniscient writer" is hardly relevant, for there is no concealed information to impart either as thoughts or as secreted material, and the text seems to have an independent existence of its own. There are four "settings" involved: a compartment in a train moving along the French Mediterranean coast, an observation tower overlooking the city of Cannes, a section of the beach at Cannes together with an adjoining part of the city, and a series of photographs in a book.

Although there is no plot in the accepted sense of the term, one might venture to say that the book exhibits a new concept of plot consisting in the manner statements about the setting (that is, words connected with the setting) and a half dozen characters (functions or names) are combined in order to produce a given effect on the reader. In other words, the structure of the fiction is also its plot. *L'Observatoire de Cannes* is made up of thirty-one brief chapters, the first and the last two being set in the train compartment, as are three others spaced out in between. As the text shifts to tower, beach, and city, with photographs providing an articulation, one notices that most of the words and phrases of the initial compartment setting are used again, with or without variations. That recalls the process adopted by Ollier in *La Mise en scène* several years earlier, but in Ollier's text only a few descriptions are repeated, while Ricardou reuses words, in a number of cases being concerned only with the word in itself (e.g., a triangle might refer to the shape of a blouse's opening, of the parts of a bikini, of the areas that cannot be seen from the observation tower) or with sections of words (*-age*, as in *nuage*, *visage*, and *corsage*)—but this does not prevent him from repeating the entire word. The description of the compartment provides a vocabulary store, and its eight seats inscribe that number in the text for recurrent use. We thus have an octagonal bar on top of the tower, an eight-sided revolving stand, a beach bag with eight holes for the strap that secures it, and so forth.

The observation tower then provides the correlative on the basis of which the text develops. As the cable car goes up the hill toward the tower more and more of the scenery is unveiled at a gradually increasing distance from the hill, and at the top of the tower one enjoys an unrestricted view of the entire region. The panoramic view is then forsaken as one returns to city and beach, practically to sea level. Likewise, there is a gradual, imaginary unveiling of a young woman's body, and in the last chapter she is restored to her banal, everyday appearance in the train. Finally, what is also unveiled is the manner in which language functions in order to provide an impression (or an illusion) of the surrounding reality. This was intended by Ricardou to be demonstrated by his inserting into the novel, with practically no changes, a text that had appeared in 1961 in the fifth issue of *Tel Quel,* "Description d'un strip-tease." The original text, however, isolated as it was, could be read as its title suggested—as a representational text. When caught in the economy of the novel, it can no longer be read in such fashion.

Even such a summary account—and a detailed analysis might compel one to repeat the entire text, word for word—should demonstrate that from the start Ricardou was ahead of almost everyone else in his emphasis on textual matters. In *La Prise de Constantinople* (1965; The Taking of Constantinople) he goes even further in establishing the text's independence from the standard referents. At first, the book would seem to have no other source than the book itself and its situation in a continuum of language and literature; it generates its sentences in similar fashion as did *L'Observatoire de Cannes.* There had been a few basic outside referents in that work (the city of Cannes, the train, and so on). Perhaps no more than a few specks of dust generated Robbe-Grillet's *Dans le labyrinthe,* but those tiny referents were still something. Now there is practically nothing external, for the source of the book lies in the necessary elements of its cover, that is, the author's name, that of the publishing house he is tied to by contract, the publisher's emblem (the five-pointed star attached to an *m* of *Les Editions de Minuit*). That already provides numbers (so many letters in each name), a topic (the m[ysterious] star, which eventually becomes the setting for a science-fiction story), names (*Editions* produces Ed, Edith, and Sion—which is the French spelling for Zion), and initial time setting (*minuit*). The coincidence that gives a common series of five letters to the names of both Ricardou and Villehardouin, a chronicler of the Crusades, adds the parallel topic of the Crusades to that of space science fiction. The Fourth Crusade is selected for several precise reasons—one of them is that once the common letters have been removed from "Villehardouin" there remains "ville" and "in," suggesting the idea of penetration into a city, and that is what the soldiers of the Fourth Crusade did in Constantinople rather than going on to Jerusalem.

A minor issue needs to be dealt with here, for Villehardouin is not the only writer whose name has five letters in common with Ricardou's. One that would probably come more readily to the mind of a literary critic or historian is Victorien Sardou, the prolific playwright of the latter nineteenth century whose plays were performed all over the world. Had his name been selected, a somewhat different book would have resulted, which might have been entitled "La Prise de l'Académie." Subjective considerations must have intervened, and the situation is similar to the one faced by Raymond Roussel as explained by Michel Butor (see p. 24 above). In fact, Sardou and Ricardou are antithetical figures; Sardou has often been put down as a mere entertainer, while Ricardou, on the other hand, like the other writers I have discussed, takes scriptional activity most seriously. On occasion, one gathers the impression that he sees himself as a crusader for textuality. Hence, perhaps, Villehardouin; nevertheless, the suspicion remains that the Crusades, as a referent, were present in the writer's mind, consciously or not, before the Ricardou/Villehardouin connection was "discovered."

In keeping with the hypothesis that the book started from nothing outside of it, *rien* becomes the first word of the text; in conjunction with other elements, it suggests a statement from Mallarmé's *Un Coup de dés jamais n'abolira le hasard,* "NOTHING . . . WILL HAVE TAKEN PLACE . . . SAVE THE PLACE . . . WITH THE EXCEPTION . . . PERHAPS . . . OF A CONSTELLATION." This last word, incidentally, has twelve letters in common with Constantinople.[3] Thus, a textual interplay is immediately authorized, and even encouraged by the only other statement appearing on the first page, "Other than, perhaps, rising to the surface, the gap that such a certainty establishes." It is one that almost seems to emerge out of Mallarmé's text. As a means of working against people's linear reading habits, pages, chapters, and parts are unnumbered —also a means of preventing lecturers and reviewers from dealing with and referring to the text in conventional fashion. Since the back cover could traditionally be conceived as a sort of exit out of the linear narrative, a "left-hand" title page replaces it, on which *La Prose de Constantinople* is substituted for *La Prise de Constantinople,* thus also pointing to the textual nature of the book (within the narrative, naming a character Ed Word further emphasizes it). Where the signs *star* and *crusade* are concerned, the referents should not, of course, be visualized as the real star in space or the actual crusade; they are respectively a marking on a book's cover and the words of another book. The referents of signs in this instance are other signs—but not only in this instance, for, as Jacques Derrida and other have shown,[4] that is the way language functions, our everyday habits notwithstanding. As with several works of fiction by the other writers I have examined, it all amounts to a "Singular Book in which the hero will be invited to read the story of his own adventures . . . and of his entire life, henceforth a fictitious one." The statement occurs about one-fourth of the way into the text. Replacing the word *hero* with "reader" will bring it in line with what Sollers has said concerning readers being "signs" and needing to think of themselves as characters in fiction.[5]

There are carryovers from the preceding fiction, such as the number eight (there are eight letters in Ricardou's name, there were eight Crusades, and so forth) and erotic symbols (the triangles previously mentioned appear as chapter headings and Venus, seemingly as a planet, plays a major role). The striptease sequence also shows up again, this time with many variations. One could go on ad infinitum, describing the main body of *La Prise* (or *La Prose*) *de Constantinople* and eventually account for the existence of the entire text, but that would require many more words than this book contains. As with *L'Observatoire de Cannes*, this might actually be the only truthful way of dealing with it. Along with Sollers's *Nombres*, for instance, and in spite of the many differences between the two books, they have this in common: that one cannot "talk" about either one at a cocktail party. One can experience Ricardou's fiction, and one could give a rigorous description of one aspect or another of its textual functioning. But try as one may, Ed Word will never resemble anybody's Uncle Edward.

Les Lieux-dits (1969) is far less "extreme" in appearance, but it is based on similar principles and must likewise be read and experienced rather than talked about. The title is the common French way of referring to a country locality, sometimes a group of farmhouses, sometimes a physical feature, sometimes a place where a historic event occurred. Literally translated, however, it means "the spoken place," "the place that is called"—and the relation between language and reality once more enters the picture. One wonders, for instance, if the locality's name is really derived from the historical event that supposedly took place nearby or if that name was the source of a myth, a narrative spoken (*dit*) by the name of the place (*lieu*). There is, once more, a striptease sequence, in which the garments are taken off in alphabetical order; this is hardly noticeable until a male "character" suggests, "Before unfastening your bra [*soutien-gorge*], the order of the alphabet demands that you first get rid of your panties [*slip*]." The number eight is in evidence again as the book is divided into eight chapters, each chapter into eight sections.

Those chapters bear the names of the eight localities that are "visited," and each name comprises eight letters. When fitted into the spaces of a square grid the result looks like a defective crossword puzzle that can only be read horizontally and diagonally from top left to bottom right (Ricardou often inveighs against "diagonal" or "speed" reading), repeating the name of the fourth locality, Belcroix, thus seeming to stress its "crucial" importance. The text is organized in such fashion that, metaphorically, each of those places could be the scene of the "initial conflict," a "confrontation between the theory of language as creator and the theory of the primacy of the world." The first chapter is entitled "Banniere," and the references to a local painter called Crucis call to mind, on the one hand, the colloquial phrase *la croix et la bannière* ("a hell of a job to tackle"), and the Crusades on the other. A touch of irony is thus introduced. It is reinforced by the presence of two antagonistic species of ants whose struggles and itineraries are metaphors of the Crusades. Everything is reduced to words or, as the penultimate sentence of the book would have it, "All that, once again, today, is a metaphor." It should be stressed, however, that such an assertion is made by the painter Crucis, not by Ricardou. Or might one say that it was made by the text?

Révolutions minuscules (1971) is a set of nine short stories that might better be called vignettes. The first, for instance, entitled "Jeu," that is, "Game" or "Play"—the latter most likely in the sense of freedom for motion, as in a machine, demonstrates the play there is between appearances and their description. It also suggests gratuitousness in the sense that the signs used in such a description have no necessary bonds with their referents, not in the sense that the text might not have a relevant meaning. The demonstration is not didactic; it emerges out of Ricardou's descriptive practice. A first-person narrator opens the text as he approaches a beach, which is the goal of an imaginary journey that started with the contemplation of a painting that he refuses to describe. He mentions only the seductive effect it had on him and the various paths it proposed to his imagination, but he refuses to give any detail—except one: he remembers a beach, low-lying islands beyond a calm expanse of sea, and a dying young woman, stretched out, half naked on the nearby grass, watched over by a brown dog and a faun, and the text reads as though he had actually entered the painting. He then assures the reader that it is not a copy of Piero di Cosimo's *Death of Procris*, nor is it in the same style; nevertheless he detects what he calls a complicity between the two but can give no evidence. Nevertheless, he says his painting is a nearly exact copy of the original, whatever it may be, and he goes on to mention the sea, beach, and sand dunes that are depicted in the background of a standing young woman (earlier she had been lying down) wearing a bikini and facing the viewer. But he cannot decide whether she is really facing him or if her body is slightly slanted; there is also a problem with the lighting, which seems to come from two opposite directions at once; he solves the latter by suggesting that she is in a room with two sources of light, the seascape that is painted on one side of the room reflecting the daylight that enters from the other.

Like Alice going through the looking glass, he may be imagined as stepping through the painting's varnish and setting out on a quest for a beach that would duplicate it. Many descriptions follow, as well as considerations covering the linguistic versus realistic motivations for the search. He wonders, for instance, if a series of adjectives such as *"insaisissable, irrécusable, inépuisable, indéfinissable, indispensable, infranchissable*" is not what draws him ineluctably to the sand (*sable*) of a beach.[6] He does eventually, after acquiring a brown dog, find an appropriate beach and a beautiful woman who is not even wearing a bikini; finally, after what may have been a rape, she rises and cries out for Cosimo. But there is no one around to answer her call, not even the narrator. So "she runs away along the page [a word, identical in French and in English, that now replaces the initial *plage* ("beach")] haphazardly, among the seashells, at the risk of getting lost, in pursuit of some new game or other" (31). Nothing remains of "reality" except the words of Ricardou's vignette. In different fashion, and using a different vocabulary, every one of these texts converges on a recognition of the dominance of words over reality.

Le Théâtre des métamorphoses (1982) attempts to demonstrate the truth of the notion that theory and practice can be combined. The back-cover statement insists that the book is not a mixture (*mélange*—as of sand and clay) of various parts but a composite (*mixte*—like salt). The first section, called "Mixte," is divided into two subsections entitled "La Presse" (The Media) and "Le Texte." The first is essentially theoretical, restating a number of well-known positions involving serious writers and their difficulties with the media and critics today; the second is presented in the form of a conversation among imaginary or seemingly historical figures. To me, however, the latter device seems contrived and does not remove the impression that this is still theory. The second, "Communications," presents the text of a radio drama on the right-hand page and a commentary on the left-hand page—and, almost inevitably, the drama reads like an illustration of the theoretical commentary.

Contemporary practice has given ample evidence that the notion of genre has lost much of its significance or even usefulness. One might reasonably argue, therefore, that theory and fiction might readily fuse—the way fiction, autobiography, poetry, and commentary often have. I think the reason they have not is that theory is not a literary genre but a scientific category.

La Cathédrale de Sens (1988), like Ricardou's second book, bears an ambiguous title: it is also *La Cathédrale de sons*, as the phrase appears on the title page. The first reading, which is printed on the book's spine, would, at first glance, be referential and designate the early-Gothic cathedral located in the city of Sens, of which only the right-hand tower was completed (a fact teasingly mentioned in the text on 32 and 142); "*sens*" might also not be capitalized and one would thus be presented with a further ambiguity, a dialectic between sounds (*sons*) and meaning (*sens*), and the text confirms this possibility: "Meaning? Basically repressed within my soul . . . / Sounds. Greeted in fact without alarm" (128). Another variation, introduced in one of the more erotic short stories, is "cathédrale de seins" (130); finally, the book's back cover displays, in the space where the title might have been repeated, the phrase "*dans tous les sans,*" printed upside down. Since *sans* is a preposition this is grammatically jarring, but it could be read, phonetically, as an admonition not to neglect any level of interpretation. Taken literally, it also invites one to take into consideration all the things the text is lacking (*sans* means "without").

There are seven texts here (I expected eight . . .), six of them quite short (ten to twenty-four pages each). The first and longest, seventy-eight pages in length, is entitled "Lapsus circulaire," and while inscribed in homage to Ricardou's father, a craftsman, it might well have been dedicated to the memory of Raymond Roussel. The title suggests one of the devices mentioned in *Comment j'ai écrit certains de mes livres*, that of the deliberate "slip" of the pen changing the initial sentence of a text into its concluding one. Also played with is the device of seeking different readings of a key sentence based on sound (*Délaissez des lits qu'ornent* becomes *Des laies et des licornes* [83]) or on permutation of letters or syllables (*A la recherche du temps perdu* becomes *A la recherche du père tendu* [63]). While Ricardou is most serious in his purpose, much of this is just plain fun.

Along with the cathedral another work of art, Delacroix's painting *La Mort de Sardanapale*, plays an important generative part; while it may be the painting given to one of the characters in "Le Lapsus circulaire," it happens to be specifically mentioned in "Conte dans le goût d'autrefois" (An Old-fashioned Tale) where one is invited to taste the delicate flavor of "sardines pâles" (phonetically not far removed from "Sardanapale" [89]). The host is next described, lying on a sofa, in terms that fit Delacroix's canvas. One presumes it was chosen because of the painter's name, which can be read as a translation of the Latin *Crucis*, and this, one will recall, is the name of the fictitious painter in *Les Lieux-dits* who also shows up in *La Cathédrale de*—and I should now point out that this is the way the title reads on the book's cover; *La Cathédrale de sons* is what one sees on the title page, but the list of Ricardou's writings, as it appears in the more recent essay, *Une Maladie chronique* (1989), includes *La Cathédrale de Sens*. Another painting by Delacroix, his *Prise de Constantinople par les croisés*, was inserted near the center of Ricardou's second novel.[7]

The *Mort de Sardanapale* was inspired by Byron's *Sardanapalus;* the Romantic poet's lameness may well have produced the narrator's knee injury in "Le Lapsus circulaire," Delacroix's possibly illegitimate birth may be the source of the confusion surrounding the same narrator's origin. The two converge on the Oedipus myth, never mentioned by name but alluded to (33-34) and the dream, or myth, of one's having noble parents suggests the Freudian family romance, a suggestion that is reinforced by the impression I occasionally have that the narrator is a

patient in analysis. The person who may be his real father is introduced as
being a sort of intellectual godfather to him: he is the Count Valyre—an
obvious anagram of Valéry (11), the French poet whom Ricardou
admires and whose name eventually shows up in the text (82). If this, in
conjunction with the dedication, conjures up the possibility that "Lapsus
circulaire" is a form of autobiography, one should keep in mind that a
fictional piece of scription is necessarily biographical, up to a point.
Nevertheless, a correction is offered on pages 13-14: it is more like an
"autopsy" (that is, an *autopsy*choanalysis) or an "autography." As the
narrator puts it, "The whole substance of his person might well be . . .
nothing more than a dream deduced from such and such an intersecting
[*croisé*] arrangement of words" (in French, *croisé* readily suggests *mots
croisés*, a crossword puzzle, another game often alluded to); he then cries
out, "I am in my turn the victim of a cruci-fiction." This, however, is
spoken by a "character," not by Ricardou, and it does not lessen the
presence of bio-graphy in the text.

Simultaneously with *La Cathédrale de* a revised version of *Révolutions
minuscules* was published. The changes to the original text of the nine
vignettes are, for the most part, minor; they represent the usual improve-
ments on or strengthening of the writer's characteristic scription. Two
titles have been changed: "Sur la pierre" has become "Epitaphe"
(etymologically, "on a tomb[stone]") and "Gravitation" is now "Enlève-
ment" ("a kidnapping"). At first glance this latter change seems more
significant; indeed, the changes in this text are much more extensive
than elsewhere and result in giving the writing a stronger focus. After
what may have been a spring shower a little girl resumes her game of
hopscotch in the street as the sun begins to shine again; or perhaps she is
coming home in the subway with her mother, looking forward to playing
in the street; or perhaps she is being imagined by a man in the subway
who reads a newspaper and works on a couple of crossword puzzles
(absent in the original version, illustrated in the revised edition); or
perhaps they are all in the subway, the man trailing her, kidnapping her
when she is alone, playing in the street; or perhaps he loses her and will
have to start all over again. The text is especially disturbing in the second
version because the "descriptions" are more precise and the meaning
more elusive.

There is, furthermore, one important addition in the 1988 edition: a
hundred-page text, by way of preface, in memory of Jean Paulhan, the
critic and essayist who had been editor of *La Nouvelle revue française*. It
is entitled "Révélations minuscules, en guise de préface, à la gloire de
Jean Paulhan" and echoes the title of the *Suite en jaune à la gloire de Van
Gogh* by the painter Albert Ayme, in whom Ricardou had been much
interested for a time. An initial moment of surprise is understandable, for
there is as much difference between the pictures of Ayme and those of

Van Gogh on the one hand as there is between the works of Ricardou and Paulhan on the other. But just as Ayme is fascinated by one particular aspect of Van Gogh's practice, his use of the color yellow, so Ricardou wishes to pay tribute to the intellectual rigor and scrupulous scription of Jean Paulhan.

This preface is part autobiography, part fiction, part essay, and is in my opinion a far more successful attempt at mixing genres than was *La Théâtre des métamorphoses*. One reason for this may be that what I strictly identify as theory is absent from the text; the second may be that the scription, as carefully wrought as it is in Ricardou's other works, has achieved an idiosyncratic combination of ease and old-fashioned punctiliousness that enables the components of the text to flow together. I must say that I am not personally partial to the imperfect subjunctive (*"soit qu'ils s'y adonnassent ou bien le crussent"* [16]), or to pedantic neologisms (the abuse of which must have been called to his attention, for there is a touch of irony in attributing to someone else the coinage of *isophonohomogrammatisme* [36]), or to the inversion of the usual sequence of noun and qualifier (*"l'inédite préface"* [11]). Combined, however, they do mark his text with an unmistakable brand.

The narrative evolves about a game of bowls (a variety of bowling, without pins), known in southern France as *pétanque* (Ricardou was born in Cannes) and played on hard-packed soil instead of on a green. The autobiographical element emerges out of memories of games played in Paris among the Roman ruins of an amphitheater known as Arènes de Lutèce and located off the rue Monge. There were a dozen players involved, including the playwright Jacques Audiberti, Jean Paulhan, Claude Simon (southerners living in Paris), Ricardou himself, and others. Also listed was the well-known critic and scholar Jean-Pierre Richard who actually never joined the group. As he recognizes his lapse of memory and attempts to identify its cause, he remembers that Richard is a *pétanque* enthusiast who regretted never having participated in those games animated by Paulhan's presence and, more importantly, sees the similarity between the critic's name and his own, which might be read as "little Richard"—the suffix *ou* having a diminutive function in Provencal. Also, in a quotation attributed to Richard there is mention of "the homology between two of my most deep-seated inclinations, scription and the game of bowls" (21). The stage is thus set for having theoretical and practical considerations involving *pétanque*, many of which, arising from conversations between Paulhan and Ricardou during games, spill over into the act of writing. This is hardly the first time that games and writing have been associated and the notion is far from frivolous. I have previously mentioned the games of solitaire (Butor), chess (Roussel, Sollers), and now crossword puzzles (of which Perec was a practitioner) —not forgetting the activities of the Oulipo group, which I shall discuss briefly in connection with Perec. Defining man as a playing animal, as Johan Huizinga did in his *Homo Ludens* (1938), is no less revealing than calling man a social or a toolmaking being.

While Ricardou engages in his usual wordgames, and the one he emphasizes most in this mock preface is the symmetry between beginning and end of sentences, paragraphs, or texts (the first word of the preface is *Monumentalement* and the last are *divers vagues demi-mots, nus, mentalement*), the most striking aspect of "Révélations minuscules" is the destruction or metamorphosis of the subject. What starts out as an introduction written for the new edition of *Révolutions minuscules* gradually becomes a dialogue, first purely rhetorical, then more realistic as the reader identifies the other person as a woman (37: "que je m'en fusse alors aperçue") who finally takes over as the writer of the preface— which is signed "Noëlle Riçoeur." The irony is that this is perhaps the most "autobiographical" of Ricardou's texts. The point is, I suppose, that the subject is necessarily split; whenever one writes seriously (which does not exclude playing games and using humor) an "other" is always involved—Marcel Proust's "moi profond."

Games and humor are perhaps more obvious in this "preface" than in previous texts, through which Ricardou has given the impression (which might well have been a mistaken one) of being not only serious but even intransigent. What was interpreted as a terrorist stand (one might recall that Paulhan's famous essay *Les Fleurs de Tarbes* [1941] was subtitled "La Terreur dans les lettres" [Terrorism in Literature], something Paulhan was against), accompanied by his independence, has provoked opposition and even hostility and, in turn, has lessened his influence (which had been considerable in the seventies). Although he may, at times, have been too extreme in his judgments, he has rightly denounced a number of literary fallacies and insisted on rigorous argument based on solid evidence. Literary-minded people are not always insistent on, or even partial to such a position. I believe his role has been essentially positive; it is most noticeable and effective in the conferences he has directed at Cerisy-la-Salle.[8]

NOTES

1   The Centre Culturel International at Cerisy-la-Salle was founded in 1952 by Anne Heurgon-Desjardins (1899-1977), daughter of Paul Desjardins who had organized the famous Décades de Pontigny between 1910 and 1939.

2   See my introduction, above, and my essay, "Twelve Points from Tel Quel," *L'Esprit créateur* 14, no. 4 (Winter 1974): 291-303.

3   See Jean Ricardou, "Naissance d'une fiction," in *Nouveau roman: hier, aujourd'hui* (Paris: 10/18, 1972), 2: 379-92.

4   Jacques Derrida, *De la grammatologie* (Paris: Minuit, 1967), 65 ff.

5 Philippe Sollers, "The Novel and the Experience of Limits," in *Writing and the Experience of Limits*, trans. Philip Barnard (New York: Columbia University Press, 1983), 194.

6 Ricardou, *Révolutions minuscules* (Paris: Gallimard, 1971), 23. Subsequent references to works by Ricardou will appear in the body of the text.

7 For the role of Delacroix's painting in *La Prise de Constantinople*, see Lynn A. Higgins, *Parables of Theory: Jean Ricardou's Metafiction* (Birmingham: Summa Publications, 1984), 101-6.

8 Jean Ricardou directed, among others, the following colloquia at Cerisy-la-Salle: "Nouveau roman: hier, aujourd'hui" in 1971, "Lire Claude Simon" in 1974, "Robbe-Grillet: analyse, théorie" in 1975, and "Problèmes actuels de la lecture" in 1979.

14

Georges Perec

By 1972, Perec was known for having produced four variegated works of fiction, each one seeming like the first book of different writers. *Les Choses* (1965; *Things*) is subtitled "Une histoire des années 60," a narrative that could make one think of Stendhal and his chronicle of the 1830s. If the reference was intentional, however, it could only have been ironical, for the two main characters (there is of course no "hero"), Jérôme and Sylvie, have no real ambition aside from acquiring the material "things" of the title. They are petty bourgeois who aspire to the comforts and pleasures of the upper bourgeoisie, and the narrative that describes their activities comes close to being sociological. Actually, Jérôme and Sylvie are both psychosociologists who go about polling people as to their desires, habits, preferences, and reactions to this or that advertisement. They neither like their job nor dislike it; it pays for the "things" they want and leaves them enough free time to look for them. They are moderately happy, although realizing that their happiness hangs by a thread. They have no real political conscience even though they read the proper newspapers and magazines; they long for the days of the Spanish Civil War or the Resistance when, as they see it, choices were clear and inescapable. Somewhat hypocritically they do not acknowledge the existence of the Algerian war, which actually presents them with a choice. Only at the end do they join in a street demonstration or two—an exercise in frightened futility, and they know it. Their material ambitions, likewise, are not based on practical strategies but on dreams; they imagine themselves winning fantastic sums from the lottery or inheriting them from a forgotten rich uncle. They then decide to flee: they go to Tunisia where Sylvie has been offered a teaching job, and both manage to survive on her salary in mediocre fashion. Not long after they spend a weekend in the beautiful home of a wealthy English couple, they realize that such a home would always be beyond their reach and decide to go back to Paris and live as before. But it is also too late for that; through friends, they find a "responsible" position in Bordeaux. The book ends as they enter the dining car of the train that takes them to a life of relative ease, admiring the table settings "where the thick, escutcheoned plates will seem like the prelude to a sumptuous feast. But the meal they will be served will be utterly insipid" (130). One will have noted the future tense in this quotation: in fact, it dominates the last seven pages, giving them an aura of irrevocable destiny, in contrast with the first six pages that are permeated with the conditional of dreams.

What prevents *Les Choses* from being a mere cautionary tale is the writing itself. The economy of means, the variety of style, the irony not only keep the reader interested, amused, and alert, they also involve him or her in the sense that one realizes that the story is not just about Jérôme and Sylvie but about readers of their age, that is, approaching thirty—as Perec himself was when he wrote it.

This was followed by a narrative with a preposterous title, *Quel petit vélo à guidon chromé au fond de la cour?* (1966; What Small Bike with a Chrome-plated Handlebar Standing in the Courtyard?). It is a short piece of fiction that seems to be about a soldier who suddenly discovers that he might be shipped to North Africa during the Algerian war (obviously an inescapable presence in Perec's early texts). He begs his first sergeant to do something about it, such as running over him with a jeep so he can be hospitalized. The first sergeant, Henri Pollak, who could be called the main character and is the friend of the anonymous narrator, consults with other friends who think up a number of hare-brained schemes to keep the soldier out of the war. The one they try to carry out fails, but in the end no one knows what happened to the soldier. That matters only to the extent that he could be termed a deserter, an act that would be echoed in the lives of several other characters in later fiction. At first sight, however, the plot is of no consequence: what matters is the telling of it. It is told by Perec in what appears to be a transcription of spoken French. One soon realizes, however, that it is a very contrived version of oral French and that Perec enjoys playing with language: he has fun, and so does the reader, who may be forgiven for thinking of Raymond Queneau. The soldier, whose fear of war is the pretext for the whole thing, bears an undecidable name. Queneau, in *Le Dimanche de la vie*, managed to provide about forty different spellings for the name of one of his characters; twelve years after *Quel petit vélo*, in *La Vie mode d'emploi*, twenty different pronunciations are given for one character's name, and there are also a number of possible spellings for that same name ranging from Kleinhof to Cinoc (as he is known in the text). The latter is identical in pronunciation to "*sinoc*" or "*sinoque*," a

colloquialism for "crazy." Such undecidability is related to Cinoc's
Jewishness, since officials "needed little encouragement to seem
somewhat illiterate and rather hard of hearing when it came to giving
identification papers to a Jew."[1] Perec's soldier, who is branded not as a
Jew but as different is given more than sixty different spellings for his, all
beginning with "Kara," going from Karaphon to Karabibine. But what
about the bike with chrome-plated handlebars? What bike?

Un Homme qui dort (1967; *A Man Asleep*) is, like Michel Butor's *La
Modification*, written in the second person—although in the more
familiar "*tu*" form rather than the formal "*vous.*" While it seems, at first,
quite different from the two preceding books, it actually hovers somewhere in between. It is not composed in a variant of spoken French, but
there are sections that benefit from being read aloud. The main character,
who is nameless, is not intent on acquiring "things," quite the contrary—
his dream is to withdraw from the world, detach himself from all earthly
considerations. The result, however, is that even though his path is the
opposite of that of Jérôme and Sylvie his life is eventually bound to be the
same as theirs, and there is nothing either one of them could have done
about it. On the penultimate page of the text whoever speaks gives a
quotation from Sophocles (who is not identified as the source), unless it
be from the epigraph to Robbe-Grillet's *Les Gommes:* "Time who sees all
has found you out against your will."

That kind of subdued echo from another writer can be detected a
number of times. After the initial brief remark, "As soon as you shut your
eyes, the adventure of sleep commences" (a negative echo or perhaps a
contradictory response to the first sentence of Maurice Roche's *Compact*,
published the previous year), there follows a forty-seven-line sentence
that has a Proustian aura about it. Later one thinks of Maurice Blanchot's
title when encountering the phrase "l'attente et l'oubli" (28); a line by
Lamartine appears at the bottom of page 44, Rimbaud is invoked on page
48 through the mention of a "*bateau ivre*" and Harrar; a section begins on
page 79 with the same words that initiate Diderot's *Neveu de Rameau*.
The bells that toll the hours from the church of Saint Roch recall those
that are heard throughout the night from a nearby convent in Butor's
Passage de Milan. There are also reverberations of Baudelaire, Raymond
Queneau, Albert Camus, and Claude Simon. On pages 152-53 Perec has
inserted a brief summary of Melville's "Bartleby the Scrivener" (without
mentioning writer or title) and half a dozen pages before the end he
suggests that no wandering *Rachel* will rescue the anonymous main
character from the *Pequod's* wreck.

In several respects *Une Homme qui dort* marks a turning point in
Perec's work. The assimilation of lines by other writers is developed in
extraordinary fashion in his masterpiece, *La Vie mode d'emploi* (1978),
the title of which reads like a response to this early work's statement,

"You are not surprised to discover that there is something wrong, that, to speak bluntly, you don't know how to live, you never will" (H 24)—and I shall discuss that text presently. References to crossword puzzles (72) emphasize his concern with linguistic play, practicing a particular version of solitaire reveals an interest in complex riddles, both of which are illustrated in subsequent works. All that is related to the Ouvroir de Littérature Potentielle, better known as Oulipo, a "research" group whose conception harks back to the Raymond Queneau colloquium at Cerisy-la-Salle in 1960; its actual birth, signified by the first meeting of the group, took place on November 24 of the same year.[2] The better-known members were Queneau and Marcel Duchamp and the group has included one American, Harry Mathews, since 1973. The cofounder of Oulipo was a mathematician, François Le Lionnais; the combination Queneau–Le Lionnais might possibly account for the mixture of rigor and playfulness (sometimes verging on black humor) that characterizes the activities of the group. Perhaps less obviously comical, Jacques Roubaud, a mathematician, poet, and more recently novelist (whom I mentioned with reference to Jean Pierre Faye and the *Change* collective, and in whose fiction humor does come to the surface) joined the Oulipo in 1966; he has specifically mentioned the troubadours as models (he has written about them and the legends of King Arthur and the Grail) and the sonnet as a privileged form.

Queneau's own *Cent mille milliards de poèmes* (1961), although elaborated earlier, appeared a year after the birth of Oulipo; it is a collection of ten sonnets, each line of which is printed on an individual strip of the page and bound to the spine on its left side. Any first line may thus be followed by any second line, and so forth, and as a result the number of different sonnets that can be read is ten to the fourteenth power; the time required for reading the complete set, devoting eight hours a day and two hundred days a year to the book, would amount to more than one million centuries. So much for combinatory literature, potentiality, and long-term fun. Italo Calvino, who became a member in 1972, said that the Oulipo sailed "under the banner of hoaxing and practical joking."[3]

While members of the Oulipo do not indeed care to become victims of what Sartre called "*l'esprit de sérieux*," there is, nevertheless, a serious background to their activities, and this may be seen through the imposition of constraints. "Writing under constraints" is how Roubaud defines their method. As most everyone realizes, that has been nearly inseparable from the practice of literature but usually not emphasized as such. Called rules or definitions, constraints were part of the accepted canon, like the definition of the sonnet, for instance. When new, more visible constraints are added critics take notice and react—often unfavorably. The French *rhétoriqueurs* of the fifteenth century have not fared well at the hands of traditional literary historians; Gongorism and preciosity have fared even worse. But as Claude-Edmonde Magny noted with reference to Jean Giraudoux's *préciosité* (and I have alluded to this in connection with Maurice Blanchot and Jean Pierre Faye), preciosity is the outcome "of a secret despair facing the irremediable imperfection of the world."[4] It is a protest against evil—even though such a stance might not be fully conscious. The difference with the Oulipo and the reason for the latter's playfulness—at least, I should think, in the mind of Raymond Queneau— is that in the long run, no matter what we do in the world it is of no real consequence, for the world will eventually come to its inevitable end— beyond which there is nothing.

One of the activities related to the Oulipo is known as PALF, that is, "Production Automatique de Littérature Française."[5] The idea is to take a text and replace each word with its dictionary definition; if the result is unsatisfactory, one does the same thing again and again. A variation on this is to replace each noun with the seventh (or any other numeral) noun following it in a given dictionary, or each verb, or both, and so forth. A refusal of the given text, or the world it stands for, is quite clear.

Perec joined the group in 1967 as an associate member. *La Disparition* (1969) would seem to be directly influenced by his interest in the Oulipo; it is a lipogram, which Webster defines as "a writing composed of words not having a certain letter or letters." This book is a fascinating tour de force in that it is written without making use of the vowel *e*, the one most frequently used in French as in English. The narrative is prefaced with a sonnet by Roubaud, from which, in addition to other constraints germane to the sonnet form, the letter *e* is also missing. The writing of *La Disparition* constituted quite a challenge, an exalted form of play, and its surprising aspect is that Perec managed to make it readable. The book relates a series of burlesque, preposterous adventures that are more or less disconnected and in which a number of "characters" disappear (including one named Voyl, who might have been called *"voyelle"* [vowel], if the vowel *e* had not been banned) and also features the device I emphasized in connection with *Un Homme qui dort*—drawing on names, characters, parodic episodes or summaries, and other references to well-known writers (Proust, Kafka, Lowry, Roussel, Wilde, Melville, and so forth), in this instance in order to enhance the knowledgeable reader's amusement. Scholars will no doubt busy themselves unraveling that multitude of threads. A few years later *Les Revenentes* (1972; The Ghosts) marked the return of that vowel and the elimination of others (resulting in the unavoidable misspelling of the title)—something like the return of the repressed, and this indeed would seem to invite a thematic, psychoanalytic interpretation.

The suggestion that beneath the superficial, commonplace occurrences of life, "Another thread had always run, forever present, always kept at a distance" (H 32), as if it were repressed, is also conveyed in a later work, *W ou le souvenir d'enfance* (1975; *W, or The Memory of Childhood*). The thread may be related to Perec's Jewishness, of which he seems not to have been overly conscious at first but which keeps cropping up in various, puzzling fashions beginning with *Un Homme qui dort.* The last fourth of this book is marked by a tone that is bitter, even violent, beginning with the exclamation that begins a section: "Free like a cow, like an oyster, like a rat!" (H 119). The rat, as a metaphor, initiates a nine-page development, after which the notion of "monster" creeps in and fills the following pages with a litany that insults practically all categories of human beings, "your fellow creatures, your brothers" (128). They include "the exiles, the outcasts, those who have been excluded, the bearers of invisible stars" (129). The allusion to the stars Jews were forced to wear during the Nazi occupation of France is obvious, and the statement that begins the next paragraph is disturbing: "You follow them, you watch them closely, you hate them" (129). The Jewishness and cruelty of Georges Perec have posed problems for critics.[6]

A man who sleeps is bound to dream. *La Boutique obscure* (1973; The Dark Store) is a collection of 124 dreams, or rather what can be remembered of them, sometimes in the shape of a narrative, sometimes less than that. The dreams supposedly took place between May 1968 and August 1972, a relatively short period of time, but one during which, assuming Perec had only one dream per night (a very conservative assumption), he should have had well over fifteen hundred dreams. One supposes that less than 10 percent were remembered or worth noting; over 90 percent have disappeared, like the letter *e* in *La Disparition.* While this is intriguing it is mainly a problem for psychoanalysts to worry about. I cannot help noting, however, that a number of the dreams that are recorded (or invented—but is there really a difference?), including the first and the last, involve scenes of concentration camps, police actions, and arrests of civilians by the Nazi SS. Now Georges Perec was born in 1936 and his father, who enlisted in 1939, died at the front in 1940, the day the armistice between France and Nazi Germany was signed, when Georges was four years old. The boy was evacuated to Grenoble (he had relatives nearby) through the offices of the Red Cross in 1942; his mother was arrested in 1943 and never heard of since. My point is that Georges Perec as a child could have had no immediate, conscious experience of concentration camps, arrests, or deportations. These were part of a dark aura that surrounded his childhood; it affected his personality and un-settled his identity in a way that he could not immediately comprehend. If one is tempted, with respect to some of the dreams related in *La Boutique obscure* and other writings as well, to speak of the return of the repressed, one might point out that what was involved was more like a collective repression.

Espèces d'espaces (1974; Species of Spaces) could be viewed as an illustration of such a repression in that it is a description of the spaces in which we live or move about, as they are now, without historical or ideological considerations. There is the space of the page on which one writes, the bed in which one-third of life is spent (the suggestion that it is also the space of dreams, fears, and desires is not enlarged upon), the room, the apartment, and so forth, until one reaches the world and space itself, in the abstract. The constraints are not strong enough, however, and there are two pages on unlivable space that include instructions for planting trees and bushes around the gas chambers at Auschwitz.

With *W ou le souvenir d'enfance* one is confronted with Perec's life as a child during the occupation and with the experience of a totalitarian state, although the latter is presented in allegorical form. The composition of the book is intriguing. It is made up of two seemingly distinct narratives, told in alternating chapters—on the one hand a kind of adventure story leading to the description of the island called W and its people devoted to Olympic-like sports, and an autobiography on the other. In other words, fiction versus reality. The fictional tale, however, begins in the most realistic fashion; the reality of the autobiography is challenged at the outset of the second chapter: "I have no childhood memories" (13). The narrator added at the bottom of the same page that he challenged anyone to question him about his childhood, for History (with a capital H and a large ax—"H" and "ax," as I pointed out in connection with one of Sollers's texts, are pronounced the same in French) had already answered in his stead: war and camps have replaced childhood memories. Indeed, as he tries to tell about his childhood he finds he must ask relatives what happened; he also discovers that his own memories are often contradicted by what other people recall. He remembers injuries that no one else does, and false accusations involving actions of which he says he was innocent. Following one such instance, a bee stung him on the thigh and his leg immediately began to swell alarmingly: "For all my schoolmates, and above all for myself, that sting was *evidence*" of guilt. Somehow, the Jewish experience of persecution followed by self-deprecation seeps through those pages and produces a tension between the actual life of Georges Perec between the ages of four and eight and his reshaping of it in his midthirties. On one level, this tension is mirrored in the contrast between an "autobiographical" text he wrote when he was in his late teens and reproduced here (42-49), followed by many corrections that represent the "truth" as he saw it in 1970-74 when W was being written.

Going back to the fictional narrative, one notices a few telling correspondences. For instance, identical turns of phrase give the (different) month, day, and hour of birth for Georges Perec and Gaspard Winckler (the fictional narrator). Both actual and fictional narrators trace the decision to write and publish W, which is described by one as "a" (not "the") story of his childhood (14), by the other as the account by "the only guardian, the only living memory, the only remnant" (10) of a given world, to an incident that took place in Venice some years before. The latter fictional statement should be tied to what Perec says concerning his scription: "I write: I write because we have lived together, because I was one of them, a shadow among their shadows, a body among their bodies; I write because they have left within me their indelible imprint, the trace of which lies in its scription: their memory is dead to scription; scription is the memory of their death and the affirmation of my life" (59). The fictional Gaspard Winckler explains that he deserted from the army, was taken in charge by an organization of conscientious objectors who provided him with a new identity (his present one) and a passport. The passport was a real one, and the original Gaspard was a deaf-mute child who subsequently disappeared after (or perhaps before) a shipwreck in the vicinity of the Tierra del Fuego islands. The false Gaspard Winckler is urged to go and find out what happened to the real one. The parallel with the autobiography is obvious: the six-year-old Perec "deserted" occupied Paris and his Jewishness (of which he was hardly aware), was taken in charge by the International Red Cross and sent to the nonoccupied Grenoble area, where he was given a new identity as a pupil in a Catholic school. When he wrote *W ou le souvenir d'enfance* he tried to find out who the "real" Georges Perec was.

The book is divided into two parts. While the "autobiographical" narrative continues more or less chronologically and still somewhat spasmodically, the "fictional" narrative breaks off without saying anything about the narrator's decision, how he reached the southern tip of South America and was able to land on a nearly inaccessible island. It begins the second part in a make-believe manner that presages its allegorical nature: "There would be, over there, at the other end of the world, an island. It is called W" (89). It was settled in the nineteenth century by a man named Wilson, about whose identity contradictory stories are told (identity is a leitmotiv in *W*). At first the narrative continues by providing a favorable, although seemingly detached description of life on W(ilson) island. It is a country devoted to sport and the glorification of the body. Gradually, though, one is reminded of the Nazi's attitude toward physical prowess and their contempt for the human individual, and in the end, after describing how children enjoy a pampered life before being suddenly thrust into the brutal atmosphere of adult life, the tone changes: "Very few attempt suicide, very few become truly insane. Some never stop howling, but most remain silent, relentlessly so" (190). This last sentence could remind one of Bartleby's stance and justify enlarging the scope of the satire beyond the obvious condemnation of fascist totalitarian regimes (Pinochet is mentioned on the book's last page) to a commentary on life in our Western society as well as its intense competitive spirit.

If one is to believe Perec's "autobiographical" narrative, his fictional counterpart, Gaspard Winckler, had already been the main character of his first unpublished novel, "Le Condottiere"; Winckler then permeated the text of the monumental *La Vie mode d'emploi* (1978; *Life: A User's Manual*), in which his wife Marguerite dies in 1943, the year Perec's mother disappeared, bound for Auschwitz. It is intriguing to think of Winckler as a sort of mirror image of Perec as it is to muse on the initial letter of his name, which is the same as that of the Tierra del Fuego island and has been, in the book and in the title, reduced to that initial. Perec, perhaps as a consequence of his activities in the Oulipo, was fascinated by the material qualities of the letters of the alphabet. In *W ou le souvenir d'enfance* he commented on the only French substantive to be represented by a single letter, *x* (105), referring to a sawbuck table, on the importance of the symbol in mathematics, where it stands for the unknown, on the geometric transformations that change an *x* into a swastika as well as into the Star of David. There is also the one that, by rotating the lower half of the *x*, transforms it into a *w*. It all entailed a phantasmatic geometry of which "the basic figure was the double *v*, whose multiple entanglements delineate the major symbols of my childhood history." (One might add that *w* is not a French letter, just as Perec's parents were originally Polish.) The final chapter of *La Vie mode d'emploi* shows the dead Bartlebooth seated before an almost completed jigsaw puzzle, and "the black hole for the piece that still needs to be fitted in is in the nearly perfect shape of an *x*. But the piece that the dead man holds between his fingers has the shape, long foreseeable in its very irony, of a *w*" (600).

There are basically two ways of approaching *La Vie mode d'emploi*, according to one's bent. If one is a scholar and/or a devotee of puzzles of various kinds, mathematical, linguistic, or literary, the text will be analyzed in order to discover the rules and constraints that presided over its composition. If one is an amateur, in the best sense of the term, one will seek the pleasure of the text, whether it be ethical or aesthetic, and describe the emotions that are experienced. Either approach is valid, and although I favor the latter I believe some information about the former will enhance one's pleasure. In this instance there has been (and still is) such critical emphasis on the composition of the work that I need only sum up what scholars have discovered without repeating the details.[7]

After a preamble (to be repeated word for word at the outset of chapter 44), in which the nature and practice of the more complex, sophisticated jigsaw puzzles are examined, the first chapter then takes the reader to a Paris apartment building where a woman from a real-estate agency is climbing the stairs, looking carefully at everything, on her way to a small apartment that has just been put on the market. Upon completing the second or third chapter, the reader realizes that the lives of tenants and former tenants of the building will be accounted for—but in what order? Perec decided to rely on the solution to a chess problem: what path must the knight follow in order to touch every square of the board; he then adapted that solution to his imaginary building's architecture. Next came the major constraint. Essentially, it required that in making up the stories that would involve his tenants Perec, by means of mathematical permutations (Queneau had a passion for mathematics, which was also the basis for the architecture of such works as Ollier's *La Mise en scène* and Butor's *Degrés*), arrive at a list of forty-two objects (some of which might be quotations) or themes that must be included in each chapter. As he himself explained: "Thus, in chapter 23, I had to use a quotation from Jules Verne and one from Joyce. The one, or rather the several quotations from Verne pertained to the library (134), which is Captain Nemo's, and the list of tools that reproduces that of the magic chest in *The Mysterious Island*. The house Leopold Bloom dreams about at the end of *Ulysses* has become the dollhouse on page 135."[8] One will recall that quoting the texts of other writers is a practice that began with *Un Homme qui dort*. The question that logically follows, for which it might not be possible to provide an answer, is, why those particular writers, why those specific themes, why those precise objects?

On page 695 of *La Vie mode d'emploi* there is a postscript that lists thirty writers (including Perec himself) whose texts, "sometimes slightly modified," have been inserted into his own. Among the half-dozen projects he enumerated in 1976 and which his premature death in 1982 prevented from completing, there is that of "Le Roman du XIXe siecle": starting from a standard anthology of nineteenth-century French literature he planned "to unify its components in order to end up with a narrative whose chapters would contain fragments out of *Adolphe, Attala*, and so forth, down to Zola."[9] Michel Butor had already practiced this form of unemphasized quotations in *Portrait de l'artiste en jeune singe* (1967) and *Illustrations II* (1969) and asserted in the issue of *L'Arc* featuring his work (also in 1969) "A [literary] work is *always* a collective work." He has not, however, generalized the process of incorporating other texts into his own to the extent that Perec has. *La Vie mode d'emploi* includes Butor among those he has borrowed from, and quotations from seven books have been identified, thus suggesting a certain affinity in the two writers' stance as to the act of scription. Also, the reader who begins the book is almost bound to notice the similarity, superficial as it may be, with Butor's *Passage de Milan*.

As was the case with Raymond Queneau's *Le Chiendent* (1933), it is quite possible that few if any critics would have noticed such architectural features if the writer himself had not called attention to them. Sources are the just-mentioned postscript to *La Vie mode d'emploi*, a number of interviews, and contributions to literary reviews. Once readers have become acquainted with those compositional secrets, they can go back to the text and discover (or imagine) a number of clues they had overlooked. It thus seems possible that descriptions in the present tense might be those of a painting—the one that Serge Valène, a painter who was a tenant in the building, had contemplated doing but never did. Another painter, Hutting, also a tenant, had planned a series of twenty-four paintings, to be executed at the rate of one per month in a predetermined order. They were to be portraits, whose subjects, while playing a determining part, were merely one of their basic elements; the first and last names of the subjects together with their profession were to be the starting point of each picture: "Subjected to various linguistic and numerical processings, the buyer's identity and profession would successively determine the painting's size, the number of figures, the predominant colors, the 'semantic field' . . . the central theme of the anecdote, the secondary details (historical and geographic allusions, clothing, accessories, and so forth), and finally the price" (356). Valène's project, detailed in chapter 51, which was to include 179 topics, all of which can be identified as being part of *La Vie mode d'emploi*, did not materialize; Perec is the one who completed it in words, following a method similar to Hutting's.

Putting aside such complex matters dealing with the composition of the book, one can now resume one's reading of the first chapter and learn that the vacant apartment was that of Gaspard Winckler who died two years earlier (the "chronological indications" at the end of the volume disclose that it was in 1973). Perhaps one has noticed that the chapter begins in a very tentative manner, with verbs in the conditional, like the beginning of *Les Choses*, "Yes, it could begin this way, right here, just like that, in a somewhat slow and ponderous fashion, in this neutral space that belongs to everyone and to no one," before firming up on the second page with verbs in the future tense, like the end of *Les Choses:* "Yes, it shall begin here: between the fourth and the fifth floor, 11 rue Simon-Crubellier." The street, an imaginary one, can nevertheless be precisely located on a map of Paris, for it is surrounded by actual streets, and its "history" is given on pages 570-71. It is impregnated by the surrounding reality and thus quite emblematic of Perec's books—and not only his: the fictitious lycée of Butor's *Degrés* is similarly implanted in the reality of Paris. While other tenants' names are mentioned, this first chapter focuses on Winckler's name and apartment, for it is his death that has belatedly caused the real-estate agent's visit, and it ends with a tantalizing statement: "Gaspard Winckler is dead, but the slow vengeance that he has so patiently, so meticulously contrived has not yet been fully sated" (22). A few minutes and 578 pages later, Percival Bartlebooth, a wealthy Englishman who bought an apartment in the building in 1929, dies as he is about to complete a jigsaw puzzle; he dies, unable to figure out how to fit a *w* into the unknown—the space shaped like an *x*.

The generic subtitle of *La Vie mode d'emploi* is *"romans,"* in the plural. There are indeed many independent narratives in the book; they emerge in associative fashion, much the way secondary narratives do in some of Raymond Roussel's works. What links them is that their protagonists have at one time or other lived in the apartment building or are related to someone who does or has. Nevertheless, it is the story of Bartlebooth and that of the Bartlebooth-Winckler relationship that helps in bringing it all together. Bartlebooth's name is a compound of Melville's Bartleby, who first showed up in *Un Homme qui dort*, and Valery Larbaud's millionaire, A. O. Barnabooth. Bartlebooth's wealth was matched only by the indifference to what wealth generally allows one to do. He "decided one day that his entire life would be organized around a single project, the arbitrary necessity of which would have no other end but itself" (157). He planned to spend ten years learning how to do watercolors (he knew it would take that long because he had no aptitude) and twenty years to travel around the earth painting five hundred watercolors of seaports; each one was to be sent back to Paris where Winckler would transform them into jigsaw puzzles. Back in the rue Simon-Crubellier, Bartlebooth would finally spend twenty years putting the puzzles together again; permanently glued, they would be sent to the place where they had been painted, the watercolor dissolved, and the paper, in its original whiteness, returned to Paris. Another metaphorical circle in contemporary French fiction has once more been completed.

Fifty years of his life would thus be fully occupied by an undertaking as complex and difficult as it was futile. In the end, all trace of his activity would have been eradicated. In contrast to the many who aspire to leave a record, a monument testifying to their presence on earth, and fail, Bartlebooth wished that there be nothing left—and he, too, failed. The agent of his undoing was Gaspard Winckler, for solving a jigsaw puzzle is not a solitary activity: "Every gesture made by the puzzle solver, the puzzle maker had made before; every piece he takes and picks up again, examines, fondles, every combination he tries and tries again, every trial and error, every intuition, every hope, every discouragement, have been determined, calculated, studied by the other" (18, 251).

What the book does not tell the reader, however, is what prompted Winckler to seek revenge, what Bartlebooth had done to arouse such deep, slow-burning passion. The question's importance is attested by the recurrence of the theme throughout *La Vie mode d'emploi*. It crops up in the story of Elizabeth de Beaumont, who lived with her mother on rue Simon-Crubellier for only one year, as a teenager, and ran away; she then turned up in England working as an au pair and taking care of the five-year-old son of a Swedish diplomat; she accidentally, carelessly, or intentionally let the boy drown in the bathtub and fled. The mother, who arrived shortly afterward, committed suicide. The father, who only returned home two days later, vowed to find Elizabeth: he "swore to devote [his] life, wealth, and wit" (188) to avenging his wife and son. After six years of a relentless search, three-quarters of his wealth having been spent, and on the verge of insanity, he finds out where she is and kills her and her husband. Elizabeth, for her part, had soon realized that he was pursuing her and did her best to elude him; in the end, however, she gave up. She wrote him to say that she would stay in one place, that it was hopeless trying to escape, because (and this is a significant detail) "luck and money have been, and will always be, on your side" (197). She did not mention obstinacy, although that is a theme often present in the narratives of La Vie mode d'emploi, not necessarily connected with revenge, not necessarily leading to success. Bartlebooth's life might be cited as an example of obstinacy leading nowhere.

A second story of an avenging quest is that involving Oswald Zeitgeber, who murdered the forty-nine inhabitants of an African village in order to gain access to a graveyard of elephants whose ivory made him fabulously rich. Another man had "incessantly tracked him down for twenty years, unremittingly searching for the evidence of his guilt: now he had found it" (288). It would be hard to forget Hélène Gratiolet, whose father owned the apartment building. After he died in 1917 she sold her share of the inheritance, got married, and emigrated to the United States where her husband was killed by three thugs. She found out who they were, where they were, followed them until she could methodically kill them one by one. It all started, in a way, because she had felt slighted in her father's will.

Bartlebooth was a millionaire, of course, but money as a motive for revenge is, in Winckler's case, never mentioned. At this point we should probably keep in mind what Perec himself told one of his interviewers: "It is once again necessary to start from the metaphor of the jigsaw puzzle or, if one prefers, that of an unfinished book, of an unfinished 'oeuvre' within a literature that will never be completed."[10] Each book is like the individual pieces of the puzzle, which have no meaning in themselves but must be related to the whole. The various narratives of La Vie mode d'emploi do not yield their full meaning when considered individually; each "roman" relates to the entire set of "romans." Likewise, that book considered alone does not yield its full meaning, for it must be considered in the context of all the other books written by Perec.

The characters, or rather the words that bring forth characters in the reader's mind, are one of the more obvious links. Perec, in the novel he was working on at the time of his death, 53 Jours (posthumously published, in fragmentary fashion, in 1989), suggested that the various transformations that are effected between one novel and the next "do not have the same effect on the progress of the story as, for instance, having a major character circulate from one book to another" (108-9).

One recalls that Gaspard Winckler is the distorted mirror image of Perec himself in *W ou le souvenir d'enfance*, that he is connected with the unknown, the lack of identity, the *x*. He is the one who bears witness to the atrocities that characterize life on W(ilson) island. There is nothing in the text of *La Vie mode d'emploi* that might allow one to state that Gaspard is Jewish or that he is not; he has no relatives that anyone knew about, and after his death it takes a lawyer several months to dig up a distant cousin; he is connected with the darker side of life, as evidenced by his making what was known as "the Devil's rings" and "Witches' mirrors" (50, 51). Bartlebooth, on the other hand, is related to Melville's Bartleby, hence to Perec's *Un Homme qui dort*, the man who sleeps while the holocaust takes place. Bartlebooth himself, protected, like Barnabooth, by his wealth, seems completely unaffected by the Second World War during which he continues to travel, paint his watercolors, and send them to Winckler (sometimes through the good offices of the Swedish diplomatic services). The plight of the Jews is illustrated in one of the *romans*, the one telling the story of Appenzzell, the anthropologist who left for Sumatra in 1932 in order to study an isolated tribe by becoming a part of it. He soon discovered that they would not accept him. After that traumatic experience of rejection, he found he could not return home in Austria because he was a Jew and the Anschluss had been accomplished. He disappeared, and his mother who refused to wear the star identifying Jews during the German occupation managed to escape to the unoccupied zone, only to be killed in 1944 in the Vercors.

As I see it, Jewishness in Perec's work seems to function as a catalytic agent bringing together and exacerbating a sense of otherness, of injustice, prompting a desire for revenge. At first, the otherness could not be rationally accounted for. As he noted in *W ou le souvenir d'enfance*, "How could it have happened that . . . during Christmas night, I was the only child left in a school that was practically filled, not with sick children, as originally intended, but with refugee children" (162). He did not realize it at the time, but the reason was that he was Jewish and had no immediate family. On the whole, in the light of some of the stories told in *Le Vie mode d'emploi* and the one subsequently related in *Un Cabinet d'amateur* (1979; An Art Lover's Collection), it would seem that it is injustice that matters, whether suffered by a Jew or a non-Jew.

That 1979 fiction is about a German immigrant to the United States who made a fortune in the brewery business in the latter part of the nineteenth century and decided he would rival or better the art collections of people like Duveen in England or Mellon in America. He soon discovered, however, that the paintings he had begun to collect were either worthless or fakes. With the help of his nephew who had studied art in Boston and a couple of experts he then put together a complex machinery to provide authentication for the initial items in his collection as well as for all the subsequent fakes that he purchased or manufactured afterwards. His revenge was posthumous, as his paintings were auctioned off after his death and very profitably sold to wealthy individuals, foundations, and museums; later, the nephew wrote a letter to all buyers explaining what had happened. A double irony is in evidence here. First, the title of the book refers to a painting representing the brewer, Hermann Raffke, in the midst of his collection, a painting in which all the "original" works were imitated; it turns out that this is the only original painting of the lot—now unavailable as it was placed in a sealed vault facing Raffke's mummified body. Second, Raffke was full of "patriotic" feelings for his old country and an admirer of the emperor William II; providentially, he died before the First World War was begun and in all likelihood he was not Jewish. The final lines of *Un Cabinet d'amateur* point out that, like the paintings of Raffke's collection, "most of the details of this fictional narrative are false, and it was conceived for the sole pleasure, and the sole thrill, of pretending" (90). Such is sublimated revenge.

A fondness for puzzles, including crossword puzzles (of which he contributed quite a few to periodicals), mathematics, playing with language merged with the theme of revenge in *La Vie mode d'emploi* and were perhaps intended to be fused together in *53 Jours*. As this work is unfinished, there is no way of knowing in what shape Perec would eventually have published it had he lived long enough to do so. The themes can be identified, and all those I just mentioned are present. The architecture would appear to be less associational, more integrated, drawing the reader into the narrative's fabric. Indeed, while the epigraph to *La Vie mode d'emploi*, taken from Jules Verne's *Michel Strogoff*, "Keep your eyes open, keep them fully open," suggests the position of a spectator, the reader of *53 Jours* (supposedly the time it took Stendhal to write *La Chartreuse de Parme*) is taken in hand by a narrator who, through an intermediary, the local consul (this takes place in a former French African colony), has been given a manuscript drafted by a mystery-novel writer named Serval who claimed his life was in danger and if anything happened to him the explanation could be found in the manuscript. Serval has disappeared, the manuscript is the unfinished text of a mystery entitled "The Crypt"; we read it, only to find that references to other mystery novels are embedded in it, making the problem more difficult to solve.

By the end of the first part, we understand that Serval was implicating the consul in a scandal and, to protect himself, the consul kills Serval and arranges things so that the narrator will seem guilty of the murder. At the outset of the second part we learn that what we have just read is an unfinished manuscript entitled "53 Jours," found in Grenoble (Stendhal country, in addition to being Perec's temporary country as a child) in the abandoned car of a man called Serval, a businessman and former Resistance hero. This manuscript is supposed to contain clues that will solve the mystery of Serval's disappearance. Thanks to Stendhal, Balzac, and others, the reader may decide that the man who disappeared was not Serval but an impostor who took his place after he was killed a few weeks before the liberation of Grenoble. The text becomes a sort of avenging machine that sets in motion a number of complex, dizzying devices that enable one to arrive at the truth. *La Vie mode d'emploi* played on the reader's emotions as well as his mathematical, puzzle-solving imagination; *Un Cabinet d'amateur* emphasized the pleasure of putting together a complex fiction. In spite of echoes from the French colonial wars of this century and of the deadly underground struggles during the occupation, what evidence there is points to a novel more in the spirit of *Un Cabinet d'amateur*. As Robert Pinget might have said, Perec, in polishing and rewriting *53 Jours* (perhaps under another title), would have done his best to produce an object of art, one that pleased him emotionally and thrilled him intellectually. It is a pity he was not given the chance.

NOTES

1 *La Vie mode d'emploi* (Paris: Hachette, 1978), 361. Further references to Perec's work will be given in the body of the text with the following abbreviations: *Un Homme qui dort*, H; *La Vie mode d'emploi*, V.

2 See Paul Fournel, *Clefs pour la littérature potentielle* (Paris: Denoël, 1972); the collective works *Oulipo: la littérature potentielle* (Paris: Gallimard, 1973) and *Oulipo: Atlas de littérature potentielle* (Paris: Gallimard, 1981); Jacques Bens, *Oulipo 1960-1963* (Paris: Bourgois, 1980); and in English, Warren F. Motte, Jr., trans. and ed., *Oulipo: A Primer of Potential Literature* (Lincoln: University of Nebraska Press, 1986).

3 Italo Calvino, "Cybernetics and Ghosts," in *The Literary Machine*, trans. Patrick Creagh (London: Secker & Warburg, 1987), 11.

4 Claude-Edmonde Magny, *Précieux Giraudoux* (Paris: Seuil, 1945), 42.

5 See Marcel Benabou and Georges Perec, "Le P.A.L.F.," *Change*, no. 14 (February 1973): 118-30.

6 See Marcel Benabou, "Perec et la judéité," and Claude Burgelin, "Perec et la cruauté," in *Cahiers Georges Perec, I* (Paris: P.O.L., 1985), 15-30 and 31-52. The tone that characterizes the end of *Un Homme qui dort* also dominates Patrick Modiano's *La Place de l'étoile* (see my conclusion).

7 For further information on such matters see *Texte en Main*, no. 2 (Summer 1984) and no. 6 (Winter 1986), *L'Arc*, no. 76 (1979), *Cahiers Georges Perec I* (1985), and Warren F. Motte, Jr., *The Poetics of Experiment: A Study of the Works of Georges Perec* (Lexington: French Forum, 1984).

8 Perec, "Quatre Figures pour *La Vie mode d'emploi*," in *L'Arc*, no. 76 (1979): 52.

9 *Cahiers Georges Perec I*, next to last unnumbered page.

10 Georges Perec/Jean-Marie Le Sidaner, "Entretien," in *L'Arc*, no. 76 (1979): 3.

Conclusion

The Next Generation

Accounting for what is taking place in any contemporary field is extremely difficult; in one as elusive as the art of writing it may well be impossible. When I wrote *French Fiction Today* I was fortunate in that the future had been foretold. Not quite fifteen years earlier, the French periodical *Esprit* (no. 7-8, July-August 1958) and Jérôme Lindon, who directed Les Editions de Minuit, had heralded and publicized the advent of a new form of writing fiction. Most but not all the writers featured in *Esprit* were published by Lindon (Gallimard and Le Seuil brought out the others) and Les Editions de Minuit's catalog listed a number of writers now forgotten; nevertheless, the conjuncture was sufficient to convince a number of critics and ordinary readers that a fruitful crisis was at hand. We now know that Lindon and Jean-Marie Domenach, the editor of *Esprit*, were right.

Nothing similar has happened since. An issue of the *Change* collective (no. 34-35, March 1978) attempted to promote what they called a "new narrative" and its practitioners. Jean Pierre Faye urged his readers to hasten the demise of the novel, which he said was now a useless genre, and replace it with a new form of narrative that would no longer be mimetic but transformational and involved in the historical process. Whatever the merits of the theory I see no evidence that the collective was able to convince a sizable segment of the reading public or of the critical establishment. Perhaps that issue of *Change* was too heavily theoretical, perhaps they were seen as promoting their own people; perhaps there were other reasons having to do with the politics of the intellectual and literary set in Paris. At any rate, the works of fiction were generally reviewed (and often quite favorably) as individual productions, not as components of a new, homogeneous venture. More recently, several reviews have attempted to assess the literary state of affairs.

Philippe Sollers's *L'Infini* (no. 19, Summer 1987, and no. 26, Summer 1989), *Yale French Studies* (Special Issue, 1988), the *Review of Contemporary Fiction* (Spring 1989), and Maurice Nadeau's *La Quinzaine litteraire* (no. 532, 16-31 May 1989) have provided us with a multitude of names and a few evaluations. What I find striking in looking at the list of writers is their discrepancies; there are some who appear in two or three of those issues but not a single writer appears in all five.

The writers I am attempting to identify are those whose practice seems most significant and who began publishing in the late sixties or seventies and who were thus in a position to start building on what they had learned from their elders or to react against them—as often happens between one generation and the next. This new generation of French writers is a remarkably gifted one where the quality of their prose is concerned. It comprises many fine craftspeople who handle language with skill and know what they are doing. But I am also looking for texts that might provide one with a new experience in narrative prose and/or an innovative, original practice, in addition to providing new insights into the process of scription. This is where I feel that, so far, no one writer measures up to the leaders of the previous generation. When dealing with younger writers, however, it is not always possible to determine, at a given point of their development, whether they are drifting away from the promises of their first books and should be written off; or it may be that those initial publications were not right for them and they are now battling in a different direction toward a major accomplishment. Could the readers of Claude Simon's first four works of fiction realize that he was struggling in the direction of *Les Géorgiques* and *L'Acacia?*

What may well be a major characteristic of writing fiction in France at present is heterogeneity. Writers appear to be moving in all possible directions. Name a topic, a theme, a pattern, an approach—I am sure one could point to a text that corresponds to it. As always, of course, there are hacks who pander to what they think are the tastes of the public; a number of them succeed in selling their wares, but they are not the people I am interested in. In spite of the apparent confusion, however, I believe one can isolate two groups of texts located at opposite sides of the contemporary set of writings; curiously enough, both could come under the heading of a return of the repressed. What makes them different is the nature of the repressed elements. On the one hand, there is the experience of the Nazi Occupation and, more generally speaking, life in a totalitarian police state; on the other there is awareness of one's body and writing about it in a nonpornographic way.

Historians and essayists, of course, have not failed to write about the horrors of the Second World War, but following Céline, Sartre, Beauvoir, and Camus, among major examples (and probably in reaction against them), the leading French postwar writers had initially appeared to repress memories of the Occupation. (Claude Simon is exceptional in that respect, for history has played a special role in his fiction.) Some have more recently allowed events of the forties to come to the surface of their narratives, as we have seen in the instances of Duras, Robbe-Grillet, and Ollier, for example. All three, however, tell or fantasize about events they have witnessed. What is striking about the new generation is that they are too young, in most cases, to have had firsthand experience of the period. Even Georges Perec, who lived through it, was young enough to have been sheltered from the worst part of the physical experience.

Patrick Modiano was born in 1945, the year the German Nazis capitulated. His first book, *La Place de l'étoile*, came out in 1968, the year of the student uprisings—when French student demonstrators marched through Paris chanting, "We are all German Jews!"—and he has since published nearly a score of other narratives. What lured me into his work was the title and epigraph of the first. The title, to anyone familiar with Paris, could mean either "the Square (or Circle) of the Etoile" (as in Union Square or Columbus Circle)—in other words a well-known site in Paris (until it more recently became Place Charles De Gaulle)—or, in a more literal fashion, "the place of the star." The epigraph tells the story of a German officer who, during the Occupation, asks a Frenchman on a Paris street, "Where is the Place de l'étoile?" The Frenchman responds by raising his hand and pointing to the left-hand side of his chest (where the yellow star identifying him as a Jew should have been pinned). It is a most disturbing, violent book, throughout which the narrator, Raphaël Schlemilovitch (and one might ponder the semiotic implications of such a name in a book intended for mostly gentile readers), experiences the anti-Semitism of our century as he encounters mock representations of many famous figures beginning with Léon Rabatête (Lucien Rebattet, with a dash of Léon Daudet) and Dr. Bardamu (Céline) on the first page to Jean-Paul Schweitzer de la Sarthe (Sartre), whom Freud, in whose hospital Raphaël ends up, urges him to read so that he will understand that he is not a Jew but just a man among others. And he explains, "We now live in a peaceful world. Himmler is dead, how come you remember all that, you were not born" (150).

As I suggested in Perec's case, we may be witnessing the return of a collective unconscious as what had been rationally understood and accounted for finally reaches down in its fullness to the core of one's being. As Modiano, the first-person narrator of *Livret de famille* (1977; The Family Record Book), pointed out, "I was only twenty, but my memory encompassed the time preceding my birth. I was convinced I had lived in Paris during the Occupation since I remembered figures of that period as well as infinitesimal, disturbing details that are not mentioned in any history book" (96). Later on in his narrative he refers to the Occupation as "the several years that mean so much to me even though they preceded my birth" (166). Walking through the Bois de Boulogne, he comes upon the stables of the riding academy in which his father hid from the Germans and wonders why, thirty-three years later, he was still able to "smell the pernicious stench of the Occupation—that compost out of which I arose" (169). Over the years the Jewish element has become less dominant in his books and the preoccupation with the past more individual. Perhaps his writing had effected something akin to a talking cure. As Primo Levi has stated, "After Auschwitz, I had an absolute need to write, not only as a moral duty but as a psychological need."[1] Levi, of course, had had firsthand experience of Nazi torture; Modiano had not. At any rate, in *Vestiaire de l'enfance* (1989; The Childhood Coatroom), the narrator has fled Paris and changed his name after being involved in an accident reminiscent of the Chappaquiddick case—a traumatic event that impels him to write about something different and yet profoundly related. In the fiction he is writing the script of a radio serial about the *Adventures of Louis XVII* and he says he is obsessed with "the theme of the survival of people who have passed away, the hope of finding again those one has lost some time in the past" (10).

Linked to the Jewish experience during the Occupation of France, there is the more generalized background of totalitarianism, which may be removed in both space and time. This was made manifest by the publication of Danièle Sallenave's *Les Portes de Gubbio* in 1980. The title is explained two-thirds of the way into the book: Gubbio is a small Italian town north of Perugia and Assisi that harbors a street where medieval houses still stand; they feature two doors, a normal-sized one through which the living come and go, and a small, narrow one for the removal of the dead. The narrator adds, "My memory is like the houses in Gubbio, but it sometimes confuses the two doors" (229). Born in 1940 and now on the faculty of a French university, she, like Perec and Modiano, has had no direct exposure to the German atrocities of the Occupation; while she has visited Czechoslovakia and Poland, she has not experienced postwar life in Eastern Europe as a native might. The narrative of *Les Portes de Gubbio* is set there in the form of a diary written between October 1966 and June 1967, thus during the uneasy period that preceded the abortive springtime reforms in Prague in 1968.

Actually there is a primary narrator who says he has been given a document to translate. This is the diary, written by another man called S., a composer and musicologist who finds the oppressive regime too much to bear and asks for a leave, presumably to devote more time to composing music. Instead he engages in research on the life of another composer, Egon Kaerner, who died in 1937 in a psychiatric institution, the victim of a different totalitarian regime. Kaerner is highly regarded and performed throughout the world but his music is still banned in his own country. Acting as a kind of intercessor between S. and the object of his research, as well as between Sallenave and her reader, there is also an archaeologist, F., who is dying and has been cut off from his source material. S. writes: "My past, my life, my body, our friends, my father and mother, F.'s life, that of Kaerner: like an architecture of various styles"—and he would like to comprehend it all. What further complicates matters is that "ancient columns are caught, as in Rome, in the arcades of recent walls" (243). The process of discovering the facts about Kaerner is as intricate as uncovering the reality of Perec's or Modiano's childhood and identity. Again from S.'s diary: "I am henceforth like an architect who would have been commissioned to restore a palace and discovered behind the walls a complex of rooms, secret stairways, hallways that the owners never suspected existed" (ibid.). Nevertheless the distancing is greater and is perhaps symbolized by the architectural metaphors and by the fact that all the major texts involved, supposedly written by men about a male composer, were actually composed by a woman. The tone is also more philosophical when we as readers are led to wonder what we learn, or how much we learn, when we read or listen to a narrative or a musical work. Or how much do we learn when we write?

Death and oblivion dominate this book as much as they do Sallenave's first novel, *Paysage de ruines avec personnages* (1975; Landscape of Ruins with Figures), in which there is also a link with the experimental writing of the sixties. In others there is more emphasis on the meaning of life in the face of death, especially in one of the more recent ones, *Adieu* (1988). The permanence of art as opposed to individual death is asserted but not at all in the confident, grandiloquent manner I tend to associate with André Malraux. The final lines of S.'s diary in *Les Portes de Gubbio* concern Egon Kaerner: "Yes, he was immortal; but what he had been granted now, in its abominable shape, was the happiness of stones, a sort of frightful eternity, on which frost had no purchase" (308).

Sallenave has said that she needed to remove herself from the company of others and be alone so that, paradoxically, the self would disappear. We have seen something similar in Nathalie Sarraute's *Entre la vie et la mort* even though the immediate concern was quite different. Indeed, Sallenave is someone for whom, as she herself put it, the outside world exists. In that respect she is closer to Claude Simon than to her other predecessors—even though the outside world, in one shape or another, is necessarily present in all of them. Her approach is different, for she is concerned with problems of the narrative and how to have it correspond with an objective reality, which may well be impossible. In her attempt to do so, the self is put aside.

For Muriel Cerf on the other hand, the self is crucial in dealing with the outside world, which doubtlessly exists, but only as a facade to be rejected or circumvented. Her *Les Rois et les voleurs* (1975; Kings and Thieves, translated as *Street Girl*) is a powerful text stuffed with a violent although not repulsive vocabulary that accounts for a teenager's discovery of life enjoyed to the fullest accompanied by a rejection of her parents, teachers, and other components of conventional society. One is perhaps not surprised to learn that she was eighteen in 1968. A more recent work, *Doux oiseaux de Galilée* (1988; Gentle Birds of Galilee), her twelfth, is less aggressive; its style, especially toward the end, occasionally matches the romantic lyricism of the title, although it can, at times, be rather crude. Like the first-person narrator of *Les Rois et les voleurs,* this anonymous third-person storyteller attempts to make up an outside world distinct from commonly accepted reality; its characters are like "the gentle birds of Galilee that follow the Lord's journey under the bright light of Israel's sky" (262) and they reject the Passion and the Cross as symbols of suffering and unearthly salvation. In spite of her being a woman writer and a rebellious person, she does not seem to have been attracted by feminism any more than Sallenave. As will become more and more obvious, the category of "woman writer" is proving less and less relevant—and this may be one of the consequences of the feminist movement.

While Cerf's texts appear to harbor, even if somewhat reluctantly, a mythical quality, Patrick Grainville goes much further in that direction. His texts are unabashed mythmakers, his writing torrential (two recent works, *Le Paradis de orages* [1986; Heavenly Storms] and *L'Atelier du peintre* [1988; The Painter's Studio] average 400 pages each and others are not far behind), and his eroticism unbridled. There is a major character in *La Caverne céleste* (1984; *The Cave of Heaven*), an archaic, age-old enchantress of sorts, who experiences a sensuous delight in speaking; Grainville's art is that of the storyteller and, like her, he speaks on a number of levels, sometimes moving in the direction of scription. The focus of this narrative is an archaeological site in a cave in southwestern France where a 500,000-year-old human cranium has been unearthed. The story that is told amounts to a quest for origins that ends up being circular in that the presence of those ancient remains reactivates all the primitive instincts of those who are caught up in their orbit—uninhibited sexual satisfactions, hunting and killing animals (or even one's fellow man, in this instance a Basque terrorist who is hiding in the area). Nature itself joins in the fray as a raging forest fire endangers the region. With their baroque narrative these books do in spots remind one of Philippe Sollers's sexuality; *Le Paradis des orages,* however, bears an erotic epigraph borrowed from Claude Simon's *La Route des Flandres.* This, in addition to the texts themselves, suggests that he sees himself as writing on the verge of a catastrophe.

Renaud Camus is also someone who bears watching. Like the early Perec he has been proceeding almost simultaneously in several directions. In opposition to Muriel Cerf (and many others) he claims to support conventional behavior and the constraints of society. His *Journal d'un voyage en France* (1981; Diary of a Journey through France) has been described as being in "the tradition of nineteenth-century travel diaries."[2] His first work, *Passage* (1975), supposedly the first installment of "a trilogy in four books and seven volumes," contains an appendix inspired by the one in Perec's *La Vie mode d'emploi* in which Camus states that about one-fourth of his text is made up of quotations from some thirty-eight writers that he then lists; this would be in addition to the *Grand Larousse Encyclopédique* and quotations from "the author's previous works." As this is his first publication, that final notation throws an ironic light on the whole statement. As in Perec (and Queneau), the spelling of characters' names is apt to change: Anne-Marie Stretter, borrowed from Marguerite Duras on page 10, becomes Anne-Marie Straighter on page 93, and Ann-Mary Straighter on page 125. Camus himself has used several variations on his own name to sign his books.

The first volume published by Mathieu Bénézet is misleadingly and tantalizingly called *L'Histoire de la peinture en trois volumes* (1968): it is a collection of poems. Next, he brought out *Biographies* (1970), which he classified as a novel. *Dits et récits du mortel* (1977; Sayings and Tales of the Mortal Being) was more accurately characterized on its title page as a Menippean work—after the late sixteenth-century French *Satire Ménippée*, itself so named for the third-century Greek cynic writer, Menippus, whose works have been lost. All of this is pregnant with significance: the oblivion into which we are doomed to go, the refusal of literature and its division into arbitrary genres, the criticism or satire directed at the human condition. The work is fragmented (its first section is entitled "Fragments") and it manifests the notion of the split or undecidable subject. As Bénézet explains in his back-cover blurb, "For what is an 'I' if not the different voices manufacturing one's own and proper self? The other, the stranger, the excluded one represents the unreadable and incomprehensible share that lies in my 'own' speech." The appearance of the printed word on the page is variegated and occasionally reminds one of Maurice Roche's practice, but in a more restrained fashion. The title page of *L'Imitation de Mathieu Bénézet* (1978) suggests that it is a continuation of the previous volume; this time it is characterized as a "melodrame" while *Ceci est mon corps* (1979; This Is My Body) is identified as "mélange." The Christian connotations of both titles, and the fragmented continuity that is implied, together with many references to Mallarmé in the text of *Dits et récits du mortel,* imply that each book made up of fragments is in itself but a fragment of the real Book toward which Bénézet is struggling. *La Fin de l'homme* (1979; The End of Man), called "roman abandonné," could be read as a demonstration of Roland Barthes's observation that a writer is "created" by his work, not the other way around. It includes eight photos that do not "illustrate" the book but constitute integral elements of its meaning; their sobriety, verging on starkness, is also emblematic of Bénézet's texts.

Even though some of the more recent works appear to revert to a more traditional splitting of "prose" and "verse," this writer's contribution is already an original and important one. As a poet-fiction-writer, he reminds one of Jacques Roubaud, to whom I have made occasional reference, except that Roubaud is essentially a poet who more recently turned to writing fiction. Already in 1978 there was an indication that he was tempted to move in that direction as *Graal fiction* attempted to retell some of the medieval legends, as he posited Brocéliande, the magic forest of Britanny, as the birthplace of the novel. It will be interesting to see whether *La Belle Hortense* (1985; *Our Beautiful Heroine*), *L'Enlève-ment d'Hortense* (1987; *Hortense Is Abducted*), and the even more challenging *Le Grand Incendie de Londres* (1989; *The Great Fire of London*) mark a turning point or a temporary detour. The latter, from which traditional poetry is still excluded (some verse is quoted at the end but this is conventional quotation), is a heterogeneous text that brings together fiction, nonfiction, and autobiography.

To anyone reading Tony Duvert's first novel, *Récidive* (1967; Repeated Offense), it is clear that the lessons of the previous generation had been assimilated. The relationship between narrative and any possible referent is shaky or problematic and it comes as no surprise to find out that the sequence called "Rappel succinct de ce qui précède" (A brief reminder of previous events) does not at all sum up the events of the previous pages. As the text oscillates between first- and third-person narrative, the subject is put in doubt and a similar indeterminacy affects characters. Linearity also goes by the board. What I find interesting is that, as Maurice Blanchot did with *Thomas l'obscur*, Duvert published a "new version" of *Récidive* in 1976, in which the features I mentioned have been attenuated. What remains, however, is a strong presence of the flesh: a pervading sensuousness runs through the text, as it does through that of his next work of fiction, *Portrait d'homme couteau* (1969; Portrait of a Knife Man). Those two books were greeted with relative critical silence, possibly because of the combination of an elaborate scription with homosexual pornography ("something that inspires a legitimate disgust," Duvert himself wrote, ironically, on the back cover of *Paysage de fantaisie* [*Strange Landscape*] in 1973). *Journal d'un innocent*, on the other hand, renounced working in scription; there is a single, unified narrative in the first person, characters have stable referents, and so forth. As a result, journalistic reviewers praised the book and pronounced it worthy of Duvert's great French classic antecedents. What had perturbed ordinary reviewers was that Butor, Robbe-Grillet, Roche, and others had tampered with the notions of "literature," "belles lettres," and style; graphically rendered erotic acts, however, were increasingly acceptable—provided they were encased in "fine" prose.

Encountering the fictions of Eugène Savitzkaya was for me a most pleasurable experience. While his texts do not resemble the works of the earlier generation, except perhaps, fleetingly, some aspects of those by Marguerite Duras, they evidence no return to the ways of conventional fiction where matters of plot, characters, verisimilitude, and linearity are concerned. It seemed as though the literary domain had been swept through by winds out of Lautréamont and the surrealists but with results that are unlike the texts that one associates with either. What reminded me of Duras is rather subtle: it has to do with the way clauses and sentences are put together, the way a paragraph is brought to a close—or rather, the way it opens up on something else. It relates to the way meaning is generated.[3]

Savitzkaya was born in 1955 and in spite of his name or pen name he has Belgian roots (not an irrelevant detail as the surrealist wind I mentioned above may well have blown through the paintings of James Ensor and the texts of Michel de Ghelderode). He has published works of poetry and fiction, but separately; nevertheless, poetic language does permeate the fiction. The latter includes *Mentir* (1977; Telling Lies), based on his childhood; *Un Jeune homme trop gros* (1978; An Overly Fat Young Man), which is a fictional, whimsical story generated by the figure of Elvis Presley; *La Traversée de l'Afrique* (1979; Going across Africa); *La Disparition de maman* (1982); *Les Morts sentent bon* (1983; The Dead Smell Good), which is about a king who goes on a quest for a peaceful land, is more than once beheaded, is eaten up by a wild beast, but each time rises again to continue his quest; and *Sang de chien* (1988; Dog's Blood). These works frankly and wholeheartedly belong to the category French critics call the "marvelous," one that includes fairy tales. But the fairy tales Savitzkaya reminds one of are those collected by Grimm rather than those edited by Perrault, tales in which the supernatural is linked to cruelty and violence. Here, however, something childlike, in the everyday sense of the world, runs through the narrative, making it bearable. As in books by Duvert, the flesh is ever-present but it is neither erotic nor pornographic; one might call it earthy. To quote the final sentence of *Sang de chien,* "When I stink, I smell like you."

I mentioned Duras as a writer I occasionally thought of when reading Savitzkaya. When one remembers that Duras is a woman, one may hold a minute but significant clue to an important development. During the course of a dialogue between Duras and Xavière Gauthier, the two attempted to identify what in the writings of Duras issues specifically from the woman. Gauthier, referring to some of Duras's work, said, "I believe this could have been written only by a woman, but it's difficult to show."[4] The reasons that make it difficult are that so-called womanly and manly characteristics do not necessarily coincide with the biological division of the sexes and those that are termed womanly have been downgraded or repressed. Duras and Gauthier, in the spontaneity of their conversations, give excessive weight to their own uniqueness as women and the utter otherness of men. The endnotes they have added reveal that they are aware of that exaggeration, and toward the end of their first dialogue Gauthier does say, "In any case I think that male writers, in order to write, must be womanly, too. No?"—and Duras agrees.[5] Instead of going back to the man/woman dichotomy one should probably adopt the phraseology found in Julia Kristeva's theory where the symbolic modality is opposed to the semiotic one.[6] What I am driving at is that not only the texts of Savitzkaya and Duvert but many other contemporary works of fiction display what I propose to call a *gynetext*, a word Naomi Schor introduced in passing in 1976 in an essay on *Madame Bovary*.[7]

Although the appearance of a gynetext might also be interpreted as a return of the repressed and a reaction against what were mistakenly viewed as characteristic of the so-called new novel, its emergence does not signify a return to practices identified with those of the nineteenth-century novel—or more accurately of its run-of-the-mill variety. To paraphrase Louis Althusser, we should not, in the twentieth century, live and write as if Marx, Nietzsche, and Freud had not existed,[8] even though quite a few people do. As Guy Scarpetta wrote, "What is returning, after the 'era of suspicion,' is undoubtedly less psychology than the *body* (sensations, perceptions, rhythm, physical and nervous peculiarities, flavors, outbursts of sensuality, and so forth)."[9]

With male writers, the gynetext's presence tends to be more subdued as ideology changes very slowly. François Bon, for instance, is concerned with the ways in which the human body is affected by work in a factory; in *Sortie d'usine* (1982; Factory Exit), his first novel (he was born in 1953), it may not strike the reader as much because the topic almost calls for it. In reading that narrative one may, as Nathalie Sarraute suspected readers would do, start building characters and imagine the manner in which individuals react. But, as one critic remarked, in an interview with the writer, "There are strictly speaking no characters in your books, merely voices"; François Bon soon agreed: "So, at the beginning, no, there are no characters but only images, which I don't succeed in catching up with."[10] In connection with *Limite* (1985), where four "characters" describe the way their bodies are affected by a crucial event in their lives, the same critic speaks of the constraints of their working with a specific material related to their jobs, adding, "And 'working' here means a bodily experience, a close combat situation." The discontinuous narratives of *Le Crime de Buzon* (1986) and *Décor ciment* (1988) have confirmed the quality and maintained the tone of Bon's "voices." At the end of the interview from which I have already quoted, he spoke of "the obscure portion of one's self, where one must remain, and perhaps where fascination discovers its physical, founding part." Among the twentieth-century writers he feels most comfortable with, Bon has named Proust and Kafka.

Jean Echenoz, who was born in 1946, did not publish his first novel until 1979. As in the case of Alain Robbe-Grillet, his background is non-literary: he studied organic chemistry. While Raymond Roussel traveled all over the world but claimed he did not use his experience in his works, Echenoz set one of his fictions in a small Pacific island and the other in Malaysia but has visited neither place. As Lautréamont did, he relied on encyclopedias and other reference works. The results, in *Le Méridien de Greenwich* (1979) and *L'Equipée malaise* (1986; The Malaysian Venture) as well as in one that belongs chronologically in between, *Cherokee* (1983), are entertaining yarns that on occasion remind one of Raymond Queneau and contain many references to films (Queneau was also quite taken by the movies). In *Le Méridien de Greenwich*, whose setting is mostly a small island bisected by that meridian, thus causing time problems, there is also a reference to a jigsaw puzzle that brings Perec to mind; here, the pieces of the puzzle are compared to words in language, meaningless in themselves, which are assembled in order to constitute a work of literature; once assembled, however, the latter loses all interest. In 1988, Echenoz published a fifteen-page text called *L'Occupation des sols* (Holding the Lots) that is of a very different nature. One way to describe it would be to say that it is about the death of the mother and the preservation of her image—a false one.

So far, the gynetext has not surfaced in Echenoz's narratives (although it may be sensed, just below the surface, in that brief fiction), nor do I detect its presence in the texts of Jean-Philippe Toussaint. While *L'Occupation des sols* could have been a turning point for Echenoz, his recent *Lac* (1990) harks back to earlier works; Toussaint, however, born in 1957, is too young for valid predictions to be made concerning his future. On the other hand, I would say that the three fictional narratives that have already come out at the time of this writing are very original and quite promising. Each one revolves around either a bizarre decision (the narrator of *La Salle de bain* [1985; *The Bathroom*] choosing to remain in his bathtub, which after one spur-of-the-moment, unfortunate trip to Venice, he leaves only on the last page of the book), an unexpected outside event (the main character of *Monsieur* [1986], which is the only way he is referred to, passively accepts whatever happens), or impulsive reactions to minor outside events (the narrator of *L'Appareil-photo* [1988] picks up someone else's camera and, while first intending to return it, he does not). Their style is successively detached, ironic, and melancholy.

For the time being, most (but not all) instances of the gynetext will be found in the writings of women. Not in all of them, however, It does not show in Sallenave's *Les Portes de Gubbio*, nor in Muriel Cerf's texts (although she may turn out to be a borderline case). Feminist writers like

Nancy Huston and Leila Sebbar do not necessarily display it. It would be unseemly to survey, ever so briefly, the productions of some of these women without first mentioning Hélène Cixous. A year younger than Perec and Sollers, she already has a large body of work to her credit, including a doctoral dissertation on James Joyce. Much of her work has been critical, theoretical, and feminist, but it also includes fiction. The gynetext could be said to manifest the workings of the semiotic modality within the otherness of language—an otherness that social constraints have led most of us to accept as our own. This comes out most forcibly in fiction, and I should like to quote from *Dedans* (1969), one of the early texts by Cixous that deals, in part, with the relations of a child, who happens to be female (that is, immersed in the semiotic), with her father (who is at ease with the symbolic): "I have few words. My father, who had them all, left so precipitously that he did not have the time to give them to me.... Since my father became silent I have been living off my sparse heritage. In order to become acquainted with words all I have is books that are in the dark library. My mother does not talk much, and further-more her language is not the same as my father's.... Where she knows more than I do is in the area of anatomy and physiology. Even though it is useless to me here, I remember tens and tens of such words, to please her; when she enumerates and makes lists I follow her and we thus meet at the secret joints of the Human Body."[11]

The gynetext also signifies a problematic identity. As Cixous stated, in that same text, "No one knows who I am. Even I did not know, at least at the beginning" (66-67). Jeanne Hyvrard says something quite similar in *La Meurtritude* (1977): "It is not me who is writing. It is another woman. She dwells in my body" (21). Hyvrard is a feminist, her works are remark-ably illustrative of the gynetext's presence, and she is a woman; beyond all that, however, she is simply a first-rate French writer.

In addition to emphasizing the writer's body and questioning his or her identity, the presence of a gynetext affects language itself—not only the narrative, the relation of it to a referent, but also its syntax ("Words matter more than syntax," Duras said in *Les Parleuses* [11]), grammar, and vocabulary. By the last I mean treating words not as if they were transparent signs but rather as elements of the material world (some-thing already posited by Roland Barthes) that can be tampered with, turned around, and played with. The assumption is that human beings are introduced to language at the moment of the thetic, or phallic phase of their development, and this thoroughly coded and structured language is the privileged manifestation of the symbolic modality. Such a language represents the law of the Father while the semiotic modality is closer to the Mother, nature, the unconscious, the real (as opposed to "reality"). The result is that, as Kristeva puts it, "In women's writing, language appears to be seen from the distance of a foreign land."[12]

In spite of that metaphor and since women must live within a domain that is not their own, the feeling of alienation is often translated into one of imprisonment, which comes across very strongly in Jeanne Hyvrard's *La Meurtritude* (1977; Bruisedness, her third work of fiction, published simultaneously with *Les Doigts du figuier* [Fingers of the Fig Tree], following *Les Prunes de Cythère* [1975; The Plums of Cythera] and *Mère la mort* [1976; *Mother Death*]): "I come to visit you in the room for the terminally ill in the castle by the lake. That is where they keep you imprisoned. On the edge of a swamp whose name you do not know. On the edge of a swamp at the end of my sorrow. Perhaps it does have a name. It is the abode of the unnamable" (25). The narrative continues for the length of three paragraphs, a little under two pages, and leads up to the statement, "Since they have condemned me to say what they want to forget" (27). The linguistic features of the gynetext are made patent: it is an other language ("unnamable"); it has been repressed ("imprisoned," "condemned") because it might state things that society has agreed to deny ("they want to forget"). The metaphor is taken up again in a more recent text, *Canal de la Toussaint* (1985; All Saints' Day Canal): "Misunderstanding. Born of the swamp, man refuses it. He imprisons the woman who preserves its memory. It seeps out just the same" (11, 95). Hyvrard has published close to a dozen books as of this writing, and I have emphasized the gynetext as this term brings together what is most innovative about her texts—a further sapping of the notion of genre and conventional syntax while preserving power and readability. There are writings that can be discouraging to some because of their novelty and seeming opaqueness; others grip their readers and force them to keep going. Hyvrard's belong to the latter category.

Chantal Chawaf is a prolific writer who, born in 1948, has already published more than a dozen books that are in various guises predicated on a woman's experience of the body, from sexual intercourse to giving birth, and encompasses the entire gamut of the relationships between male and female. She herself has stated that her aim was "to write in the space where a literature does not yet exist because the areas sought by scription are those of a return to the body that precedes words, when the human being does not yet know how to speak or cannot speak." And she added, "In this novelistic genre . . . one proceeds in the opposite direction, backward, toward the beginning, toward life, and not toward the end, not toward death."[13] The first part of the statement places her practice squarely within the realm of what I am calling the gynetext; the second marks a difference of emphasis between her writing and that of Jeanne Hyvrard. Not that death and violence have been eliminated from her texts: *Retable* (1974), the first fiction she published, takes as its point of departure the cesarean birth of a girl whose mother and father were killed during a bombing in 1940. She is adopted by another couple and, a quarter of a century later, learns the truth. That, however, is the only narrative constituent of a text that develops in nonreferential fashion, in the manner of poetry, and syntax is bent to meet Chawaf's requirements. For instance, "It hurts, alone, very weak, born and having to walk doubting the kiss that cut across destruction and I shiver, stumble alone" (70).

The violence in *Retable* is produced by the Second World War and it testifies to a presence already noted in several writers of her generation. Her fourth work of fiction, *Le Soleil et la terre* (1977), was presented in its blurb as "the book of love and war" and it sometimes reads like a supplication to men who are also the victims of the madness they have set loose. "Man, man ... the wine of sperm that is poured in the ritual of love and life does not alleviate the blood continuously shed in the primitive ritual of war and death" (86). In her thirteenth work, *Rédemption* (1989), there is a protagonist who has murdered his wife just before the narrative begins. He is incapable of simply enjoying his body, of sharing that enjoyment; he has metaphorically become a vampire who hates women. Nevertheless he begins a relationship with another woman who seems attracted to him in spite of what she learns or senses about him. Perversely, perhaps? I believe, rather, as the title suggests, that she pities him and, through him, men in general, who stand in need of redemption.

With Annie Ernaux, the narrative, while still concerned with the body, shifts somewhat in the direction of the social milieu. Her first book came out at the same time as Chawaf's did, in 1974. Entitled *Les Armoires vides* (translated as *Cleaned Out*), a phrase borrowed from a poem by Paul Eluard ("I have preserved fake treasures in empty wardrobes / A useless ship links my childhood to my boredom / my games to weariness"), it represents a slow flashback as the first-person narrator, a young woman, is suffering from an abortion. In *La Femme gelée* (1981; *The Frozen Woman*) fiction and autobiography have more obviously merged, as they have with Duras, Robbe-Grillet, and Sollers—but Ernaux lays greater stress on the division of labor imposed on a couple by society's ideology. *La Place* (1984) was sparked by her father's death, *Une Femme* (1987; *A Woman's Story*) by her mother's. As in previous works, there is an experience that forces the writer to go back in time and attempt to figure out how she got there, who she is, and who we are. As she does so, she will try to write in a direct manner, without symbols and metaphors, without the aid of poetic prose. When she uses the latter, it is done ironically, as in the first sentence of *La Femme gelée:* "Fragile, diaphanous women, soft-handed fairies, slender inspirations of the home that silently bring forth order and beauty, voiceless women, submissive women, search as I might I find few of them in the landscape of my childhood."

The personal psyche and the body of previous literature are the fonts from which most writing springs. For some, if not for most, literature is more important, although they can never suppress what comes from the psyche. Michel Butor is perhaps typical of this group as he searches through an imaginary universal library in order to locate the empty shelf he is destined to fill. Or, as Danièle Sallenave put it, "The true nature of art . . . is that it makes us contemporaries of the dead."[14] The gynetext's strong links to the body will inevitably cause some practitioners to give more emphasis to the psyche as it has been shaped or damaged by the family and the social environment. Ernaux is obviously one such, and she has noted: "It is quite easy for me to see with whom I am *not* contemporary —novelists who draw their inspiration from fiction."[15]

Marie Redonnet belongs in the same company; she became a writer after much psychic suffering and it was only after a long analysis that she broke her silence with the simultaneous publication of *Doublures* (Stand-ins), a series of twelve brief tales, and *Le Mort & Cie* (1985), a poetic sequence of some five hundred three-line stanzas. I am reminded of the "sort of catastrophe" whose presence Blanchot identified as often being at the source of scription. This was immediately followed by a fictional "triptych," *Splendid Hotel* (1986), *Forever Valley* (1986), and *Rose Mélie Rose* (1987). The title of the first comes out of Rimbaud's *Illuminations*, and this is acknowledged by means of an epigraph. It constitutes the only literary reference in a text that is all but "literary" in the usual sense of the word. The narrator, a woman, has inherited from her grandmother a hotel the latter had built near a swamp; she tries to manage it with the presence (rather than the help) of her two sisters, Ada and Adel, but everything deteriorates, especially the plumbing, and after a while the toilets no longer function. The text is made up mostly of short one-clause sentences of which the following is typical: "I have succeeded in getting rid of the spiders. Ada no longer dreams. But she has pains in her belly. She can no longer stand my washing her. She doesn't want me to clean her room. The salesmen no longer visit her. I don't know what to do" (45). Eventually the narrator's sisters die, the hotel keeps deteriorating—and existing, after a fashion.

Forever Valley is also a first-person narrative, told by a sixteen-year-old illiterate woman who lives in the parsonage of an abandoned church in the mountains, near a border. Much of her activity consists in digging around the parsonage, under the priest's supervision, looking for the dead. On Saturdays she "works" at the local dance hall, patronized by men from the customs service. The priest dies, a good friend dies, the dance hall closes because a dam has been built and the village of Forever Valley is now under water. The style is very similar to that of *Splendid Hotel.* With *Rose Mélie Rose*, however, it becomes just a little less simple and at the outset the narrative reads like a fairy tale. The narrator, Mélie, was found in a cave, just after she was born, by an old woman named Rose; they live together until Rose dies, twelve years later, as Mélie is about to have her first period and the main narrative gets under way. Rose has left her an address in a nearby town, on her way to which her various adventures begin. At the end of the book she gives birth to a girl she names Rose, has a hemorrhage, and probably dies, covered by sand, in a car that was abandoned on a beach. She has left her child in the cave where she herself was found. The time that elapsed between the two events is equal to the time Redonnet herself spent in analysis. The circularity of the narrative is evident (a feature I identified in many works of the previous generation), as it proceeds from birth to birth, Rose to Rose, woman to woman. Even though linked with death, the blood that suffuses its beginning and its end, menstrual and postnatal, could be called the blood of life as it is involved with the reproductive process. The presence of a yacht called *La Reine des fées* may or may not be an ironic reference to Spenser's *The Faerie Queene;* conscious or not, such a literary allusion could be interpreted as signaling Redonnet's entry into "literature," that is, her acceptance of aesthetic concerns in addition to her more fundamental ones.

My survey of writers could go on and on. Why not mention all those who were enumerated in the periodicals I have recorded? On the other hand, to repeat what I wrote in the original 1972 introduction, I have no desire to produce an encyclopedia and while it may be more hazardous to offer my personal choice (as the editors of *L'Infini, Yale French Studies*, the *Review of Contemporary Fiction*, and *La Quinzaine* have doubtless also done), I enjoy the challenge—and the gamble.

NOTES

1   See E. J. Dionne's "Driven to Write by the Unexpected," a brief interview with Levi that accompanied Alvin H. Rosenfeld's review of Levi's *The Periodic Table. New York Times Book Review*, 23 December 1984, p. 9. Maurice Blanchot had made a similar remark, taking a short story by Jean Paulhan as a point of departure: "One should not conclude, on the basis of this narrative, that literature must necessarily have a crime at its source, or simply a theft. It does, however, suppose a collapse, a sort of catastrophe." See "Le Paradoxe d'Aytré," in *La Part du feu* (Paris: Gallimard, 1949), 75.

2   See Pierre Force and Dominique Jullien, "Renaud Camus," in *After the Age of Suspicion: The French Novel Today (Yale French Studies*, Special Issue, 1988): 285-90.

3   I have developed this and related points in "Is There a New Novel Today," *Three Decades of the French New Novel*, ed. Lois Oppenheim (Urbana: University of Illinois Press, 1986), 152-73.

4   Marguerite Duras and Xavière Gauthier, *Les Parleuses* (Paris: Minuit, 1974), 19.

5   Ibid., 51.

6   See Julia Kristeva, *Revolution in Poetic Language*, trans. Margaret Waller (New York: Columbia University Press, 1984), 25 and passim.

7   Naomi Schor, "Pour une thématique restreinte / Ecriture, parole et différence dans *Madame Bovary*," *Littérature*, no. 22 (May 1976): 46.

8   See Louis Althusser, *Lire le Capital* (Paris: Maspero, 1970), 1: 10ff. For those who might be inclined to question this on account of the 1989-1990 events in Eastern Europe, I would point out that members of the Communist party have not usually been serious readers of Marx—and that is why French intellectuals, for instance, who joined the Party after reading Marx very soon left it.

9   Guy Scarpetta, *L'Impureté* (Paris: Grasset, 1985), 289.

10   Sonia Nowoselsky-Müller, "Côté Cuisines (entretien avec F. Bon)," *L'Infini*, no. 19 (May 1987): 55-62.

11   Hélène Cixous, *Dedans* (Paris: Grasset, 1969), 53-56.

12   Julia Kristeva, "Oscillation du 'pouvoir' au 'refus,' " *Tel Quel*, no. 58 (Summer 1974): 100.

13   "Chawaf, Chantal," in *Le Dictionnaire*, ed. Jérôme Garcin (Paris: François Bourin, 1988), 122-23.

14   "French Novelists on Their Writing," *Review of Contemporary Fiction* 9, no. 1 (Spring 1989): 214.

15   Ibid., 211.

Selected Bibliography

1. Raymond Roussel

FICTION

La Doublure. Paris: Lemerre, 1897; rpt. Paris: Pauvert, 1963.
La Vue. Paris: Lemerre, 1904; rpt. (with *Le Concert* [1903] and *La Source* [1904]) Paris: Pauvert, 1963.
Impressions d'Afrique. Paris: Lemerre, 1910; rpt. Paris: Pauvert, 1963. (*Impressions of Africa.* Trans. Lindy Foord and Rayner Heppenstall. Berkeley: University of California Press, 1967.)
Locus solus. Paris: Lemerre, 1914; rpt. Paris: Pauvert, 1963. (*Locus Solus.* Trans. Rupert Copeland Cunningham. Berkeley: University of California Press, 1970.)
Nouvelle impressions d'Afrique. Paris: Lemerre, 1932; rpt. Paris: Pauvert, 1963.
Comment j'ai écrit certains de mes livres. Paris: Lemerre, 1935; rpt. Paris: Pauvert, 1963. (*How I Wrote Certain of My Books.* Trans. Trevor Winkfield, with an introduction by Kenneth Koch, two essays by John Ashbery, and a translation of canto 3 of *New Impressions of Africa.* New York: State University of New York, 1977.)
Epaves. Ed. François Caradec, with an essay by Michel Leiris. Paris: Pauvert, 1972.
(*Selections from Certain of His Books.* Ed. and trans. John Ashbery, Harry Mathews, et al. London: Atlas Press, 1991.)

CRITICISM (in French)

Amiot, Anne-Marie. *Un mythe moderne: "Impressions d'Afrique" de Raymond Roussel.* Paris: Lettres Modernes, 1977.
Caradec, François. *Vie de Raymond Roussel.* Paris: Pauvert, 1972.
Caburet, Bernard. *Raymond Roussel.* Paris: Seghers, 1968.
Durham, Carolyn A. *L'Art romanesque de Raymond Roussel.* York, SC: French

Literature Publications Company, 1982.

Ferry, Jean. *Une Etude sur Raymond Roussel.* Preface by André Breton. Paris: Arcane, 1953.

———. *Une Autre Etude sur Raymond Roussel.* Paris: Collège de Pataphysique, 1967.

Foucault, Michel. *Raymond Roussel.* Paris: Gallimard, 1963.

Houppermans, Sjef. *Raymond Roussel: Ecriture et désir.* Paris: Corti, 1985.

Leiris, Michel. *Roussel l'ingénue.* Fata Morgana, 1987.

Sciascia, Leonardo. *Actes relatifs à la mort de Raymond Roussel.* With essays by Jean Ricardou and Gérard-Julien Salvy. Paris: L'Herne, 1972.

Special issues of periodicals: *L'Arc,* no. 68 (1977); *Mélusine,* no. 6 (1984).

CRITICISM (in English)

Brotchie, Alastair, ed. *Raymond Roussel: Life, Death & Works.* London: Atlas Press, 1987.

Foucault, Michel. *Death and the Labyrinth: The World of Raymond Roussel.* Trans. Charles Ruas. Garden City, NY: Doubleday, 1986.

Heppenstall, Rayner. *Raymond Roussel.* Berkeley: University of California Press, 1967.

2. Nathalie Sarraute

FICTION

Tropismes. Paris: Denoël, 1939; rpt. Paris: Minuit, 1957. (*Tropisms.* Trans. Maria Jolas. New York: Braziller, 1967.)

Portrait d'un inconnu. Paris: Robert Marin, 1947; rpt. Paris: Gallimard, 1956. (*Portrait of a Man Unknown.* Trans. Maria Jolas. New York: Braziller, 1958.)

Martereau. Paris: Gallimard, 1953. (*Martereau.* Trans. Maria Jolas. New York: Braziller, 1959.)

Le Planétarium. Paris: Gallimard, 1959. (*The Planetarium.* Trans. Maria Jolas. New York: Braziller, 1960.)

Les Fruits d'or. Paris: Gallimard, 1963. (*The Golden Fruits.* Trans. Maria Jolas. New York: Braziller, 1964.)

Entre la vie et la mort. Paris: Gallimard, 1968. (*Between Life and Death.* Trans. Maria Jolas. New York: Braziller, 1969.)

Vous les entendez? Paris: Gallimard, 1972. (*Do You Hear Them?* Trans. Maria Jolas. New York: Braziller, 1973.)

"Disent les imbéciles." Paris: Gallimard, 1976. (*"fools say."* Trans. Maria Jolas. New York: Braziller, 1977.)

L'Usage de la parole. Paris: Gallimard, 1980. (*The Use of Speech.* Trans. Barbara Wright. New York: Braziller, 1983.)

Enfance. Paris: Gallimard, 1983. (*Childhood.* Trans. Barbara Wright. New York: Braziller, 1985.)

Tu ne t'aimes pas. Paris: Gallimard, 1989. (*You Don't Love Yourself.* Trans. Barbara Wright. New York: Braziller, 1990.)

CRITICISM (in French)

Allemand, André. *L'OEuvre romanesque de Nathalie Sarraute.* Neuchâtel:
Editions de la Baconnière, 1980.
Cranaki, Mimica, and Yvon Belaval. *Nathalie Sarraute.* Paris: Gallimard, 1965.
Micha, René. *Nathalie Sarraute.* Paris: Editions Universitaires, 1966.
Tison-Braun, Micheline. *Nathalie Sarraute ou la recherche de l'authenticité.*
Paris: Gallimard, 1971.

CRITICISM (in English)

Besser, Gretchen R. *Nathalie Sarraute.* Boston: Twayne, 1979.
Minogue, Valérie. *Nathalie Sarraute and the War of the Words.* Edinburgh: The
University Press, 1981.
Temple, Ruth Z. *Nathalie Sarraute.* New York: Columbia University Press, 1968.
Watson-Williams, Helen. *The Novels of Nathalie Sarraute: Towards an Aesthetic.*
Amsterdam: Rodopi, 1981.

3. Maurice Blanchot

FICTION

Thomas l'obscur. Paris: Gallimard, 1941. (*Thomas the Obscure.* Trans. Robert
Lamberton. Barrytown, NY: Station Hill, 1988.)
Aminadab. Paris: Gallimard, 1942.
Les Très-haut. Paris: Gallimard, 1948.
L'Arrêt de mort. Paris: Gallimard, 1948. (*Death Sentence.* Trans. Lydia Davis.
Barrytown: Station Hill, 1978.)
Thomas l'obscur (Nouvelle version). Paris: Gallimard, 1950. (*Thomas the Obscure*
[New Version]. Trans. Robert Lamberton. New York: David Lewis, 1973.)
Au moment voulu. Paris: Gallimard, 1951. (*When the Time Comes.* Trans. Lydia
Davis. Barrytown: Station Hill, 1984.)
Le Ressassement éternel. Paris: Minuit, 1951; rpt. Paris: Gordon & Breach, 1970.
(*Vicious Circles.* Trans. Paul Auster. Barrytown: Station Hill, 1985.)
Celui qui ne m'accompagnait pas. Paris: Gallimard, 1953. (*The One Who Was
Standing Apart from Me.* Trans. Lydia Davis. Barrytown: Station Hill, 1988.)
Le Dernier homme. Paris: Gallimard, 1957. (*The Last Man.* Trans. Lydia Davis.
New York: Columbia University Press, 1987.)
L'Attente l'oubli. Paris: Gallimard, 1962.
La Folie du jour. Montpellier: Fata Morgana, 1973. (*The Madness of the Day.*
Trans. Lydia Davis. Barrytown: Station Hill, 1981.)

CRITICISM (in French)

Collin, Françoise. *Maurice Blanchot ou la question de l'écriture.* Paris: Gallimard,
1971.
Laporte, Roger, and Bernard Noël. *Deux Lectures de Maurice Blanchot.*

Montpellier: Fata Morgana, 1973.
Levinas, Emmanuel. *Sur Maurice Blanchot.* Montpellier: Fata Morgana, 1975.
Londyn, Evelyne. *Maurice Blanchot, romancier.* Paris: Nizet, 1976.
Madaule, Pierre. *Une Tâche sérieuse?* Paris: Gallimard, 1973.
Wilhem, Daniel. *Maurice Blanchot: la voix narrative.* Paris: U.G.E., 1974.
Special issues of periodicals: *Critique,* no. 229 (June 1966); "Lire Blanchot I,"
   Gramma, no. 3-4 (1976); "Lire Blanchot II," *Gramma,* no. 5 (1977).

CRITICISM (in English)

Shaviro, Steven. *Passion and Excess: Blanchot, Bataille, and Literary Theory.*
   Tallahassee: Florida State University Press, 1990.
Special issues of periodicals: "Flying White: The Writings of Maurice Blanchot,"
   SubStance, no. 14 (1976).

4. Marguerite Duras

FICTION

Les Impudents. Paris: Plon, 1943.
La Vie tranquille. Paris: Gallimard, 1944.
Un Barrage contre le Pacifique. Paris: Gallimard, 1950. (*The Sea Wall.* Trans.
   Herma Briffault. New York: Pelligrini & Cudahy, 1953.)
Le Marin de Gibraltar. Paris: Gallimard, 1952. (*The Sailor from Gibraltar.* Trans.
   Barbara Bray. New York: Grove, 1966.)
Les Petits Chevaux de Tarquinia. Paris: Gallimard, 1953. (*The Little Horses of
   Tarquinia.* Trans. Peter DuBerg. London: Calder, 1960.)
Des Journées entières dans les arbres. Paris: Gallimard, 1954. (*Whole Days in the
   Trees.* Trans. Anita Barrows. New York: Riverrun, 1984.)
Le Square. Paris: Gallimard, 1955. (*The Square,* in *Four Novels.* Trans. Richard
   Seaver et al. New York: Grove, 1965.)
Moderato cantabile. Paris: Minuit, 1958. (*Moderato Cantabile,* in *Four Novels.*)
Dix Heures et demie du soir en été. Paris: Gallimard, 1960. (*10:30 on a Summer
   Night,* in *Four Novels.*)
L'Après-midi de monsieur Andesmas. Paris: Gallimard, 1962. (*The Afternoon of
   Monsieur Andesmas,* in *Four Novels.*)
Le Ravissement de Lol V. Stein. Paris: Gallimard, 1964. (*The Ravishing of Lol
   Stein.* Trans. Richard Seaver. New York: Grove, 1966.)
Le Vice-consul. Paris: Gallimard, 1966. (*The Vice Consul.* Trans. Eileen Ellen-
   bogen. New York: Pantheon, 1987.)
L'Amante anglaise. Paris: Gallimard, 1967. (*L'Amante Anglaise.* Trans. Barbara
   Bray. New York: Grove, 1968.)
Détruire dit-elle. Paris: Minuit, 1969. (*Destroy, She Said.* Trans. Barbara Bray.
   New York: Grove, 1986.)
Abahn Sabana David. Paris: Gallimard, 1970.
L'Amour. Paris: Gallimard, 1971.
L'Homme assis dans le couloir. Paris: Minuit, 1980.

L'Homme atlantique. Paris: Minuit, 1982.
La Maladie de la mort. Paris: Minuit, 1982. (*The Malady of Death.* Trans. Barbara Bray. New York: Grove, 1986.)
L'Amant. Paris: Minuit, 1984. (*The Lover.* Trans. Barbara Bray. New York: Pantheon, 1985.)
La Douleur. Paris: P.O.L., 1985. (*La Douleur.* Trans. Barbara Bray. London: Collins, 1986.)
Les Yeux bleus cheveux noirs. Paris: Minuit, 1986. (*Blue Eyes, Black Hair.* Trans. Barbara Bray. New York: Pantheon, 1987.)
La Pute de la côte normande. Paris: Minuit, 1986.
Emily L. Paris: Minuit, 1987. (*Emily L.* Trans. Barbara Bray. New York: Pantheon, 1989.)
La Pluie d'été. Paris: P.O.L., 1990.

CRITICISM (in French)

Marini, Marcelle. *Territoires du féminin avec Marguerite Duras.* Paris: Minuit, 1977.
Pierrot, Jean. *Marguerite Duras.* Paris: J. Corti, 1986.
Ricouart, Janine. *Ecriture féminine et violence: une étude de Marguerite Duras.* Birmingham: Summa, 1991.
Seylaz, Jean-Luc. *Les Romans de Marguerite Duras.* Paris: Lettres Modernes, 1963.
Tison-Braun, Micheline. *Marguerite Duras.* Atlantic Highlands, NJ: Humanities Press, 1984.

CRITICISM (in English)

Selous, Trista. *The Other Woman: Feminism and Femininity in the Work of Marguerite Duras.* New Haven: Yale University Press, 1988.
Willis, Sharon. *Marguerite Duras: Writing on the Body.* Urbana: University of Illinois Press, 1987.

5. Claude Simon

FICTION

Le Tricheur. Paris: Sagittaire, 1945.
Gulliver. Paris: Calmann-Lévy, 1952.
Le Sacre du printemps. Paris: Calmann-Lévy, 1954.
Le Vent. Paris: Minuit, 1957. (*The Wind.* Trans. Richard Howard. New York: Braziller, 1959.)
L'Herbe. Paris: Minuit, 1958. (*The Grass.* Trans. Richard Howard. New York: Braziller, 1960.)
La Route des Flandres. Paris: Minuit, 1960. (*The Flanders Road.* Trans. Richard Howard. New York: Braziller, 1961.)
Le Palace. Paris: Minuit, 1962. (*The Palace.* Trans. Richard Howard. New York:

Braziller, 1964.)
Histoire. Paris: Minuit, 1967. (*Histoire*. Trans. Richard Howard. New York: Braziller, 1968.)
La Bataille de Pharsale. Paris: Minuit, 1969. (*The Battle of Pharsalus*. Trans. Richard Howard. New York: Braziller, 1971.)
Orion aveugle. Geneva: Albert Skiva, 1970.
Les Corps conducteurs. Paris: Minuit, 1971. (*Conducting Bodies*. Trans. Helen R. Lane. New York: Viking, 1974.)
Triptyque. Paris: Minuit, 1973. (*Triptych*. Trans. Helen R. Lane. New York: Viking, 1976.)
Leçon de choses. Paris: Minuit, 1975. (*The World about Us*. Trans. Daniel Weissbort. Princeton: Ontario Review Press, 1983.)
Les Géorgiques. Paris: Minuit, 1981. (*The Georgics*. Trans. Beryl and John Fletcher. New York: Riverrun, 1989.)
La Chevelure de Bérénice. Paris: Minuit, 1984.
L'Invitation. Paris: Minuit, 1987. (*The Invitation*. Trans. Jim Cross. Elmwood Park: Dalkey Archive, 1991.)
L'Acacia. Paris: Minuit, 1989. (*The Acacia Tree*. Trans. Richard Howard. New York: Pantheon, 1991.)

CRITICISM (in French)

Ricardou, Jean, ed. *Claude Simon: analyse, théorie*. Paris: 10/18, 1975.
————. *Lire Claude Simon*. Paris: Les Impressions Nouvelles, 1986. (Reprint of above with updated bibliography.)
Roubichou, Gérard. *Lecture de "l'Herbe" de Claude Simon*. Lausanne: L'Age d'Homme, 1976.
Sarkonak, Ralph. *Claude Simon: les carrefours du texte*. Toronto: Editions Paratexte, 1986.
Starobinski, Jean, Georges Raillard, Lucien Dällenbach, and Roger Dragonetti. *Sur Claude Simon*. Paris: Minuit, 1987.
Sykes, Stuart W. *Les Romans de Claude Simon*. Paris: Minuit, 1979.
Special issues of periodicals: *Entretiens*, no. 31 (1972); "La Terre et la guerre dans l'œuvre de Claude Simon," *Critique*, no. 414 (November 1981).

CRITICISM (in English)

Birn, Randi, and Karen Gould, eds. *Orion Blinded: Essays on Claude Simon*. Lewisburg: Bucknell University Press, 1981.
Britton, Celia. *Claude Simon: Writing the Visible*. Cambridge: Cambridge University Press, 1987.
Duncan, Alastair B., ed. *Claude Simon: New Directions*. Edinburgh: Scottish Academic Press, 1985.
Evans, Michael. *Claude Simon and the Transgressions of Modern Art*. New York: St. Martin's, 1988.
Fletcher, John. *Claude Simon and Fiction Now*. London: Calder & Boyars, 1975.
Gould, Karen. *Claude Simon's Mythic Muse*. Columbia, SC: French Literature Publications, 1979.

Jiménez-Fajardo, Salvador. *Claude Simon.* Boston: Twayne, 1975.

Loubère, J. A. E. *The Novels of Claude Simon.* Ithaca: Cornell University Press, 1975.

Sarkonak, Ralph. *Understanding Claude Simon.* Columbia: University of South Carolina Press, 1990.

Special issues of periodicals: *Review of Contemporary Fiction* 5, no. 1 (Spring 1985).

6. Robert Pinget

FICTION

Entre Fantoine et Agapa. Jarnac: La Tour de Feu, 1951; rpt. Paris: Minuit, 1966. (*Between Fantoine and Agapa.* Trans. Barbara Wright. New York: Red Dust, 1982.)

Mahu ou le matériau. Paris: Robert Laffont, 1952. (*Mahu or the Material.* Trans. Alan Sheridan-Smith. London: Calder, 1966.)

Le Renard et la boussole. Paris: Gallimard, 1953.

Graal Flibuste. Paris: Minuit, 1956.

Baga. Paris: Minuit, 1958. (*Baga.* Trans. John Stevenson. London: Calder, 1967.)

Le Fiston. Paris: Minuit, 1959. (*Monsieur Levert.* Trans. Richard Howard. New York: Grove, 1961.)

Clope au dossier. Paris: Minuit, 1961. (*Clope.* Trans. Barbara Wright. London: Calder, 1963.)

L'Inquisitoire. Paris: Minuit, 1962. (*The Inquisitory.* Trans. Donald Watson. New York: Grove, 1966.)

Quelqu'un. Paris: Minuit, 1965. (*Someone.* Trans. Barbara Wright. New York: Red Dust, 1984.)

Le Libera. Paris: Minuit, 1968. (*The Libera Me Domine.* Trans. Barbara Wright. New York: Red Dust, 1978.)

Passacaille. Paris: Minuit, 1969. (*Passacaglia.* Trans. Barbara Wright. New York: Red Dust, 1978.)

Fable. Paris: Minuit, 1971. (*Fable.* Trans. Barbara Wright. New York: Red Dust, 1980.)

Cette voix. Paris: Minuit, 1975. (*That Voice.* Trans. Barbara Wright. New York: Red Dust, 1981.)

L'Apocryphe. Paris: Minuit, 1980. (*The Apocrypha.* Trans. Barbara Wright. New York: Red Dust, 1986.)

Monsieur Songe. Paris: Minuit, 1982. (*Monsieur Songe.* Trans. Barbara Wright. New York: Red Dust, 1987.)

Le Harnais. Paris: Minuit, 1984.

Charrue. Paris: Minuit, 1985.

L'Ennemi. Paris: Minuit, 1987. (*The Enemy.* Trans. Barbara Wright. New York: Red Dust, forthcoming.)

Du Nerf. Paris: Minuit, 1990.

CRITICISM (in French)

Praeger, Michèle. *Les Romans de Robert Pinget: une écriture des possibles.* Lexington, KY: French Forum, 1986.
Special issues of periodicals: "Autour de Pinget," *bas de casse*, no. 2 (1980).

CRITICISM (in English)

Henkels, Robert M., Jr. *Robert Pinget: The Novel as Quest.* University, AL: University of Alabama Press, 1979.
Special issues of periodicals: *Review of Contemporary Fiction* 3, no. 2 (Summer 1983).

7. Alain Robbe-Grillet

FICTION (excluding the *ciné-romans*)

Les Gommes. Paris: Minuit, 1953. (*The Erasers.* Trans. Richard Howard. New York: Grove, 1964.)
Le Voyeur. Paris: Minuit, 1955. (*The Voyeur.* Trans. Richard Howard. New York: Grove, 1958.)
La Jalousie. Paris: Minuit, 1957. (*Jealousy.* Trans. Richard Howard. New York: Grove, 1959.)
Dans le labyrinthe. Paris: Minuit, 1959. (*In the Labyrinth.* Trans. Richard Howard. New York: Grove, 1960.)
Instantanés. Paris: Minuit, 1962. (*Snapshots.* Trans. Bruce Morrissette. New York: Grove, 1968.)
La Maison de rendez-vous. Paris: Minuit, 1965. (*La Maison de Rendez-Vous.* Trans. Richard Howard. New York: Grove, 1966.)
Projet pour une revolution à New York. Paris: Minuit, 1970. (*Project for a Revolution in New York.* Trans. Richard Howard. New York: Grove, 1972.)
Rêves de jeunes filles. Photographs by David Hamilton. Paris: Robert Laffont, 1971. (*Dreams of a Young Girl.* Trans. Elizabeth Walter. New York: Morrow, 1971.)
Les Demoiselles d'Hamilton. Photographs by David Hamilton. Paris: Robert Laffont, 1972. (*Sisters.* Trans. Martha Egan. New York: Morrow, 1973.)
La Belle captive. With reproductions of works by René Magritte. Lausanne: Bibliothèque des Arts, 1975.
Construction d'un temple en ruines à la déesse Vanadé. Etchings by Paul Delvaux. Paris: Le Bateau Lavoir, 1975.
Topologie d'une cité fantôme. Paris: Minuit, 1976. (*Topology of a Phantom City.* Trans. J. A. Underwood. New York: Grove, 1977.)
Temple aux miroirs. Photographs by Irina Ionesco. Paris: Seghers, 1977.
Souvenirs du triangle d'or. Paris: Minuit, 1978. (*Recollections of the Golden Triangle.* Trans. J. A. Underwood. New York: Grove, 1986.)
Un Régicide. Paris: Minuit, 1978. (*A Regicide.* Trans. John Calder. London: Calder, 1990.)

Traces suspectes en surface. Lithographs by Robert Rauschenberg. New York: Tatyana Grosman, 1979.

Djinn: Un trou rouge entre les pavés disjoints. Paris: Minuit, 1981. (*Djinn.* Trans. Yvone Lenard and Walter Wells. New York: Grove, 1982.)

Le Miroir qui revient. Paris: Minuit, 1984. (*Ghosts in the Mirror.* Trans. Jo Levy. New York: Grove Weidenfeld, 1991.)

Angélique ou l'enchantement. Paris: Minuit, 1988. (*Angelique.* Trans. Jo Levy. London: Calder, 1991.)

CRITICISM (in French)

Alter, Jean. *La Vision du monde d'Alain Robbe-Grillet.* Geneva: Droz, 1966.

Bernal, Olga. *Alain Robbe-Grillet ou le roman de l'absence.* Paris: Gallimard, 1964.

Jaffe-Freem, Elly. *Alain Robbe-Grillet et la peinture cubiste.* Amsterdam: Meulenhoff, 1966.

Leenhardt, Jacques. *Lecture politique du roman: "La Jalousie" d' Alain Robbe-Grillet.* Paris: Minuit, 1973.

Miesch, Jean. *Robbe-Grillet.* Paris: Editions Universitaires, 1965.

Morrissette, Bruce. *Les Romans d'Alain Robbe-Grillet.* Paris: Minuit, 1963.

Ricardou, Jean, ed. *Alain Robbe-Grillet / Colloque de Cerisy / Analyse-Théorie.* Two volumes. Paris: 10/18, 1976.

Special issues of periodicals: *Obliques,* no. 16-17 (1978).

CRITICISM (in English)

Fletcher, John. *Alain Robbe-Grillet.* London: Methuen, 1983.

Jefferson, Ann. *The Nouveau Roman and the Poetics of Fiction.* Cambridge: Cambridge University Press, 1980.

Leki, Ilona. *Alain Robbe-Grillet.* Boston: Twayne, 1983.

Morrissette, Bruce. *Alain Robbe-Grillet.* New York: Columbia University Press, 1965.

———. *Intertextual Assemblage in Robbe-Grillet from "Topology" to "The Golden Triangle."* Fredericton, NB: York, 1979.

———. *The Novels of Robbe-Grillet.* Ithaca: Cornell University Press, 1975.

Stoltzfus, Ben. *Alain Robbe-Grillet and the New French Novel.* Carbondale: Southern Illinois University Press, 1964.

———. *Alain Robbe-Grillet: The Body of the Text.* Rutherford: Fairleigh Dickinson University Press, 1985.

8. Claude Ollier

FICTION

La Mise en scène. Paris: Minuit, 1958. (*The Mise-en-Scène.* Trans. Dominic Di Bernardi. Elmwood Park: Dalkey Archive, 1988.)

Le Maintien de l'ordre. Paris: Gallimard, 1961. (*Law and Order.* Trans. Ursule

Molinaro. New York: Red Dust, 1971.)
Eté indien. Paris: Minuit, 1963.
L'Echec de Nolan. Paris: Gallimard, 1967.
Navettes. Paris: Gallimard, 1967.
La Vie sur Epsilon. Paris: Gallimard, 1972.
Enigma. Paris: Gallimard, 1973.
Our ou vingt ans après. Paris: Gallimard, 1974.
Fuzzy Sets. Paris: 10/18, 1975.
Marrakch médine. Paris: Flammarion, 1979.
Mon double à Malacca. Paris: Flammarion, 1982.
Une Histoire illisible. Paris: Flammarion, 1986.
Déconnection. Paris: Flammarion, 1988. (*Disconnection.* Trans. Dominic Di Bernardi. Elmwood Park: Dalkey Archive, 1989.)
Feuilleton. Paris: Julliard, 1990.

CRITICISM (in French)

Houppermans, Sjef, ed. *Recherches sur l'oeuvre de Claude Ollier.* Groningen: C.R.I.N., 1985.

CRITICISM (in English)

Special issues of periodicals: *SubStance,* no. 13 (1976); *Review of Contemporary Fiction* 8, no. 2 (Summer 1988).

9. Michel Butor

FICTION

Passage de Milan. Paris: Minuit, 1954.
L'Emploi du temps. Paris: Minuit, 1956. (*Passing Time.* Trans. Jean Stewart. New York: Simon & Schuster, 1960.)
La Modification. Paris: Minuit, 1957. (*A Change of Heart.* Trans. Jean Stewart. New York: Simon & Schuster, 1959.)
Le Génie du lieu. Paris: Grasset, 1958. (*The Spirit of Mediterranean Places.* Trans. Lydia Davis. Marlboro: Marlboro Press, 1986.)
Degrés. Paris: Gallimard, 1960. (*Degrees.* Trans. Richard Howard. New York: Simon & Schuster, 1962.)
Mobile. Paris: Gallimard, 1962. (*Mobile.* Trans. Richard Howard. New York: Simon & Schuster, 1963.)
Réseau aérien. Paris: Gallimard, 1962.
Description de San Marco. Paris: Gallimard, 1963. (*Description of San Marco.* Trans. Barbara Mason. Fredericton: York, 1983.)
Illustrations. Paris: Gallimard, 1964.
6 810 000 litres d'eau par seconde. Paris: Gallimard, 1965. (*Niagara.* Trans. Elinor S. Miller. Chicago: Regnery, 1969.)
Portrait de l'artiste en jeune singe. Paris: Gallimard, 1967.

Paysage de répons suivi de "Dialogues des règnes." Paris: Castella, 1968.
Illustrations II. Paris: Gallimard, 1969.
La Rose des vents. Paris: Gallimard, 1970.
Où. Paris: Gallimard, 1971.
Travaux d'approche. Paris: Gallimard, 1972.
Illustrations III. Paris: Gallimard, 1973.
Intervalle. Paris: Gallimard, 1973.
Matière de rêves. Paris: Gallimard, 1975.
Illustrations IV. Paris: Gallimard, 1976.
Matière de rêves II: Second sous-sol. Paris: Gallimard, 1976.
Matière de rêves III: Troisieme dessous. Paris: Gallimard, 1977.
Boomerang. Paris: Gallimard, 1978. (*Letters from the Antipodes.* Trans. Michael
    Spencer. Athens: Ohio University Press, 1981.)
Envois. Paris: Gallimard, 1980.
Matière de rêves IV: Quadruple fond. Paris: Gallimard, 1981.
Explorations. Lausanne: Editions de l'Aire, 1981.
Les Naufragés de l'arche. Paris: La Différence, 1981.
Exprès (Envois 2). Paris: Gallimard, 1983.
Avant-goût. Chavagne: Ubacs, 1984.
Chantier. Gourdon: Dominique Bedou, 1985.
Matière de rêves V: Mille et un plis. Paris: Gallimard, 1985.
Avant-goût II. Chavagne: Ubacs, 1987.
Le Retour du boomerang. Paris: P.U.F., 1988.
Avant-goût III. Chavagne: Ubacs, 1989.
L'Embarquement de la reine de Saba. Paris: La Différence, 1989.

CRITICISM (in French)

Charbonnier, Georges. *Entretiens avec Michel Butor.* Paris: Gallimard, 1967.
Dällenbach, Lucien. *Le Livre et ses miroirs dans l'œuvre de Michel Butor.* Paris:
    Minard, 1972.
Helbo, André. *Michel Butor: vers une littérature du signe.* Brussels: Complexe,
    1975.
Jongeneel, Else. *Michel Butor: le pacte romanesque.* Paris: Corti, 1988.
Raillard, Georges. *Butor.* Paris: Gallimard, 1968.
———, ed. *Michel Butor.* Paris: 10/18, 1974.
Santschi, Madeleine. *Voyage avec Michel Butor* [interviews]. Lausanne: L'Age
    d'Homme, 1982.
Skimao and Bernard Teulon-Nouailles. *Michel Butor: qui êtes-vous?* Lyon: La
    Manufacture, 1988.
Van Rossum-Guyon, Françoise. *Critique du roman: Essai sur "la Modification" de
    Michel Butor.* Paris: Gallimard, 1971.
Waelti-Walters, Jennifer. *Alchimie et littérature: a propos de "Portrait de l'artiste
    en jeune singe" de Michel Butor.* Paris: Denoël, 1975.
Special issues of periodicals: *L'Arc,* no. 39 (1969); "Ecrire avec Butor," *Texte en
    Main,* no. 2 (Summer 1984); "Michel Butor: Regards critiques sur son oeuvre,"
    Oeuvres & Critiques 10, no. 2 (1986).

CRITICISM (in English)

Lydon, Mary. *Perpetuum Mobile: A Study of the Novels and Aesthetics of Michel Butor.* Edmonton: University of Alberta Press, 1980.

McWilliams, Dean. *Michel Butor: The Writer as Janus.* Athens: Ohio University Press, 1978.

Oppenheim, Lois. *Intentionality and Intersubjectivity: A Phenomenological Study of Butor's "La Modification."* Lexington: French Forum, 1980.

Spencer, Michael C. *Michel Butor.* New York: Twayne, 1974.

Waeli-Walters, Jennifer. *Michel Butor.* Victoria: Sono Nis Press, 1977.

Special issues of periodicals: *World Literature Today* 56, no. 2 (Spring 1982); "Butor Studies," *Kentucky Romance Quarterly* 32, no. 1 (1985); *Review of Contemporary Fiction* 5, no. 3 (Fall 1985).

10. Jean Pierre Faye

FICTION

Entre les rues. Paris: Seuil, 1958.

La Cassure. Paris: Seuil, 1961.

Battement. Paris: Seuil, 1962.

Analogues. Paris: Seuil, 1964.

L'Ecluse. Paris: Seuil, 1964.

Les Troyens. Paris: Seuil, 1970.

Inferno, versions. Paris: Seghers/Laffont, 1975.

L'Ovale (détail). Paris: Seghers/Laffont, 1975.

Les Portes des villes du monde. Paris: Belfond, 1977.

Commencement d'une figure en mouvement. Paris: Stock, 1980.

CRITICISM (in French)

Partouche, Maurice. *Jean Pierre Faye.* Paris: Seghers, 1980.

Ronat, Mitsou. *Faye.* Lausanne: L'Age d'Homme, 1980.

11. Philippe Sollers

FICTION

Le Défi. In *Ecrire* 3. Paris: Seuil, 1957.

Une Curieuse solitude. Paris: Seuil, 1958. (*A Strange Solitude.* Trans. Richard Howard. New York: Grove, 1959.)

Le Parc. Paris: Seuil, 1961. (*The Park.* Trans. A. M. Sheridan-Smith. New York: Red Dust, 1969.)

Drame. Paris: Seuil, 1965. (*Event.* Trans. Bruce Benderson and Ursule Molinaro. New York: Red Dust, 1987.)

Nombres. Paris: Seuil, 1968.

Lois. Paris: Seuil, 1972.
H. Paris: Seuil, 1973.
Paradis. Paris: Seuil, 1981.
Femmes. Paris: Gallimard, 1983. (*Women.* Trans. Barbara Bray. New York: Columbia University Press, 1990.)
Portrait du joueur. Paris: Gallimard, 1984.
Paradis II. Paris: Gallimard, 1987.
Le Cœur absolu. Paris: Gallimard, 1987.
Les Folies françaises. Paris: Gallimard, 1988.
Le Lys d'or. Paris: Gallimard, 1989.

CRITICISM (in French)

Barthes, Roland. *Sollers ecrivain.* Paris: Seuil, 1979.

CRITICISM (in English)

Barthes, Roland. *Sollers Writer.* Trans. Philip Thody. London: Athlone, 1987.

12. Maurice Roche

FICTION

Compact. Paris: Seuil, 1966. (*Compact.* Trans. Mark Polizzotti. Elmwood Park: Dalkey Archive, 1988.)
Circus. Paris: Seuil, 1972.
CodeX. Paris: Seuil, 1974.
Opéra bouffe. Paris: Seuil, 1975.
Mémoire. Paris: Belfond, 1976.
Macabré. Paris: Seuil, 1979.
Maladie mélodie. Paris: Seuil, 1980.
Camar(a)de. Paris: Arthaud, 1981.
Ecritures. Montmorency: Carte Blanche, 1985.
Je ne vais pas bien mais il faut que j'y aille. Paris: Seuil, 1987.
Qui n'a pas vu Dieu n'a rien vu. Paris: Seuil, 1990.

CRITICISM (in French)

Maxence, Jean-Luc, ed. *Maurice Roche par les autres.* Paris: L'Athanor, 1978.
Paris, Jean. *Maurice Roche.* Paris: Seghers, 1989. (With a selection of Roche's texts.)
Pierssens, Michel. *Maurice Roche.* Amsterdam: Rodopi, 1989.
Special issues of periodicals: *SubStance,* no. 17 (1977); "Autour de Maurice Roche," *La Nouvelle barre du jour* (April 1985).

13. Jean Ricardou

FICTION

L'Observatoire de Cannes. Paris: Minuit, 1961.
La Prise de Constantinople. Paris: Minuit, 1965.
Les Lieux-dits. Paris: Gallimard, 1969.
Révolutions minuscules. Paris: Gallimard, 1971; Paris: Impressions Nouvelles, 1988. (A new version, to which has been added "Révélations minuscules, en guise de préface, à la gloire de Jean Paulhan.").
Le Théâtre des métamorphoses. Paris: Seuil, 1982.
La Cathédrale de Sens. Paris: Impressions Nouvelles, 1988.

CRITICISM (in English)

Higgins, Lynn A. *Parables of Theory: Jean Ricardou's Metafiction.* Birmingham: Summa Publications, 1984.

14. Georges Perec

FICTION

Les Choses. Paris: René Julliard, 1965. (*Les Choses: A Story of the Sixties.* Trans. Helen R. Lane. New York: Grove, 1967; *"Things: A Story of the Sixties" and "A Man Asleep."* Trans. David Bellos and Andrew Leak. Boston: Godine, 1990.)
Quel petit vélo à guidon chromé au fond de la cour? Paris: Denoël, 1966.
Un Homme qui dort. Paris: Denoël, 1967. (In *"Things: A Story of the Sixties" and "A Man Asleep."*)
La Disparition. Paris: Denoël, 1969.
Les Revenentes. Paris: René Julliard, 1972.
La Boutique obscure. Paris: Denoël/Gonthier, 1973.
Espèces d'espaces. Paris: Galilée, 1974.
W ou le souvenir d'enfance. Paris: Denoël, 1975. (*W, or The Memory of Childhood.* Trans. David Bellos. Boston: Godine, 1988.)
Alphabets. Paris: Galilée, 1976.
Je me souviens. Paris: Hachette, 1978.
La Vie mode d'emploi. Paris: Hachette, 1978. (*Life: A User's Manual.* Trans. David Bellos. Boston: Godine, 1987.)
Un Cabinet d'amateur. Paris: Balland, 1979.
53 Jours. Paris: P.O.L., 1989.
L'Infra-ordinaire. Paris: Seuil, 1989.
Vœux. Paris: Seuil, 1989.
Je suis né. Paris: Seuil, 1990.

CRITICISM (in French)

Magné, Bernard, ed. *Cahiers Georges Perec I*. Paris: P.O.L., 1985.
Special issues of periodicals: *L'Arc*, no. 76 (1979).

CRITICISM (in English)

Motte, Warren F., Jr. *The Poetics of Experiment: A Study of the Works of Georges Perec*. Lexington: French Forum, 1984.
Schwartz, Paul. *Georges Perec: Traces of His Passage*. Birmingham: Summa, 1989.

15. The Next Generation

a) MATHIEU BÉNÉZET

Biographies. Paris: Gallimard, 1970.
Dits et récits du mortel. Paris: Flammarion, 1977.
L'Imitation de Mathieu Bénézet. Paris: Flammarion, 1978.
La Fin de l'homme. Paris: Flammarion, 1979.
Ceci est mon corps. Paris: Flammarion, 1979.
Nous ces photographies. Non. Rennes: Ubacs, 1984.
Ceci est mon corps, 2. Paris: Flammarion, 1985.
Roman journalier. Paris: Flammarion, 1987.

b) FRANÇOIS BON

Sortie d'usine. Paris: Minuit, 1982.
Limite. Paris: Minuit, 1985.
Le Crime de Buzon. Paris: Minuit, 1986.
Décor ciment. Paris: Minuit, 1988.
Le Calvaire des chiens. Paris: Minuit, 1990.

c) RENAUD CAMUS

Passage. Paris: Flammarion, 1975.
Echange. Paris: Flammarion, 1976.
Travers. Paris: Hachette, 1978.
Tricks. Paris: Hachette, 1979.
Buena Vista Park. Paris: Hachette, 1980.
Journal d'un voyage en France. Paris: Hachette, 1981.
Eté. Paris: Hachette, 1982.
Roman roi. Paris: P.O.L., 1983.
Roman furieux. Paris: P.O.L., 1986.
Journal romain. Paris: P.O.L., 1987.
Le Bord des larmes. Paris: P.O.L., 1990.

d) MURIEL CERF

L'Antivoyage. Paris: Mercure de France, 1974.
Le Diable vert. Paris: Mercure de France, 1975.
Les Rois et les voleurs. Paris: Mercure de France, 1975. (*Street Girl.* Trans. Dominic Di Bernardi. Elmwood Park: Dalkey Archive, 1988.)
Hiéroglyphes de nos fins dernières. Paris: Mercure de France, 1977.
Le Lignage du serpent. Paris: Mercure de France, 1978.
Les Seigneurs du Ponant. Paris: Mercure de France, 1979.
Amérindiennes. Paris: Stock, 1979.
Une Passion. Paris: Jean-Claude Lattes, 1981.
Maria Tiefenthaler. Paris: Albin Michel, 1982.
Une Pâle beauté. Paris: Albin Michel, 1984.
Dramma per musica. Paris: Albin Michel, 1986.
Doux oiseaux de Galilée. Paris: Albin Michel, 1988.
La nativité à l'étoile. Paris: Albin Michel, 1989.
Primavera Toscana. Paris: Sand, 1989.

e) CHANTAL CHAWAF

Rétable, followed by *La Rêverie.* Paris: Des Femmes, 1974.
Cercœur. Paris: Mercure de France, 1975.
Blé de semences. Paris: Mercure de France, 1976.
Le Soleil et la terre. Paris: Pauvert, 1977.
Rougeâtre. Paris: Pauvert, 1978.
Maternité. Paris: Stock, 1979. (*Mother Love, Mother Earth.* Trans. Monique Nagem. New York: Garland, 1990.)
Landes. Paris: Stock, 1980.
Crépusculaires. Paris: Ramsay, 1981.
Les Surfaces de l'orage. Paris: Ramsay, 1982.
La Vallée incarnate. Paris: Flammarion, 1984.
Elwina, le roman fée. Paris: Flammarion, 1985.
L'Intérieur des heures. Paris: Des Femmes, 1987.
Rédemption. Paris: Flammarion, 1989. (*Redemption.* Trans. Monique Nagem. Elmwood Park: Dalkey Archive, forthcoming.)
L'Eclaircie. Paris: Flammarion, 1990.

f) TONY DUVERT

Récidive. Paris: Minuit, 1967.
Portrait d'homme couteau. Paris: Minuit, 1969.
Interdit de séjour. Paris: Minuit, 1969.
Le Voyageur. Paris: Minuit, 1970.
Paysage de fantaisie. Paris: Minuit, 1973. (*Strange Landscape.* Trans. Sam Flores. New York: Grove, 1975.)
Récidive. Nouvelle version. Paris: Minuit, 1976.
Journal d'un innocent. Paris: Minuit, 1976.
Quand mourut Jonathan. Paris: Minuit, 1978.

L'Île atlantique. Paris: Minuit, 1979.
Un Anneau d'argent à l'oreille. Paris: Minuit, 1982.
Abécédaire malveillant. Paris: Minuit, 1989.

g) JEAN ECHENOZ

Le Méridien de Greenwich. Paris: Minuit, 1979.
Cherokee. Paris: Minuit, 1983. (*Cherokee.* Trans. Mark Polizzotti. Boston: Godine, 1987.)
L'Equipée malaise. Paris: Minuit, 1986.
L'Occupation des sols. Paris: Minuit, 1988.
Lac. Paris: Minuit, 1990.

h) ANNIE ERNAUX

Les Armoires vides. Paris: Gallimard, 1974. (*Cleaned Out.* Trans. Carol Sanders. Elmwood Park: Dalkey Archive, 1990.)
Ce qu'ils disent ou rien. Paris: Gallimard, 1977.
La Femme gelée. Paris: Gallimard, 1981. (*The Frozen Woman.* Trans. Tanya Leslie. New York: Four Walls Eight Windows, forthcoming.)
La Place. Paris: Gallimard, 1984. (*A Sense of Place.* Trans. Tanya Leslie. New York: Four Walls Eight Windows, forthcoming.)
Une Femme. Paris: Gallimard, 1988. (*A Woman's Story.* Trans. Tanya Leslie. New York: Four Walls Eight Windows, 1991.)

i) PATRICK GRAINVILLE

La Toison. Paris: Gallimard, 1972.
La Lisière. Paris: Gallimard, 1973.
L'Abîme. Paris: Gallimard, 1974.
Les Flamboyants. Paris: Seuil, 1976.
La Diane rousse. Paris: Seuil, 1978.
La Dernier Viking. Paris: Seuil, 1980.
Les Forteresses noires. Paris: Seuil, 1982.
La Caverne céleste. Paris: Seuil, 1984. (*The Cave of Heaven.* Trans. Dominic Di Bernardi. Elmwood Park: Dalkey Archive, 1990.)
Le Paradis des orages. Paris: Seuil, 1986.
L'Atelier du peintre. Paris: Seuil, 1988.
L'Orgie, la neige. Paris: Seuil, 1990.

j) JEANNE HYVRARD

Les Prunes de Cythère. Paris: Minuit, 1975.
Mère la mort. Paris: Minuit, 1976. (*Mother Death.* Trans. Laurie Edson. Lincoln: University of Nebraska Press, 1988.)
La Meurtritude. Paris: Minuit, 1977.
Les Doigts du figuier. Paris: Minuit, 1977.

Le Corps défunt de la comédie. Paris: Seuil, 1982.
Auditions musicales certains soire d'été. Paris: Des Femmes, 1984.
La Baisure, followed by *Que se partagent les eaux.* Paris: Des Femmes, 1985.
Canal de la Toussaint. Paris: Des Femmes, 1986.
Le Cercan. Paris: Des Femmes, 1987.
La jeune morte en robe de dentelle. Paris: Des Femmes, 1990.

k) PATRICK MODIANO

La Place de l'étoile. Paris: Gallimard, 1968.
La Ronde de nuit. Paris: Gallimard, 1969. (*Night Rounds.* Trans. Patricia Wolf. New York: Knopf, 1971.)
Les Boulevards de ceinture. Paris: Gallimard, 1972. (*Ring Roads.* Trans. Caroline Hillier. London: Gollancz, 1974.)
Villa triste. Paris: Gallimard, 1975. (*Villa Triste.* Trans. Caroline Hillier. London: Gollancz, 1977.)
Livret de famille. Paris: Gallimard, 1977.
Rue des boutiques obscures. Paris: Gallimard, 1978. (*Missing Person.* Trans. Daniel Weissbort. London: Jonathan Cape, 1980.)
Une Jeunesse. Paris: Gallimard, 1981. (*Trace of Malice.* Trans. Anthea Bell. Boston: Godine, 1990.)
De si braves garçons. Paris: Gallimard, 1982.
Quartier perdu. Paris: Gallimard, 1984.
Dimanches d'août. Paris: Gallimard, 1986.
Remise de peine. Paris: Seuil, 1988.
Vestiaire de l'enfance. Paris: Gallimard, 1989.
Voyage de noces. Paris: Gallimard, 1990.

l) MARIE REDONNET

Le Mort & Cie. Paris: P.O.L., 1985.
Doublures. Paris: P.O.L., 1986.
Splendid Hotel. Paris: Minuit, 1986.
Forever Valley. Paris: Minuit, 1987.
Rose Mélie Rose. Paris: Minuit, 1987.
Tir & Lir. Paris: Minuit, 1988.
Silsie. Paris: Gallimard, 1990.

m) JACQUES ROUBAUD

Graal fiction. Paris: Gallimard, 1978.
Le Roi Arthur. Paris: Hachette, 1983.
La Belle Hortense. Paris: Ramsay, 1985. (*Our Beautiful Heroine.* Trans. David Kornacker. Woodstock, NY: Overlook, 1987.)
L'Enlèvement d'Hortense. Paris: Ramsay, 1987. (*Hortense Is Abducted.* Trans. Dominic Di Bernardi. Elmwood Park: Dalkey Archive, 1989.)
Le Grand incendie de Londres. Paris: Seuil, 1989. (*The Great Fire of London.* Trans. Dominic Di Bernardi. Elmwood Park: Dalkey Archive, 1990.)

L'Exil d'Hortense. Paris: Seghers, 1990.
La Princesse Hoppy ou le conte du Labrador. Illus. Jean-Claude Castelli. Paris: Hatier, 1990.

n) Danièle Sallenave

Paysage de ruines avec personnages. Paris: Flammarion, 1975.
Le Voyage d'Amsterdam. Paris: Flammarion, 1977.
Les Portes de Gubbio. Paris: Hachette, 1980.
Un Printemps froid. Paris: P.O.L., 1983.
La Vie fantôme. Paris: P.O.L., 1986. (*Phantom Life.* Trans. Lydia Davis. New York: Pantheon, 1989.)
Conversations conjugales. Paris: P.O.L., 1987.
Adieu. Paris: P.O.L., 1988.

o) Eugène Savitzkaya

Mentir. Paris: Minuit, 1977.
Un Jeune homme trop gros. Paris: Minuit, 1978.
La Traversée de l'Afrique. Paris: Minuit, 1979.
La Disparition de maman. Paris: Minuit, 1982.
Les Morts sentent bon. Paris: Minuit, 1984.
Capolican, un secret de fabrication. Paris: Arcane 17, 1987.
Sang de chien. Paris: Minuit, 1988.

p) Jean-Philippe Toussaint

La Salle de bains. Paris: Minuit, 1985. (*The Bathroom.* Trans. Nancy Amplioux and Paul De Angelis. New York: Dutton/Obelisk, 1990.)
Monsieur. Paris: Minuit, 1986.
L'Appareil-photo. Paris: Minuit, 1988.

Index

Franken, Ruth, 210
Freud, Sigmund, 61, 74, 79, 107, 153, 308, 315
Frye, Northrup, 123

Gaddis, William, 156
Gary, Romain, 177
Gauthier, Xavière, 87, 314-15
Genette, Gérard, 148
George, Henry, 222, 226
Ghelderode, Michel de, 314
Gide, André, 18, 29, 191, 218, 223
Giono, Jean, 52, 223
Giraudoux, Jean, 10, 15, 16, 54-55, 178, 222-23, 225, 237, 294
Gogh, Vincent van, 267, 286-87
Goldmann, Lucien, 46, 86
Gorz, André, 177
Gracq, Julien, 10, 53, 57, 243
Grainville, Patrick, 311, 339
Guesde, Jules, 226
Guyotat, Pierre, 10

Hamilton, David, 159, 160
Heath, Stephen, 46
Hegel, Georg Wilhelm, 50, 256
Heidegger, Martin, 47n7, 50
Heppenstall, Rayner, 149
Hérold, Jacques, 208-9
Hokusai, 211
Homer, 231, 235
Hugo, Victor, 19, 161, 216
Huguenin, Jean-René, 242
Huizinga, Johan, 288
Huston, Nancy, 317
Hyvrard, Jeanne, 317, 318, 339-40

Ionesco, Irina, 160

Jacob, Max, 29
Jakobson, Roman, 119n8
Jefferson, Thomas, 202
Johns, Jasper, 160
Joyce, James, 105, 132, 166, 231, 249, 254, 258, 268, 299, 317

Kafka, Franz, 57-58, 235, 249, 294, 316
Kaufmann, Walter, 8
King, Martin Luther, 203
Kircher, Athanasius, 193
Klossowski, Pierre, 10, 60
Kolár, Jiri, 217

Kristeva, Julia, 25, 74, 87, 264, 315, 317

Lacan, Jacques, 61, 74, 79, 107, 153, 218, 263
Lamartine, Alphonse de, 292
La Motte Fouque, Friedrich de, 222
Lao-tzu, 253, 263
Larbaud, Valery, 10, 301
La Rochefoucauld, Duc de, 244
Lautréamont, Comte de, 183, 214, 314, 316
Leblanc, Maurice, 183
Le Clézio, J. M. G., 10
Leiris, Michel, 24
Le Lionnais, François, 293
Leroux, Gaston, 183
Levi, Primo, 309
Lévi-Strauss, Claude, 107
Lindon, Jérôme, 306
Lowry, Malcolm, 270-71, 294

Mabille, Pierre, 247
Mably, Gabriel Bonnet de, 239
Magnasco, Alessandro, 217
Magny, Claude-Edmonde, 54, 223, 294
Magritte, René, 159, 160
Mailer, Norman, 7
Mallarmé, Stéphane, 49, 52, 154, 183, 187, 203, 247, 251, 257, 268, 281, 312
Malraux, André, 51, 92, 103, 127, 263, 310
Manet, Edouard, 153-54, 245
Mao Tse-tung, 254, 263
Martin du Gard, Roger, 72
Marx, Karl, 272, 315, 322n8
Masson, André, 63, 208
Mathews, Harry, 293
Matthews, J. H., 16
Mauriac, Claude, 11-12, 45
Mauriac, François, 43-44, 95, 103, 191, 230, 243, 274
McCarthy, Mary, 34
Melville, Herman, 214, 256, 292, 294, 297, 301, 303
Menippus, 312
Mercier, Vivian, 10-11
Merleau-Ponty, Maurice, 110
Milton, John, 271
Miró, Joan, 112
Modiano, Patrick, 305n6, 308-9, 310, 340
Monet, Claude, 211-12
Montaigne, Michel de, 260
Montherlant, Henry de, 86
Morrissette, Bruce, 143, 146, 153, 159

MODERN FRENCH LITERATURE FROM DALKEY ARCHIVE

Albert-Birot, Pierre. *Grabinoulor*	Cloth, $20.00
Cerf, Muriel. *Street Girl*	Cloth, $19.95
Cholodenko, Marc. *Mordechai Schamz*	Cloth, $19.95
Ernaux, Annie. *Cleaned Out*	Cloth, $19.95
Grainville, Patrick. *The Cave of Heaven*	Cloth, $19.95
Navarre, Yves. *Our Share of Time*	Paper, $9.95
Ollier, Claude. *Disconnection*	Cloth, $19.95
Ollier, Claude. *The Mise-en-Scène*	Cloth, $20.00
Queneau, Raymond. *The Last Days*	Cloth, $19.95
Queneau, Raymond. *Odile*	Cloth, $19.95
Queneau, Raymond. *Pierrot Mon Ami*	Paper, $7.95
Roche, Maurice. *Compact*	Cloth, $19.95
Roubaud, Jacques. *The Great Fire of London*	Cloth, $21.95
Roubaud, Jacques. *Hortense Is Abducted*	Cloth, $19.95
Roubaud, Jacques. *Some Thing Black*	Cloth, $19.95
Simon, Claude. *The Invitation*	Cloth, $15.95

New French Fiction: a special issue of the *Review of Contemporary Fiction* with fiction by Roubaud, Cerf, Grainville, Roche, Cholodenko, Navarre, Ernaux, Bénézet, Chawaf, Rezvani, Hyvrard, Savitzkaya, Le Clézio, Sallenave, Vautrin, Boulanger, and Modiano   Paper, $8.00

Available at better bookstores or directly (add $1.50 postage) from

Dalkey Archive Press
1817 N. 79th Avenue
Elmwood Park, IL 60635